W9-AAG-317

Adventure Guide to

Venice
& the Veneto

Marissa Fabris

HUNTER

Hunter Publishing, Inc.
130 Campus Drive
Edison, NJ 08818-7816
☎ 732-225-1900/800-255-0343/fax 732-417-1744
www.hunterpublishing.com
comments@hunterpublishing.com

IN CANADA
Ulysses Travel Publications
4176 Saint-Denis
Montreal, Québec H2W 2M5 Canada
☎ 514-843-9882, Ext. 2232/fax 514-843-9448

IN THE UK
Windsor Books International
The Boundary, Wheatley Road
Garsington, Oxford OX44 9EJ England
☎ 01865-361122/fax 01865-361133
ISBN 1-58843-519-9
© 2006 Hunter Publishing, Inc.
Manufactured in the United States of America

Front cover, *Venice* (Superstock); back cover and spine photos,
Carnival masks (www.cadelsolmaschere.com)
All other color photos by author, unless otherwise indicated.
Maps by Toni Wheeler © 2006 Hunter Publishing, Inc.
Index by Nancy Wolff

4   3   2   1

Contents

19.99
10.00
- 9

Introduction

■ Discovering the Veneto

Writers, painters, historians and philosophers have long been inspired by the dramatic landscapes of the Veneto Region and, by translating astute observations on canvas or in print, have captured the beauty of a land and a people that have evolved over many centuries.

Situated in Italy's northernmost zone, few other regions boast such diverse landscapes. From the low sandy coastline where the Veneto meets the Adriatic Sea, to the mighty Alpine peaks, rolling hills, thermal springs and lagoon systems, the varied landscape makes for lively getaways any season of the year.

Veneto, a name that derives from Veneti, a pre-Roman people who once inhabited the area, is divided into seven provinces: Belluno, Padua, Rovigo, Treviso, Venice, Verona and Vicenza.

Although the Venetian Republic's rule over its mainland territories officially ended in the late 18th century, the presence of its rule is still evident throughout the Veneto today. One of the most telling reminders is the winged lion of St. Mark, which was once Venice's official emblem.

One of the great cultural cities of the world, Venice's geographical location contributed to its naval and commercial dominance in the Mediterranean for centuries and the Republic's subsequent wealth.

The history of Venice, or *La Serenissima*, drastically affected the entire Veneto region and it is impossible, if not inaccurate, to fully appreciate the many towns and their achievements without putting them in their proper context.

During Venice's golden age, aristocrats brought their wealth to the Veneto countryside and commissioned architects to build agricultural estates and country homes. Today, more than 4,000 villas remind us of that period, the most famous of which were designed by 16th-century architect Andrea Palladio.

The Veneto is considered by many to be one of Italy's most artistically rich regions, from Palladio's significant architectural contribution in Vicenza to the art of Giotto and Mantegna in Padua and the ancient Roman ruins in Verona.

The Veneto's depth, however, extends far beyond its artistic treasures. From *grappa*, Bassano del Grappa's distilled liquor, and Valdobbiadene's sparkling *Prosecco* wine, to Asiago's cheese from mountain dairies, and seafood from the lagoon, the Veneto is a food- and wine-lovers' delight.

Nearly nine million visitors are attracted to the Veneto each year. The eastern shore of Lake Garda, Riviera degli Olivi, offers visitors Mediterranean scenery against an Alpine backdrop, while Montegrotto Terme and Bibione, famous for their thermal springs and mineral baths, cater to travelers with a more relaxed vacation in mind. The seaside resorts of Caorle and Jesolo are ideal locations for water sports and relaxation alike, and the Dolomite Mountains offer perfect conditions for skiing, hiking, cycling and more.

■ A Land of Infinite Wonders

Geography

 The Veneto is one of Italy's most topographically diverse regions, boasting Alpine zones, plains, lakes, lagoons and islands within a surface area of 18,364 square kilometers (7,063 square miles). Italy's eighth-largest region, the Veneto shares its borders with Austria to the

The Veneto Region

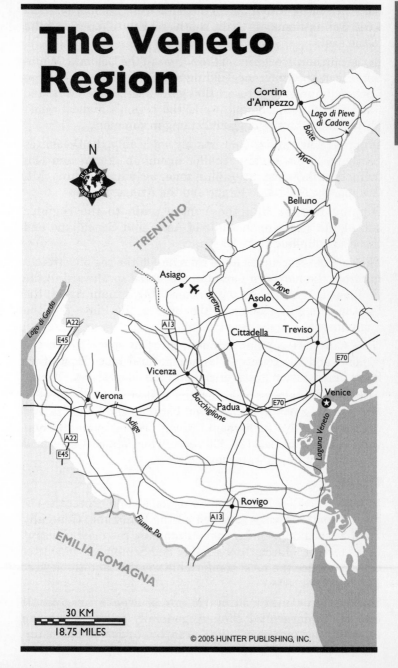

N

Cortina
d'Ampezzo
Lago di Pieve
di Cadore

Boite

Mae

Belluno

TRENTINO

Asiago

Brenta

Piave

Asolo

Treviso

Cittadella

E70

Vicenza

Bacchiglione

Padua

E70

Venice

Verona

Adige

A22

E45

A22

E45

Laguna Veneto

Lago di Garda

A13

Rovigo

A13

Fiume Po

EMILIA ROMAGNA

30 KM

18.75 MILES

north, Trentino-Alto Adige to the northwest, Lombardy to the west, Emilia-Romagna to the south and Friuli-Venezia Giulia to the east.

In the northernmost zone of the region sit the Dolomite Mountains, best known for ideal skiing conditions in towns such as Cortina d'Ampezzo (a resort that gained fame when it hosted the 1956 Winter Olympics) and the region's highest peak, Marmolada (the site of glacial skiing in summer).

Dropping down in size but certainly not beauty, the Dolomites gently slope toward the smaller mountain groups and plateaus that form the pre-Alpine zone, including Belluno, Mt. Grappa, the Mt. Baldo Range and the Asiago plateau.

Dipping further into the Veneto plain to the region's sub-Alpine zone are the hills of Asolo and Conegliano and those surrounding Lake Garda.

The vast plain occupies more than half of the region, stretching from the northern mountainous areas southward to the Po River and is crossed by northern Italy's main rivers: the Po, the Adige, the Livenza, the Brenta, the Piave and the Tagliamento.

Lake Garda, a popular summer vacation spot, is both the region's and the country's largest natural lake. Most other lakes in the region are artificial and considerably smaller.

Although the plains make up the majority of the Veneto's landscape, lagoon systems found between the Po Delta and the mouth of the Tagliamento River form an extensive network dating back nearly 6,000 years, when Venice was formed as a result of rising water levels.

Climate

 Travelers to the Veneto region should expect the climate to vary as much as the landscape. Generally speaking, spring and autumn are the most pleasant times to visit. March through May and September and October experience the most comfortable weather and the fewest number of tourists.

The region's many climatic zones create an overall temperate-continental climate, generally milder along the Adriatic coast and near Lake Garda, but coldest in the mountainous areas. Inland towns are typically colder in winter and warmer in summer than Venice.

The time of year for your travels will depend on what you want to do – be it an adventure along the Adriatic in June, in the Dolomites in December or in Venice for Carnevale.

■ Understanding the People

Population

 In a country with nearly 57 million inhabitants, about 4½ million people inhabit the Veneto region, the majority concentrated in and around the areas of Treviso, Padua and Vicenza.

Many people assume that Venice has the highest population in the region, but there is in fact no one city that is dramatically more populated or more economically-important than others in the Veneto.

Due in part to the region's shared borders and proximity with other countries, there are several minority groups in the Veneto, including Austrians, Germans, Slovenians and French.

Language

Italian is both the country's and the region's official language, although the Venet dialect (one that varies from town to town within the region) is also commonly spoken.

For years people have debated whether or not the dialect is a language, since it was the official language of the Venetian Republic. Although the language has strong Latin roots, it also contains many words of Germanic origin, especially in the more mountainous zones.

Other small, isolated linguistic zones exist where Cimbri, an ancient Bavarian dialect, and Ladin, another dialect heavily influenced by German, are spoken.

Italian remains the dominant spoken language, but travelers to Venice and other large cities in the region can often find shopkeepers and locals who speak English.

Religion

For centuries in Italy, religion has influenced and been influenced by many other aspects of life – namely culture, politics and economics. From the early days of the Kingdom of Italy, there was a strong Catholic presence in the Veneto. The religious importance is easily identified in cities and towns throughout the region, not only in chapels and basilicas, but also in villas, palaces and town squares.

■ The Veneto's Place in Time

A Brief History

 The Veneto was once inhabited by the Veneti and the Euganei people until, in the third century BC, the Romans conquered the local inhabitants as they worked their way northward to subdue France and Germany. The Romans established Verona as a base for their northward expansion and left the city with more significant marks of Roman rule than any other city in the region.

Though experts agree that the Venetian lagoon was created nearly 6,000 years ago, Venice itself remained mostly uninhabited, except for small numbers of fishermen, until the fifth century AD. When barbarian Goths looted their way southward to Rome, they drove many people away from the Veneto mainland and forced them to take refuge on the coastal Venetian islands.

During the fifth century, people began establishing villages on the islands and trade links began with the Byzantine Empire. Venice was officially founded when the relic of St. Mark the Evangelist was stolen from Alexandria in Egypt and brought to Venice. At that point, St. Mark became the patron saint of the city, establishing Venice as part of Christendom.

As the centuries passed, trade significantly developed with the East and Venice became a powerful crossroads between east and west. In the ninth century AD, Venice gained its independence from the Byzantine Empire and, by the early

11th century, it developed into a powerful city-state, trading with Christian forces during the Crusades.

Piazza San Marco was the trade hub and the source of mounting wealth for the Republic, but the powerful Republic acknowledged that it needed to secure and maintain sufficient control over the mainland, *terra firma*, in order to control trade through rivers and mountain passes into northern Europe.

The Venetian Army set out to conquer family dynasties such as the Scaligeri of Verona and the Visconti of Milan in order to lay its claim to the mainland.

By the early 13th century, Venice had flourished into a true maritime Republic and ruled the Byzantine Empire. It exercised control over the eastern Mediterranean, though it did not officially rule Venetia until the 15th century.

The Republic took Cyprus in 1489, though many were growing tired of the Republic's expansion. In 1508, Pope Julius II, the Kings of France and Spain and the Holy Roman Emperor Maximilian joined together to form the League of Cambrai, with the intent to conquer cities of the Veneto and halt Venetian territorial expansion.

Venice continued to dominate the Eastern Mediterranean with its monopoly on Mediterranean trade and controlled northeastern Italy for over than 200 more years.

The Turks became a significant threat to Venice and, in 1570, they took Cyprus back. Having recognized that it was imperative to depend on more than the sea for its wealth, Venice shifted its focus to agricultural development on the mainland.

As the Venetian Republic increased its influence over the Veneto region, nobles began to commission architects such as Andrea Palladio, to design villas and farming estates in the Veneto as vacation retreats.

The Venetian Republic was ruled by the Doge, a leader established for life to reign over the Republic along with his Council of 10 and the Grand Council of 2,000 members. This government maintained its force until Napoleon invaded in 1797 and the Doge and his Grand Council resigned, officially bringing the Venetian Republic to an end.

The serious decline of the Republic started long before Napoleon's invasion, however, when aristocratic Venetians squandered wealth on lavish lifestyles. Shortly after, Napoleon offered Venice to his allies the Austrians, and looted the city. The Austrian rule inspired many to join the Risorgimento and rise up against Austrians in order to unite Italy.

By 1804, Napoleon took Venice back from the Austrians and established himself as King of Italy but, again in 1814-15, the Austrians drove the French out of Venice during a volatile period. In the First Italian War of Independence in 1848, Venice revolted against Austrian Rule, though it was not until 1866 that Venice and the Veneto were finally freed, allowing Venice to reconstruct.

With the opening of the Suez Canal in 1869, and then the construction of the Port of Marghera, some old trade routes were revived. By the turn of the century, Venice was once again becoming a fashionable spot where the wealthy vacationed at the new beachside resorts.

Cities and small towns of the Veneto alike felt the effects of both World War I and World War II. The main cities of Treviso, Verona, Vicenza and Padua were bombed and other towns badly scarred. With Nazi occupation, people resisted and formed partisan groups. Combat was often fierce in the mountains, especially around Monte Grappa, Asiago and Belluno.

Art & Architecture

Among the most notable artistic achievements in the Veneto region are those that date to the Byzantine Gothic period as a result of the commerce route and ties with Constantinople and the East.

During the early 14th century, **Giotto** arrived in Padua to fresco the Scrovegni Chapel with what became his masterpieces. Though not Venetian by birth, he left an extraordinary mark on the region and influenced other painters of that period.

By the 15th century, artists such as **Andrea Mantegna**, and **Jacopo**, **Gentile** and **Giovanni Bellini** marked the dawn of the Renaissance abandoning the Byzantine techniques for fresh ones that added perspective and dimension to paintings.

The golden age of Venetian painting came later in the 16th century with painters **Jacopo Tintoretto**, **Jacopo da Bassano**, **Lorenzo Lotto**, **Paolo Veronese** and **Titian**.

The great architect **Andrea Palladio**, the most famous in the region and most influential of his time, designed many structures throughout the region during the century, including Villa Barbaro, the Ponte Vecchio in Bassano, and the Olympic Theater in Vicenza. Commissioned by aristocrats to build elegant structures, Palladio's designs have been studied, admired and replicated continually over the centuries.

UNESCO & the Veneto

The cultural branch of the United Nations, UNESCO, has awarded the prestigious title of World Heritage Site to many places throughout the world based on their historical and artistic heritage, nearly two-thirds of which exist in Italy. Several places in the Veneto are on this list, including Venice and its Lagoon (1987), the City of Vicenza and the Palladian Villas (1994), the Botanical Garden in Padua (1997) and the City of Verona (2000).

■ The Veneto Today

Economy

Once almost entirely dependent on agriculture, the Veneto's economy is now oriented toward high-tech industry and fashion. The prosperity of the Veneto's economy depends on manufacturing clothing, textiles and footwear, metal engineering, woodworking and furniture. There are several industrial districts in the region, but its primary source of income is from the industrial hub centered in Mestre and Porto Marghera near Venice. Among the region's best-known clothing manufacturers are Benetton and Diesel.

Another important aspect that has contributed to this cosmopolitan region's prosperity is the agricultural and food industry. Among the Veneto's many food products awarded the DOP (Denomination of Protected Origins) are Asiago cheese, radicchio (red chicory) and extra virgin olive oil from Garda. Wine grapes cultivated in the Veneto contribute to the production of numerous wines, many of which are DOC (Denomination of Controlled Origin) wines, such as Valpolicella and Soave. Tourism in the Veneto is another significant source of income and further enhances the economy's status.

Government

Since the monarchy was dissolved in 1946 by popular referendum, Italy established a democratic republic with a bicameral parliamentary system headed by the prime minister.

A founding member of the European Union, Italy is administratively divided into 20 regions, including the Veneto, and approximately 100 provinces.

Established in 1970, the Veneto reserves the power to vote for a regional council that ultimately has limited governing powers over the region and reports to the centralized government. And each of the seven provinces in the Veneto has a prefect appointed by the central government to represent provincial matters.

■ A Lively Culture

Holidays, Festivals & Celebrations

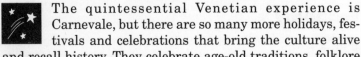
The quintessential Venetian experience is Carnevale, but there are so many more holidays, festivals and celebrations that bring the culture alive and recall history. They celebrate age-old traditions, folklore and customs.

From operas to symphonies and dance to theatrical events, the major cities and some of the Veneto's smaller towns have an impressive cultural scene and performers of the highest caliber bring their talent to the region each year.

■ Food & Drink

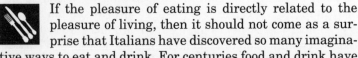
If the pleasure of eating is directly related to the pleasure of living, then it should not come as a surprise that Italians have discovered so many imaginative ways to eat and drink. For centuries food and drink have been an integral part of the Venetian culture and perhaps a central catalyst for social development.

Mealtime is traditionally social and Veneti hardly ever forego an opportunity to enjoy deliciously prepared foods or the chance to be in the company of family and friends.

Meals – *Colazione* (breakfast) is traditionally the smallest meal for Veneti and hardly consists of anything more than tea, espresso or cappuccino, sometimes accompanied by a *brioche* (a cream- or jelly-filled pastry), fresh fruit or toast. Many people also enjoy *caffè latte* (a bowl of warm milk, coffee and day-old bread). Cereals and fruit juices have become increasingly popular among the younger generations. Breakfast, taken at home or at a bar, is rarely more than a light morning snack. If you need a heartier breakfast to jump-start your day, hotels typically cater to international guests with continental-style breakfasts consisting of breads, cold cuts, cheese, fruit, cereal and yogurt.

Customarily, Italians return home from school or work for *pranzo* (lunch), traditionally the largest meal of the day. This meal consists of *antipasti* (appetizers), a *primo piatto* (first course), a *secondo piatto* (second course) with *contorni* (side dishes) and sometimes *frutta* (fruit) or a *dolce* (dessert). Although shunned in some cultures, it is acceptable in Italy to consume an aperitif, a glass of wine or a digestive drink during the midday meal. More and more people now, particularly the younger generations, opt for quicker lunches on-the-go and have a *panino* or *tramezzino* (sandwich) at lunchtime.

The evening meal, *cena*, is often smaller than lunch, consisting of either a first course or a second course. With more people on the go for the midday meal, however, it is becoming increasingly common to consume a light lunch and a larger meal in the evening.

Courses – Meals often begin with antipasti, consisting of fresh vegetables, seafood and meats served either warm or cold. The *primo piatto* can consist of anything from pasta or soup to *risotto* (a rice-based dish) or *polenta* (made from white

DINING PRICE CHART	
Price per person for an entrée	
€	Under €5
€€	€5-€12
€€€	€13-€20
€€€€	€21-€30
€€€€€	Over €30

or yellow maize and grown abundantly in the Veneto).

As with pasta, risotto can be prepared in assorted ways with fresh meats, vegetables, seafood and cheeses. Polenta is cooked in liquid form, left to set, then either served hot or sliced and grilled as a first course topped with a sauce, as a side dish or with a soup. Pasta dishes can be found on almost any restaurant's menu and are always a popular choice for a first course. Soups are often a less-filling option for a first course and people who eat pasta at lunchtime commonly opt for soup in the evening.

Depending on your appetite, you may have room for a *secondo piatto* comprised of grilled, roasted, boiled or stewed chicken, rabbit, lamb, duck, fowl, beef, pork or seafood. Meats and fish are typically served with *contorni* such as roasted potatoes, green vegetables and an *insalata mista* (mixed salad).

A meal is hardly complete without a *dolce* (dessert) and restaurants often serve a signature dessert in addition to a *gelato* (ice cream) and *macedonia di frutta* (mix of fresh fruit and white wine). Locally grown fruits such as kiwis, berries, apples, peaches and cherries complement many desserts.

If you're not sure what to order, ask for a *piatto misto* (mixed plate) of either antipasti or primi. Not all restaurants are willing to do this but when they are, this is a great way to sample a few different dishes for a reasonable price.

Seasonal Cooking – The abundance of crops cultivated in the Veneto provides restaurants and markets with the freshest seasonal products year-round. The most seasonal meat, produce, fish and cheese dictate every menu and it is rare that any restaurant will offer customers the same menu in June that they do in November. Even though it has become increasingly possible to find many ingredients year-round, most Italians cook with predominantly seasonal ingredients in order to create dishes with the most refined flavors.

Fish markets are typically closed on Monday. Steer clear of ordering fish-based meals on Monday as they are probably not fresh.

In the Veneto region many restaurants showcase *asparagi bianchi* (white asparagus from Bassano del Grappa) in the springtime, *radicchio* (red chicory from Treviso) in the winter and *funghi* (wild mushrooms) in the fall and winter.

Veneto's Cuisine – People around the world consider themselves intimately familiar with Italian cuisine, but few know how differently foods are prepared from one region to another. You would be disappointed if you came to the Veneto in search of red-sauce-based pasta dishes prepared with heavy cheeses and meats. The Veneto's cuisine is based largely on several key ingredients produced in the region and it differs from the mountains to the sea as much as the landscape does.

Around the Venetian lagoon some of the oldest, most characteristically Venetian dishes are based on seafood. Cuisine in the mountainous zones, especially around Cortina d'Ampezzo and Comelico, is largely influenced by Austro-Hungarian cooking. Some ingredients commonly used in mountain cooking are poppy seeds, barley, mushrooms and cheeses from mountain dairies. Lake Garda's cuisine is highly regarded for its diversity – it benefits from ingredients grown in the mountains near Monte Baldo, the rich agriculture from the hills around Verona, the premium extra virgin olive oil from Garda's Riviera degli Olivi and Garda's fresh trout, carp, eel and other fish.

> **Tip:** *Contorni* (side dishes) are often not included in the price of your second course. What appears to be an inexpensive meal may turn out to be more than what you expected, so be mindful of whether or not sides are included.

Wine, Spirits & Other Beverages

 The long list of wines, spirits and other beverages produced in the Veneto are the product of premium ingredients and imaginative people who have developed drinks for all occasions, drinks to accompany each course and others to stand alone as their own course. A good blend of Italy's climate, soil and viticulture traditions have led to Italy's importance in wine production and the Veneto contributes to that. The country's wine history dates back several thousand years, as suggested by evidence from the early civilizations of the Etruscans and the Greeks. A large number of Italians are employed in the wine industry.

Aperitivi (aperitifs) can be served along with an antipasto, but many Italians stop for one at a bar before lunch. *Prosecco*, a dry sparkling wine served either as an aperitif or with dessert, is produced near Conegliano in the province of Treviso. Another popular before-dinner drink, the *Bellini* (named after the 16th-century painter) is a Venetian concoction – a mix of Prosecco and white peach nectar. Then there is the non-alcoholic alternative, *Crodino*, a bitter beverage that can be enjoyed alone or mixed with either white wine or soda. Martini and Campari are also popular aperitivi, although they are not specific to the Veneto region.

It may be easy to overlook the *sorbetto* or *sgroppino* after a filling meal but this drink, typically made with *panna* (cream) ice cream, Prosecco and Vodka or another liquor of choice, is much-loved. It is generally served as a palette cleanser between the first and second courses, although many people choose it in lieu of a dessert.

Caffè is served following dessert and the *espresso*, a shot of strong Italian coffee, is the most popular. Some enjoy *caffè con latte* (coffee with milk), while others prefer *caffè corretto* (espresso with a shot of liqueur).

The *digestivo* (digestive drink) announces the close to a meal and the region's most popular is *grappa*, made from distilled grape leaves. Montenegro and Ramazzotti are also popular digestives from other regions in Italy.

A large selection of non-alcoholic drinks such as soft drinks, *frullati* (milk shakes made with fruit), *spremute* (fruit juices), *sugi di frutta* (fruit nectar) and *aqua* (water) are always available. If you prefer still water, remember to ask for *non-gazzata* or *naturale*. Otherwise, you'll be disappointed by the bubbly mineral water your waiter will probably bring.

Did you know? The Veneto region produces the largest quantity of DOC (Denomination of Controlled Origin) wines in Italy and Verona is the region's leader.

Veneto's Eateries – There is a large assortment of eateries throughout the Veneto and many factors that will likely influence where you choose to eat, including your budget, time of day, itinerary and location. Travelers can find some international cuisine and fast food establishments in Venice and a few other large cities in the Veneto, but the overwhelming majority of dining establishments in the region serve regional Italian cuisine.

One of the most casual places to stop for a quick bite on the go is a *bar*. Contrary to its name, a bar serves more than alcoholic beverages and is one of the most popular locales usually open from early in the morning until late in the evening. Bars generally serve standard fare, from breakfast pastries, sandwiches and mini-pizzas to coffee, juices and liquors. They don't always have tables.

The *caffè*, however, is similar to the bar and does typically have tables. It's an inexpensive option and a popular spot for Italians to read the daily paper or meet friends for a drink.

> **Tip:** One of the surest ways to look like a tourist is to ask for a *cappuccino* after your meal. Drink it with breakfast, mid-morning or afternoon but not after a meal.

Another quick option for breakfast is the *pasticcerìa* (pastry shop), where you can buy a breakfast pastry.

The *gelateria* is perhaps the most coveted of all eateries among tourists who can't seem to get enough of *gelato*, Italy's ice cream.

The *tavola calda* is an economical option at lunchtime where pasta, meat, vegetables and more are served informally (often buffet-style) and cheap. This is a good place to eat, particularly if you are dining solo or on the go.

For an informal, moderately priced evening meal, the *pizzeria* is a great option. In the Veneto, *pizzerie* typically serve personal-sized thin-crust pizzas topped with a variety of fresh ingredients, but sometimes offer a selection of pastas and salads. These are not generally open in the afternoon and restaurants that double as pizzerias will usually serve pizza only for the evening meal.

If you're craving a pizza for lunch, look for a *pizza al taglio*, where pizza is sold by the slice.

A popular alternative to the pizzeria in the Veneto, especially for dinner and late-night snacks, is the *bruschetteria*. Topped similarly to a pizza and often served on a wooden paddle, a *bruschetta* is made with toast.

Trattorie are typically family-owned establishments, known for home-cooked meals and good values. They offer regional specialties but often have limited menus in order to maintain the highest quality foods at minimal costs. A trattoria is a casual option for either lunch or dinner, but remember that they are open from about noon until 2 or 3 pm, then close again until dinner.

Ristoranti range from the casual to the upscale. These establishments offer customers moderately priced to expensive meals and some require reservations, especially on weekends. Although a tie is not usually required for men, jackets sometimes are. It is a good idea to inquire about the recommended dress code when making reservations.

> **Historic Interest:** For a list of restaurants and hotels in Italy with special historic interest, visit www.localistorici.it.

As Italy's leading producer of DOC wines, there are plenty of places in the Veneto to enjoy a glass of wine. The *enoteca* (wine bar) is popular in late afternoon and evening and serves wines and spirits, along with some simple food to accompany drinks such as cheeses, cold meats and sandwiches.

Similar to the enoteca is the *bacaro*, typical to Venice. Venetians love to stop here for tapas-like *cicheti* accompanied by a glass of wine or, as they call it, an *ombra*.

Tourist Trap: Keep in mind that any eatery you choose in a tourist hot spot could drain your budget and often leave you disappointed. For the most satisfying, budget-friendly meals, avoid restaurants in popular city squares and main thoroughfares. Travel outside of city limits if you can but, if not, find an eatery where there seem to be more locals and fewer tourists.

Understanding Menus – Reading a menu in another language can be particularly overwhelming for travelers and unless you find yourself in a major tourist center, don't expect a restaurant to have a menu translated in English. This shouldn't discourage you, however. Servers are usually willing to explain menus and accommodate specific needs. Since meals are frequently prepared after you place your order, don't feel uncomfortable asking to have food prepared to accommodate dietary needs or personal tastes, within reason. Likewise, if you prefer to eat appetizers and then a second course, or perhaps only a first course, tell your server. It is not uncommon for a waiter to approach your table and recite a menu rather than hand you one. Unfortunately you cannot see the prices, but if you are overwhelmed, ask to see a menu (that may or may not exist).

Pane e Coperto – A bread and cover charge is typically tacked onto your bill (usually per person), although some restaurants have done away with this. Rumors have circulated about whether or not restaurants charge this fee if you don't touch the breadbasket on your table. With the rare exception, you'll be charged whether you eat the bread or not.

Tipping – Taxes and service charges are typically included in your meal so tipping is not obligatory. Some regard tipping as showy and doing so will almost certainly single you out as a tourist. Tipping is at your discretion. That said, by all means tip your server if you feel especially satisfied with your service.

When to Dine – Since many stores, museums and restaurants close for several hours each afternoon, it is helpful to know the times Italians sit down to dine and schedule your meals accordingly. Breakfast is usually eaten in the early morning; lunchtime begins around noon and can last until about 2 pm. Dinners are not generally served before 7 pm and continue until 10 pm or later, depending on the establishment.

Good Value: It can be more economical to eat larger meals at lunchtime than at dinnertime. Consider opting for a sit-down meal in the middle of the day when many shops and museums are closed, then grab a light dinner in the evening. The *menu fisso* (fixed menu) can be a good, economical option as well.

Festive Dishes – It seems that religious holidays have traditionally spurred an exceptional dose of creativity in kitchens across the Veneto. Early in the calendar year, Veneti celebrate the feast of Carnevale with arguably more pomp and circumstance than in any other region in Italy. This festive period that culminates on *Martedì Grasso* (Fat Tuesday) has historically been a time for overindulgence.

Two of the most famous desserts in Venice and throughout the Veneto during Carnevale are *fritole* (often called *frittelle*), soft pastries made with fruit or cream, and *crostoli* or *galani*, ribbons of deep-fried dough topped with powdered sugar and sometimes filled with jam.

Tip: Mealtime is typically less rushed and more relaxed in Italy than what many travelers are accustomed to. If you are in a rush, notify the server at the beginning of the meal. Otherwise, relax and enjoy not feeling pressured to eat and run.

During the period of Lent, leading up to Easter, there is a greater emphasis on seafood and fish, and it is common for

Veneti to eat *frittate* (omelettes) prepared with a variety of fresh vegetables in lieu of meat.

While lamb is a popular second course for Easter dinner, eel is a Venetian specialty for Christmas Eve dinner and Christmas Day menus inevitably include turkey, duck or veal roasts.

There are many popular Christmas desserts originating in the region, such as the *Pandoro* (a Christmas cake from Verona), *Nadalin* (star-shaped sweet bread from Verona) and *Nadale lasagna* (sweet lasagna from the mountain town of Cadore made with poppy seeds and walnuts).

Associations

Unione Ristoranti del Buon Ricordo

(www.buonricordo.com). First established in 1964 by 12 restaurants in Italy in order to preserve and promote regional cuisine, *Buon Ricordo* unites Italy's premier restaurants and organizes various initiatives and events year-round. Today, 17 of the organization's 110 restaurants are in the Veneto region, and patrons who order the restaurant's specialty dish are given the *Buon Ricordo* plate as a memento.

Slow Food

(www.slowfood.com). This Italian association was founded in 1986 and developed into a popular international movement in Paris by 1989. The aim is to protect traditional food and the agricultural heritage, to rediscover regional cooking, while rejecting fast food and the fast life worldwide. This grassroots effort represented by the snail symbol focuses on tourism, food, wine and agriculture. It aims to generate public awareness through various initiatives, including themed dinners, taste education workshops, tours and exhibitions, in addition to publishing books and magazines.

■ Accommodations

Types of Accommodations

 Affittacamere – If you like the idea of meeting the locals and enjoying a bit of independence during your visit, consider staying in someone's private home. Tourist offices typically have a list of rooms for rent in private homes, although they do not rate these in the way hotels are rated.

Agriturismo – Agricultural tourism (the farm stay) has become increasingly popular in Italy over the past several years and there are many such establishments in the Veneto countryside that offer great alternatives to the standard hotel room. The principle

HOTEL PRICE CHART	
Based on a double room for two	
€	Under €50
€€	€50-€80
€€€	€81-€120
€€€€	€121-€190
€€€€€	Over €190

mission of these operating farms is agricultural production, but in addition many sell their products in their *azienda* (store), have dining facilities where they welcome visitors, offer guest rooms and organize recreational activities. Some people wrongly assume that a vacation at a farmhouse will cost much less than a hotel. Although this is often the case, farmhouse vacations can also be quite luxurious and charming (in other words, pricey). Amenities can vary greatly – some rooms are equipped with a private bathroom, television, telephone, air-conditioning and satellite TV, while others have little more than a wash basin, leaky roof and rickety floor boards. One of the most attractive features of farm stays is that homegrown products are typically served in the farmhouse dining room. Meals and beverages should consist of two-thirds farm produce and products not produced on-site usually come from nearby farms. Not all farmhouses provide meals, but many provide *spuntini* (snacks). Agriturismi offer a great option for those seeking genuine hospitality and fresh products. Some have guest rooms with either private or shared bathrooms, or they have apartments with bathrooms, a kitchen and other amenities. While their guest rooms are usually open during the week, their azienda and dining facility are usually open to the general public from Fri-Sun. Several agriturismi have been included in this guide but, for a more comprehensive list or to learn more about farm stays in Italy, visit the following sites:

■ www.agriturist.it

■ www.terranostra.it

■ www.turismoverde.it

■ www.italyfarmholidays.com.

Albergo – There is generally little difference between an albergo and a hotel, other than size (an albergo is typically smaller). You'll find fewer alberghi than hotels in your travels.

Apartments and Villas – Independent travelers who plan to ground themselves in one spot for a week or more find apartment and villa rentals very attractive. Similar to other types of accommodations, these can run the gamut from simple to lavish. They often have kitchen facilities and more space than a standard hotel room and are typically more economical for longer periods of time (the larger your family or group, the more economical this can be). If you do your research in advance, this can amount to an enjoyable vacation. But likewise, pictures can be deceiving and an 18th-century historical villa once inhabited by a noble Venetian family may have lost its charm, to say the least. Tourist offices often have lists of apartment and villa rentals in the area, but there are also several companies that specialize in such rentals. These include:

■ **Doorways, Ltd.** (www.villavacations.com)

■ **The Best in Italy** (www.thebestinitaly.com)

■ **Vacanza Bella** (www.vbella.com)

■ **Rent Villas** (www.rentvillas.com)

■ **Carefree Italy** (www.carefreeitaly.com)

■ **My Italian Vacation** (www.myitalianvacation.com)

■ **Villas International** (www.villasintl.com).

Bed and Breakfasts – These are small establishments that generally include warm hospitality and breakfast. You will come across a handful of them in the Veneto region, but they have not taken off in Italy the way they have in other countries. Unlike affittacamere, bed and breakfasts are usually officially recognized.

Campeggio and Villagio Turistico (Campsites and Tourist Villages) – Camping is quite popular around Lake Garda and near the sea, but if you didn't pack your tent or arrive with your trailer, there are plenty of tourist villages that rent bungalows and trailers. Similar to hotels, campsites are classified with a star system based on services and amenities.

This economical option is a good choice for families, but hardly translates into the type of wilderness camping many Americans are familiar with. Campgrounds and tourist villages often have large facilities with swimming pools, supermarkets, game rooms, bars, sports tournaments, planned excursions and evening entertainment.

- For more information regarding camping in Italy: www.camping.it.

Hotels and Resorts – Ranging from simple one-star lodgings to the deluxe five-star establishments, hotels are the most popular type of accommodations. Remember that stars are granted based on a facility's amenities and don't necessarily translate into charm. Ask to see your room before actually accepting it. Be sure to request a room with a shower or a bath if that's what you're after.

Locande – This is usually a family-run inn, but the term can also refer to some dining establishments.

Ostelli – Hostels offer travelers of all ages budget accommodations. In addition to the single-sex communal rooms, some also offer private family rooms. Additionally, most hostels impose curfews (though not all enforce them). If you're looking to save a few euros, this could be a place to do it. If you value your privacy, however, you'll be better accommodated in an inexpensive hotel. Check Hostelling International's website (www.hiayh.org) for more details about this option.

Pensioni – Once very popular throughout Italy, there are very few of these that still exist, and those that have the name *pensione* are typically small one-, two- or three-star hotels.

Religious Institutions – Some religious institutions, including monasteries and convents, offer budget accommodations to travelers throughout Italy. Accommodations are usually very modest and often single-sex. Curfews are often imposed.

Rifugi – Mountain travelers, particularly hikers and cyclists, find *rifugi* (mountain huts) to be convenient places to spend the night. There are scores of these throughout the Dolomite Mountains and it is easy to plan extended trips in the mountains with overnights at rifugi.

High Season/Low Season

Generally speaking, high season in most large cities and towns is in the summertime. Low season is November-March for most large cities and April-May and September-November in ski resort towns. Prices are consequently higher during the peak season and low during off-season.

> **Caution:** Many accommodations close during off-season, particularly in the mountains, by the sea and by the lake. If you're planning a trip during an off-period, finding somewhere to stay may take more effort but there are usually at least a few places that remain open year-round or that alternate periods of closure.

■ Adventures & Activities

The Veneto region offers travelers all manner of adventures from the cultural, intellectual sort right down to the seat-of-your-pants thrilling variety. Whether planning your itinerary entirely around a particular activity like a week-long cycling holiday or a language immersion course, or if you're trying to offset your museum and church-heavy itinerary with some off-the-beaten track activities, there are a tremendous number of opportunities to help you broaden your experiences, live the culture and acquaint yourself with the locals. This book highlights cultural adventures (language lessons, mask-making workshops, wine tastings, cooking courses, painting classes), sports adventures (hiking, biking, horseback riding, golf, skiing, hang-gliding, rock climbing, white-water rafting), adventures for the soul (spas), family adventures (amusement parks), driving adventures and many other types of activities to help you discover more about the land, and about yourself.

Some of the most popular adventures in the Veneto are horseback riding, skiing, spelunking and wildlife watching in the mountains, sailing and kayaking along the Adriatic coast and Lake Garda and bicycle riding and hiking through the foothills near Asolo.

Other activities such as language and culinary lessons offer cultural enthusiasts a chance to witness the culture from a more intimate perspective, while actively participating in it. Travelers can benefit from courses at numerous public and private culinary and language institutes throughout the Veneto.

Spa, beach and golf retreats may not conjure up images of an active holiday, but the variety of sports and leisure activities at these locations allows visitors to experience the Venetian culture firsthand.

The diverse landscape in the Veneto region is what makes it a prime location for adventure travel. After all, there are few regions where it is possible to windsurf at a beach resort today and, after driving a few hours, ski on a glacier tomorrow.

The important thing about adventure travel is that it should be exactly that – an adventure, an opportunity to experience things with a greater sense of passion and spirit.

Hiking

There are several hikes included in this guide so a few general hiking safety tips might be in order.

- Whether in the Dolomite Mountains, the Euganean Hills or near Lake Garda, be sure to select itineraries that are appropriate for your fitness and ability levels.

- Know the technical nature and the length of the trail before setting out on it and plan for a safe return during daylight hours.

- If hiking in a group, take into account the skill levels of all hikers and plan accordingly.

- Bring appropriate equipment and clothing for the hike and weather. Be prepared for changes in weather, since conditions can change drastically in the mountains.

- Bring along a first aid kit.

- Never go out alone on an excursion and always leave behind details of your itinerary (even if only with your hotel clerk).

- Study your path well.
- Remember to respect the environment on your hike and don't wander off paths.

Special Interest Trips

Bike Riders Tours (www.bikeriderstours.com)
Ciclismo Classico (www.ciclismoclassico.com)
Epiculinary (www.epiculinary.com)
Shaw Guides (www.shawguides.com)

■ Travel Essentials

Planning Your Trip

Animals

 Customs allows the entry of dogs and cats as long as the owner presents a certificate of origin and health that has been issued by the appropriate health authorities. The certificate must show proof that the animal has received a rabies vaccination within the last 11 months and at least 20 days prior to the date on the certificate with details regarding the breed, age, sex and color of the pet, as well as information about the owner. Check with an Italian consular office for more information before traveling. Other animals that require documents include parrots, parakeets, rabbits and hares. Dogs must be kept on a leash or muzzled in public and it is at the customs official's discretion to require a health exam upon entry if they are unsure of the animal's health or origin.

Currency, Credit Cards, ATMs, Traveler's Checks, Banking

 Since January 1, 2002 the euro replaced the lira as the Italian monetary currency. It is possible to exchange your currency for euros at banks or designated exchange shops (*Change / Cambio / Wechsel*) in airports, railway stations or around town. An easier way to go about this is by using your ATM card at machines that say

Bancomat, where you are able to withdraw euros directly from your account, based on the current exchange rate.

Most shops, restaurants and hotels accept major credit cards, but this is not always the case so be sure to look for the credit card symbols posted on an establishment's window or ask in advance. Another option is using Traveler's Checks that you can exchange or use for payment of goods in lieu of money. Although you should be able to use traveler's checks at most hotels and shops, I've heard many a story about travelers who haven't been able to use them in shops. If you feel safer, change them in a bank or foreign exchange office. To find out the current exchange rate, check the universal currency converter at www.xe.net/currency.

Electrical Current/Adaptors

 Italy's electrical current is 220 volts, much the same as many other European countries. The plugs have two round prongs and, although some hotels have hairdryers for your use, it is best to purchase an appropriate adaptor and a transformer if you plan to use your own electrical appliances during your trip.

Passport Regulations, Visas & Documents

 EU citizens must possess a valid identity document and non-EU citizens must have a valid passport in order to enter the country. Citizens of the USA and Canada need only a valid passport in order to enter Italy if they are staying for 90 days or less and will not be working. Beyond this, visitors can go to a *questura* (police station) and request a 90-day extension (for tourist purposes) or apply for an appropriate visa (for work or study). See www.agenziadogane.it.

Time Difference

Italy is in the Central European Time zone (CET), one hour ahead of Greenwich Mean Time (GMT) and six hours ahead of Eastern Standard Time (EST).

Travel Insurance

You'll have to weigh the circumstances yourself to determine whether or not you should invest in a travel insurance plan. You may be able to go through your personal insurance company for this; otherwise, there are plenty of companies out there that provide travel insurance. Depending on the plan, this could cover trip delays, interruption and cancellation due to a variety of issues.

What to Pack

 Italians tend to dress up rather than down so, when in doubt, opt for the smarter looking outfits rather than the more casual ones, unless your trip will be primarily devoted to sports activities. During summer months, the weather across the Veneto is warm and sometimes humid (though cooler in the mountain regions, where you'll need a jacket). If your plans include visits to churches, remember to pack appropriate clothing (See *Churches*). Generally speaking, you won't find many locals wearing shorts or sneakers and travelers who want to blend in should bring along dresses, skirts and pants (for women) and slacks (for men). The same goes for dining out – while most restaurants won't impose a jacket and tie dress code, you won't find patrons in jeans and sneakers. In winter, expect cold temperatures, even near the Adriatic coast, which sees a lot of rainfall and some snow during the winter months. I don't have to tell you what to expect in the Dolomites during winter, but don't underestimate the cold and snow. Year-round, it's always a good idea to travel with an umbrella since unexpected rain showers are not uncommon.

When to Visit

 The mean annual temperature in the Veneto region is 13.2°C/55.8°F; January temperature is 4.9°C/41°F and July is 22.1°C/72°F. There are an average of 79 days of rain per year.

■ Arriving in the Veneto

By Plane

 There are several airports in the Veneto, although the primary airport with domestic and international flights is Marco Polo in Venice. Malpensa Airport in Milano is another major one, with international and domestic flights flying in and out daily. The other airports listed below handle less air traffic daily but may be good options for travelers coming from other locations throughout Europe.

Airports: Venice – Aeroporto Civile Venezia-Tessera Marco Polo (☎ 041-2609260); **Milan** – Aeroporto Intercont. Malpensa-Varese (☎ 027-4852200); **Verona** – Aeroporto Civile Verona-Villafranca (☎ 045-8095666); **Treviso** – Aeroporto Treviso-S. Giuseppe (☎ 0422-315123).

Airlines: Italy's primary air carrier is **Alitalia** (☎ 848865642, www.alitalia.it), but many other carriers fly into and out of Italy's airports, including **Air France** (☎ 848884466, www.airfrance.fr), **American Airlines** (☎ 0642741240, www.aa.com), **British Airways** (☎ 848812266, www.britishairways.com), **Continental Airlines** (☎ 0269633256, www.continental.com), **Delta Airlines** (☎ 800864114, www.delta.com), **Iberia** (☎ 848870000, www.iberia.com), **KLM** (☎ 800877318, www.klm.com), **Lufthansa** (☎ 0665684004, www.lufthansa.it), **Ryan Air** (www.ryanair.com), **Sabena** (☎ 848801616, www.sabena.com) and **Swissair** (☎ 848849570, www.swiss.com).

By Train

Arriving in the Veneto by train from other European cities is simple, particularly if you are on a direct train to Venice or Verona from Paris, Lyons, Brussels, Zurich, Munich, Hanover, Berlin and Vienna. The Eurostar and InterCity trains travel between the major cities, while the Inter-Regional, Regional and local trains are convenient for traveling shorter distances. Italy's railway system is operated by Ferrovie dello Stato and details can be found at **www.trenitalia.com**. First- and second-class tickets may be purchased at railway stations and must be validated in a ticket machine on the platform prior to boarding a train. Trains that travel greater distances have buffet cars and sleeper cars; certain trains also transport bicycles.

By Car

Anyone entering Italy must possess valid documents for their vehicle (car, motorcycle or trailer), including the proper registration and the international insur-

Above: Spring in the Dolomites

Below: The Dolomites

*Above: The trail to the dinosaur tracks at the foot
of Monte Pelmo begins here*

Below: Belluno, with Ponte della Vittoria (webdolomiti.net, Giovanni Vanz)

Above: Belluno, with its Duomo (webdolomiti.net, Giovanni Vanz)

Below: San Vittore church, Feltre (webdolomiti.net, Giovanni Vanz)

Porta Oria in Feltre (webdolomiti.net, Giovanni Vanz)

ance card (green card). The primary border crossings with Austria, Switzerland, France and Slovenia are open 24 hours a day every day.

■ Exploring

By Car

 A network of motorways (indicated by the letter A) and state and provincial roads (indicated by SS or SP) bisect the Veneto region. The primary motorways are **A4** (Torino-Trieste), **A22** (Brennero-Modena), **A13** (Bologna-Padova), **A31** (Vicenza-Thiene) and **A27** (Mestre-Belluno). State and provincial roads are indicated by blue signs with white lettering and numbers, while motorways have green signs with white lettering and numbers.

> **Tip:** When arriving in a city or town, follow signs for the *centro* (city center).

ACI: Italy's ACI (Automobile Club d'Italia) is similar to AAA in the USA and offers roadside assistance. They can be reached by calling 116 free of charge from any telephone. You can reach them 24 hours a day, but highways also have emergency phones every two km in the event you need mechanical or medical assistance. For information regarding weather conditions, tolls, customs, currency and other important highway tips, call ☎ 06-491716.

Tolls: Be prepared to pay tolls on Italy's motorways.

Driver's License: Valid licenses from other countries are recognized in Italy, and a US or Canadian license must be accompanied by a translation or international license (AAA or CAA can help). If you arrive in Italy without this, contact the ACI (Automobile Club d'Italia) to obtain it.

Driving in Tunnels: Slow your speed, turn on the fan and lights and keep right. You'll likely encounter many of these tunnels (*gallerie*) when driving in the mountains.

Gasoline (benzina): Most gas stations distribute *benzina senza piombo* (unleaded gasoline) or *gasolio* (diesel).

Seat Belts: These are mandatory for driver and passengers in the front and back seats.

Mountain Driving: Snow tires may be used between November 15 and March 15 and you'll find these absolutely necessary if your travels take you through the mountains during the snowy season. It is mandatory in some zones to have snow chains on tires as well during winter.

Cellular Phones: It is prohibited to use cell phones while driving unless using hands-free equipment.

Speed Limits: 50 km/hour on urban roads; 90 km/hour on secondary and local roads; 110 km/hour on main roads outside city limits; 130 km/hour on motorways.

> **Tip:** By law, on highways drivers must drive on the right and pass on the left, only stopping for emergencies in designated parking areas.

Children: Children under 12 years old must be in the back seat and in child seats as appropriate.

By Bus

 Each of the Veneto's seven provinces has its own system of bus transportation that links the major cities with many of the province's smaller towns, and links that province's capital city with those of other provinces. Most bus drivers do not sell tickets on board; you should purchase tickets in advance at tobacconists, bars, newsstands or at the bus station, then validate them in the orange box when you board the bus. Tickets usually expire within one hour of validation so travel must be completed in that time (some exceptions). Be prepared to pay a fine if a control agent comes around to check for tickets and you don't have one that has been validated.

By Train

 The Veneto railway's network covers approximately 1,234 km and its primary lines are Milano-Venezia, Milano-Trieste and Milano-Udine. As with buses, it is necessary to purchase tickets before boarding the train from the train station ticket window, then validate the ticket in the yellow box on the platform. By neglecting to validate your ticket, or boarding without a ticket at all, you may be fined if a ticket agent is on board.

DISTANCES BETWEEN MAIN CITIES	
Cortina and Venice	102 miles
Milan and Venice	176 miles
Padua and Venice	23 miles
Verona and Venice.	75 miles

■ Useful Resources

Admission Fees

 All admission fees for museums and churches included in this guide are for full-price adult tickets (*biglietti interi*), unless otherwise specified. There are generally reduced tickets available for children and large groups.

Business Hours

 The following hours are listed as a general guideline, but may vary slightly from one place to another.

Banks: Mon-Fri (8:30 am-1/1:30 pm and 2:30/3 pm-4/5 pm; some Sat service).

Post Offices: Some are open Mon-Fri (8 am-2 pm), Sat (9:30 am-1 pm). Others are open Mon-Fri (8 am-7 pm), Sat (9:30 am-1 pm).

Shops: Traditionally, shops are open Mon through Sat from 9:30/10 am until about 12:30 pm and reopen again at 3 or 4 pm, remaining open until 7:30/8 pm. Many shops, however, particularly in larger cities, do not close at lunchtime and instead maintain continuous hours. This can vary slightly depending on the season (some shops remain open longer during summer) and the destination (shops in popular tourist cities sometimes open on Sunday as well).

Restaurants: Generally, eating establishments are open for lunch from noon until 2 or 3 pm and for dinner from 7 until about 11 pm. These hours may also vary, particularly in tourist destinations. Most restaurants are closed one day each week, although many remain open seven days a week during high season.

Gas Stations: Most gas stations are open from 8 am-1 pm and 2:30-7:30 pm, but now many have *fai da te* (self-service), where you may use credit cards or euros and pump gas yourself 24 hours a day.

Pharmacists: Mon-Sat (8:30 am-12:30 pm and 4-8 pm); some Sunday service.

Churches

Most churches strictly enforce a dress code (no sleeveless tops or shorts; skirts must be below the knee) and hardly make exceptions for the unknowing tourist. This is a matter of respect, so if your plans include church visits, save yourself the hassle and dress appropriately. As another measure of respect, church visits are off-limits during religious services.

Emergencies

Any of the following telephone numbers may be called free of charge from public or private telephones.

- Police (Carabinieri) – 112
- Police (Polizia di Stato) emergency police help – 113
- Fire Department – 115
- Customs and Excise (Guardia di Finanza) – 117
- Medical Emergency – 118
- Phone Directory – 12
- ACI (Automobile Club d'Italia) – 116
- International Inquiries – 176

Holidays

 The following is a list of public holidays. Many public offices, museums and shops close for these occasions.

January 1 – New Years

January 6 – Epiphany

Easter

Easter Monday
April 25 – Liberation Day
May 1 – Labor Day
June 2 – Republic's Day
August 15 – Assumption
November 1 – All Saints Day
December 8 – Immaculate Conception
December 25 – Christmas Day
December 26 – Boxing Day

Internet Cafés

Rather than depleting your funds on phone card purchases, find one of the many Internet cafés scattered throughout the country (particularly in major cities) to stay in touch.

Personal Health & Safety/Security

 Italy does not require its visitors to have particular vaccinations prior to entry, and no vaccinations are required prior to reentry in the US or Canada. In the event of an emergency, travelers should go to the nearest emergency room (*pronto soccorso*). It is wise to have a health insurance policy when you travel.

Postal Service

Post offices throughout Italy offer various services in addition to mailing letters and packages. These include paying bills, sending telegrams and faxes. You can purchase stamps from either a post office or a tobacco shop.

Registering in Italy

Tourists must, by law, register with the Italian police within three days of their arrival. Hotels generally see that this is done by requesting to hold your passport when you arrive, but if your plans include staying with friends or family, or in a place that doesn't request your documents, stop into a police station within the first three days of your stay.

Going Metric

To make your travels in this region easier, we have provided the following chart that shows metric equivalents for the measurements you are familiar with.

GENERAL MEASUREMENTS

1 kilometer = .6124 miles

1 mile = 1.6093 kilometers

1 foot = .304 meters

1 inch = 2.54 centimeters

1 square mile = 2.59 square kilometers

1 pound = .4536 kilograms

1 ounce = 28.35 grams

1 imperial gallon = 4.5459 liters

1 US gallon = 3.7854 liters

1 quart = .94635 liters

TEMPERATURES

For Fahrenheit: Multiply Centigrade figure by 1.8 and add 32.

For Centigrade: Subtract 32 from Fahrenheit figure and divide by 1.8.

Centigrade	Fahrenheit
40°	104°
35°	95°
30°	86°
25°	77°
20°	64°
15°	59°
10°	50°

Saints Days

 In addition to holidays, cities and towns around Italy observe Saints Days, typically in honor of a town's patron saint. It's rather difficult to plan your trip around these, but don't be surprised if you arrive in a smaller town only to find everything from the tourist office to the town museum closed for the day. The main saints days around the Veneto are:

- Vicenza (January 22 – San Vincenzo Martire)
- Verona (April 12 – San Zeno)
- Venice (April 25 – San Marco)
- Treviso (April 27 – San Liberale)
- Padua (June 13 – Sant'Antonio)
- Belluno (June 29 – San Pietro)
- Rovigo (June 29 – SS. Pietro e Paolo)

Telephones

 Italy's international code is 39, which must be dialed prior to the telephone number when calling from abroad.

In order to place international telephone calls from Italy, first dial the international code of the country you are trying to reach, followed by a telephone number.

Public telephones are widely available in Italy and public phones require a *carta telefonica* (phone card), which may be purchased at newsstands, bars and tobacco shops.

Calls within Italy must begin with a city's prefix (041 in Venice), except for cellular phones, which should not begin with a zero.

VAT & Tax-Free Shopping

Purchases made for goods in European Union shops include a tax called VAT (Value Added Tax). The tax rate varies depending on the product and could be anything from 20% for clothing to 4% on bread. By law, non-European Union residents are entitled to refunds on purchases in Italy that total €154.94 or more. Look for the Tax Free Shopping sign displayed in store windows and shop in these stores for hassle-free refunds. For more information: Global Refund (www.globalrefund.com) or Premier Tax Free (www.premiertaxfree.com).

■ Useful Resources

Embassies – **US** (Via Vittorio Veneto, 119/A, Rome, Italy, ☎ 0646741), **Canada** (Via G.B. de Rossi 27 and Via Zara 30, Rome, Italy, ☎ 06445981), **Great Britain** (Via XX Settembre 80, Rome, Italy, ☎ 06-42200001) and **Australia** (Via Antonio Bosio 5, Rome, Italy, ☎ 06852721).

Consulates – For lost passports and other such issues. **US** (Via Principe Amadeo 2/10, Milan, ☎ 02-290351), **Canada** (Via Vittor Pisani 19, Milan, ☎ 02-67583420 or 02-67583422) and **Great Britain** (Piazzale Donatori di Sangue 2/5, Venezia-Mestre, ☎ 041-5055990).

ENIT (630 Fifth Avenue, Suite 1565, New York, NY 10111, ☎ 212-245-4822, www.italiantourism.com, www.enit.it). Ente Nazionale Italiano per il Turismo is the Italian State Tourist Board and promotes Italy's tourism around the world.

Italian Cultural Institute (2025 M Street NW, Suite 610, Washington, DC, 20036, ☎ 202-223-9800, www.italcultusa.org). This organization's mission is to promote Italian culture and civilization.

Italian Trade Commission (33 East 67th Street, New York, NY, 10021, ☎ 212-980-1500, www.italtrade.com). Also known as the Italian Institute for Foreign Trade, this organization is responsible for promoting trade, business and industry between Italy and other countries.

National Italian American Foundation (1860 19th St. NW, Washington, DC, 20009, ☎ 202-387-0600, www.niaf.org). NIAF's goal is to preserve Italian American heritage and culture.

Tourist Offices – The principal cities and towns in each of the Veneto's seven provinces have tourist offices that are at travelers' disposal and generally provide maps, brochures and advice.

The Province of Belluno

Belluno is a richly diverse province, from its more densely populated southern district between Feltre and Longarone, where the land rises steadily through the valleys and dense forests to the crests of the jagged Dolomite Mountains.

Belluno

Much of the province was under Austrian rule for many years and consequently was significantly impacted by their culture. While Italian is predominantly spoken in the zone, there are pockets where the language has significant German influence.

Celebrated for its shimmering peaks, dramatic vertical rock faces, lively resort towns, Alpine hamlets and world-class ski resorts, the Dolomite Mountains are a retreat for intrepid climbers, skiers, mountaineers and all manner of outdoors enthusiasts.

Chair lifts and cable cars connect mountain refuges. During winter, these are the perfect way to access well-groomed slopes and, in summer, the extensive trail network. Much of the Belluno province can only be accessed on foot.

> **Did You Know?** Dolomite, a mineral composed of calcium and magnesium carbonate, was discovered by the French geologist Deodat de Dolomieu in the 18th century and named in his honor. The name was later given to the section of the Alps where the mineral is present in great quantities.

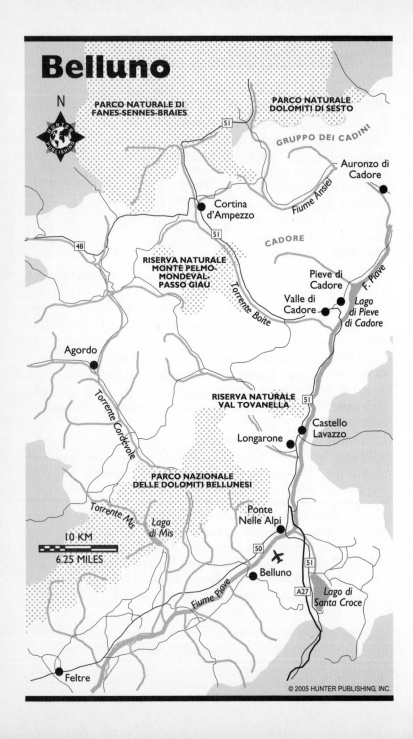

■ Getting There & Getting Around

 By Car: The best way to access the Belluno province's towns from Venice is by taking the **A27** motorway north to Belluno. Just past Belluno, the A27 turns into **SS51**, which continues north to Pieve di Cadore and then on to Cortina d'Ampezzo. To reach **Feltre** from Belluno, follow **SS50** southwest. The best road for reaching towns in the **northwest** part of the province is by following **SP203** from Belluno through Agordo and Rocca Pietore.

 While the Dolomites are in their glory in winter months and the mountains draw large crowds for skiing and other snow sports, roads (particularly mountain passes) are sometimes impassable. A great deal of caution should be exercised when driving through the zone during winter months. Check the weather predictions so you don't get stranded.

 By Bus: Dolomiti Bus (www.dolomitibus.it) operates throughout the province of Belluno. All towns included in this chapter can be accessed by Dolomiti Bus lines, but keep in mind that exploring the zone can be a challenge without a car.

 By Train: The main railway stations in the province are in Feltre, Belluno, Calalzo, Ponte nelle Alpi and Longarone. These stations are along the Padua-Calalzo line. Trains travel frequently between these cities and a few times daily between them and Venice. It takes approximately two hours to reach Belluno from Venice and 2½ hours to reach Calalzo from Venice.

By Plane: The nearest airport to the Belluno province with domestic and international flights daily is Venice's Marco Polo. From here visitors have the option of continuing on to the province by train or by bus. For details: www.veniceairport.it.

■ Adventures

Skiing

Dolomiti Superski: The Dolomiti Superski (www.dolomitisuperski.com) is a network of 1,220 km of ski slopes and 450 lifts that, from early December until spring, make it possible to ski one of the largest ski circuits in the world. By purchasing a Ski Pass, you're entitled to ski on any of the myriad slopes in the network and travel between towns and ski centers by bus. There are many different ski pass combinations for adults and children. The ski circuit covers: Cortina d'Ampezzo, Plan de Corones, Alta Badia, Val Gardena/Alpe di Siusi, Val di Fassa/Carezza, Arabba/Marmolada, Alta Pusteria, Val di Fiemme/Obereggen, San Martino di Castrozza/Passo Rolle, Valle Isarco, Tre Valli and Civetta. It is also possible to purchase a ski pass for one of the 12 zones that the Dolomiti Superski covers. In addition to the network, there are 16 tours around the Dolomiti Superski zone that allow skiers and non-skiers alike to discover various historical and cultural aspects of the zone using the lifts and cablecars as well as the buses.

■ Food & Drink

Mountain dishes in the Belluno province are hearty, traditional and Austrian-inspired due to the zone's proximity to and relationship with Austria.

There are several dishes you're likely to find on menus throughout the zone including *casunzei* (ravioli-like pasta prepared with either pumpkin, spinach or potatoes), *canderli* (dumplings), *spres frit* (fried cheese) and barley soup.

Puina (dialect term for polenta), *lamon* beans, mushrooms, wild herbs, poppy seeds, smoked ricotta and Schiz cheese are all ingredients commonly used in preparing dishes in the mountains.

If it's too cold to sample the world-famous locally produced *gelato*, try a *strudel di mele* (apple strudel) or another apple- or berry-based dessert.

Note: November and May are virtually dead months in most mountain towns, and you'll be lucky to find the occasional hotel or restaurant open.

■ Websites

www.infodolomiti.it

www.provincia.belluno.it

www.sellaronda.com

www.dolomiti.it

■ Vocabulary

Passo – mountain pass

Via ferrata – "Iron-way," anchored steel cable climbing trail

Sciovia – ski lift

Seggovia – chair lift

Ovvavia – two-passenger cab lift

Sentieri – paths

Passegiate – passages/walks

Camminate – walks

Rifugio – mountain refuge

Motoslitte – snowmobiles

Ciaspe – snowshoes

Racchette da neve – snowshoes

Sciare — to ski

> **Note:** Most *rifugi* are only open from mid-June to mid-October, weather permitting. Some are also open for skiers during the winter season.

■ Belluno

Looking out over the Piave valley, the *Città Splendente* (shining city), as it is often called, may have derived its name from the Celtic words *belo-dunum*, meaning splendid city. Positioned where the Dolomites fade into the plateau, the placid

Belluno

town of Belluno serves as a gateway where the Piave and the Ardo Rivers converge in the Piave Valley.

Belluno had its share of unwelcome visitors over the years, including the Longobards and the Goths, but prospered after voluntarily becoming part of the Venetian Republic in the early 15th century.

Still standing are Belluno's two gates, the medieval **Porta Dojona** to its north (left) that once served as its main gate, and **Porta Ruga** to its south.

For centuries the broad **Piazza dei Martiri** (known as *Campedél* until its name was changed in honor of partisans) was the town center. Locals continue to gather in the low-key square's cafés and shops and the otherwise tranquil atmosphere is interrupted by the occasional passing city bus. Just outside the square, nearby mountains peek out from above the Gothic and Renaissance buildings along the main street, **Via Mezzaterra**.

Belluno's artistic achievements include the splendid frescoes by Cesare Vecellio and Francesco Frigimelica in the Gothic church of **Santo Stefano** and several works by Palma il Giovane, Jacopo Bassano and Cesare Vecellio in the 16th-century **Duomo**.

Getting Around

The best way to reach Belluno's town center is by parking in the public paying lot and taking *le scale mobili* (the escalator) up to the city center (Mon-Thurs, 6:30 am-10:30 pm; Fri and Sat, 6:30 am-12:30 am; Sun and holidays, 8 am-10:30 pm).

Sightseeing

Museo Civico (Palazzo dei Giuristi, Piazza Duomo 16, Belluno, ☎ 0437-944036, May-September, Tue-Sun, 10 am-1 pm and 4-7 pm; Oct-April, 9 am-1 pm and 3-6 pm, €2.30). Belluno's civic museum houses a collection of archeological objects dating back to prehistoric times as well as an art gallery with 15th- to 20th-century paintings by many artists who lived or worked in Belluno, including Palma il Giovane, Domenico Tintoretto and Placido Fabris.

Tourist Office

IAT - Belluno
Piazza dei Martiri 8
Belluno
☎ 0437-940083

■ Feltre

The Alps to its north and the pre-Alps to its south didn't safeguard Feltre from being conquered and destroyed repeatedly over the years by barbarian invaders. After suffering great losses, the one-time Roman-controlled town finally moved its city center to a hilltop, the Colle delle Capre, in order to better fortify it.

But it was not only the Romans, Visigoths and Longobards that were interested in the town. After the League of Cambrai sacked it in the 16th century, the Venetian Republic came to its rescue and kept the peace for several hundred years.

Today the low-key university town contains richly frescoed medieval palazzi, a large number of which sit along Feltre's main roads, Via Mezzaterra and Via Lorenzo Luzzo. The frescoes, though disappearing with the passage of time, relate mythological and religious tales.

Sightseeing

 Archeological Zone (Duomo, ☎ 0439-83879, March-Oct, Sat and Sun, 10 am-1 pm and 4-7 pm; free admission). Beneath Feltre's cathedral are excavated ruins from the pre-Roman period, including a commercial and residential quarter of what was then the Roman center of Feltria.

Museo Civico (Via Luzzo 23, Feltre, ☎ 0439-885241, Tue-Fri, 10:30 am-12:30 pm and 4-7 pm; Sat and Sun, 9:30 am-12:30 pm and 4-7 pm; closed Mon. Museum opens and closes one hour earlier in afternoon during winter. €4). Feltre's civic museum displays an interesting collection of medieval and archeological objects on its ground floor and upstairs houses an art gallery with paintings by several artists, including Cima da Conegliano, Gentile Bellini and Palma il Giovane.

> **Great Value:** Purchase a combined ticket for both the Museo Civico and the Carlo Rizzarda Museum of Modern Art for €5.

Carlo Rizzarda Museum of Modern Art (Via Paradiso 8, Feltre, ☎ 0439-885234, Tue-Fri, 10:30 am-12:30 pm and 4-7 pm; Sat and Sun, 9:30 am-12:30 pm and 4-7 pm; closed Mon. Museum opens and closes one hour earlier in afternoon during winter. €4). In the early 20th century, Carlo Rizzarda acquired an extensive collection of modern artwork for his home, much of which is on display at his museum in Feltre. The collection includes paintings, furniture and other decorative artwork by Wildt, Casorati, Scarpa and Marussig, as well as some of his own wrought iron pieces.

Adventures

Festivities

 The lively celebration of the **Palio di Feltre** takes place the first weekend of August each year with processions, concerts, markets, horse races and a rivalry in good spirit between the town's districts.

Cultural Adventures

Euro Studi Veneto (Via Tofana Prima 5, Feltre, ☎ 0439-81821, www.italiaservice.com). Many travelers intent on learning Italian during their visit leave disappointed because most language schools offer courses that last a minimum of four weeks, longer than most travelers' visits. Euro Studi Veneto, however, offers two-week courses (as well as individual lessons) that explore both language and culture. Accommodations are not included in the program fee but the staff does assist participants in finding lodging.

Horseback Riding

 Centro Equestre del Vinchetto di Cellarda – Associazione Turismo Equestre Feltrino (Via Caorame 18, Feltre, call 1-7 pm, closed January, ☎ 0439-390094). Just outside of Feltre, this equestrian center offers horseback riding lessons on a regular basis as well as organizing a variety of excursions, including one to the zone's Venetian villas.

Dining Out

 Pedavena Birreria (Via Vittorio Veneto 78, Pedavena, ☎ 0439-304402, www.labirreriapedavena.com, 10 am-2 am, closed Mon from Oct-June only, and closed two weeks in November, €€). In 1888, the three Luciani brothers from Canale d'Agordo – Luigi, Sante and Giovanni – came to Pedavena in search of good water to build a beer production plant that they later opened in 1896. The plant was later restructured and since 1975 has been part of the Holland-based Heineken International Group. The brewery produces a wide variety of draught beers, including the popular long-aging *Birra del Centenario* (centennial brew). Today, the brewery is a popular place to stop for a beer, enjoy a meal and listen to live music. The best place to do it between April and September is outdoors in the beer garden.

Accommodations

 Hotel Doriguzzi (Viale Piave 2, Feltre, ☎ 0439-2003, www.hoteldoriguzzi.it, €€). A comfortable hotel centrally located in the Bellunese town of Feltre, the Doriguzzi has simple, modern rooms and a pleasant staff. Request one of the spacious upstairs rooms with sloped ceilings and skylights that let plenty of light in.

Shopping

Feltre's primary general market is Tuesday morning, but there is also a smaller market on Friday mornings. Both unfold near the Duomo on Via Campogiorgio Campomosto.

Tourist Office

IAT - Feltre
Piazzetta Trento e Trieste 9
Feltre
☎ 0439-2540

■ Longarone

Straddling the border of the Veneto and Friuli-Venezia Giulia regions, Longarone is in the verdant Vajont Valley where, on Oct 9, 1963 at 10:39 pm, catastrophe struck in the form of a landslide plummeting from the slopes of Toc Mountain into the artificial lake of the Diga del Vajont (Vajont Dam), provoking a massive wave that took more than 1,900 lives in Longarone and nearby towns.

In the hours and days following the tragedy, emergency workers, soldiers, the Italian Red Cross and volunteers arrived in the zone to begin rescue efforts, but they discovered that the deluge of water led to far more dead than wounded.

The landslide essentially created two waves – one eastward toward the center of the Vajont Valley and the other westward toward the Piave Valley between Longarone's center and the nearby towns of Rivalta, Pirago, Faé and Villanova, where the greatest number of lives were lost.

The destruction was tremendous, but great efforts were made to rebuild the destroyed towns. Driving through today, there is an obvious contrast in construction between the towns in the valley that were destroyed and those that were spared. Follow the road up to the top of the dam, where there is a memorial to the victims and a rather chilling reminder of what took place on that night in 1963.

Getting There

 You'll need your own vehicle to reach the memorial site at the top of the dam in Longarone. The best way to reach Longarone is by taking the **A27** north from Venice toward Belluno and then the **SS51** north, exiting at Longarone. From here follow signs as you travel through the small town and climb roads leading to the top of the dam.

■ Cadore

Pieve di Cadore, Tai di Cadore, Lozzo di Cadore

The small attractive mountain town of Pieve di Cadore was the birthplace of the famous Renaissance painter Tiziano Vecellio, better known as Tiziano (Titian).

The modern optical industry has roots in the Cadore zone, which continues to be an important center for eyeglass production today. Many prominent eyeglass and sunglass manufacturers are in Cadore and you'll notice the factories and factory shops as you travel through the zone.

Sightseeing

Casa Natale di Tiziano (Via Arsenale, Pieve di Cadore, open summer only, Tue-Sun). Not far from Pieve di Cadore's main piazza sits the 15h-century house where Renaissance painter Tiziano Vecellio lived with his noble family for many years. Titian studied drawing and painting before being sent to stay with relatives in Venice where he became a student of Giorgione and left a tremendous impact on the city of art. The great painter died in Venice in 1576.

Museo dell'Occhiale (Via degli Alpini 35, Tai di Cadore, ☎ 0435-500213, Sept-June, Mon-Sat, 8:30 am-12:30 pm; July and August, Mon-Sat, 8:30 am-12:30 pm and 4:30-7:30 pm). The local optical industry has led eyeglasses to become an important symbol of Cadore. This museum (located just outside of Pieve di Cadore in Tai di Cadore) chronicles the history of optical science and design from the Middle Ages to the present day, offering insight into the technology and evolution of eyeglasses. Exhibits showcase more than 2,600 pieces, documenting seven centuries of optical history, more than 120 years of which have been in Cadore.

Belluno

Adventures

Driving Adventure

Pian dei Buoi – From Lozzo di Cadore's town center, follow signs toward the Pian di Buia and Tita Poa. The Pian dei Buoi is a plateau about 1,800 meters/5,900 feet above sea level that offers panoramic views of the Dolomite mountains (including Tre Cime di Lavaredo and the Marmarole group on clear days), as well as surrounding valleys. **Timing:** It takes about one hour by car to reach the plateau from Lozzo's town center along an asphalt road. **Caution:** This road is extremely narrow and steep and should not be traveled in poor weather, after dusk or when the roads are slick. **Times:** Due to the narrowness of the road, the absence of a guardrail and the traffic that passes through here during summer months, traffic flow is restricted between July 1 and August 31. Traffic may ascend only from 9 am until 1 pm and must descend between 2 and 5 pm. It is open to two-way traffic from 5 pm until 9 am, but it is not advisable to travel the road after dusk. **Other:** If you have an interest in exploring and a good mountain map, many trails begin along this road.

On Foot

Sentiero Botanico di Tita Poa – This well-marked botanical trail, dedicated to a Lozzo man who used this path until he was 105 years old, is easy to reach from Lozzo di Cadore's town center by following signs for the Tita Poa and Pian dei Buoi. It takes approximately two hours to walk the well-marked trail that winds through the wooded slopes near Lozzo di Cadore. Signs on the trail highlight various flora, vegetation and bird-watching zones (great if you can read Italian or the Ladino-Cadorino dialect). The trail is relatively easy, but hiking boots are recommended.

Accommodations

Hotel al Sole (Via Municipio 26, Pieve di Cadore, ☎ 0435-32118, www.dolomiti.it/alsole, breakfast included, €€€). In Pieve di Cadore's intimate town center, al Sole is a pleasant hotel that offers guests the option of standard hotel rooms or mini apartments in its adjacent residence. Rooms are spacious and the restaurant serves good traditional fare. Unlike many other hotels in mountain regions, this one remains open year-round.

Hotel al Pelmo (Via Nazionale 56, Pieve di Cadore, ☎ 0435-500900, www.pelmo.it, €€). The friendly Trevisian owners at the Pelmo run a small hotel with 43 rooms, many of which have splendid views of the surrounding mountains. They offer guests unfussy but pleasant rooms and they organize day trips around the Belluno province. Their handy online booking service allows potential guests to select room options and dates, as well as to view rooms of their choice.

Shopping

Eyeglass shops are abundant in the Cadore zone, particularly along the road leading from Pieve di Cadore to Auronzo.

Tourist Office

IAT - Cadore
Piazza Venezia 20
Tai di Cadore
☎ 0435-31644

■ Sappada

Just a few kilometers from the Friuli-Venezia Giulia region, and only a few more from the Austrian border sits the sunny resort town of Sappada, comprised of 15 *borgate* (villages). Perched above the main town center is the old town center, *Sappada Vecchia*, where antiquity is reflected in the traditional *Blockbau*-style wooden homes in five of Sappada's *borgate*: Cottern, Fontana, Hoffe, Kratten and Soravia.

Best-known in the mountains for its unique Carnival celebrations, Sappada is an attractive resort town that offers its winter guests a good network of ski trails, ski schools, rental agencies, hotels and restaurants (many concentrated in Borgata Bach). Summertime visitors find plenty in the way of hiking, biking and outdoor adventure.

Quick Stopover: On the road to Sappada from Santo Stefano di Cadore you'll see signs for the Cascata Aquatona along the main road. Make a quick stop here and walk to the covered bridge to see the torrent in the ravine below that cuts through several meters of rock.

Adventures

In Winter

 For the Family: Nevelandia (Via Bach 96, Sappada, ☎ 0435-469554, Dec-Mar, €10). This family snow fun park opened in 2004 offers a variety of snow activities geared to children and families, from sledding and ice skating to snow tubing and ski lessons.

Snowmobile Rental: Motoslitte Tour (Via Bach 96, Sappada, ☎ 0435-469585, www.motoslittetour.com). Located at the Ristorante-Baita Mondschein, Motoslitte Tour rents snowmobiles and offers daytime and evening snowmobile excursions in Sappada and the surrounding zone for adults and children. Enthusiasts should inquire about the 90-km Gran Tour excursion.

Downhill Skiing: Sappada has 20 km of downhill skiing, with trails of varying difficulty. There are five chairlifts and 11 ski lifts, runs for children and beginners, plenty of ski rental shops, a good network connected by a ski bus (see *Ski Pass Office* below) and two ski schools (see below).

Cross-Country Skiing: Sappada was the site of the 1994 Cross Country Skiing World Cup and has five separate trails for cross-country skiers.

Ski Pass Office (Via Palù 88, Sappada, ☎ 0435-469554). If you're considering skiing in Sappada, a ski pass will allow you to access many different ski centers in the network by ski bus. High season rates begin at €23 for one day.

Note: Ski slopes are generally open from 9 am until 4:20 pm, conditions permitting.

Ski Schools: Scuola Italiana Sci-Ski Team (Borgata Soravia 2, Sappada, ☎ 330-298392, www.ski-team.it) and **Scuola Italiana Sci - Sappada** (Borgata Palu 19, Sappada, ☎ 0435-469288, www.scuolascisappada.com) offer adults and children group lessons for €110 (two hours a day for five days) and one-hour private lessons for €30 in high season.

Rentals: Many shops rent skis, snowboards, sleds and other snow equipment, including **Kratter Punto Sport** (Via Bach 55, Sappada, ☎ 0435-469102, www.puntosportkratter.com).

In Summer

In addition to 60+ km of walking trails in and around Sappada, there are also mountain bike trails (stop into the tourist office for a map) and shops that rent mountain bikes, including **Kratter Punto Sport** (see *Ski Rentals*).

Sorgenti del Piave – Follow the eight-km hike from Cima Sappada to the Val Sesis to discover the place where the Piave River originates. If you're up for this hike, stop into the tourist information center for a map.

Adventures for the Soul

Le Terme delle Dolomiti (Via Valgrande 43, Padola di Comelico, ☎ 0435-470153, www.termedelledolomiti.it). At least as far back as the 1800s, the thermal waters from the Dolomites that emerge at Valgrande in Comelico were noted for their curative properties. Although the center is somewhat out of the way, if you're staying in Sappada, after a few days of skiing your tired muscles will thank you for the treat. The modern thermal center, in the Valgrande in Comelico, offers a variety of treatments and services, including thermal cures, massages, a Turkish bath and aesthetic treatments.

Traditional Adventures

Since 1804, people have been gathering the third weekend of September each year to make a pilgrimage to the **Santuario di Santa Maria** in the Austrian town of Luggau. Initially done by locals to give thanks to the Virgin for sparing them from the plague, this beautiful nine-hour excursion to Austria is a telling act of devotion. Join local on Saturday before dawn in the historical center of Cima Sappada, then head to the source of the Piave River and continue toward Luggau. The weekend pilgrimage concludes in Sappada on Sunday evening with a mass of thanksgiving.

Dining Out

Elena (Via Palù, Sappada, ☎ 0435-66238, €€). This restaurant and pizzeria along Sappada's main road serves up generous portions of hearty, traditional dishes. The *raviolini alla Sappadina* (herb-filled ravioli topped with poppy seeds and smoked cheese) is good, if a bit unusual for its distinct smoky flavor; for a second course, try the grilled sausage served with polenta and mushrooms. Not surprisingly, pizza is only served in the evening.

Ristorante-Baita Mondschein (Via Bach 96, Sappada, ☎ 0435-469585, www.ristorantemondschein.it, €€). The cuisine may be traditional in its style at this mountain lodge but the chef keeps the quality anything but typical, highlighting fresh seasonal ingredients in his regional dishes. This is a favorite among locals and returning vacationers.

Accommodations

Hotel Haus Michaela (Borgata Fontana 40, Sappada, ☎ 0435-469377; open Dec-Easter and May-Oct; breakfast included; major credit cards accepted; €€€). In the heart of Sappada, this Alpine-style hotel has rooms and small apartments as well as a good list of amenities, including a Turkish bath, sauna and fitness center. It's a nice place to stay anytime of year, but you will particularly enjoy this in summer since it is Sappada's only hotel with an outdoor pool. If you want to explore the zone on a bike, ask to rent one of their mountain bikes.

Pensione Fontana (Borgata Soravia 51, Sappada, ☎ 0435-469174, €€). The hospitable Fontana family has been welcoming guests into their 15-room *pensione* for many years and, if you're lucky, you'll meet the sweet Signora Pia who, in her grandmotherly way, will make you feel right at home. Depending on your preference, you can choose between half- and full board. The locale is very convenient to the ski lifts and cross-country skiing.

Shopping

The general market is held in Sappada on Thurs mornings during summer months.

Tourist Office

IAT - Sappada
Borgata Bach 9
Sappada
☎ 0435-469131

Websites

www.sappadadolomiti.com

www.sappada-plodn.com

■ Auronzo & Misurina

Among the Dolomites' most famous peaks, the Tre Cime (three peaks) di Lavaredo crown Auronzo di Cadore and its 11 villages, including Misurina. Nature lays a thick blanket of snow from fall until spring on the luminous slopes of Monte Agudo in Auronzo and on Tre Cime di Lavoredo's tallest peak, while the Alpine air freezes a reflection of the impressive mountains in Misurina's lake.

And when winter melts in Auronzo di Cadore as the flowers and plant life start to emerge, the land radiates an extraordinary beauty, familiar yet decidedly different from other seasons. Trees come back to life, revealing densely wooded areas where, centuries ago, wood was cut down and taken to Venice for the construction of ships.

The resort towns offer fine hotels and restaurants, and are part of the Dolomiti Superski circuit, with world-famous ski slopes and excellent facilities.

Adventures

Driving Adventures

 Strada Panoramica delle Tre Cime di Lavaredo – Whether you opt to go on foot, by car (depart from Misurina, €€) or by bus, your visit to the zone would not be complete without discovering the Tre Cime di Lavaredo. Accessible between June and Oct (weather-permitting), the panoramic road leading to the Tre Cime departs from Misurina. It stops at 2,320 m above sea level near the **Rifugio Auronzo** (Località Forcella Longeres, Misurina, ☎ 0435-39002, June-Sept, €), where you can park and either enjoy a meal or spend the night, before continuing on paths that lead closer to the Tre Cime. The **Rifugio Lavaredo** (☎ 0435-39135) is about 30 minutes away from the Rifugio Auronzo on foot along a path beneath the Tre Cime. **Timing:** If you're planning to drive this, the road is open in June between 8 am and 7 pm, in July, August and Sept between 6 am and 8 pm and in Oct from 8 am until 5 pm.

Passo Tre Croci – This scenic mountain pass links Misurina with Cortina and opens onto a splendid panorama of Monte Cristallo and the Marmarole group. For better views, take the chair lift up to Cristallo's **Rifugio Lorenzi** (☎ 0436-866196).

Adventure Sports Operators

Guide Alpine Tre Cime (Località Loita, Misurina, ☎ 333-8420220, Ufficio Turistico, Via Roma 24, Auronzo, ☎ 0435-9359, www.guidetrecime.com). This group of mountain guides helps visitors discover the spirit of the Dolomites through a variety of year-round events in the zone, including snowshoeing and skiing excursions in the winter and mountain hikes in high Alpine passes and rock climbing in summer. They offer activities for all age and skill levels as well as personal instruction.

In Winter

Ice Skating: Stadio del Ghiaccio (Via Roma, Auronzo, ☎ 0435-9544, 10 am-noon, 2-4 pm and 9-11 pm; closed May, June and Nov). Rent a pair of skates and spend an hour or two on the ice in Auronzo's covered ice stadium which hosts occasional ice hockey games, speed skating events and ice shows. Skate rentals cost €6.80 and admission to the rink is €4.20 per person, per session. Skating lessons can be arranged beginning at €8. Note that stadium hours may change during scheduled events.

Go-Carting on Ice: Auronzo Ice Kart (Via Roma 24, Località Palus San Marco, Auronzo, ☎ 328-6904653, www.auronzoicekart.com). By day or night, Auronzo's ice-kart track is one of the hottest places to be in town. Half-hour go-carting sessions on the 500-meter circuit begin at €55 per person.

Sledding: Centro Sleddog Marmarole (Località Palus S. Marco, Auronzo, ☎ 338-7598202, renatoalberoni@libero.it, Dec-Mar). Set out on the European Sleddog 2004 Championship circuit on husky-drawn sleds, either alone or in the company of a group. In addition to excursions, the *Centro* will arrange lessons for adults and children.

Snowmobile Rentals & Excursions: Tre Cime Service (☎ 333-3142212, www.trecimeservice.it). There are several ways to reach Tre Cime di Lavaredo, but none may be as exhilarating as by snowmobile. Departures are from the parking lot at the Loita ski lift.

Downhill Skiing: Auronzo's downhill skiing consists of five lifts and eight ski runs on Monte Agudo, while Misurina has two lifts and five ski runs on Col de Varda. Auronzo di Cadore and Misurina are part of Cortina's circuit on the Dolomiti Superski network and thus are well connected by bus.

Cross-Country Skiing: Centro Sci Fondo at Palus San Marco (☎ 0435-99603) is Auronzo's center for cross-country skiing with 53 km of cross-country skiing, a ski school, rentals and nighttime skiing. **Centro Sci Fondo Misurina** (☎ 0435-9359) is Misurina's center for cross-country skiing, with a school and rentals.

In Summer

 Horseback Riding: Cortes Ranch (Via Val d'Ansiei 33, Località Palus S. Marco, Auronzo, ☎ 0435-497060, June-Oct) offers half- and full-day excursions on horseback for all skill levels. This agriturismo is situated along the road approximately six km from Misurina.

Boat Rentals: Paddle boats can be rented on Lago di S. Caterina in Auronzo and on Lago Misurina in Misurina.

Panoramic Journey: Take a *seggiovia* (chairlift) from Taiarezze in Auronzo to Monte Agudo and follow a short path to the **Rifugio Monte Agudo** (☎ 0435-9336, mid-July-early

Sept and Dec-Mar) at 1,573 m above sea level. The views of the Val d'Ansiéi are marvelous as you look across from the Croda dei Toni to the Tre Cime di Lavaredo.

Accommodations

 Hotel Juventus (Via Padova 26, Località Villapiccola, Auronzo, ☎ 0435-9221, www.dolomiti-hotel.it; closed Nov, €€€) and **Hotel Auronzo** (Via Roma 30, Auronzo, ☎ 0435-400202, www.dolomitihotel.com, €€€) are both located in Auronzo near Lake Caterina and have many rooms and mini-apartments overlooking the lake.

Tourist Office

IAT – Auronzo di Cadore
Via Roma 10
Auronzo di Cadore
☎ 0435-9359

Websites

www.auronzodinverno.com

www.auronzo.com

www.tre-cime.info

■ Cortina d'Ampezzo

Since hosting the Winter Olympics in 1956, the chic mountain resort of Cortina has become one of Italy's premier getaways and a hot-spot for the jet-set crowd.

Famously upscale Cortina radiates elegance everywhere you turn. But in spite of its fashionable boutiques on Corso Italia, its varied skiing and world-renowned restaurants and hotels, the town has retained its Alpine identity, thanks in part to strict zoning laws that have governed the city since the Middle Ages.

Barely 40 km from the Austrian border, Cortina was a literary salon of sorts for intellectuals and artists like Hemingway and De Chirico in the 30s and 40s.

Development in the 1950s brought the finest winter sports facilities, from the Olympic ice rink and the ski jump to the bobsled track and miles and miles of well-groomed ski slopes.

Tucked into the Boite Valley, Cortina is surrounded by the blue-gray peaks of Croda da Lago, Nuvolau, Tofane, Cristallo, Cinque Torri and Sorapis, where winter sports enthusiasts, including nobility and celebrities, enjoy prime ski conditions by day and exceptional dinners and entertainment by night.

Adventures

Driving Adventure

Passo Giau: Of all of Belluno's scenic mountain passes, Passo Giau (2,236 m) is one of the loveliest, with dramatic views of a number of majestic Dolomite peaks. The drive connects Selva di Cadore and Cortina d'Ampezzo and can be started at either end. From Selva di Cadore take SP638 to SS48. Along the drive you'll see meadows, dense forests and rugged mountain peaks but the climax of the route is at the **Hotel Giau** (see *Accommodations*), which sits at the highest point of the mountain pass. This is an ideal place to stop for a midday drink on the outdoor terrace, where you can bask in the high-altitude sun and enjoy the panoramic views. If you're driving this in the winter, consider renting a snowmobile near the Hotel Giau (see *Winter Adventures*).

> **Note:** I once drove this route in mid-May and was amazed to find that the territory was still completely blanketed in deep snow.

Adventure Sports Operators

Cortina Adrenalin Center (Pista Olimpica di Bob, Località Ronco, Cabina S, Cortina d'Ampezzo, ☎ 0436-860808, www.adrenalincenter.it). Since 1990, the Cortina Adrenalin Center has proven how much adventure and excitement Cortina has to offer once the snow melts. From rafting, kayaking and canyoning to taxi-bobbing, mountain biking and hydrospeed, there is an adventure for every age and ability level. And, if you like obstacle courses, try the exciting Adrenalin Park. With their office located at Cortina's bob track, the Adrenalin Center has been a popular draw in Cortina for visitors in search of adventures in the snow too. Whether it be a relaxing excursion on *ciaspes* (snowshoes), followed by a traditional mountain meal, bobsledding on Cortina's bob track, nighttime sled rides, or snow rafting, you can rely on the 20-plus instructors here for their safely designed programs and knowledgeable instruction.

Guide Alpine-Scuola d'Alpinismo (Corso Italia 69/a, Ciasa de Ra Regoles, Cortina d'Ampezzo, ☎ 0436-868505, www.guidecortina.com, 5:30-9:30 pm). Guide Alpine is a group of 25 mountain guides who lead participants on a variety of mountain adventures, including ski mountaineering, snowshoeing, ice climbing and off-trail skiing in winter, as well as free-climbing, iron-way trail climbs and orienteering in summer. Some excursions include overnight stays at mountain refuges and there are also children's programs and a climbing school to choose from.

In Winter

 Ice Skating: Stadio Olimpico del Ghiaccio (Via dello Stadio 1, Cortina d'Ampezzo, ☎ 0436-4380, January-Apr, 10:30 am-12:30 pm and 3:30-5:30 pm). Now indoors, Cortina's Olympic Ice Stadium that was built when the town hosted the 1956 Olympics is open to the general public for skating during the winter and early spring only. The cost for one session is €5 or €8.50 with skate rental. It is also the site of many ice hockey and skating performances and events.

Snowmobiling: Moto Snow Cortina (Località Passo Giau, Colle Santa Lucia, ☎ 348-7920620). Located in Passo Giau just across from the Hotel Giau, Moto Snow Cortina rents snowmobiles, sleds and snowshoes to explore the beautiful mountain pass and surroundings.

Bobsledding: (See *Cortina Adrenalin Center* above)

Cross-Country Skiing: Centro Sportivo Fiames (Via dei Campi 8, Località Fiames, ☎ 0436-4903). Cortina's cross-country ski center is comprised of extensive ski tracks in addition to equipment rentals and Cortina's cross-country ski school, **Scuola Fondo Ski Cortina**, which offers private and group ski lessons. There are several different tracks, including a beginner track, two- , three- , five- and 7.5-kilometer tracks, and a 30-km track along what was once the railway from Cortina to Dobbiaco. A one-day ticket to the cross-country circuit is €3 and a weeklong Dolomiti Nordic Ski Pass begins at €10 per person. Inquire about special offers – during the 2004/2005 season, the tracks were illuminated for two hours on Wednesday evenings and the ski school offered complimentary lessons.

Downhill Skiing: Cortina offers skiers 140 km of downhill slopes, the majority of which are graded medium difficulty (but more than a quarter of which are easy). Cortina's main downhill ski centers are Faloria, Cristallo-Mietres, Tofana, Socrepes-Pocal and Falzarego-Cinque Torri. All of Cortina's ski centers can be accessed by bus but some say the skiing here isn't at its prime too early or too late in the season.

Belluno

SKI & SNOWBOARDING SCHOOLS

Scuola Sci Cortina (locations at Corso Italia, Ciasa de Ra Regoles, ☎ 0436-2911; Località Socrepes, ☎ 0436-867381; Località Pocol, ☎ 0436-3496, www.scuolascicortina.it).

Scuola Sci Dolomiti-Cortina (Via Roma 91, ☎ 0436-862264, www.dolomitiscuolasci.com).

Scuola di Sci Azzurra (Via Ria de Zeto 8, Funivia Faloria Cortina d'Ampezzo, ☎ 0436-2694, www.azzurracortina.com).

Scuola Snowboard (Via XXIX Maggio, 10/b, Cortina d'Ampezzo, ☎ 0436-878261, www.boarderline.it). Private and group lessons as well as snowboard rentals.

Ski Pass: **Ski Pass World Cortina** (Via Marconi, Cortina d'Ampezzo, ☎ 0436-862171, Mon-Sat, 8:30 am-12:30 pm and 3:30-7:30 pm).

RENTALS

Snow Service (locations at Via XXIX Maggio 11, near Largo Posta, ☎ 0436-866635; Corso Italia 206, ☎ 0436-868679; Via Marconi 14, near the Stazione,

☎ 0436-862467; Sciovia Lacedel, ☎ 0436-2221, www.snowservice.it). They rent skiing and snowboarding equipment in addition to sleds and snowshoes.

Shop & Rent-Scuola Sci Cortina (Piazzetta S. Francesco 2, Ciasa de Ra Regoles, ☎ 0436-2503, www.scuolascicortina.it) sells and rents ski and snowboard equipment and has a repair shop.

In Summer

● Mountain Biking

Centro Mountain Bike (Località Fiames, ☎ 0436-867088, 8:30 am-7 pm) and **Cicli Cortina** (Località Majon 148, ☎ 0436-867215, 8:30 am-7 pm) rent mountain bikes beginning at €6 for one hour and €25 for a full day.

● On Foot

Following are a few exceptionally scenic hikes that are popular and widely considered to be among the best in the zone. I've included these particular hikes (in order of increasing difficulty) for their proximity to Cortina, a popular base for many mountain travelers, but note that several of these are difficult trails and *vie ferrate* that require great technical aptitude and a good fitness level in addition to the proper equipment (including a helmet and harness). Prior to setting out on a trail, it is best to consult a CAI (Club Alpino Italiano) map and a local guide, particularly if your plans include extensive hiking.

> **Warning:** Do not underestimate the level of difficulty of *vie ferrate* and begin trails early in the day in good weather only.

Orme dei Dinosauri (The Dinosaur Track Hike) – To reach the beginning of trail 472, follow SS251 from Selva di Cadore southeast until you reach the **Rifugio Staulanza** at Forcella Staulanza. This easy trail at the foot of Monte Pelmo leads to fossilized dinosaur tracks from the Triassic period. It was once believed that this area was at about sea level and there were numerous herbivore and carnivore dinosaurs that roamed the area. An enormous rock formation fell from the side of Monte Pelmo, broke into many pieces and exposed the dinosaur tracks that were discovered in the late 20th century. **Timing:** Allow approximately one hour to reach the tracks and another hour to retrace your steps back.

Giro di Nuvolau – Depart from Passo Giau along trail 452, an easy-moderate trail. Follow the trail to **Rifugio Averau** (from where you can see Marmolada, Civetta and Cinque Torri), then pick up trail 439 and head to **Rifugio Scoiattoli** (you can see rock climbers scaling nearby rock faces). From here, continue on trail 439 to **Rifugio Cinque Torri**, from where you have great views of Cinque Torri (Five Towers). Then take trail 443 back to Passo Giau.

> **Note:** If you want to visit one of the oldest rifugi in the zone and enjoy great views of Austria and Switzerland on a clear day, take the 30-minute route from Rifugio Averau to Rifugio Nuvolau on 439 (one of the more remote rifugi in the area) and then retrace your steps.

Giro Classico del Monte Pelmo – This trail begins at Rifugio Staulanza at Forcella Staulanza, near Selva di Cadore. Follow trail 472 toward Rifugio Venezia, a moderate-easy trail. From here you can either retrace your steps back or, for an expert trail and via ferrata, take trail 480 to Forcella Val d'Arcia and continue on trail 480, then pick up trail 468 until you reach trail 472 which takes you back to Rifugio Staulanza.

Passo Falzarego – Park at the cable car parking lot and either take the cable car to **Rifugio Lagazuoi** (Lagazuoi, Cortina d'Ampezzo, ☎ 0436-867303), which was used as an operations base during the filming of the movie *Cliffhanger* with Sylvester Stallone, or follow trail markers for Galleria Lagazuoi (Lagazuoi tunnels). These tunnels were built during World War I as a protected access route and they spiral up inside the mountain toward Rifugio Lagazuoi. The rifugio's panoramic terrace offers great views of the surroundings and is a good place to stop for lunch. If you want to continue exploring the zone on foot, the rifugio is a good base for a large trail network that leads both north toward Lagazuoi's summit and east toward the **Gallerie di Castelletto** and the World War I open-air museum. This museum consists of reconstructions of World War I trenches, access routes and living and operating quarters for both the Italian and Austro-Hungarian front lines.

> **Note:** Trails from the rifugio range from moderate to expert level.

Sorapis – Begin trail 215 at Passo Tre Croci and follow it to **Rifugio Sorapis A. Vandelli**, about a three-hour hike (this is graded easy). The rifugio is at the base of the Sorapis peaks and near Lago di Sorapis at 1,923 meters above sea level. For more of a challenge, continue on trail 215/244 to **Rifugio Tondi D. Faloria**, a trail that transitions from moderate difficulty to expert. The total time needed to reach Rifugio Tondi D. Faloria is about six hours. Retrace steps back.

Monte Cristallo – From Cortina d'Ampezzo, head east on SS48 toward Passo Tre Croci and stop at the **Ristorante Rio Gere** (1,680 meters) and a chair lift where you can park. **Take the lift to Rifugio San Forca** (2,235 meters). From here, you can continue to **Capanna Guido Lorenzi** (2,932 meters) either by taking the *ovvavia* (standing ski lift) or by following the hiking trail (this is graded difficult/expert). From Capanna Guido Lorenzi, there are four expert trails (two of which are vie ferrate). The most famous via ferrata leads to the summit of **Monte Cristallo** (3,221 meters) and even though it takes less than two hours to reach Monte Cristallo, it is very technical and should be started before noon in good weather conditions. There are exceptional views from here. Don't leave before signing your name in the book.

> **Note:** The non-hikers in your group may enjoy the atmosphere and the views from Rifugio San Forca and Rifugio Capanna Guido Lorenzi while you set off on foot. There is a fee for both the chair lift and the ovvavia. If you intend on embarking on the via ferrata to Monte Cristallo, it is recommended to take the ovvavia to Capanna Guido Lorenzi rather than hiking there.

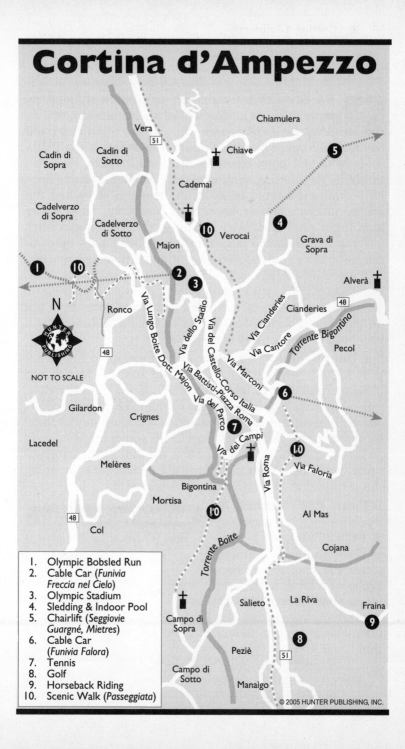

Dining Out

 Ra Stua (Via Grohmann 2, Cortina d'Ampezzo, ☎ 0436-868341, closed Wed in low season, €€€). Stroll by Ra Stua on a chilly winter night and you'll be lured into one of Cortina's oldest restaurants (circa 1930), if not by the fabulous aromas wafting out the door, than certainly by the glowing *caminetto* (grill/fireplace) visible near its entrance. Restored in 2002, the majolica stove and the warm, intimate atmosphere were preserved, as was the unfailingly good food. With a blazing grill, you might have guessed that their specialties include grilled meats, meat on the spit and the much-loved *Fiorentina* (Bistecca Fiorentina, or Florentine-style steak). The pasta is homemade, and, thanks to a lively young management, dishes are innovative. Many of their products, including their wine, come from the owner's family farm, *Vitis & Vita* in the Euganean Hills. A very good choice any day of the week.

Da Beppe Sello (Via Ronco 68, Cortina d'Ampezzo, ☎ 0436-3236, www.beppesello.it, closed Tue, late Mar to late May, and late Sept to late Nov, €€€). If you're in search of refined mountain cuisine, search no more. Da Beppe Sello is one of the favorites in Cortina and is a *Ristorante del Buon Ricordo* for good reason (see page 39). If you're in the habit of ordering *Buon Ricordo* dishes when you dine at their restaurants, you'll take their collector's plate home after enjoying the savory *carré di cervo saporito* (deer meat).

Il Ponte (Via Franchetti 8, Cortina d'Ampezzo, ☎ 0436-867624, €€). Just off Corso Italia, this bar and pizzeria is a popular gathering spot for locals in the evenings and, fortunately, it's open during low season. The pizza selection is typical and their *pizza marinara con olive nere* (my typical order) was very good.

DINING PRICE CHART	
Price per person for an entrée	
€	Under €5
€€	€5-€12
€€€	€13-€20
€€€€	€21-€30
€€€€€	Over €30

Accommodations

 If notoriously over-priced Cortina doesn't fit into your budget, consider staying in a hotel outside of Cortina's center where rates are more reasonable. If you're planning a trip during off-season, call the tourist office for a list of hotels that will be open during your visit, since Cortina's hotels tend to alternate their periods of closure each year.

HOTEL PRICE CHART	
Based on a double room for two	
€	Under €50
€€	€50-€80
€€€	€81-€120
€€€€	€121-€190
€€€€€	Over €190

Hotel Passo Giau (Passo Giau, Colle S. Lucia, ☎ 0437-720130, June 20-Sept 20, €€€). Operated by the Alpine guide Diego Valleferro and his family, the hotel and restaurant is on the Passo Giau at the base of the Nuvolau cliffs. You don't get much better than this in terms of scenery from your hotel window, but this is only on option if you're visiting between June 20 and Sept 20. If you're planning hiking excursions in the zone, you'll find Diego and his son to be an excellent resource. There is an outdoor terrace where you can sit with an espresso or an aperitif and soak up the mountain sun in the company of many others since this is a favorite stopover, particularly with motorcyclists.

Hotel de la Poste (Piazza Roma 14, Cortina d'Ampezzo, ☎ 0436-4271, www.delaposte.it; closed Nov and May; breakfast included; major credit cards accepted; €€€€). In 1835, Gottardo Manaigo began accommodating visitors who arrived in carriages on mail routes into his home, and over time it evolved into a guesthouse. In the heart of Cortina, de la Poste is still operated by the same family which for decades has preserved its status as one of Cortina's most refined hotels. Many of the nicest rooms have balconies overlooking the town center.

Hotel Ancora (Corso Italia 62, Cortina d'Ampezzo, ☎ 0436-3261; breakfast included; major credit cards accepted; €€€€). Since its inception in 1826, the legendary Hotel Ancora has been heralded for its hospitality and sophistication. Rooms are elegantly furnished with antiques and rich décor; some have balconies and Jacuzzis. They have several restaurants that are well-respected for their fine cuisine, but whether or not you're a guest here, one of the nicest pastimes in Cortina is sipping a caffè or aperitif in the Terrazza Viennese overlooking the Corso Italia.

Hotel Meuble Villa Neve (Via B. Franchetti 18, Cortina d'Ampezzo, ☎ 0436-2228, www.villaneve.dolomiti.com; open year-round; breakfast included, €€€). By some standards this hotel might not be considered the best value for the euro, but its convenience to the town center outweighs the somewhat noisy rooms (Via Franchetti is well-trafficked) and scanty breakfast spread. If you're traveling during low season when nearly all other hotels are closed, it's a good option.

Nightlife & Entertainment

 Cortina is a sophisticated town with a lively nightlife and displays its colorful spirit everywhere from concerts and discos to piano bars and jazz clubs.

Enoteca Cortina (Via del Mercato 5, Cortina d'Ampezzo, ☎ 0436-862040, www.enotecacortina.com). This wine bar is a popular place to spend a more intimate evening enjoying a glass of the finest Italian and international wines accompanied by cheese and salumi plates or other appetizers in the company of friends.

Blu Room (Largo delle Poste 8, Cortina d'Ampezzo, ☎ 0436-4366, www.blunotte.it; open Christmas-Easter and August; €15-25 cover charge). This cosmopolitan club is a hit with the 25-35 crowd for its cultured food, music and dancing. If you want the dancing minus the frills, try their other club, **Area Disco** (Via Ronco 82, Cortina d'Ampezzo, ☎ 0436-867393; €15-25 cover charge), Cortina's popular discoteca that draws a younger crowd.

Shopping

Corso Italia is Cortina's glamorous core where, sooner or later, every visitor passes through to splash out obscene amounts of money (or at least window shop) at one of the upscale boutiques. This pedestrian zone also has several artisan craft shops where you can find traditional crafts. One of these is **Artigianato Artistico Ampezzano** (Corso Italia

87, 9 am-12:30 pm and 4-7:30 pm; closed Sun and Mon; major credit cards accepted).

Cortina's general market takes place Tue and Fri mornings in Piazzale della Stazione.

Tourist Office

IAT – Cortina d'Ampezzo
Piazzetta S. Francesco 8
Cortina d'Ampezzo
☎ 0436-3231

Websites

www.cortinadampezzo.it

www.cortinavirtualtour.com

www.cortina.com

■ Arabba

At the base of the Sella mountain chain and at the tip of the Upper Agordino district between the Passo Pordoi and the Passo Campolongo, Arabba is one of the Dolomite's most visited ski resorts, yet it has somehow preserved its low-key atmosphere. The town has continued to develop, with many new apartments and hotels sprouting up frequently but, in spite of its growth, Arabba has not traded in its Alpine character and traditions for tourism. The village has many of the facilities and services that you'd expect from a larger tourist resort, but has retained the charm of a small mountain village.

Don't Miss: Keep an eye out for the ruins of  the **Castello di Andraz** along SP48 on the way to Livinallongo and Arabba. This cliff-fortress dates back to circa 1000 AD. Overlooking the Livinalongo meadows, according to legend, it was built by three sisters and used as a lookout point. Over the centuries it served as a fortress and a noble residence.

As part of the Dolomiti Superski network, Arabba is a great departure point for skiing in the Sellaronda group and on the Marmolada. This quaint town has several cafés, restaurants, pubs and bars that balance out a day spent on the ski slopes.

Adventures

In Winter

 Downhill Skiing: Arabba has 52 km of downhill ski slopes and is connected with the Sella Ronda mountain group, as well as the four mountain passes of Gardena, Pordoi, Campolongo and Sella. Arabba's mountain is Portavescovo, at 2,478 m above sea level, and Marmolada can be accessed from here as well.

Ski Schools: Scuola Italiana Sci-Arabba (Passo Campolongo-Passo Pordoi, ☎ 0436-79160, www.scuolasciarabba.com). Arabba's ski school offers group and private skiing, carving and snowboarding lessons for adults and children. Private lessons begin at €30 for one person for an hour and €210 for one person for a full day. If you can find a second person to schedule a private lesson with, it's a much better deal and you still get plenty of one-on-one attention. Group courses for adults begin at €58 for one day and €120 for five days in high season.

Ski rentals: Ski Service da Nico (Via Piagn 2, Arabba, ☎ 0436-79445, www.skiservicearabba.com). Da Nico is *the* place to rent ski and snowboard equipment in Arabba and have your own equipment serviced.

Snowmobile rentals: Snowmobiles can be rented near the **Plan Boé hut** (☎ 0436-79339) during high season, and daytime and evening excursions on snowmobiles can be arranged.

Accommodations

Hotels

 Hotel Alpenrose (Via Precomun 24, Arabba, ☎ 0436-750076, www.alpenrosearabba.it, €€€). Just outside of Arabba's town center, the Alpenrose offers guests well-appointed mountain-style lodging in bright, comfortable rooms. Rooms have pine furniture and tile bathrooms, many with beamed ceilings and hardwood floors. The hotel has a restaurant as well as a wellness center with a Turkish bath and sauna.

Apartments

Villagio Precumon-House Service Arabba (Via Salesel di Sotto 81, Livinallongo, ☎ 0436-780142, www.hsarabba.it, €€). The characteristically Alpine Precumon Village, new in 2004, consists of one- , two- and three-room apartments that can accommodate up to seven guests. The spacious apartments were carefully designed to include all modern comforts that the most discerning travelers expect. The village's proximity to the slopes makes it perfect for those who value convenience. This is ideal for families and groups who prefer independence and privacy and plan on staying for at least a week. If you did not pack your own, be prepared to pay an extra fee for towels and bed linens.

Belluno

HISTORICAL INTEREST

From May of 1915 until November of 1917, the Austro-Hungarian/Italian front lines passed through the highest peaks in the Dolomites, making for some of the most brutal and bloody battles of the Great War. Trenches, forts and tunnels were constructed by soldiers to defend themselves from not only the enemy soldiers, but the wind, the snow and the bitter cold as well. Many of these still remain in the zone today, and the **Giro Sciistico della Grande Guerra 1914-1918** is a ski itinerary (part of the Dolomiti Superski) that traces the front lines and passes around the Col di Lana (3,452 m).

Tourist Office

IAT – Arabba
Via Boe
Arabba
☎ 0436-79130

Website

www.arabba.it

■ Marmolada

Winter Adventure - Glacial Skiing

On the doorstep of the Trentino-Alto Adige region, Marmolada makes skiing under the summer sun supremely doable and the activity of choice for so many ski enthusiasts. Dubbed *Queen of the Dolomites*, the glacier reigns over the Agordino district and the entire Veneto region from 3,342 m above sea level (the highest peak in the Dolomites).

Just above the small town of Rocca Pietore sits the *Malga Ciapela*, the primary base for accessing Marmolada's main 12-km slope known as **La Bellunese** at Punta Rocca (3,270 m) by cable car, in addition to the Padon ski area. A few bars and hotels surround Malga Ciapela.

Ski Schools

 Scuola Italiana Sci-Rocca Marmolada (Rocca Pietore, ☎ 0437-722060, www.marmolada.com/scuolascimarmolada). They offer individual and group ski and snowboard lessons for adults and children in addition to ski excursions. Group lessons start at €100 for six three-hour lessons and individual lessons begin at €34 for one hour.

Sightseeing

 Museo della Grande Guerra (Serauta cable car station, www.museo.marmolada.com, 9:30 am-3:30 pm, conditions permitting; free admission). The highest museum in Europe sits at 2,950 m in the Serauta cablecar station below Marmolada's summit. Dedicated to all soldiers who gave their lives fighting on the glacier, the museum exhibits war relics, including personal photographs, documents, weaponry, uniforms and equipment.

Accommodations

 Hotel Principe Marmolada (Malga Ciapela, ☎ 0437-522971, www.giemmehotels.com; breakfast included; major credit cards accepted; €€€-€€€€). The most convenient place to stay if your plans include skiing Marmolada, this is a 73-room hotel with understated, modern rooms (some with balconies), a restaurant, pool, fitness center and live entertainment during high season. If you're looking for comfort, accessibility and style, you'll find them all here.

Tourist Office

IAT - Rocca Pietore
Via Roma 15
Rocca Pietore
☎ 0437-721319

Website

www.marmolada.com

Belluno

Province of Padua

■ Padua

Situated where the Brenta and the Bacchiglione Rivers converge, Padua was founded as a fisherman's village in the fourth century BC. Later, during the Roman period, *Patavium*

(as it was then known) was allied to the Romans against the Gauls and was one of the Roman Empire's most prosperous towns.

The 13th century gave birth to a university town that would become a burgeoning center of education and art in the Middle Ages and the Renaissance, marked by luminaries such as Galileo, Dante, Giotto and Donatello.

By the 16th century, the Serene Republic of Venice took Padua under its control. It later came under Napoleon's control, followed by that of Austrians.

Long considered one of Italy's golden cities of art, this frescoed town exhibits many impressive works by great medieval and Renaissance artists and today is a spirited cultural center animated by university students, intellectuals, artists and travelers.

Saint Anthony, associated with Padua for his 13th-century works and the subsequent construction of a basilica in his honor, is the patron saint of lost and found objects. His feast day is June 13th.

Getting There

By Car: Padua is easily accessible from either the **A4** highway linking Milan and Venice (exit at Padova Ovest or Padova Est), or from the **A13**, which connects Bologna with Padua (exit at Padova Sud). The **SS47** connects Padua with Cittadella and Bassano but, like many state roads, this is heavily trafficked during peak hours.

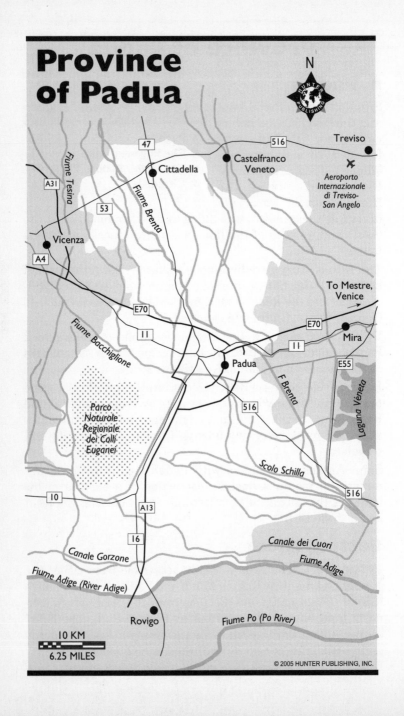

By Bus: Padua's main bus station for SITA buses is located at Piazzale Boschetti, behind the Parco dell'Arena and the Scrovegni Chapel. **SITA** buses (☎ 049-8206811, www.sita-on-line.it) connect many towns throughout the province of Padua and additionally make several stops in the provinces of Venice and Rovigo.

 By Train: Padua is on the Venezia-Milano and the Venezia-Roma railway lines. Trains between Padua and Venice run several times each hour and take approximately 30 minutes. For timetables and fares: www.trenitalia.com.

 By Plane: The nearest airport to Padua with domestic and international flights daily is Venice's Marco Polo, about 42 km from Padua. Trains and buses connect to Padua from the airport. For details: www.veniceairport.it.

Getting Around

 On Foot: Padua's city center is fairly expansive and its Corso del Popolo (the main road, which turns into Corso Garibaldi, Via VIII Febbraio, Via Roma and Via Umberto I), connects the railway station in the northern part of town to Prato della Valle in the south. Most major sites can be accessed from Corso del Popolo but, since they are not centralized, wear a comfortable pair of shoes and allow extra time to tour the city.

 By Bike: Padua is a fairly large city and bicycles make it much easier to visit the sites in less time. Bicycles can be rented at the **Railway Station** (☎ 348-7016373), at the **Piazza del Santo** (seasonal, ☎ 049-8753087) and from **Noleggio Biciclette di Padova** (Via Sauro, ☎ 049-650662).

By Car: Traffic is generally congested in and around Padua during the day and the best bet for travelers arriving by car is to park and travel the city on foot or by bus. The major **parking lots** in the city are the **Parcheggio Prato della Valle** (Piazza Rabin) on the south end of town, **Parcheggio Stazione FS** (at the railway station) and **Parcheggio Via Sarpi**. Parking at these lots is free for PadovaCard holders.

The PadovaCard offers an excellent way to explore the sites of Padova without draining your budget. This discount card is good for 48 hours and offers access to most of the city and many of the province's important attractions for free or reduced fees. Many of the museums, villas, castles, boat trips and gardens accept this card, as well as bed and breakfasts, shops and tour agencies. The non-refundable, non-transferable PadovaCard can be used for one adult and one child under the age of 12 and costs €13. To purchase, stop at the region's tourist information offices. For more information, see www.turismopadova.it/padovacard.

For travelers interested in **car rentals**, both **Hertz** (☎ 049-8752202) and **Avis** (☎ 049-664198) are located at the railway station.

By Taxi: Padua's principle taxi stop is in front of the railway station. If you find yourself around town and in need of a ride, don't expect to hail a cab. Instead, call the 24-hour service at ☎ 049-651333, www.taxipadova.com. **Radio Taxi Padova** also offers services to transport handicapped passengers and has shuttle buses (☎ 049-8704425) that travel to and from the airport in Venice.

By Bus: APS is the urban bus line that runs throughout the city and its outer limits and is an alternative to traveling the city on foot. Most APS buses depart from the railway station, including lines 3 and 8, which both make stops along Corso Garibaldi and at Prato della Valle. A valid PadovaCard can be used in lieu of a bus ticket to travel on APS buses.

Look Out For: The **Metrobus** is a modern tram system that will offer a speedy alternative to traveling around town. The construction of the tram system in Padua's city center was still in progress at time of publication but, once in motion, three separate blue tram lines are expected to improve travel within the city center.

Above: Basilica di San Antonio in Padua (courtesy of Danesin)

Below: One of Giotto's frescoes in Padua's Scrovegni Chapel (courtesy of Danesin)

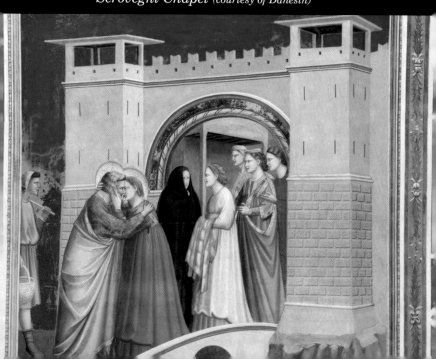

Above: Chapel and ruins in the Delta del Po, Rovigo

Below: The Asolo countryside

Above: Palladio's Villa Emo Capodilista in Fanzolo di Vedelago, Treviso

Below: Prosecco vineyards

Padua

1. Giardini dell'Arena; Piazza Eremetani
2. Pollini Concert Hall; Museo della 3a Armate; Porta Altinate; Piazza Garibaldi
3. Piazzale Boschetti; Bus
4. Porta Portello
5. Porta Ponte Molino; Piazza Petrarca; Chiesa e Scuola del Carmine
6. Giardini della Rotonda
7. Porta Savonarola
8. Porta San Giovanni
9. Porta Saracinesca
10. Giardino Trieste
11. Chiesa di San Leopoldi
12. Piazzale Santa Croce
13. Porta di Santa Croce
14. Prato della Valle; Basilica di Santa Giustina
15. Orto Botanico
16. Basilica del Santo; Oratorio di San Giorgio
17. Porta Pontecorro; Piazzale Pontecorro; Parco Treves
18. Palazzo Zabarella; Chiesa di San Francesco
19. Tomba di Antenore
20. Università (Palazzo del Bò)
21. Municipio; Piazza delle Erbe
22. Stabilimento Gran Caffé Pedrocchi; Piazza della Frutta
23. Teatro Verdi; Chiesa di S Nicolò; Piazza dei Signori; Torre dell'Orologio; Loggia della Gran Guardia
24. Piazza Duomo; Cattedrale e Battistero
25. Osservatorio Astronomico (la Specola)

i Padua Tourist Board

▪▪▪▪▪▪ City Walls

▪▪▪▪▪▪ Walking Tours

NOT TO SCALE
© 2005 HUNTER PUBLISHING, INC.

Sightseeing

 Prato della Valle, said to be one of Europe's largest piazzas, was a swampland until Andrea Memmo had it redesigned and transformed into a commercial center in 1767. The *prato* (field), a large grassy island surrounded by a canal, has four stone bridges connecting it to the surrounding square and 78 statues honoring great Paduan citizens. Today this pedestrian zone is the site of markets, concerts, sports and cultural events and is a popular spot to bask in the sun, read a book, skate or relax.

Basilica di Santa Giustina (Prato della Valle, ☎ 049-8751628; summer 7:30 am-noon and 3-8 pm; winter 8 am-noon and 3-5 pm). The eight cupolas of the Basilica di Santa Giustina, a structure rebuilt by Benedictine friars in the 16th century, dominate the south side of the Prato della Valle. Among the finest works of art contained in the basilica is Veronese's altarpiece from 1575 representing the *Martyrdom of Santa Giustina*.

Orto Botanico (Via Orto Botanico 15, ☎ 049-8272119; Apr-Oct, 9 am-1 pm, 3-6 pm; Nov-Mar, 9 am-1 pm; €4). This serene Renaissance garden, established in 1545 by the University of Padua's faculty of medicine, is considered the oldest university garden in the world and exhibits a fascinating collection of plants from around the globe. The oldest plant in the garden, a palm from 1585 commonly referred to as the *Goethe palm* after the German writer, is enclosed in a glass house in the circular garden where two other plants from the 1700s, a ginkgo and a magnolia, are also found.

Basilica di Sant'Antonio (Piazza del Santo, ☎ 049-8789722, www.basilicadelsanto.org). This Romanesque-Gothic basilica honors Friar Anthony from Lisbon, who died outside Padua in 1231 and was later beatified. Construction on the basilica, with its eight Byzantine inspired domes, began shortly after his death and was completed in the early 14th century. One of Italy's largest pilgrim shrines, drawing millions of pilgrims each year, it contains Saint Anthony's marble tomb in the **Cappella di Sant'Antonio**, along with many votive offerings by people who have attributed restored health to *il Santo*, as he's com-

Madonna & Child, by Donatello in the Basilica di Sant'Antonio

monly referred to. Many relics from his life, including his tongue, vocal chords and tunic, can be seen in the **Capella delle Reliquie** behind the main altar. Donatello's 15th-century crucifix and sculptures on the high altar and his series of bronze reliefs illustrating the life of *il Santo*, are among the basilica's many important works of art.

Oratorio di San Giorgio and the Scuola del Santo (Piazza del Santo, ☎ 049-8755235; winter 9 am-12:30 pm and 2:30-5 pm; summer 9 am-12:30 pm and 2:30-7 pm; €2, reduced admission with the PadovaCard). Travelers who visit the basilica and neglect the other buildings in the Piazza del Santo miss some of Padua's most precious fresco cycles. The admission fee is well worth paying to see late 14th-century frescoes by Altichiero da Zevio and

Jacopo Avanzo in the **Oratorio** and Titian's early 16th-century frescoes (see right) depicting the lives of St. George, St. Catherine and St. Lucy in the **Scuola**.

Musei Antoniani (Piazza del Santo, ☎ 049-8225656; winter 10 am-1 pm and 2-5 pm; summer 9 am-1 pm and 2:30-6:00 pm, closed Mondays; €2.50, reduced admission with PadovaCard). This museum houses important works of art that have been made for the basilica over the centuries, including paintings, sculpture and tapestries.

Gattamelata (Piazza del Santo). Rising above the stalls in Piazza del Santo is Donatello's 15th-century equestrian statue, Gattamelata. Cast in bronze, this work is recognized

Padua

Statue of Gattamelata in the Piazza del Santo

for its substantial impact on the development of Renaissance sculpture.

Battistero del Duomo (Piazza del Duomo, ☎ 049-656914; Nov-Mar, 10 am-6 pm; Apr-Oct, 10 am-7 pm; €2.50, reduced admission with the PadovaCard). The baptistery's cycle of 14th-century frescoes by Giusto de'Menabuoi illustrating biblical stories from the Old and New Testaments is a remarkable work and makes the baptistery more impressive than the neighboring cathedral.

Piazza dei Signori – Many cafés, pastry shops and small boutiques line this square but its character is defined by the **Palazzo del Capitanio**, a former Carrara palace rebuilt in the 17th century as a residence for the city's government representatives, and its **Torre del Orologio** with an astronomical clock from 1344.

Palazzo della Ragione (Enter from Via VIII Febbraio, Tue-Sun: 9 am-7 pm, ☎ 049-8205006; free admission with the PadovaCard except during exhibitions). This early 13th-century palace built as the seat of Padua's parliament separates the **Piazza della Frutta** and **Piazza delle Erbe**, two lovely squares that host the daily fruit and vegetable market. **Il Salone**, the palazzo's upper floor, is a massive hall with a vibrant cycle of 15th-century astrological and religious frescoes by Nicolò Miretto that replaced Giotto's frescoes, destroyed in a 1420 fire. The wooden sculpture of a horse (a replica of the Gattamelata) was commissioned to be pulled in a public procession and later placed in the great hall that measures a vast 81 m long. Today, the ground floor of the palazzo is a covered market with many food shops.

Palazzo del Bo (Via VIII Febbraio, ☎ 049-8273044; guided visits Mon, Wed, Fri, 3:15 and 4:15 pm; Tue, Thurs, Sat, 10:15 and 11:15 am; €3). The Palazzo del Bo, named after an inn that once stood on this site called *Il Bo*, is the main seat of

Italy's second-oldest university, the University of Padua, founded in 1222. The guided tour is well-worth taking to see Galileo's desk and pulpit where he taught from 1592-1610, as well as the world's oldest anatomy theater (1594). Another famous 16th-century professor who taught at the university was Gabriele Fallopio, after whom the Fallopian tubes were named. The first female university graduate, Elena Lucrizia Cornaro Piscopia, received her degree from here in 1678, and her statue is in the courtyard. Don't be surprised to see recent graduates who just received their *laurea* (degree) emerging from here and congregating outside in ridiculous costumes reciting peculiar verses. This is a rite of passage and tradition among university graduates, and you might enjoy being a spectator.

> **Tip:** Because this is one of the main sites for graduation ceremonies and other official university events, tours are occasionally cancelled, so plan ahead.

Caffé Pedrocchi-Piano Nobile (Via VIII Febbraio 15, ☎ 049-8205007, www.caffepedrocchi.it; 9:30 am-12:30 pm and 3-6 pm, closed Mon; €4, free admission with the PadovaCard). This fashionable historic café, often referred to as the *café without doors*, has been a Padua landmark since the 19th century and today is still very much a part of the social heart of the city. Commissioned by a famous coffee maker, Antonio Pedrocchi, and designed by Venetian architect Giuseppe Jappelli in 1831, the neoclassical café has been an important gathering place for intellectuals over the years, including Eleonora Duse, Luigi Barzini and Stendhal. The grand café was the site of a student uprising in 1848 and its *piano nobile* is used for lectures, concerts and exhibitions. Its rooms are decorated in various styles, including Egyptian, Roman, Greek, and Etruscan. There is also a ballroom dedicated to the architect's friend, Rossini. The café is a chic place

Padua

to see and be seen with a prosecco or espresso in hand and occasionally it hosts live musical events.

Chiesa degli Eremitani (Piazza Eremitani, ☎ 049-8756410, 8:30 am-5 pm daily). Don't forget to look up when you enter this Romanesque church or you're likely to miss one of the church's finest characteristics, its 14th-century vaulted wooden ceiling. Unfortunately, Andrea Mantegna's frescoes of the lives of St. James and St. Christopher from the 15th-century were destroyed in a WWII bombing raid, but fragments remain on display in the church.

Musei Eremitani (Piazza Eremitani, ☎ 049-8204551; Feb-Oct, 9 am-7 pm; Nov-Jan, 9 am-6 pm; closed Mon; €10, free admission with the PadovaCard). Located in what was formerly the cloisters of the convent of the Eremitani friars, the civic museums exhibit a rich collection of 14th- to 19th-century art, including Bellini's 15th-century *Portrait of a Young Senator*, as well as many Etruscan, Roman and Egyptian objects. The **Bottacin Museum** has an interesting collection of Venetian coinage and rare Roman medallions.

Capella degli Scrovegni (Piazza Eremitani, ☎ 049-2010020, www.cappelladegliscrovegni.it; €11 admission, €1 booking fee, free admission with the PadovaCard). The pinnacle of Padova's rich collection of historical and artistic monuments, the Scrovegni Chapel was built by Enrico Scrovegni in 1303 to spare his deceased usurer father from the hell wished upon him by Dante in his *Inferno*. The chapel,

surrounded by the ancient Roman amphitheater, is famed for an impressive cycle of frescoes painted by the great Florentine artist Giotto between 1303 and 1305, narrating scenes from the lives of Mary and Jesus. Among the most important panels in the early Renaissance cycle are the *Nativity* (left), the

Lament Over the Dead Christ (above) and the *Last Judgment*, in which Enrico is shown offering the chapel to the Madonna.

> **Tip:** Be sure to book your visit to the chapel 72 hours in advance or there is little chance of entering, especially during summer months.

Osservatorio Astronomico-Museo La Specola (Vicolo dell'Osservatorio 5, ☎ 049-8293469, www.pd.astro.it/museo-laspecola; guided visits only, Sat, 11 am and 4 pm; Sun, 4 pm; €7, reduced admission with the PadovaCard). Instituted by the Republic of Venice in the 18th century for the University of Padua, the Astronomical Observatory is located in one of Ezzelino da Romano's medieval towers in the southern outskirts of the city. Many original telescopes, globes, clocks and other astronomical instruments are on display here.

Tour Operators

Guida ASCOM (Passagio de Gasperi 3, ☎ 049-8209711, www.guidepadova.it) has a number of authorized tour guides on hand who offer guided visits to the city and the province. Guides specialize in different walking itineraries and speak multiple languages.

CitySightseeing Padova (City Sightseeing Italy, ☎ 049-8704933, www.city-sightseeing.it, €13). New in 2004, this hop-on hop-off double-decker tour bus begins at the Basilica del Santo and stops at 11 destinations throughout the city, including Piazza dei Signori, Piazza Garibaldi, Piazza Eremitani and Prato della Valle. The hour-long tour operates daily from May until Sept, 9 am until 8 pm, and Oct through Apr, from 9:30 am until 7 pm. Tickets can be purchased on board and are valid for 24 hours; included are headsets with a guided tour in seven languages, including English.

> **Time Saver:** If you're pressed for time, hop on the number 8 bus at the railway station and take it to **Prato della Valle**. It's easy to work your way back to the northern part of the city from here while stopping at the major sites.

Adventures

On Water

Several tour companies operate river cruises that leave from Padua to tour the city's canals as well as several nearby towns in the province. The tours that depart from Porte Contarine and Portello take place in the spring and summer months and generally last between an hour and a full day.

Delta Tour (Via Toscana 2, ☎ 049-8700232, www.deltatour.it). A popular tour to explore the city is *From 1300 to 1500: Discovering Padua through the Footsteps of Giotto*, a combination of a walking tour, a group lunch and a boat trip, leaving from Porte Contarine. The tour lasts from 9:30 am until 5 pm and is a great way to explore the city from two perspectives. Another tour, *Navigating Padua: The City of Saint*

Anthony, highlights the splendor of Padua's walls, palaces, churches, and monuments from on-board *La Padovanella.* This tour from Porte Contarine (available during the day or evening) lasts less than two hours and costs €13 per person. Delta Tour also offers full-day trips to the Euganean Hills, Venice and the Po Delta.

Il Burchiello (Via Orlandini 3/5, ☎ 049-8763044, www.ilburchiello.it). The Burchiello is one of the most popular ways to tour the villas along the Brenta Canal from Stra to Venice. For departures from Padua (Wed, Fri and Sun), meet at Piazzale Boschetti at 8:15 am and travel by bus to the Villa Pisani in Stra where the full-day tour commences. Passengers also visit the Barchessa Valmarana di Mira and the Villa Foscari di Malcontenta, stopping for lunch in Oriago. The tour ends in Venice at approximately 6:30 pm and passengers may return to Padua by bus or train.

Festivities

Marathon of Saint Anthony (www.maratonasant-antonio.com). The last Sunday of April each year, runners take to the streets of Vedelago in the province of Treviso and travel through eight towns before reaching Padua (the final leg of the race follows in the footsteps of Saint Anthony on his final trip). For those interested in participating in shorter races, there are non-commpetitive 12- and five-kilometer races, a children's marathon and a race for the disabled beginning in Prato della Valle. This event kicks off a week-long program of festivities that take place in the Prato della Valle.

Culinary Adventures

● **Cooking Classes**

Peccati di Gola (Via Gattamelata 136/A, ☎ 049-773933, www.infotech.it/peccatidigola/). What better souvenir to return home with than a working knowledge of Veneto cooking? The skilled instructors at Peccati di Gola impart their love of cooking to students through a variety of themed classes, such as "Torte Salate," which highlights several pastry-based meals, including *torta di asparagi* and *crostata al pesto*. Instructors help students refine their kitchen know-how while developing a genuine appreciation for local cuisine and the valuable role seasonal ingredients play in creating delicious dishes. Classes are small and taught in the home of one of the instructors from 6:30-9:30 in the evening, beginning with the instruction and preparation of dishes and culminating in a dinner. Classes last for one or two nights and generally cost €50 per person.

Cultural Adventures - Linguistic

Bertrand Russell (Via E. Filiberto 6, ☎ 049-654051, www.bertrand-russell.it; closed two weeks in Dec-Jan). Since 1975 this language institute has been helping students and professionals from around the globe discover Padua and the Italian language. Their teaching method is one of total immersion, with classes taught solely in Italian. The beginner, intermediate, advanced and superior level classes last four weeks (80 hours) but can be prorated for a shorter period, and individual lessons are possible for €25 per hour. All text materials are included in the enrollment fee and accommodation in either an apartment or with a family can be arranged as necessary. The enrollment fee covers guided visits to the city as well as certain cultural courses, such as art history and cooking classes.

Dining Out

Alchimia (Prato della Valle 117, ☎ 049-654088, www.alchimia.pd.it; Tue-Sat, 10 am-2 am; Sun, 2 pm–2 am, closed Mon; reservations recommended; €€-€€€). In early 2004 Alchimia opened its doors onto one of Europe's largest squares, almost immediately becoming Padua's new hot spot. But don't be fooled by the size of the restaurant when you first enter. The wine bar gives way to another dining room, a courtyard with a few tables, and my absolute favorite, the lounge room. Kick back on a sofa in front of the fireplace with a cocktail in hand and enjoy the hip cosmopolitan atmosphere. The ambience, enhanced by artwork from local artists covering the walls (many are for sale),

DINING PRICE CHART	
Price per person for an entrée	
€	Under €5
€€	€5-€12
€€€	€13-€20
€€€€	€21-€30
€€€€€	Over €30

shouldn't overshadow the food. Grapefruit is highlighted in several unusual antipasto dishes, including *gamberetti, rucola e pompelmo rosa* and *speck e pompelmo*. The penne prepared with a vegetable sauce is very good as well.

Ristorante Antico Brolo (Corso Milano 22, ☎ 049-664555; closed Mon and one week in Aug; major credit cards accepted; €€€). Located in Padua's city center is one of Italy's 40 *Ristoranti di Buon Ricordo*, renowned for its fine cuisine, served in an elegant atmosphere. If you're prepared to splurge, the Chateaubriand prepared with balsamic vinegar is one of the restaurant's most acclaimed dishes.

Parterre Café & Restaurant (Via Matteotti 21, ☎ 049-8788802; Tue-Fri, 11 am-2 am; Sat and Sun, 5:30 pm-2 am; closed Mon and three weeks in Aug; €€-€€€). One of Padua's more cosmopolitan eateries, Parterre is a chic place catering primarily to a business clientele. The chef puts a Mediterranean flair on the evening menu with dishes like paella. The *tagliata di manzo* is a prime cut of beef prepared with balsamic vinegar and rosemary and is particularly good. Its continuous hours make this a convenient choice for dining at off-peak times.

De Gustibus (Via N. Tommaseo 62, ☎ 049-8762438, www.degustibus.co.it; opening hours vary for the restaurant and the bistro; major credit cards accepted; €€). Specializing in Mediterranean cuisine, DeGustibus is an eclectic bistro and restaurant only a short walk from the train station. Its casual atmosphere attracts patrons for cocktails with nightly happy hour from 6-10 pm, but it's also popular for Sunday brunch. Try the *pasta al forno con scamorza e melanzane* (pasta prepared with eggplant and cheese) at lunchtime. If you're interested in putting your Italian skills to the ultimate test, combine dinner and a movie for a reasonable price with the cinema menu. There are some outdoor tables here but, since the restaurant is located on a busy road, I'd recommend a table indoors.

Per Bacco (Piazzale Ponte Corvo 10, ☎ 049-8754664, www.per-bacco.it; lunch, 10 am-2:30 pm; dinner, 7 pm-midnight; closed Mondays and two weeks in Aug; €€). Come for the wine, but stay for the food. The owner, Franco Favero, has a true passion for wine, particularly Tuscan wines, and stocks his enoteca's cellar with nearly 1,000 different Italian wines (all which can be ordered by the glass). If you're not in the neighborhood when they have a wine tasting scheduled, request one. The friendly staff is more than happy to arrange a tasting for small groups and will tailor it to your tastes. Their Tuscan-influenced menu changes frequently, but their signature meat dishes, *Bistecca Fiorentina* and *Tagliata di Chianina,* are usually available and always excellent.

Ponte Corvo (Piazzale Ponte Corvo 5, ☎ 049-8763819; lunch, 12-2:30 pm; dinner, 7-11:30 pm; €€). Only a five-minute walk from the basilica, this restaurant and pizzeria has a large selection of pizzas and salads and a fixed price midday menu that is a good value. Try their special half-pizza, half-calzone or their house specialty, *pasta fagioli.*

Ristorante Brek (Piazza Cavour 20, ☎ 049-8753788, www.brek.com; lunch, 11:30 am-3 pm; dinner, 5:30-10 pm; major credit cards accepted; €-€€). Just a few steps off Padua's main thoroughfare is an economical eatery for travelers on the go. But don't let the cafeteria-style dining fool you. Dishes here are prepared fresh upon request and can satisfy any appetite. Choose from fresh pasta and risotto dishes, meats, vegetables, salads and desserts. This self-service establishment's hours make it a good choice for an early lunch or dinner. There is also a children's menu and several vegetarian dishes to accommodate all tastes.

Graziati (Piazza della Frutta, 40, ☎ 049-8751014, www.graziati.com; closed Mon; €). Since 1919 this pastry shop in the Piazza della Frutta has been luring in passersby to sample its famously delectable selection of pastries, pralines, cakes and candies. Their two signature pastries are the *mille foglie* (layers of ultra-thin pastry with a rich pastry-cream) and the *pazientina* (a large bundle-like dessert made with Pan di Spagna, Zabaglione cream and covered in chocolate) – both too tempting to pass up.

Accommodations

Hotels

Hotel Grand Italia (Corso del Popolo 81, ☎ 049-8761111, www.hotelgranditalia.it; major credit cards accepted; €€€€). Built in the early

1900s, this charmingly restored Art Nouveau building is one of the city's most luxurious sleeps. The marble staircase is the focal point of the elaborate foyer and adds dimension to the hall's elegance. Rooms are tastefully furnished and if you're in the market for additional pampering, inquire about the four business suites.

Hotel Al Fagiano (Via Locatelli 45, ☎ 049-8750073, www.alfagiano.it; major credit cards accepted; €€). One of this hotel's best qualities is that each room is uniquely decorated, some with hand-painted furniture and modern artwork that put a livelier twist on the standard hotel room. The singles feel a bit cramped but, overall, rooms are comfortable and airy. This small hotel on a side street near the basilica is run by an attentive, friendly staff. There were plans to expand the hotel at time of publication so inquire about the new rooms when booking. Breakfast and parking are available but not included in the price.

Hotel Corso (Corso del Popolo 2, ☎ 049-8750822, htlcrs@virgilio.it; breakfast included; major credit cards accepted; €€-€€€). This mid-sized modern hotel located in a restored early 20th century building is a five-minute walk from the train station and convenient to the city center. My only criticism is that many of the rooms facing out onto the main road are somewhat noisy. If you're a light sleeper, ask for the quieter rooms, 234 and 236 (singles). Room 349 has a better view of the city center.

Casa del Pellegrino (Via M. Cesarotti 21, ☎ 049-8239711, www.casadelpellegrino.com; closed late Dec until mid-Jan; major credit cards accepted; €€). A stone's throw from the basilica, this hotel was formerly known as the Golden Eagle in the

HOTEL PRICE CHART	
Based on a double room for two	
€	Under €50
€€	€50-€80
€€€	€81-€120
€€€€	€121-€190
€€€€€	Over €190

Padua

1700s and catered to many illustrious visitors such as Emperor Joseph II of Austria in 1775 and Emperor Ferdinand IV, King of the Two Sicilies. Many pilgrims who travel to the basilica opt to stay here in the modest yet comfortable accommodations. Be sure to request a bathroom *with* a shower if that's what you prefer since not all rooms come equipped, though they do have television, phone and air conditioning. Breakfast and parking are also available but not included. Several rooms have a view of the basilica, including 147 and 145 (doubles) and 149 and 150 (singles).

Apartments

Palazzo Papafava dei Carraresi (Via Marsala 59, ☎ 049-661049, www.deicarraresi.it; €€€). Indulge yourself in an apartment at the Palazzo Papafava dei Carraresi, an 18th-century palace once owned by the Papafava brothers in the early 19th-century who were descendents of the powerful Carrara family. The luxurious apartment features frescoes of the *Iliad* and *Odyssey*, high stuccoed ceilings, a fireplace, marble columns and a marble bathtub, to name only a few of the elements that make this an ideal place for a romantic getaway.

Bed & Breakfasts

Koko Nor (Via Selva 5, ☎ 049-8643394, www.bandb-veneto.it/kokonor; reductions for PadovaCard holders) and **Wigwam Holiday Club** (Via Amerigo Vespucci 46, ☎ 339/4198162, www.wigwam.it) are both associations that help link travelers with the genuine hospitality of bed and breakfasts in Padua and throughout the province.

Budget Accommodations

Ostello della Gioventu (Via Aleardo Aleardi 30, ☎ 049-8752219, www.ctgveneto.it/ostello, 7-9:30 am and 4-11 pm; handicap-accessible; €). This no-frills hostel in a quiet neighborhood near the Prato della Valle, is a good option for budget-conscious travelers. There are segregated rooms for men and women, with eight bunk beds, family rooms that sleep four and handicap-accessible rooms. Each guest is provided a closet, linens and breakfast included in the price. Bathrooms and shower facilities are on each floor and there is also a laundry room and a television lounge with computers. The maximum stay at the hostel is five nights and the multilingual staff is friendly. Packed lunches are available upon request.

Shopping

Open air markets are held daily (except for Sun) in the **Piazza della Frutta**, **Piazza delle Erbe** and **Piazza Signori**, selling fresh vegetables, fruits, flowers, clothing and household goods.

The large market held on Saturday in **Prato della Valle** sells plants, household items, handmade crafts, clothing and leather goods.

Prato della Valle also hosts a popular antiques market the third Sunday of each month.

Nightlife & Entertainment

 Padua hosts many cultural events year-round, including musical concerts, operas, theatrical and dance performances. The main venues are the **Teatro Verdi** (Via dei Livello 32, ☎ 049-87770213), the **Auditorium Cesare Pollini** (Via Carlo Cassan) and the **Sala dei Giganti al Liviano** (Piazza Capitaniato, ☎ 049-8750644). For details about schedules and purchasing tickets for these events, contact the tourist information center.

Associazione Amici della Musica di Padova (Via San Massimo 3, ☎ 049-9756763, info@amicimusicapadova.org). Musical performances run from Oct through Apr and are primarily held at the Sala dei Giganti al Liviano. Inquire about the Domenica in Musica, Sunday morning performances at discounted prices.

Nightclubs

Banale (winter, Via Bronzetti 8; summer, Via dell'Ippodromo 3, ☎ 049-8717518, www.banale.org). This nightclub is a popular spot that draws a large university crowd but, depending on the entertainment, the club can also attract an older audience.

AUTHOR'S PICK One of my favorite evening activities in Padua doesn't cost a cent. **Prato della Valle**'s beat changes when the sun goes down and I find that it is more exciting to be where all the excitement is, than to go looking for it. Grab an ice cream and a bench and enjoy.

Tourist Offices

IAT
Railway Station
infostazione@turismopadova.it
☎ 049-8752077

IAT
Galleria Pedrocchi
infopedrocchi@turismopadova.it
☎ 049-8767927

IAT
Piazza del Santo
infosanto@turismopadova.it
☎ 049-8753087
Seasonal (Apr-Oct)

Useful Websites

www.padovando.com
www.turismopadova.it
www.padovanet.it

■ I Colli Euganei: The Euganean Hills

Only a short drive from Padua, the conically shaped Euganean Hills are dotted with archaeological sites, medieval fortresses, castles, abbeys, Venetian villas, gardens, thermal resorts and golf courses. The verdant hills offer active travelers an abundance of activities, whether enjoying the panorama on a mountain biking or horseback riding excursion or discovering the varied flora and fauna on a nature hike.

Ancient cobbled-street villages with their stone buildings and centuries-old churches are perched on the slopes of unspoiled hills marked by vineyards, olive groves and chestnut trees.

Arquà Petrarca, right, known only as Arquà until 1868 when the name was officially changed in honor of the great poet, is one of the most picturesque in the zone, retaining its charming medieval character. This town is a perfect place to spend a lazy afternoon, strolling the narrow streets, admiring old medieval buildings and stopping at enotecas to taste the local wine.

The Euganean spa area is the densest zone of spa waters in Europe, and is renowned for its thermal waters that originate in the pre-Alpine zone miles north of the volcanic Euganean hills, and then emerge in the hills at 85-87°C/187°F. Evidence suggests that the therapeutic waters rich in salt, bromine and iodine, that create the hot bubbling thermal springs in the hills, have existed for over 2,000 years. The two main bath towns are **Montegrotto** and **Abano Terme** but the ancient Roman origin is particularly apparent in **Montegrotto** where remains of a Roman bath complex and theater were discovered.

Abano is the larger and better developed of the two spa towns known for its famous mud therapy. For a quieter, lower-key spa experience, Montegrotto has several four- and five-star hotels and excellent spa facilities and activities, but is a smaller town. The main road leading from the train station to the town center has many tourist shops, cafés and restaurants.

The hills are characterized by hamlets and towns that have their own unique charm, scenery, culture, cuisine and history waiting to be discovered.

Getting There

 By Car: The best way to reach the hills from the north or south is by taking the **A13** (Padova-Bologna) and exiting at Terme Euganee. From Venice or Milan on the **A4**, exit at Padova Ovest and head in the direction of Abano, Montegrotto and Teolo.

 By Bus: SITA buses travel from Venice's airport to Montegrotto Terme, making stops at Padua and Abano Terme. Buses from the airport run several times daily, take less than two hours to arrive in Montegrotto and the one-way fare costs approximately €4. SITA buses run more frequently throughout the day from Padua to the hill towns. Another SITA line travels between Este and Padova and stops at Arquà Petrarca.

 By Train: The province's main station is in Padua, but in the hills there are stations at Montegrotto Terme, Battaglia Terme and Monselice. Both the Venezia-Bologna line and the Padova-Monselice-Mantua lines stop at these stations.

 By Plane: The nearest airport with domestic and international flights daily is Venice's Marco Polo. For details: www.veniceairport.it.

Getting Around

 On Foot: The hill towns are all relatively small and can easily be seen on foot, but traveling between them requires a bike, car or bus.

 By Bike: The information centers in Abano Terme and Montegrotto have several bikes for rent (free with the PadovaCard). This is a great way to explore those towns but, for other hill towns, bike excursions are the best option.

 By Car: The best way to experience the hills is certainly by car. There are so many charming villages and majestic landscapes that shouldn't be overlooked. Allow at least a day to drive around the hills at a relaxed pace. The roads are not heavily trafficked and it is worth having a car in order to make the most of your visit to the hills.

 By Bus: SITA buses travel between the hill and spa towns regularly throughout the day.

Sightseeing

 Archaeological Zone (Montegrotto). Excavated remains of immersion pools and Roman baths, as well as a Roman theater, are among the best preserved remains from the Roman period in the region and are located along the main road leading from Montegrotto's railway station to the town center.

Abbazia di Praglia (Bresseo di Teolo, ☎ 049-9999322; guided visits daily in afternoons; free admission). The 15th- to 16th-century abbey complex built on the site of an 11th-century monastery is on an ancient road leading to Este at the foot of the hills and just outside the small town of Teolo. Italy's largest community of monks lives in the four-cloister complex. They grow herbs and plants and have an

ancient book restoration workshop. The landscape surrounding the abbey is characterized by vineyards, vegetable gardens, orchards and an apiary. The monk-led tour also stops into the 16th-century library, with nearly 100,000 books and 17th-century paintings by Zelotti on the wooden ceiling.

Villa Giardino Barbarigo-Pizzoni Ardemani (Via Barbarigo 15, Valsanzibio, ☎ 049-8059224, www.valsanzibiogiardino.it; Mar-Nov, 10 am-1 pm and 2 pm-sunset; €8, reduction with PadovaCard). This Italian-style Baroque garden was brought to grandeur in the mid-1600s by the Venetian aristocrat Zuan Francesco Barbarigo and his son Antonio. Fountains, statues, cascades and fishponds ornament the garden, but one of its most impressive features is the boxwood maze.

Casa di Petrarca (Via Valeselle 4, Arquà Petrarca, ☎ 0429-718294; Mar-Oct, 9 am-12:30 pm and 3-7 pm; Nov-Feb, 9 am-12:30 pm and 2:30-5:30 pm, closed Mon; €3, free admission with PadovaCard). The famed poet Francesco Petrarca  spent the final four years of his life in this charming medieval residence where visitors can still see the desk and chair where he wrote. Visit his red Verona marble sarcophagus in front of the church in the town center.

Castello del Catajo (Via Catajo 1, Battaglia Terme, ☎ 049-8759326; Mar-Nov, Sun and Tue, 3-7 pm; Dec-Feb upon request; €7, reduction with PadovaCard). This castle, designed by architect Andrea della Valle in the 16th century, was once the villa of the Obizzi family. Zelotti's frescoes adorn the castle's walls and the castle's large park offers beautiful views of the hills.

Museo della Navigazione Fluviale (Via Ortazzo 63, Battaglia Terme, ☎ 049-525170; Sat and Sun, 10 am-noon and 3-7 pm; reduction with PadovaCard). Located along a canal in the town of Battaglia Terme, this small museum dedicated to navigation has an interesting display of boats and nautical equipment. The museum is a little hard to find, so follow signs off Via Maggiore carefully.

Villa Emo Capodilista (Via Montecchia, Selvazzano Dentro, ☎ 049-637294, www.lamontecchia.it; Mar-November, Wed and Sat at 4 and 5:30 pm; €5.20, reduced admission with PadovaCard). This 16th-century villa, designed as a hunting lodge by Dario Varotari (a student of Veronese) is now on the grounds of a sizable wine estate and is open to visitors. Tours depart in front of the wine shop.

Castello di San Pelagio/Museo dell'Aria e dello Spazio (Via San Pelagio 34, Due Carrare, ☎ 049-9125008, www.museodellaria.it; summer, 9 am-12:30 pm and 2:30-7 pm; winter, 9 am-12:30 pm and 2-6 pm; closed Mon, weekend visits only in Dec and Jan; guided tours; €7). In the small town of Due Carrare (formed by joining Carrara S.

Giorgio and Carrara S. Stefano) a medieval castle that in the 18th century was transformed into the villa of the Zaborra family, today hosts a unique museum dedicated to the history of flight. On a guided tour, visitors can see models of planes, hot air balloons, uniforms, engines and other flight-related objects, watch a film highlighting 20th-century flight and tour the surrounding gardens.

Adventures

On Foot

Founded in 1989, the **Parco Regionale dei Colli Euganei** is characterized by volcanic hills dating back nearly 35 million years and is made up of 15 municipalities. Several interesting archaeological sites and museums dot the park, dominated by large expanses of chestnut and oak trees and some Mediterranean flora. There are more than 200 trails that make up the entire trail network, 20 of which are marked and maintained by the park for excursions.

Brochures with detailed maps and explanations of the official 20 trails and territory are available at tourist offices in the zone but here are a few particularly interesting trails.

#6: Il Sentiero del Monte Ricco e Monte Castello

This five-km walk is relatively easy, takes two-three hours to complete and is a nice way to spend a relaxing afternoon exploring the hills. The point of departure for this trail is at the Monselice train station. One of the prettiest sites on this itinerary is the terrace of Ercole that offers beautiful panoramic views of the hills. The ideal times of year to walk this trail are spring and autumn.

Padua

#11: Il Sentiero del Monte Cinto

This five-km trail begins at the **Museo Geopaleontologico di Cava Bomba**, a geological and paleontologic museum in Cinto Euganeo (Via Bomba, ☎ 0429/647166) at the foot of Monte Cinto. Once a kiln and mining complex, there are now many interesting geological collections on display here as well as limestone mining tools. At its best in the springtime, this trail is moderately difficult, with some uphill tracts that wind around Monte Cinto. There are remains of a medieval fortification on Monte Cinto, but the highlight of this trail is **Buso dei Briganti**, a large rock formation that over the years has served as a guard tower, fort and hideout for outlaws. (This is accessible from the main trail, but recommended only for experts due to its level of difficulty).

Family Adventures

Casa delle Farfalle & Bosco delle Fate (Via degli Scavi 21, ☎ 049-8910189, www.butterflyarc.it and www.boscodellefate.it; Apr-Sept, 9:30 am-12:30 pm, 2:30-5:30 pm; Feb, March, Oct and Nov, 9:30 am-12:30 pm and 2-4 pm; €7; guided visits cost €26 for two hours; reduced admission with the PadovaCard). Enter the Amazon, Indo-Australian and African tropical gardens in the Butterfly Arc and discover more than 400 butterflies from around the globe. An educational demonstration and video presentation engage children, who can then journey into a mythological, magical land of sprites, gnomes and fairies in the adjacent **Bosco delle Fate**, where ancient legends are recreated.

Minigolf Montegrotto (Via Caposeda, Montegrotto, ☎ 049-793406; March-Oct, 3:30 pm-midnight) and **Minigolf Aponense** (Via Ghislandi 5, Abano Terme, ☎ 049-667205; Mon-Fri, 5-7 pm and 8:30 pm-1 am; Sat and Sun from 3:30 pm-1 am).

On Bikes

Centro Euganeo Escursioni in Mountain Bike (Via Previtali 54, Abano Terme, ☎ 049-8666677, www.centroescursionimtb.org). The Euganean Hills are brimming with adventure and the experienced team at Centro Euganeo knows exactly where to find it. These official guides, members of Italy's Accademia Nazionale di Mountain Bike, help travelers discover the territory's landscape through their bold itineraries that incorporate mountain biking with history, culture and gastronomy. Inquire about their scheduled evening rides.

On Horseback

 Centro Equestre Montagnon (Via Mezzavia 49, Montegrotto, ☎ 049-793289; two hours €25, half-day €50, full day €75). Enjoy the beauty and tranquility of the picturesque Euganean hills on horseback with Centro Equestre Montagnon, a member of Italy's Associazione Natura a Cavallo. Guided tours led by a father-and-son team depart the center, located about a 10-minute walk from the Montegrotto train station. Call ahead to schedule an excursion.

Adventures for the Soul

 From thermal baths to mud therapy, the curative qualities of the waters in the Euganean Hills bath towns are used to promote health, beauty and relaxation and regenerate the body and soul.

Hotels in Montegrotto and Abano Terme offer visitors a variety of spa treatments and facilities, as well as sports activities and traditional Euganean cuisine.

Montegrotto and Abano Terme both have several public pools, but many hotels open the doors of their spa facilities to outside visitors. The public pools are generally less expensive than private hotel facilities, and most hotels charge between €10 and €20 per day. Certain hotels only offer this service during low season and weekends, while others are off-limits to children.

● Public Pools

Sporting Center (Via Romana 104, Montegrotto Terme, ☎ 049-793400; summer, 9:30 am-6 pm; €7.50-8.50).

Piscina Comunale (V.V. da Feltre, Abano Terme, ☎ 049-812418, €4-5 or adults).

● Private Pools

International Berta (Largo Traiano 1, Montegrotto Terme, ☎ 049-8911700; 9 am-7:30 pm, Mon-Sat, €15; Sun, €20; 50% reduced admission for children).

Miramonti (Piazza Roma 19, Montegrotto Terme, ☎ 049-8911755; 9 am-7 pm, adults only, low season only, Mon-Fri, €16; Sat and Sun, €19).

Preistoriche (Via Castello 5, Montegrotto Terme, ☎ 049-793477; 9 am-10 pm, Thurs until 7 pm, Mon-Sat, €18; Sun, €23).

Bristol Buja (Via Monteortone 2, Abano Terme; 8 am-7 pm by reservation only, Mon-Fri, €16; Sat and Sun, €18).

Golf

Golf Club della Montecchia (Via Montecchia 12, Selvazzano Dentro, ☎ 049-8055550; closed Mon). What better way to top off a relaxing stay in the hills than with a round of golf at the Golf Club della Montecchia, just north of Abano Terme. This 27-hole course on the grounds of the Villa Emo Capodilista has a modern clubhouse with a pool and is open to golf lovers year-round. To arrive from A4, exit Padova Ovest and follow signs toward Selvazzano.

Golf Club Padova (Via Novera 57, Valsanzibio, ☎ 049-9130078, www.golfpadova.it). Located near the Villa Barbarigo, this scenic 27-hole golf course, open since 1962, with its last nine holes added in 2003, has a clubhouse, pool, tennis courts and a restaurant.

With Wine

The Euganean Hills are a prime production zone for 13 DOC (Denomination of Controlled Origin) wines, including Cabernet Franc, Fior d'Arancio, Moscato, Novello, and Serprino. The **Strada dei Colli Euganei** (the Euganean Wine Road) leads through the Euganean Hills' small towns, where there are numerous places to taste and purchase locally produced wines, sample characteristic local cuisine and find charming accommodations. Stop by a tourist information office for a complete list of wineries, farms and restaurants along the route.

■ Check the website www.stradavinicollieuganei.it.

During the springtime, many *cantine* (wine cellars) in the hills have designated days for tastings and tours of their establishments *(cantine aperte)*. Ask a tourist office for a list.

Enoteca da Loris/L'Azienda Agrituristica Bressanin Loris (Via Valleselle 3, Arquà Petrarca, ☎ 0429-718188, 9 am-12:30 pm and 2-7 pm; closed Mon). Turn left when you exit Petrarch's courtyard and after a few steps you'll find yourself in front of the Bressanin family's enoteca and farm. Sample their olive oil, wine, liquor-soaked jujubes (brown olive-sized fruits used in marmalades), chestnut honey and *biscotti alle giuggiole*, cookies with jujubes. One of their most popular products is the *Fior d'Arrancio Barrichato* (a liqueur).

Azienda Agricola Sturaro F & L (Via Noiera 50, Galzignano Terme, ☎ 049-9130142, 8:30 am-12:30 pm, 3-7:30 pm). This family-run winery produces seven types of wine, the most famous being the Cabernet and the Serpino. The rustic tasting room has a large banquet table with a bar and can accommodate up to 20 people. If you're interested in country-style accommodations, inquire about the bed and breakfast.

Villa Egizia (Via Galzignana 40, Battaglia Terme, ☎ 049-525149, www.villaegizia.com). This small villa, named after the wife of a 19th-century knight who previously owned the property, is located in the midst of vineyards and wine cellars along SP25 on the way to Galzignano Terme. For the last several years it has been under the ownership of a Paduan family and produces several reds, whites, spumantis and grappas. Their Profumo dei Colli Moscato Secco is one of their more popular varieties. Wine tastings and a tour of their cantina can be arranged upon request.

Festivities

 Festa della Giuggiola is celebrated the first week of Oct each year in Arquà Petrarca in honor of the jujube fruit. Numerous vendors display local agricultural products, including jujubes and jujube-based products as well as other seasonal goods like chestnuts, pomegranates and wine.

Food & Drink

 Since the 1900s, city dwellers have been retreating to the Euganean Hills on weekends to savor the rich flavors in restaurants, enotecas and agriturismi. There are many products that mark traditional dishes of the hills such as the delicately fragrant olive oil (often exhibiting traces of almonds and greens), cherries, dwarf peas from Arquà Petrarca, and jujubes. There are also several honeys produced in the hills such as the chestnut and balsamic-apple honey that are used in many classic recipes. Game is another important element of their local cuisine.

La Montanella (Via dei Carraresi 9, Arquà Petrarca, ☎ 0429-718200, www.montanella.it; 12:30-2:30 pm and 7:30-10 pm; closed Tue for dinner, all day Wed, Jan and two weeks in Aug; major credit cards accepted; €€€). Perched on a hilltop amidst the vineyard-clad hills of Arquà Petrarca, La Montanella first opened in the '50s as a bar in the town center. With such great demand for their dishes, the owners decided to transform it into a restaurant on a nearby hilltop where it has been ever since. The Borin family's game dishes are among the most requested, including the famous 17th-century recipe *paparo alla frutta* (a duck roast prepared with pears and grapes) and *risotto alla quaglia* (rice with quail). Their impressive wine list includes more than 500 Italian and international wines, ranging in cost from €12 to €700 per bottle. To top off an exquisite meal, try the *torta di pere con crema e amaretto* (cake with pears, cream and amaretto) or their homemade ice cream. Their farm is the source for much of their produce, including fruits for the marmalades, liquors and sinful grappa-soaked fruit that the lady of the house, Biancarosa, is famous for. Although there are several large dining rooms, a lovely veranda room and an expan-

DINING PRICE CHART	
Price per person for an entrée	
€	Under €5
€€	€5-€12
€€€	€13-€20
€€€€	€21-€30
€€€€€	Over €30

sive terrace nestled between olive trees overlooking the hills, don't assume a table will be waiting for you – this is one of the most highly acclaimed restaurants in the region and reservations are a must.

Verbena (Via Montirone 21, Abano Terme, ☎ 049-8669505; closed Wed; major credit cards accepted; 11 am-3 pm and 6 pm-1 am; €€). Tucked into a quiet back street in one of Abano's pedestrian zones, Verbena is a reasonably priced eatery with a large selection of dishes highlighting locally grown products. Their wine list features a wide selection of wines from the hills that complement dishes like *lasagnette con radicchio e salsiccia* (lasagna prepared with radicchio and sausage) and the *orrechiette con cime di rapa* (pasta with broccoli rape).

Al Bosco (Via Cogolo 8, Montegrotto Terme, ☎ 049-794317, 12-2:30 pm, 7:30-10 pm; closed Wed and three weeks in Jan; major credit cards accepted; €€€). An outdoor table will buy you more than just an excellent meal with Al Bosco's fantastic views of the hills. Just outside of Montegrotto, it fuses rich local flavors to create dishes like *pappardelle di castagne col sugo di capriolo* (pasta prepared with a chestnut and venison sauce). There are several pasta dishes prepared with *al bosco* sauces (using ingredients such as mushrooms and chestnuts) and the meats are grilled to perfection.

Pub Sassofono Blu (Montegrotto, 11:30 am-3:30 am, closed Mon; major credit cards accepted; €€). In a muraled building in a shopping square behind the tourist information center, this places specializes in oversized pizzas that are great for sharing. Popular with locals, its kitchen keeps its doors open throughout the day so, if you find yourself hungry when most other restaurants are closed, stop in. Try the *gnochetti alla rucola e gorgonzola*.

Accommodations

Hotels & Resorts

Grand Hotel Terme Trieste & Victoria (Via P. D'Abano 1, Abano Terme, ☎ 049-8665100, www.gbhotels.it, €€€€€). Hospitality and elegance are two of the Grand Hotel Terme Trieste & Victoria's finest attributes. The sophisticated hotel in a beautifully restored historic building is steeped in *fin de siècle* charm. Its spa facilities are world-class and their rejuvenating spa packages are among the zone's finest.

Hotel Terme Miramonti (Piazza Roma 19, Montegrotto Terme, ☎ 049-8911755, www.relilax.com, €€€€). The personalized service at Miramonti is outstanding, but the hotel is best known for its Relilax Spa. Guests can participate in personalized aqua gym lessons, intensive mud treatments and group fitness lessons. Only the finest ingredients are used to prepare dishes that reflect the local cuisine, while paying particular attention to good nutrition. There are several organized programs, such as the health and beauty program and the anti-stress program, that are part of all-inclusive weeklong stays.

Terme di Galzignano Resort (Viale delle Terme 82, ☎ 049-9195555, www.galzignano.it). Discerning travelers will find everything at their fingertips at the Terme di Galzignano Resort in the Euganean Hills. Located on SP25 about 15 km from

HOTEL PRICE CHART	
Based on a double room for two	
€	Under €50
€€	€50-€80
€€€	€81-€120
€€€€	€121-€190
€€€€€	Over €190

Padua, the complex's four hotels, Hotel Sporting, Hotel Splendid, Hotel Majestic and Hotel Green Park, all offer top-notch spa facilities and spacious accommodations. Guests don't have to walk far to play a round of golf on the nine-hole golf course, shop in the complex's boutiques, use the six thermal pools, enjoy the open-air poolside buffet in the summer and entertainment in the evening. Visitors can dine at any of the hotel's restaurants, but the Hotel Green Park's restaurant is recognized for its fine cuisine and is a favorite with guests.

Hotel Terme Montecarlo (Viale Stazione 109, Montegrotto Terme, ☎ 049-793233; breakfast included; major credit cards accepted; €€€). Tap into Montegrotto's therapeutic waters at Montecarlo, conveniently located near the spa town's train station and archaeological zone. Well-equipped with all modern amenities, its spa center offers physiotherapy massages, thermal ozone baths, mud baths, underwater massages and anti-stress massages.

Apartments

La Montecchia (Via Montecchia 16, Selvazzano Dentro, ☎ 049-637294, www.lamontecchia.it, €€€€). La Montecchia wine estate encompasses the **Villa Emo Capodilista**, as well as several country houses, vineyards and private gardens. Guests may choose between the spacious houses with kitchens, **Casa del Prete** (once the residence of the castle's priest), **Casa di Nando** and **Casa di Maria**. In addition to these weeklong vacation house rentals, there is an exclusive suite in the villa suitable for a romantic getaway for two. Inquire about wine-tastings.

Bed & Breakfasts

Chez ViVi B&B (Via Palazzine 16, Arquà Petrarca, ☎ 0429-776098, www.chezvivi.it). Enjoy a taste of genuine hospitality in one of the Colli Euganei's most charming towns, Arquà Petrarca. Chez Vivi's spacious, cozy rooms are tastefully decorated and feel like a bedroom rather than a hotel room. The friendly owners, Franco and Vivian, expose guests to the Euganean lifestyle and provide everything needed for a relaxing stay. Lounge in the garden, cool off in the pool or hop on a bike and head for the hills.

Associazione Culturale Euganean Life International (Via Prosdocimi 14, Este, ☎ 0429-56156, www.bandb-veneto.it/euganeanlife; reduction with the PadovaCard). Searching for a unique stay in the Euganean Hills? Let the Associazione Culturale Euganean Life International help you find what you're looking for. Their list of accommodations includes villas, apartments and cottages throughout the hills.

Shopping

The weekly general market takes place in Abano Terme on Wednesday in the Piazza Mercato and on Thursday in Montegrotto Terme along Viale Stazione.

An antique market takes place the second Sunday of each month in Montegrotto along Viale Stazione.

Nightlife & Entertainment

 Parco Magnolia in Abano Terme, the **Abbazia di Praglia** and the **Castello di Catajo** are a few of the most popular sites for cultural and musical events during the summer in the hills. Stop by the tourist information center for a list of events.

Speak Easy (Piazza Repubblica 4, Abano Terme, ☎ 049-8669040; closed Thurs; Bar/Caffé, 9 am-1 am, Piano Bar, 9 pm-3 am). By day, it's Abano's grand café, by night, a lively piano bar. Stop into the café for sweets, *tramezzinis* (sandwiches) and coffee. When the sun sets, make your way upstairs to the cosmopolitan piano bar overlooking the Piazza Repubblica for cocktails and live music.

King's Club (Via Monte Ceva 7, Abano Terme, ☎ 049-667895; closed Tue). Drop by the town's new sophisticated nightclub for cocktails, live music and a great time.

Tourist Offices

IAT
Via Pietro d'Abano 18
Abano Terme
☎ 049-8669055

IAT
Viale Stazione 60
Montegrotto Terme
☎ 049-793384

Ente Parco Colli Euganei
Via Fontana 2
Arquà Petrarca
☎ 0429-777145

Ente Parco Colli Euganei
Via Rana Cà Mori
Este
☎ 0427-612010

Websites

www.parcocollieuganei.com
www.ristorantoripadovani.it
www.termeeuganee.it
www.abanomontegrotto.com

■ Bassa Padovana: Este, Monselice, Montagnana

Strategically vital during medieval times, Monselice, Este and Montagnana are the main towns in what is today known as the Bassa Padovana (Lower Paduan Plain).

After World War II, Monselice, at the base of the volcanic hills, became a commercial center for the Bassa Padovana. Its main town square, Piazza Mazzini, with its Torre Civico, is encompassed within the defensive walls and is a delightful spot to visit.

Another town in the zone, Este was a center of the Paleoveneti people, and has been recognized for centuries for its ceramics production. Excavations here have uncovered the remains of the Ateste, who were conquered by Romans in the fourth century BC.

Close to the border of the province of Verona and influenced over the centuries by both provinces, Montagnana is celebrated for its well-preserved 14th-century walls and its sweet DOC prosciutto. Among the best-preserved walled towns in all of Europe, the walls were completed by the Carraresi family in the 14th century, and have 24 towers and four gates. Two castles stand here, the **Rocca degli Alberi**, which was built in 1362 to defend from the west and is now a youth hostel, and the **Castello di San Zeno**, right, the town's oldest fortification. It dates from the Ezzelino era and guards the eastern periphery at the Porta Padova.

Getting There

By Car: Take the **A13** (Padova-Bologna) and exit at Monselice to reach Monselice, Este or Montagnana. From the **A4** (Milano-Venezia), exit at Soave and follow in the direction of Montagnana-Padova.

Padua

By Bus: There are several SITA buses that run in this zone. One line runs daily from Padua to Montagnana and stops in Monselice and Este. Monselice's bus station is in the center of town at Largo Carpanedo 4. In Este the station is along Via San Girolamo and in Montagnana at Via Circonvallazione.

 By Train: The railway station in Monselice is on Via Trento e Trieste, in Este on Via Principe Amedeo and in Montagnana on Viale Spalato. There are frequent trains between Padua and Monselice along the Venezia-Bologna line and, from there, subsequent connections to Este and Montagnana.

 By Plane: Monselice, Este and Montagnana can be accessed from Venice's Marco Polo airport. A bus runs every half-hour from the airport to Padua and, from there you can transfer to the line that serves Montagnana, Este and Monselice. Or take a train from Venice to any of these towns. For details: www.veniceairport.it.

Getting Around

 On Foot: It's easy to get around in all three of these towns on foot but a car or SITA bus is the best way to travel between them.

Sightseeing

 Castello di Monselice (Via del Santuario 24, Monselice, ☎ 0429-72931; guided tours once each hour, Apr-Nov, 9 am-noon and 3-6 pm; Dec-Mar, by appointment only; closed Mon; reduced admission with PadovaCard). Once used by Ezzellino da Romano, then by the Carrara and Marcello families, this restored castle was built in different stages from the 11th to 16th centuries. The Castelletto was the earliest part, followed by the Tower of Ezzelino built in the

13th century, then the Palazzo Marcello built in the 15th century. Finally the castle library was built in the 16th century. Tour the castle's armory, private apartments and medieval kitchen to see period furnishings that help recreate the life of the Middle Ages.

Castello dei Carraresi (Este, Apr-Sept, 8 am-11 pm; Oct-March, 9 am-5 pm; free admission). Built in the 14th century by Umbertino da Carrara. Visitors can stroll through lovely public gardens and see the remains of Este's ancient castle and walls.

Museo Nazionale Atestino (Via Guido Negri, Este, ☎ 0429-2085, 9 am-8 pm, closed only for Christmas, New Years and May 1; €2). Located in the 16th-century Mocenigo Palace, built between the 16th and 18th centuries, the museum's 11 rooms cover the city's history from the Paleolithic period to the Middle Ages. It is said to have one of Italy's greatest collections of pre-Roman and Roman artifacts, with ancient funerary urns, bronze vases and jewelry. The exhibits are organized in chronological order, starting from the Bronze and Iron Ages, leading up to medieval and modern times. One of the rooms on the ground floor contains a painting by Cima da Conegliano representing the *Virgin with Child* and a fresco of the *Crucifixion* by a painter from the Giotto school.

Time Saver: This is a museum not to be missed, but since it is almost always open, plan to stop in Este in the early afternoon when most other places are closed for lunch.

Garden of Villa Emo (Via Rivella, Monselice, ☎ 0429-781987, www.villaemo.it; Sat, 2-7 pm; Sun, 10 am-7 pm; reduced admission with the PadovaCard). This 16th-century villa designed by Scamozzi with its elegant gardens is classically Italian, exhibiting many design elements from the Renaissance period. Located on the road toward

Battaglia Terme, the garden is lovely to visit any time of year but truly comes alive in the month of June.

Castello di San Zeno (Piazza Trieste 15, Montagnana, ☎ 0429-804128. Guided tour of museum: winter – Tue, 3-6 pm, Wed-Sat, 9:30 am-12:30 pm and 3-6 pm, Sun, 10 am-1 pm and 3-6 pm; summer – Tue, 4-7 pm, Wed-Sat, 9:30 am-12:30 pm and 4-7 pm, Sun 10 am-1 pm and 4-7 pm; €1). In this former Ezzelino da Romano castle at the Porta Padova, visitors can see several rooms, including a civic museum that chronicles Montagnana's history.

Adventures

On Foot in Monselice

 Santuario Giubilare delle Sette Chiese (Via Sette Chiese). Beginning at the tourist information center, follow Via Santuario from the base of the hill to Via Sette Chiese. Pass through the **Porta Romana** (also known as Porta Santa), which is the entrance gate to the sacred sanctuary of seven churches built in 1651. The noble Venetian Duodo family commissioned Vincenzo Scamozzi to build these churches between 1605 and 1615, and asked Pope Paolo V to consider a pilgrimage to these seven churches as equivalent to a pilgrimage to Rome's seven basilicas (look for the inscription *Romanis basilicas pares*, referring to its connection with Rome). After passing through the porta, follow the hill toward the six small pilgrim churches on the left that contain works by Jacopo Palma the Younger and Giovanni Carlo Loth. Just past the sixth church is the large Villa Duodo from the early 1600s designed by Scamozzi and the Church of San Giorgio. This church contains many relics and is the site of a pilgrimage each Valentine's Day. The walk to the final church takes approximately 20 minutes and is easily accessible.

> **Bonus Adventure:** For the more adventurous, take the steps that climb the hill and lead to an archaeological site and the remains of the **Mastio Federicano**, a great 13th-century tower. For information about the latter part of the walk, ☎ 0429-72931.

On Bikes

 Bike Point (Piazza Vittoria 6, Monselice, ☎ 0429-72370, www.bikepoint.it, 8:30 am-12:30 pm and 3-8 pm, closed Sun). Rent a set of wheels and explore the Colli Euganei's landscapes on your own or request a guided excursion. Rentals cost between €5 and €10 per day and excursion fees vary depending on the number of participants and the itinerary. Guides are trained in bike safety, mechanics and first aid, but keep in mind that most have a limited knowledge of English.

ESTE CERAMICS

 Este's ceramic production dates back to the prehistoric age and has been an integral part of the town's cultural and economic development, as it is considered one of Italy's most important centers for ceramic production. Evidence suggests that ceramics were widely produced during the Roman period and that the second half of the 18th century was the golden age of Este's ceramic production. Some factories continue to produce traditional styles, often employing ancient techniques and molds, while others have developed modern methods and motifs. Stop into the factory shops in the industrial zone along SS10 to find the perfect souvenirs of your stay here.

Ceramica Estensi (Via A. Volta 26, Este, ☎ 0429-4848, Tue-Sat, 9 am-12:30 pm and 3-7:30 pm; closed Sun and Mon). Since 1975 Ceramica Estensi has been known for its extensive production of both classic and modern ceramics. Visit their showroom in the main building to see popular patterns on display before heading to the large tent around back where there is a fine selection of ceramics for sale at factory prices.

Ceramica Euganea (Viale Industrie 13, ☎ 0429-50352, Este, Mon-Fri, 8 am-noon, 2:30-7 pm,

Padua

Sat, 9 am-noon and 1:30-7 pm; closed Sun). This ceramics factory established in 1969 prides itself on its unique production of hand-painted pieces. The shop is small but well known for its traditional ceramic jugs, vases, plates and lamps.

Festivals

Giostra della Rocca (Monselice, Sept). Join locals in celebrating Monselice's medieval history at the Giostra della Rocca, held each Sept. The festival is marked by colorful costumes, a medieval market exhibiting arts and crafts, challenges that the nine *contrade* (regions) of the town engage in and, the highlight of the event, a medieval procession through the historic town center.

Food & Drink

A few dishes are unique to Monselice, including *Torta di Federico II*, an almond and honey cake named after the 13th-century ruler.

Due to Montagnana's proximity to the provinces of Verona and Vicenza, its dishes exhibit traces from all

DINING PRICE CHART	
Price per person for an entrée	
€	Under €5
€€	€5-€12
€€€	€13-€20
€€€€	€21-€30
€€€€€	Over €30

three regions. Montagnana is most known for its *prosciutto di Montagnana*, a sweet ham.

Hostaria San Benedetto (Via Andronalecca 16, Montagnana, ☎ 0429-800999, www.ristorantesanbenedetto.it; noon-2 pm and 8-10 pm, closed Wed; major credit cards accepted; €€€). In an 18th-century building at the center of the historic town, this restaurant owned by the Rugolotto family is known for their wonderful preparation of classic Veneto dishes and creative twists on local specialties. Begin with a sample of locally made prosciutto, then try the *tortelli di patate e funghi con sugo di coniglio* (pasta with potatoes and mushrooms, topped with a rabbit sauce). The *tortino alle nocciole con crema di castagne*, one of their most delectable homemade desserts, is prepared with hazelnuts and chestnut cream. The owners occasionally organize dinners with a theme that highlight particular seasonal products, complemented by local wines.

La Torre (Piazza Mazzini 14, Monselice, ☎ 0429-73752, 12:30-2 and 7:30-10 pm, closed all day Mon, Sun for dinner, and in Aug; major credit cards accepted; €€). In the heart of the medieval town just inside the walls is a well-known restaurant with a good selection of local specialties. The *penne con radicchio* is exceptionally good, as are their homemade ravioli filled with seasonal ingredients.

Prosciutteria Duomo (Piazza V. Emanuele 50, Montagnana, €). Drop into this informal eatery near the cathedral for prosciutto tastings accompanied by appropriate wines or aperitifs. Savor paper-thin slices of prosciutto on warm freshly baked bread in any of their sandwiches. The *panino* with *prosciutto crudo*, brie cheese and *carcioffi* (artichokes) is very good. If you're not interested in sampling prosciutto, try one of their large salads.

Accommodations

Hotels

 Hotel Castello (Via S. Girolamo 7/A, Este, ☎ 0429-602223, www.imieiviaggi.com/hotelcastello; €€). This small establishment across from the public gardens in the medieval town center is a simply decorated establishment with only 12

HOTEL PRICE CHART	
Based on a double room for two	
€	Under €50
€€	€50-€80
€€€	€81-€120
€€€€	€121-€190
€€€€€	Over €190

Padua

rooms, most of which have a view of the castle. Rooms are spacious, but the brightest ones are *al angolo* (on the corner).

Hotel Aldo Moro (Via G. Marconi 27, Montagnana, ☎ 0429-81351, www.hotelaldomoro.com; closed two weeks in Aug; €€€). This family-operated establishment just off the main square has 34 charming rooms, with nice bathrooms and parquet floors. Some rooms have wood-beamed ceilings. Its restaurant is well known locally for its regional cooking and features an extensive wine list and notable service.

Agriturismi

Agriturismo Brolo di Ca' Orologio (Via Ca' Orologio 7/A, Baone, ☎ 0429-50099, www.caorologio.com; €€). If an authentic farm holiday removed from the intensity of city life is what you have in mind, Ca' Orologio is the ideal retreat. This tranquil country spot in an attractively restored loft beside a 16th-century villa, offers guests rooms and apartments that can be rented by the night (with a two-night minimum) or by the week. The warm, genuine hospitality of owner Maria Gioia, her homemade wine and olive oil, the peacefulness of the surrounding hills and the comfortably furnished accommodations make this a relaxing getaway that is still within commuting distance of the region's main cities.

Budget Accommodations

Rocca degli Alberi (Via Matteotti 106, Montagnana, ☎ 0429-81076, Mar-Oct, handicap-accessible rooms; €). This hostel is located within Montagnana's city walls and is in one of the city's two castles built by the Carrara family in the 14th century to protect against attacks from Verona. The larger rooms have eight beds but there are also private rooms for four.

Monastero di San Salvaro – Il Regno della Pace (Via Pozzotto 1, Urbana, ☎ 0429-809216, www.ostellosansalvaro.it; €). This hostel just six km south of Montagnana near the border of the province of Verona, is an inexpensive place to find tranquility in the countryside. Originally an 11th-century monastery, it is a good base for travels in the region. There are large rooms as well as private rooms intended for families. Additionally, there is a restaurant here and the **Museo delle Antiche Vie**, showcasing the history of the zone's ancient roads and vehicles. Entry to the museum is free Sunday from 4 until 6 pm.

Nightlife & Entertainment

 Opera in Arena takes place in August at the Martinelli-Pertile arena in Montagnana. Stop into the Montagnana tourist information center for details.

Shopping

Monselice: Open-air markets are held Mon and Fri in the Piazza Mazzini. An exhibition of medieval arts and crafts at the **Mercatino della Rocca**, takes place the last Sat of each month in Piazza Mazzini from May until Sept (the rest of the year this is a flea market).

Montagnana: A large antique market is held the third Sunday of the month (except July and Aug).

Este: The third Sunday of each month there is an antique market in the historic center. Also, see *Este Ceramics* above.

La Bottega del Miele/Bravape (Piazza Beata Beatrice 8, Este, ☎ 0429-3764, www.bravape.com, closed Tue). This specialty shop in Este's town center sells locally produced honey and honey-based products such as liquors, creams, vinegar, grappa-soaked fruits and soaps.

Tourist Offices

IAT
Via del Santuario 6
Monselice
☎ 0429-783026

IAT
Via G. Negri 9
Este
☎ 0429-600462

IAT
Castel S. Zeno
Montagnana
☎ 0429-81320

Padua

Tip: Montagnana is a quiet town (even on market days) and is a good place to stop over for a prosciutto tasting at lunchtime.

■ Cittadella

Founded as a military outpost for Padua in the Middle Ages, Cittadella was responsible for protecting Padua's northern territory from Castelfranco Veneto, an enemy city in today's province of Treviso. Long considered one of Europe's best-preserved military constructions, its massive walls built in 1220 are 1,461 m/4,820 feet long and 2.1 m/6.6 feet thick, with 32 towers and four gates. Cittadella makes for a good stopover on the road from Padua to Bassano and is an ideal place to spend a low-key afternoon sightseeing.

Aerial view of Citadella

Sightseeing

Walking Tour: One of the best starting points to explore Cittadella's historic area is at the information center located in the **Casa del Capitano** (Captain's House) near the Porta Bassanese. From here, you can walk along the walls, the **Camminamento di Ronda**, more than half-way around the medieval town until you reach the **Torre di Malta**. Built in 1251 by the tyrant Ezzelino da Romano, it was used as a prison until he was driven out of the territory and prisoners were set free. Today the tower houses an archaeological museum with artifacts from the city's early history dating back to the Bronze Age, including tools and ceramics. The walk and tower are open Sat

Torre di Malta

and Sun, 3-7 pm, and weekdays upon request. The self-guided tour of the walls, including a visit to the museum, is €2, but it's closed on rainy days. Guided tours in English cost €25.

Continue on to the center of town and the **Duomo**, the neoclassical cathedral built in the 18th and 19th centuries dedicated to the Saints Prosdocimo and Donato. The museum and art gallery are open 9:30 am-12 pm and 3:30-6:30 pm daily. Closed Mon afternoons.

Getting There

 By Car: There are two main state roads leading to Cittadella. The **SS47** (Valsugana) runs north-south and connects Trento and Padua; the **SS53** (Postumian Way) runs east-to-west connecting Vicenza and Treviso. These major roads from Bassano, Vicenza, Padua and Treviso are united in the one-way traffic ring surrounding the walls of Cittadella. There are two entrance gates to the historic center, the **Porta Bassanese** and the **Porta Padovana**, to the north and south respectively, while the two exit gates are **Porta Vicentina** and **Porta Trevisiana** to the east and west. The gates were once decorated with frescoes and the Padua gate at one time served as the main entrance to the city.

 By Bus: Buses are not permitted within Cittadella's walls. Bus stops are located outside the walls and near the town's gates. Cittadella is served by **SITA** buses along the Padova-Bassano line and also by the **La Marca** buses along the Treviso-Vicenza line.

 By Train: Cittadella's train station is a short walk outside Porta Padovana and is a convenient stop since Cittadella is on both the Treviso-Vicenza and the Padua-Bassano lines. Trains run frequently (at least one per hour) between Padua and Cittadella and take 35-45 minutes.

 By Plane: The nearest airport to Cittadella with domestic and international flights daily is **Venice's Marco Polo**. For details: www.veniceairport.it.

Padua

Getting Around

On Foot: The best way to explore the small historic center is on foot, and parking within the city walls, mostly at metered spots, is usually easy to find.

Don't Miss: There are public gardens surrounding Cittadella's walls between the Porta Vicentina and the Porta Padovana. Also, the city has plans to place boats in the canal soon.

Adventures

Culinary Adventures – Cooking Classes

Peccati di Gola (Via Montello 6, ☎ 049-402634 or 388-8488387, www.infotech.it/peccatidigola). See *Padua Culinary Adventures* for details.

Food & Drink

La Polentina, a 19th-century Cittadella recipe, is a simple yellow cake prepared with almonds and pine nuts, dusted with powdered sugar and often sold packed in small wicker baskets or cartons.

Taverna degli Artisti (Via Mura Rotta 9, ☎ 049-9402317, www.tavernadegliartisti.it; lunch, 12-2:30 pm, dinner, 7:30-11 pm; closed Mon for dinner, all day Tue and three weeks in Aug; major credit cards accepted; €€). A popular choice with the theater crowd since it opened in 2000, this taverna is on a side street directly across from Cittadella's *Teatro Sociale.* The young owners, Roger and Elisabetta, work hard to put a twist on classic Paduan dishes and change their menu daily. A Cittadella native, Roger spent years working in several renowned restaurants in Tuscany and Lombardy before moving to Paris, where he developed another passion – art. That inspired the taverna's motif. Artwork from local and international artists is on display in the dining rooms.

DINING PRICE CHART	
Price per person for an entrée	
€	Under €5
€€	€5-€12
€€€	€13-€20
€€€€	€21-€30
€€€€€	Over €30

All pastas are homemade, but the tortelloni, filled with seasonal ingredients, are prepared differently each day and are a favorite. Another great choice is the *salsiccia trentina con carciofi, tartufo e polenta* (sausage prepared with artichokes and truffles served with polenta).

Enoiteca Ai Bei (Piazza Scalco 10, ☎ 049-9403500; lunch, 11 am-3 pm, dinner, 6 pm-2 am; closed Thurs; €€). Since the 1800s this small enoteca behind town hall has been a popular gathering place for locals. The name *enoiteca* indicates its dual function as both an enoteca and an osteria. There is a large selection of Italian wines, most priced at €1-5 per glass. Several organized wine tastings are held each month, often accompanied by dinner, but the owners will also schedule individual tastings upon request.

Osteria al Portego (Località Pozzetto 122, along SS47, ☎ 049-9403383; lunch, 12-3:30 pm, dinner, 6:30 pm-1 am; closed Mon; €€). Located along the SS47 from Bassano just before you enter the city walls, this osteria promises good food at a reasonable price. Sit in any of the rustic dining rooms that are tastefully decorated with black and white period prints or, when the weather permits, enjoy seasonal dishes outdoors.

Accommodations

 Hotel Filanda (Via Palladio 34, ☎ 049-9400000, filanda@tin.it, breakfast included, fitness center, restaurant, handicap-accessible rooms, €€-€€€). Once a 19th-century silk factory, the Hotel Filanda has been fully restored and since 1994 has been a full-service modern hotel. Only a short walk outside the Porta Vicentina, the 70 comfortably appointed rooms are equipped with all modern amenities. The hotel restaurant, **San Bassiano**, is well known among locals for its fine regional cuisine and in summer, guests can dine outdoors in the garden. The spa facilities, including sauna, Jacuzzi and Turkish bath, make this reasonably

HOTEL PRICE CHART	
Based on a double room for two	
€	Under €50
€€	€50-€80
€€€	€81-€120
€€€€	€121-€190
€€€€€	Over €190

Padua

priced hotel an ideal stopover on the road from Bassano to Padua.

Hotel Roma (Via Garibaldi/second floor, entrance on Stradella Castellan, ☎ 049-9402889, www.hotelroma-cittadella.it; breakfast included; €€). This restored 18th-century palazzo is the only three-star hotel in Cittadella's historic center and is a good value. The rooms are simply furnished but the exposed wood beams in certain rooms enhance the décor.

Nightlife & Culture

 Teatro Sociale (Via Indipendenza; information, ☎ 049-9413449, tickets, ☎ 348-0090061). Performances by the Cittadella Philharmonic, along with an array of other theatrical and musical events, are held in the Teatro Sociale whose structure was designed by Giuseppe Japelli, the architect who designed the famed Caffé Pedrocchi in Padua. If your trip doesn't coincide with a performance, be sure to visit the theater with its remarkable interior frescoed by Francesco Bagnara, credited for his work in Venice's Teatro La Fenice. It's open for visits Tue-Sat, 10 am-12 pm.

Shopping

The **general market** takes place Monday mornings in Cittadella's historic center.

The **antique market** is the third Sunday of the month and the **general market** takes place the second Sunday of the month, except in July and Aug.

> **Parking Tip:** Cittadella's historic center is closed to traffic Monday mornings for the weekly market and on Sunday for markets and other events. It is possible to enter only near the Porta Padovana to park at the lot in Campo della Marta. Cars may also park between Porta Bassanese and Porta Trevisiana, as well as between Porta Trevisiana and Porta Padovana outside the walls.

Local Resources

IAT Cittadella
Casa del Capitano
Porta Bassanesi 2
☎ 049-9404485
Closed Tue

Padua

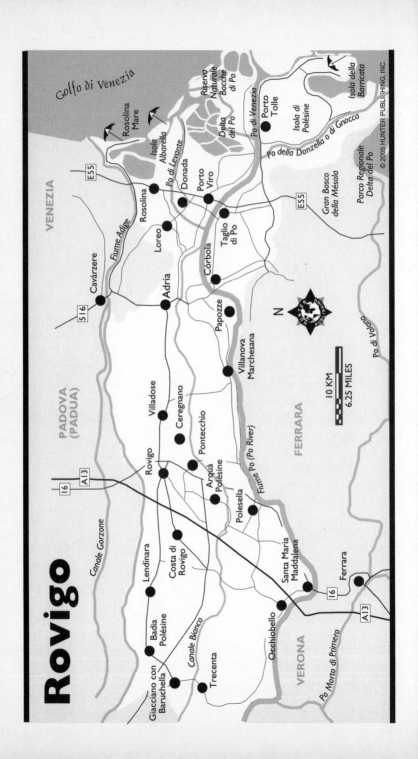

Province of Rovigo

■ Rovigo

Almost certainly the least known of Veneto's provincial capitals (and consequently the least visited), this medieval industrial

town surrounded by flatlands has a remarkably different pulse than its counterparts. Although Rovigo lacks the charm that has come to define cities like Venice and Verona, it does possess a few exceptional works of art, such as the brilliantly frescoed church **La Rotonda**, that arguably place it in a sphere with Italy's other great artistic centers.

Ruins of Rovigo's ancient defense system, including the **Torre Dona** and **Torre Mozza**, are today found within an unattractive public garden, and two of the city's gates are still standing. Rovigo's main square **Piazza Vittorio Emanuele II**, houses the **Accademia dei Concordi**, another one of the city's more refined attractions.

Rovigo's economic problems are immediately noticeable upon entering city limits, but the benefit of this is that you'll find reasonably priced (if a bit unrefined) accommodations and restaurants. While Rovigo is probably not the ideal base for a Venetian holiday, it merits a short visit, particularly if you have an interest in 17th-century art.

Getting There

By Car: From Padua, take the **A13** south toward Rovigo and follow signs to the city center. From Venice, the quickest route to Rovigo is by taking the **A4** to Padua and then picking up the **A13**.

By Bus: The main bus station in Rovigo is in Piazza Cervi. **SITA** buses travel from both Venice and Padua to Rovigo. It takes approximately one hour to reach Rovigo from Padua by bus (these buses leave about once an hour) and from Venice's Piazzale Roma it takes two hours to reach Rovigo with a connection in Padua (one or two buses leave each hour on this route).

 By Train: Rovigo's train station is in Piazza Riconoscenza and is on the Venezia-Bologna, Rovigo-Verona and Rovigo-Chioggia lines. Rovigo is approximately one hour by train from Venice and a half-hour from Padua (trains between these locations run twice an hour on average).

 By Plane: The nearest airport to Rovigo with domestic and international flights daily is **Venice's Marco Polo**, approximately 90 km from Rovigo. From here visitors have the option of continuing on to Rovigo by train or by bus. For details: www.veniceairport.it.

Sightseeing

 La Rotonda (Piazza XX Settembre 37, ☎ 0425-24914; winter, 8 am-noon and 3:30-7:30 pm; summer, 8 am-noon and 4-8 pm, free admission). Commonly known as La Rotonda, the octagonal church of Santa Maria del Soccorso was designed in  1594 by Francesco Zamberlan of Bassano (a friend of Palladio). The building was completed in 1603 but its dome  was demolished due to structural problems and was replaced by a sloped roof circa 1606. The church's architecture is simple, but this simplicity is countered by the rich cycle of frescoes that adorn the walls along with sculptures and a gilded wooden altar carved by

Fresco in La Rotonda by Padovanino

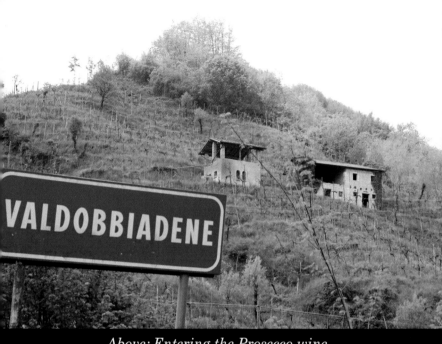

Above: Entering the Prosecco wine production zone of Valdobbiadene

Below: Molinetto della Croda in Refrontolo

Above: Palladio's Villa Barbaro in Maser, near Asolo

Below: Venice's Grand Canal

Above: Colorful Burano

Below: Gondola production at the Squero Canaletto

View of Venice from the northern lagoon

Fresco detail in La Rotonda
by Francesco Maffei

Giovanni Caracchio. The sumptuous frescoes of many 17th-century artists, including Francesco Maffei (one of the great Venetian painters of that period), make this one of Rovigo's greatest treasures. The three large windows on each of the eight sides illuminate the church, and there are three entrances, the primary one facing east. Outside, the brick bell tower designed by Baldassare Longhena stands 57 m/185 feet high and was completed in 1774.

Accademia dei Concordi (Piazza Vittorio Emanuele II 14, ☎ 0425-21654 or 0425-27991, www.concordi.it; Sept-June, Mon-Fri, 9:30 am-noon and 3:30-6:30 pm, Sat and Sun, 10 am-noon; July and Aug, Mon-Sat only, 10 am-1 pm; €2.59). The Accademia itself was founded in 1580 but it wasn't until the 19th century that it housed the *pinacoteca* (art gallery) first established with an extraordinary collection given by the Venetian art collector Count Casilini. Venetian art from the 15th-18th centuries represents the majority of the gallery's collection, though there are also paintings by 16th-century artists from Ferrara, interesting 18th-century portraits of illustrious Rovigo citizens and, on the third floor, a picture gallery of the Episcopal Seminary. A few works are particularly worth seeing, including an altarpiece by Dosso Dossi and his brother Battista Dossi, *La Madonna col Bambino e Cinque Santi,* and the 18th-century *Vedute con Rovine Classiche* by Luca Carlevarijs.

Ask to visit the *deposito,* a warehouse where an extensive collection of paintings by Italian and foreign artists are stored on large panels.

Museo dei Grandi Fiumi (Piazzale S. Bartolomeo 18, ☎ 0425-25077, www.museograndifiumi.it; Tue-Fri, 9 am-1 pm, Sat and Sun, 10 am-1 pm and 4-7 pm, €3). The restored monastery of San Bartolomeo houses this museum devoted to the Po and Adige Rivers' impact on civilization in the Polesine zone, dating back to the Bronze and Iron Ages.

Dining Out

 Rovigo's fare is, unsurprisingly, based on fish. Two popular dishes that highlight eel are *anquilla in umido* and *anguilla alla vallesana*. Risotto dishes are also quite popular here, prepared with seasonal vegetables or fish. *Polenta e coniglio* (polenta and rabbit) and *fagioli in potacin* (slow cooked beans) are commonly found on menus.

Queen Elizabeth Pub (Corso del Popolo 233, ☎ 0425-24979, 6 pm-2 am, closed Mon, €€). This bar and pizzeria along Rovigo's main thoroughfare serves inexpensive local fare. Don't be fooled by the small menu though. Choose between *gnocchi, tagliatelle, garganelli* and other pastas and then select your preferred sauce, such as a speck and gorgonzola sauce, a butter sage sauce or a simple red sauce. They also offer several types of risotto and fish dishes, and a range of pizzas made in the wood oven.

Accommodations

 Hotel Cristallo (Viale Porta Adige 1, ☎ 0425-30701, www.bestwestern.it/cristallo_ro; breakfast included, handicap-accessible rooms; €€). Hotel Cristallo offers most of what you'd expect from a member of the Best Western chain, including clean, comfortable rooms with air conditioning, telephones, televisions and mini-bars. Its proximity to the train station makes this a good choice if you're arriving by train.

Shopping

Rovigo's **general market** takes place Tuesday in the town center, Thursday in Piazza Vittorio Emanuele II and Saturday in the Commenda Est quarter of town.

Nightlife

 Teatro Sociale (Piazza Garibaldi 14, ☎ 0425-25614 or 0425-27853; box office, 10 am-1 pm and 4-7:30 pm). Constructed in the early 19th century, this theater is Rovigo's main stage for a variety of musical and theatrical performances.

Tourist Office

IAT
Via H. Dunant 10
Rovigo
☎ 0425-386290

Websites

www.provincia.rovigo.it

www.rovigo.net

■ Delta del Po (Po Delta)

Rovigo

A short day trip from Venice or Padua will reveal one of Italy's most expansive unspoiled territories, the Delta del Po, which extends over both the Veneto and Emilia-Romagna regions. The Po River subdivides into six branches that weave through the landscape (Po di Levante, Po di Maistra, Po di Pila, Po di Tolle, Po di Donzella and the Po di Goro) and its delta encompasses several towns, including Adria, Ariano Polesine, Porto Tolle and Rosolina.

The flat, rural landscape that extends out to the Adriatic is characterized by a labyrinth of canals, flood plains, dunes, islets, lagoons, sandbanks and marshlands, where many rare or unique species of bird and wildlife nest in the unpolluted habitat of the delta.

Always at the mercy of the forces of nature, life in the delta developed centuries ago around fishing and agriculture. The fertile soil of this agriculturally rich land produces maize, soy, rice, sugar beets, wheat, melons and garlic that all contribute to the zone's economy.

In 1997 a national park was established in the Delta del Po in an effort to protect and promote the territory.

A drive through the zone is particularly pretty on a spring day when the delta's many poppy fields are in full bloom.

Getting There

 By Car: To reach the Po Delta from Padua or Venice, follow **SS309** (known as the *Romeo*), the state road that runs along the coast past Chioggia to the Po Delta. From Padua, however, take **SS516** to **SS309**. SS309 is the main access road to the Delta region and many smaller towns, including Rosolina, Adria and Porto Tolle can be accessed from here. From Rovigo, follow **SP443** toward Adria and follow signs for the Delta.

 By Bus: SITA buses connect Rovigo with Adria and several lines pass through the principal delta towns on a regular basis, including Adria, Adriano Polesine, Porto Viro and Loreo.

 By Train: The main railway stations in the Po Delta region are at Adria, Rosolina and Loreo. Adria, Loreo and Rosolina are on the Rovigo-Chioggia line and Adria is on the Mestre-Adria line.

 By Plane: The nearest airport to the Po Delta with domestic and international flights daily is **Venice's Marco Polo**. For details: www.veniceairport.it.

Getting Around

SITA buses run regularly throughout the zone and connect the various towns but, since it is not heavily trafficked, it is pleasant to explore by car or bicycle.

Sightseeing

 Museo Archaelogico Nazionale (Via Badini 59, Adria, ☎ 0426-21612; Mon-Sat, 9 am-7 pm, Sun, 2-7 pm; €2). Adria's archaeological museum exhibits a notable collection of ancient ceramics, bronze pieces, gold jewelry from the Etruscan period and refined glass dishes from the Roman Period.

Sacca degli Scardovari. You'll need a car to get here, but it is worth a drive to this fishermen's village near the Oasi di Ca' Mello (See *Adventures on Foot*) to see fishermen hard at work mussel farming.

Adventures

On Bikes

Girodelta-Bike Rentals (Via Matteotti, Ca' Tiepolo, ☎ 0426-82501 or 338-8155581). Vittorio Cacciatori organizes guided excursions around the Po Delta by bicycle and canoe. If you can't (or don't want to) decide between the two, why not do both? Sign up for a combination *bici & barca* excursion and explore the zone by bike and boat. If you're not interested in a guided tour and prefer to explore on your own, it is possible to rent bicycles (€8.50 for a full day or €6 for half-day) and kayaks. Inquire about their various itineraries. Girodelta will transport bikes and canoes to pre-selected locations upon request.

On Water

One of the best ways to explore the delta is on water and the guided tours and excursions by **Marino Cacciatori "Caparin"** (Via G. Matteoti 304, Porto Tolle, ☎ 0426-380314, www.marinocacciatori.it) or **Delta Tour Navigazione Turistica** (☎ 0498-700232, www.deltatour.it) weave through the Po's territory navigating its narrow branches and canals.

Houseboat Holidays Italia (Via C. Colombo 37, Porto Viro-Porto Levante, ☎ 0426-666025, www.houseboat.it). Why settle for another standard hotel room when you can relax in the comfort of your own boat? Houseboat Holidays Italia rents four- to 10-person houseboats by the week (shorter rentals are possible when boats are available). Although not all of the boats are luxury yachts, they do make for a unique vacation. No prior experience or licensing is necessary, but the staff does provide basic navigation and safety instruction and will advise travelers on potential routes and itineraries.

Rovigo

On Foot

 Il Giardino Botanico Litoraneo del Veneto (Porto Caleri, Rosolina Mare, ☎ 0426-68408; Apr-Sept, Tue, Thurs and Sun, 10 am-1 pm and 4-7 pm). Walk along the boardwalk and sandy pathways in this expansive botanical garden to see the flora typical of this seashore environment. There are three separate paths to choose from. The shortest one remains mostly within the wooded area and is less than a half-mile long, the intermediate walk is approximately one mile, while the longest trail is less than two miles. Bicycles are not permitted and visitors may only explore on foot.

Oasi di Ca' Mello (☎ 049-8293760). Spend an hour discovering the delta's varied flora and fauna at the Oasi di Ca' Mello, a 10-minute car ride from Ca' Tiepolo on the Po Delta's Isola della Donzella (just north of the Sacca degli Scardovari). The *volpoca* (shelduck) and *rondine* (swallow) make their home here and the rich flora includes the *prugnolo* (blackthorn) and *sambuco* (elder tree).

Beaches

 Albarella – This private island boasts the province's nicer beaches but visitors to the island must have reservations at one of its hotels, a membership or a pass in order to enter (see *Accommodations*).

Rosolina Mare – If the only thing you're interested in doing is getting your feet wet and soaking in the sun for a few hours, Rosolina Mare isn't a bad option. But if you're considering spending a few days on the beach and you're looking for more of a vacation atmosphere, the province of Venice has several better-developed beach towns, such as Caorle, Jesolo and Chioggia.

Dining Out

Fish and seafood are the main focus of many of the Po Delta's traditional dishes, particularly shellfish, cuttlefish, clams, muscles, bass and eel and these are often accompanied by polenta.

Hotel Ristorante Due Leoni (Corso del Popolo 21, ☎ 0426-372129; closed Mon and two weeks in July; €€). This is one of the finest restaurants in the zone and a great place to enjoy local dishes while exploring the Po Delta.

Accommodations

Budget

 Rifugio Po di Maistra (Via Don Aldo Spanio 3, Boccasette di Porto Tolle, ☎ 0426-385330, www.rifugiopodimaistra.com; €). Within the Delta Po Park and only a few km from the beach, this hostel offers comfortable, simple accommodations and a wide range of tourist activities. In addition to its rooms that sleep two to eight guests, accommodating a total of 34 people, the hostel also has a bar, dining room and an activity room. Some of the trips that the rifugio organizes include boat excursions, bird watching tours, canoeing trips and bike excursions.

Resorts

Isola di Albarella (Rosolina, www.albarella.it, information, ☎ 0426-332281; Capo Nord and Club House Albarella, ☎ 0426-330139, Villa and Apartment Service, ☎ 0426-332234; Golf Club Albarella, ☎ 0426-330124; Centro Ippico Albarella-Horseback Riding Center, ☎ 0426-330307). This secluded resort island just off of the province's shore feels far from the land of the delta and accommodates vacationers' diverse tastes and budgets with a wide variety of accommodations and activities to choose from. Its fjord homes and villas are among the prettiest places to stay on the island but there are also lovely cottages, apartments and two hotels. Guests have access to the marina, shops, golf course, a horseback riding center, a sports center, pools, beaches, restaurants, tennis courts and more. Evening entertainment is frequently scheduled during high season. Car traffic is restricted on the island and bicycles (available for rent) are the best way to get around. Don't be surprised to see resident peacocks and other native wildlife making their way about. If you have any hopes of visiting in August, plan well in advance.

Rovigo

Shopping

If you're interested in spotting a good bargain or sampling locally grown produce, **weekly markets** take place Monday in Rosolina Mare's Piazza S. Giorgio, Wednesday in Adria, Thursday in Porto Tolle and Saturday in Adria.

Tourist Offices

IAT Rosolina Mare
Viale dei Pini 4
☎ 0426-68012

Regional Po Delta Park
Via Marconi 6
☎ 0426-372202

Ariano Polesine ProLoco
Largo Europa 2
Porto Tolle
☎ 0426-81150

Websites

www.provincia.rovigo.it
www.parcodeltapo.org
www.deltadelpo.it
www.DeltaPoCard.it

Province of Treviso

The province of Treviso is often referred to as *La Marca Trevigiana* (or *La Marca* for short). Treviso has a prosperous economy that many prominent firms such as Benetton have contributed to over the years, and the landscape from the Sile River to the

Pedemontana zone makes Treviso an increasingly popular destination for active travelers.

■ Treviso

The colorful medieval market town of Treviso, a small city once allied to Venice, is a lively cultural center that is off the beaten path for most travelers, leaving it virtually untouched by the tourism industry and a real treasure to explore. The Sile River runs through Treviso and its willow-fringed waterways that branch off and weave lazily through the city, covered by the occasional stone bridge, give it the nickname "Little Venice."

Perhaps even more distinguishable than the canals are the magnificently frescoed facades of buildings, particularly in the **Calmaggiore** district of Treviso, that led to its reputation as the "painted city." The tradition of frescoing buildings started centuries ago when, because of a lack of stone, frescoes were applied to brick and timber (this evolved into a sort of competition among townspeople in the Middle Ages).

A walk through the bustling town center will reveal high-end boutiques in centuries-old arcaded buildings, many of which were restored after being badly damaged during World War II bombings. In the 16th century the Republic of Venice erected walls surrounding the city center to defend Treviso against enemy invasion.

Among Treviso's greatest treasures are the works of Tomaso da Modena (1325-79), who left his artistic imprint on the city through numerous frescoes in churches and other edifices.

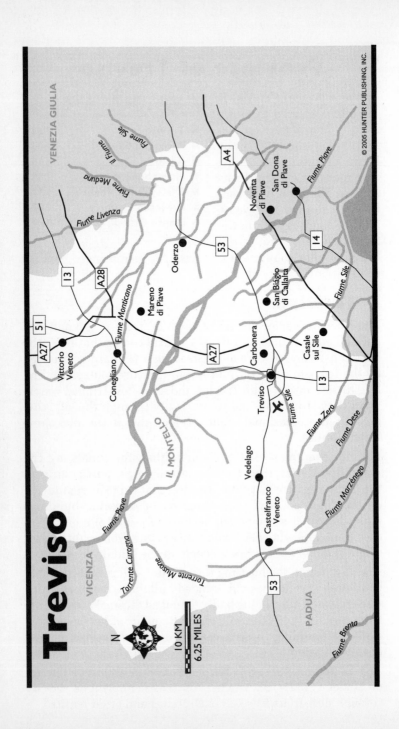

Getting There

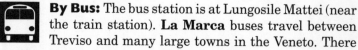

By Car: From Venice, take the **A27** to *Treviso Sud* and follow signs to the city center, or take **SS13**, a slower but direct route into the city. From Padua, take the **A4** to **A27**. From Vicenza and Verona take the **A4** to **A27** or, from Vicenza, it is possible to take the **SS53** into Treviso (slow but direct).

By Bus: The bus station is at Lungosile Mattei (near the train station). **La Marca** buses travel between Treviso and many large towns in the Veneto. There are lines that travel between Padua and Treviso, Castelfranco and Treviso and between Bassano and Treviso (passing through Montebelluna, San Zenone degli Ezzelini, Asolo and Maser). **ACTV** buses service Treviso from Venice.

By Train: Treviso's train station is at Piazzale Duca d'Aosta on the southern end of town. Trains from Venice take approximately 30 minutes to reach Treviso. From Padua, trains travel to Treviso and take about one hour. Treviso is along the Venezia-Udine and Venezia-Belluno lines.

By Plane: Venice's Marco Polo is the region's primary airport with numerous international and domestic flights daily. An alternative airport is **San Giuseppe**, only three km from Treviso's center, but it offers fewer flights daily and only connects to select destinations. www.trevisoairport.it

Getting Around

Treviso is a small city and easy to navigate on foot, but if you prefer to explore the town on wheels, consider renting a bicycle at **Pinarello** (Borgo Mazzini, ☎ 0422-543821) for €6 per day. Call ahead to reserve a bicycle.

Sightseeing

A good starting point to explore this painted city is at the **Duomo** (Piazza del Duomo, ☎ 0422-545720; Mon-Sat, 7:30 am-noon and 3:30-7 pm; Sun, 7:30 am-1 pm and 3:30-8 pm). Among Treviso's most distinc-

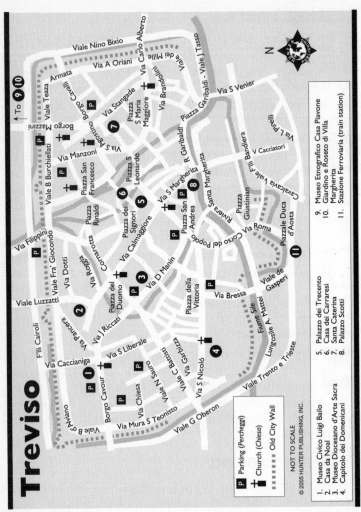

Treviso

Viale Nino Bixio

Via A Oriani

Via Carlo Alberto

Viale del Mille

Viale J Tasso

Via S Venier

Borgo Cavalli

Armata

Viale Teaza

Via Stangade

Piazza S Maria Maggiore

Via Brandolini

Piazza Garibaldi - Viale J Tasso

Borgo Mazzini

← To ⑨ ⑩

Via S Agostino

Via Manzoni

Viale B Burchiellati

Piazza San Francesco

Piazza S Leonardo

⑥

⑤

R Garibaldi

Via S Margherita

⑧

Santa Margherita

Via L Pirelli

V Cacciatori

Cavalcavia Viale F.lli Pirelli

Via Filippini

Piazza Rinaldi

Piazza dei Signori

Via Calmaggiore

Piazza San Andrea

Via S Margherita

Piazza Giustinian

Via Roma

Viale Frà Giocondo

Via Dotti

Via Roggia

Comarotta

③

Via D Manin

Riviera

Corso del Popolo

Piazzale Duca d'Aosta

Viale Luzzatti

②

Piazza del Duomo

Piazza della Vittoria

⑪

Viale de Gasperi

F.lli Cairoli

Via Pancera

Via J Riccati

Via Bressa

Via Caccianiga

Via S Liberale

Via C Battisti

Via Garbizza

Via N Sauro

Via Chiesa

Via S Nicoló

Fiume Sile

Lungosile A. Mattei

Via B di Aviano

Borgo Cavour

Via Mura S Teonisto

Via G Oberon

Viale Trento e Trieste

④

N

NOT TO SCALE
© 2005 HUNTER PUBLISHING, INC.

P Parking (Percheggi)
✝ Church (Chiesa)
▪▪▪ Old City Wall

1. Museo Civico Luigi Bailo
2. Casa da Noal
3. Museo Diocesano d'Arte Sacra
4. Capitolo dei Domenicani
5. Palazzo dei Trecento
6. Casa dei Carraresi
7. Santa Caterina
8. Palazzo Scotti
9. Museo Etnografico Casa Piavone
10. Giardino e Roseto di Villa Margherita
11. Stazione Ferroviaria (train station)

tive characteristics are the cathedral's copper domes rising up from a 12th-century structure that was reconstructed several times over the centuries. Many fine 16th-century frescoes are housed inside the cathedral, including the magnificent *Adoration of the Magi* by Pordenone and Titian's altarpiece the *Annunciation,* both found in the Malchiostro Chapel. One of the oldest parts of the cathedral is in the crypt, where marble columns from its earliest construction stand.

Don't Miss: Behind the cathedral on Via Canoniche is a beautiful paleo-Christian mosaic that attests to the city's ancient roots.

Treviso's main road, **Via Calmaggiore**, is lined with fashionable boutiques and eateries and links the cathedral with the **Piazza dei Signori**, where a clock tower rises high above the **Palazzo dei Trecento**. Evidence suggests that the city's main square served as a forum during the Roman period, though today Piazza dei Signori is lined with cafés and is a popular gathering place for locals.

Sede Museale di Santa Caterina (Via Santa Caterina, ☎ 0422-544864; Tue-Sun, 9 am-12:30 pm and 2:30-6 pm; €3). Formerly a church dedicated to Santa Caterina d'Alessandria, this structure was deconsecrated and now houses vibrant works by Tomaso da Modena, including the *Ursula Cycle*. Considered one of the great works of the 1300s, it depicts the life of St. Ursula and was painted from 1355-58 on two walls of another church, then was transferred here centuries later.

Museo Civico "Luigi Bailo" (Borgo Cavour 24, ☎ 0422-51337 or 658442; Tue-Sat, 9 am-12:30 pm and 2:30-5 pm; Sun, 9 am-noon; €3). The ground floor of this museum named after its founding director contains an interesting archaeological collection of Roman remains and ancient bronze relics, while the upstairs art gallery's finest works include Jacopo da Bassano's *Crucifixion* and a variety of works by Titian, Bellini and Lotto. At the time of publication, the museum was closed for restoration work, but many of its works are on display in the Sede Museale di Santa Caterina.

Treviso

San Nicolò (Via San Nicolò, 8 am-noon and 3:30-6 pm). This 13th-century Dominican Gothic-style church dedicated to San Nicolò is considered one of the city's most important landmarks and features Tomaso da Modena's portraits of saints on the interior columns as well as Palma the Younger's altarpiece of Sant'Agostino. The **Capitolo dei Domenicani** (Seminario Vescovile, Piazzetta Benedetto XI 2, ☎ 0422-3247, 8 am-5:30 pm) in the seminary next door contains 40 marvelous portraits depicting the personalities of Dominican friars.

Adventures

With Wine

 Treviso D.O.C. (Via del Municipio 1, ☎ 0422-583519). This wine shop near the Piazza San Vito stocks a wide range of D.O.C. wines and carries some of the most prestigious labels from wineries throughout the province. Inquire about scheduled wine events and courses.

Festivities

Radicchio in Piazza takes place the weekend before Christmas in the Piazza dei Signori and is a celebration of the famed locally grown Radicchio Rosso di Treviso (Red Radicchio of Treviso). Visitors come from all over to purchase the seasonal product and to sample traditional dishes that highlight it. For details contact **Consorzio del Radicchio di Treviso** (☎ 0422-488087) or inquire at the tourist office.

Ombralonga (www.ombralonga.it, ☎ 0422-234040). Since 1990, locals have celebrated Treviso's culinary and enological traditions with this festival.

On the third weekend of October, people take to the streets of Treviso to celebrate the inauguration of the **Fontana delle Tette** (a fountain given to the Trevisian people in 1559 by the mayor Da Ponte) that supposedly flowed for three days with wine instead of water. This festival includes a *giro* (trip) to many of Treviso's osterias, musical events, wine tastings and traditional festivities.

Did You Know? In the Veneto region, an *ombra*, which literally means shadow, refers to a glass of wine. This term is most commonly used in Venice.

Dining Out

 Trevisian cuisine salutes its territory's prized seasonal products through simple, yet refined dishes that have gained international recognition and marks of excellence. The palatable delights in the province include *radicchio rosso di Treviso*, an intense ruby-colored member of the chicory family that originates in this zone. Trevisian cuisine also features fish, particularly *trota* (trout) from the Sile River, and *chiocciole* (snails), also known as *scios* in the local dialect.

Several cheeses are particular to this zone, including *Casatella* and *Imbriago*.

Did You Know? During World War I, cheese was an important staple and since many Austro-Hungarian soldiers would pilfer for food, some Italian farmers hid cheese in the rinds of pressed grapes, where the cheese developed a dark coating and a sharper but fruity flavor. Happened upon accidentally, *formaggio imbriago* (drunken cheese) is today one of Treviso's characteristic products.

Treviso

Sopa coada, a soup of pigeon meat and bread, is a typical recipe of Treviso, but the one recipe that has lifted this city into the international spotlight is *tiramisu* (pick me up), a dessert usually prepared with either *mascarpone* or custard cream and coffee-soaked biscuits.

DINING PRICE CHART	
Price per person for an entrée	
€	Under €5
€€	€5-€12
€€€	€13-€20
€€€€	€21-€30
€€€€€	Over €30

Many fine wines are produced in the hills near Conegliano and Valdobbiadene (particularly Prosecco) as well as near the

Montello and Colli Asolani and they complement the traditional Trevisian cuisine.

La Colonna (Via Campana 27, ☎ 0422-544804, www.ristorantelacolonna.it; 12:30-3 pm and 7:30-11 pm; closed Sun night and Mon; reservations recommended; major credit cards accepted; €€€). This notable restaurant is set in a 16th-century building erected by the wealthy Rinaldi family sparing no expense. For many years it was known as the "Ostaria dai Sporchi," where the famous *vin in scuea* (wine in bowls) was served, and today it specializes in classic provincial dishes. The high-ceiling dining rooms are richly decorated and one of the restaurant's finest attributes is the fresco on the wall in the main dining room discovered during a renovation. The kitchen specializes in fish-based dishes and there are several excellent ones to choose from, including the springtime *tagliatelle mimosa* prepared with scallops and asparagus. If you can't snag a seat facing the fresco, try for one in the upstairs dining room. This restaurant is elegant but not pretentious and attracts a mostly local crowd. The adjacent wine bar, **Enoteca Odeon** serves highly acclaimed local and international wines and a *degustazione* (tasting) can be arranged upon request.

Osteria Ponte Dante (Piazza Garibaldi 6, ☎ 0422-591897; closed Sun; €€). For more than 10 years Diego has been serving up simple local fare in his small establishment along Riviera Garibaldi. Indoor seating is limited but on a warm day enjoy watching passersby on the Riviera walkway from an outdoor table. Try the *seppie in umido* (cuttlefish) or the *pasta e fagioli* (pasta and beans). The lunchtime meal is served à la carte, and if you want to sample a few dishes, request a *piatto misto* (mixed plate).

Beccherie (Piazza Ancillotto 11, ☎ 0422-540871; closed Sun evening and Mon; major credit cards accepted; €€). One of Treviso's oldest eateries, Beccherie dates back to 1875 when it was a popular spot for butchers to enjoy a bowl of tripe soup. This meeting spot for Italian patriots traveling from Venice to Lombardy and Piedmont has always served hearty Trevisian fare and one of its specialties is *zuppa di radicchio*.

Antica Osteria ai Carraresi (Via Palestro 42/A, ☎ 0422-419276; 9 am-8 pm; closed Sun; €-€€). If you're in the mood for a light lunch or you need a quick snack in the afternoon when most eateries are closed, stop into this *osteria*. Their *crostini* (small toasts) topped with seasonal ingredients are very good, as is the *fritture di pesce* (fried fish) served with polenta.

Bar Pasticceria Nascimben (Via Calmaggiore 32; closed Mon; €). A visit to Treviso would not be complete without sampling the world-famous *tiramisu* and Nascimben makes one of the best in town. If you're not up for this coffee-based dessert, try another one of their delicious pastries or a gelato instead.

Proseccheria Mionetto (Via Inferiore 2; major credit cards accepted; €-€€). Grab a table or a spot at the bar at this hip *proseccheria* near the Piazza San Vito and sample locally produced Prosecco accompanied by a small snack. Stop by for an aperitif or a late-night drink.

Accommodations

 Hotels are few and far between in this city, so if you're planning to spend the night here, book your room in advance so as not to waste time wandering. Unless your itinerary includes several days in the city, consider Treviso as a side-trip from another Veneto town.

HOTEL PRICE CHART	
Based on a double room for two	
€	Under €50
€€	€50-€80
€€€	€81-€120
€€€€	€121-€190
€€€€€	Over €190

La Colonna (Via Campana 27, ☎ 0422-544804; €€€). Run by the proprietors of the restaurant of the same name, the inn's six rooms are sophisticated and tastefully furnished. This classic is one of the town's nicer sleeps but book ahead because it is not a well-kept secret.

Al Fogher (Viale della Repubblica 10, ☎ 0422-432950; major credit cards accepted; breakfast included; €€€). This member of the Best Western chain has comfortable, standard rooms with all modern amenities. Bicycles are available for guests to explore town.

Treviso

Shopping

Markets

The **general market** takes place Tuesday and Saturday mornings in the area of Porta S. Tomaso and the Piazzale Burchiellati near Treviso's walls.

The **fish market**, dating back to the Middle Ages, takes place from Tuesday to Saturday in the *Pescheria* zone in the Cagnan Canal.

An **antiques market** takes place along Borgo Cavour the fourth Sunday of each month (except July).

Typical Goods

Treviso is known for its wrought iron and copper production. Stop into one of the small shops around town that sell these crafts or search the stalls on market day.

In a small piazza on the left side of the cathedral along **Via Calmaggiore** you can often find local artists selling oil paintings and watercolors. Many will even paint a particular Trevisian landscape on request if you have something in mind.

Nightlife & Entertainment

Ca' dei Carraresi (Via Palestro 33/35, ☎ 0422-654382). Located behind the Piazza dei Signori, this is the site of many concerts and exhibitions year-round. Contact them directly or ask the tourist information center for event details.

Teatri Spa (Piazza S. Leonardo 1, ☎ 0422-513300, www.teatrispa.it). This instrumental society of the **Fondazione Cassamarca** organizes theatrical, musical, dance and operatic performances at a variety of venues around town, including **Teatro Comunale** (Corso del Popolo 31, ☎ 0422-540480) and **Teatro Eden** (Via Monterumici, ☎ 0422-513310).

Tourist Office

IAT
Piazza Monte di Pietà 8
☎ 0422-547632

Websites

www.marcatreviso.it

www.trevisoweb.com

www.sevenonline.it/tvapt

■ Parco del Sile

Originating in Casacorba di Vedelago near the province of Padua, the Sile River stretches for approximately 95 km and is one of the longest subterranean spring rivers in the world. The Sile flows lazily in the flat countryside toward Treviso, but this changes east of the city where the river bends several times as it travels southeast toward the Adriatic.

Patrician villas, medieval churches, small hamlets, gardens and old mills dot the banks of the Sile, whose surrounding territory is important for farming.

The Sile was once an important commercial route and the territory around Treviso was called the granary of the Republic because of the mill industry located here. Many archaeological digs have uncovered evidence of farming and trading vocations as well as evidence of ancient pile-dweller villages along the river.

 Watchable Wildlife: Green woodpeckers, fan-tailed warblers and night birds of prey can be found here.

When the park was instituted in 1991 it was with the intent of protecting and preserving the territory, while furthering an appreciation and respect for the environment.

The **Cervara Oasis** in Santa Cristina is one of the park's nicest areas, marked by an ancient mill, and it is here that the river forks and creates an island that can be explored on foot or from a canoe.

The park is ideal for nature lovers with its vibrant flora, fauna and fascinating wildlife.

> **Did You Know?** A *burcio* or barge with a flat bottom, used to transport goods and navigate channels of the region, was towed by horses when it traveled upstream.

Sightseeing

 Stop at **Chiesa di Santa Cristina** (Santa Cristina di Quinto di Treviso) on the way to the Cervara Oasis to see Lorenzo Lotto's early 16th-century painting of the Madonna and Saints.

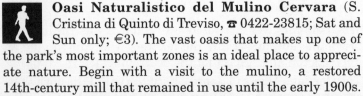

Adventures

On Water

 Canoe Club Quinto di Treviso (Vicolo Cornarotta 9, S. Cristina di Quinto di Treviso, ☎ 0422-477022). This group of canoe and kayak enthusiasts offers guided excursions along the Sile River for all skill levels. Depart from Badoere di Morgano and arrive at the Oasi Cervara. This five- to six-km voyage takes a half-day (about two hours of which are spent in water) and offers a good opportunity to learn about the Sile River's environment. Call ahead to schedule excursions.

On Foot

Oasi Naturalistico del Mulino Cervara (S. Cristina di Quinto di Treviso, ☎ 0422-23815; Sat and Sun only; €3). The vast oasis that makes up one of the park's most important zones is an ideal place to appreciate nature. Begin with a visit to the mulino, a restored 14th-century mill that remained in use until the early 1900s. Follow the **Sentiero della Rosta** (path) past the reed house, similar to those once inhabited by locals. Continuing farther into the oasis will reveal the visitor's center with several exhibits, and the ***orto botanico*** (botanical garden) where typical vegetation of the zone flourishes. This is only 15-20 minutes from Treviso by car, and a La Marca bus stops just in front of the entrance to the oasis. Allow about an hour to explore the oasis.

Watchable Wildlife: There are opportunities in the oasis to observe many species of wildlife, particularly the *germano reale* (mallard duck), the *martin pescatore* (kingfisher), above, and the *airone cenerino* (grey heron).

Tourist Office

Ente Parco Naturale Regionale del Fiume Sile
Villa Letizia
Via Tandura 40
☎ 0422-321994

Websites

www.parks.it/parco.fiume.sile

■ Asolo

"La Citta dai Cento Orizzonti"
(City of 100 Horizons) – Giosué Carducci

A mirage on the Trevisian landscape, Asolo has enchanted poets, writers and artists with its medieval charm for centuries. Little has changed over the years along Asolo's porticoed streets that reveal old palaces framed by Gothic arcades, trefoiled windows and attractive balconies. The sleepy town enjoys a privileged position in the hills, surrounded by vineyards, olive trees and ancient villas once owned by Venetian aristocrats.

Treviso

Perched on a hilltop looming over the town center is one of Asolo's icons, **La Rocca**, above, a fortress connected to the lower castle by 14th-century walls. Aqueduct, bath and theater remains discovered in Asolo are evidence of the town's importance during the Roman period when both Ptolemy and Pliny the Elder celebrated the town in their writings. The Ezzelini, Scaligeri and Carraresi left their mark on Asolo. The Queen of Cyprus, Caterina Cornaro, was in fact the daughter of a Venetian family and had married the King of Cyprus. After his death, she was forced to abdicate her throne and, as Venice wanted control of Cyprus, it is said that she was given Asolo in exchange. In 1489 the Venetian Republic sent her to rule the town.

Home to many literary figures and legendaries such as Robert Browning (who dedicated his volume of poems *Asolanda* to the town), Eleonora Duse (the divine actress of Italian theater) and Freya Stark (the English explorer), the idyllic hamlet has long been considered the *pearl of the Veneto*. Though the town has a slow pulse, it draws plenty of tourists on weekends (especially for the monthly antique market) and is hailed by many as one of northern Italy's finest treasures.

Did You Know? Cardinal Pietro Bembo wrote love letters entitled *Gli Asolani*. He coined the word *asolare* which means to pass time leisurely.

Getting There

By Car: Located in the northwestern part of the province, Asolo is easily accessible from **SS248**. Arriving by car, you have the option of either parking in Ca' Vescovo (a free lot) along SS248 and taking the shuttle or walking to the center; you can park in the Forestuzzo lot (500 m from the center); or in the Cipressina lot (300 m away). Cars may also park in the city center but there are limited

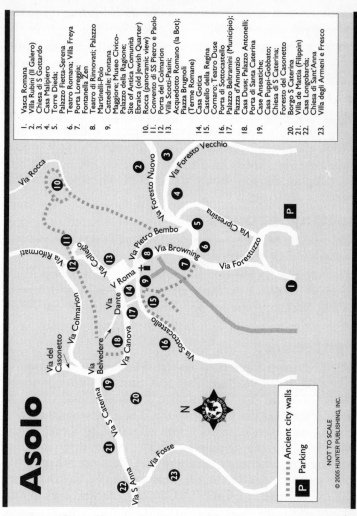

Asolo

1. Vasca Romana
2. Villa Rubini (Il Galero)
3. Chiesa di S Gottardo
4. Casa Malipiero
5. Torre Dieda;
   Palazzo Fietta-Serena
6. Teatro Romana; Villa Freya
7. Porta Loreggia;
   Fontanella Zen
8. Teatro di Rinnovati; Palazzo
   Martinelli-Polo
9. Cattedrale; Fontana
   Maggiore; Museo Civico-
   Palazzo della Ragione;
   Site of Antica Comunità
   Ebraica (old Jewish Quarter)
10. Rocca (panoramic view)
11. Convento di SS Pietro e Paolo
12. Porta del Colmarion
13. Villa Scotti-Pasini;
    Acquedotto Romano (la Bot);
    Piazza Brugnoli
    (Terme Romane)
14. Casa Gotica
15. Castello della Regina
16. Cornaro; Teatro Duse
17. Porta di Sottocastello
    Palazzo Beltramini (Municipio);
    Piazza d'Annunzio
18. Casa Duse; Palazzo Antonelli;
    Porta di Santa Caterina
19. Case Anseatiche;
    Casa Puppi-Gobbato;
    Chiesa di S Caterina;
    Foresto del Casonetto
20. Borgo S Caterina
21. Villa de Mattia (Filippin)
22. Casa Longobarda;
    Chiesa di Sant'Anna
23. Villa degli Armeni e Fresco

Ancient city walls

P Parking

NOT TO SCALE

© 2005 HUNTER PUBLISHING, INC.

spaces and roads are closed to traffic Sun, during markets and other events.

By Bus: Arriving in Asolo by bus is simple with **La Marca's** Treviso-Bassano line that runs approximately every one to two hours. Asolo also sits on the **CTM** (Vicenza's bus system) Bassano-Cornuda line. Since the buses are not permitted to enter Asolo's historic center, they stop at the Ca' Vescovo parking lot 1,500 m from the town center along SS248 and a shuttle bus connects to the center several times each hour. There is also a path leading up to the center if you prefer to walk.

 By Train: The nearest railway stations to Asolo are Bassano del Grappa, Castelfranco Veneto and Montebelluna. From these stations, Asolo is accessible by bus.

 By Plane: Venice's Marco Polo is the region's primary airport with numerous international and domestic flights daily. An alternative airport is **San Giuseppe**, only three km from Treviso's center, but it offers fewer flights daily and only connects to select destinations. www.trevisoairport.it

Getting Around

Leave the car behind and explore the small town of Asolo and its surrounding countryside on foot or bicycle.

This shop repairs bicycles and rents them for €6.50 per day. **Cicli Miotto** (Via Malombra 15, Casella d'Asolo, ☎ 0423-525125; 9 am-noon, 3:30-7:30 pm; closed Sat afternoon).

Sightseeing

 Museo Civico di Asolo (Via Regina Cornaro 74, ☎ 0423-952313; Sat and Sun, 10 am-noon and 3-7 pm; €4). Asolo's civic museum is housed in the 14th-century Loggia della Ragione. The archaeology section exhibits an interesting collection of relics from prehistoric times through the Renaissance. The art gallery contains paintings by Canova and Manera and there are other rooms in the museum devoted to two great women in Asolo's history – Eleonora Duse and Caterina Cornaro – as well a room containing treasures from the cathedral.

 Great Value: A combined ticket allows entrance to the Museo Civico di Asolo and the Gypsoteca di Possagno for €5. This ticket is valid for 30 days and also gives the holder a reduction on admission to the Villa Barbaro in Maser.

La Rocca (Sun, Apr-Oct, 10 am-7 pm; Nov-Mar, 10 am-5 pm; July and Aug, 10 am-noon and 3-7 pm; closed in inclement weather). This massive fortification on the summit of Mount Ricco dominates the sleepy town, and for centuries served to protect it from enemy invasions. The Rocca, reconstructed in the 12th or 13th century, has nine asymmetrical walls that are four m/13 feet thick and 15 m/50 feet high. One of the best vantage points from which to see the town and surrounding countryside is the Rocca. If you're fortunate enough to visit on a clear day, look across the plains for a view of the Venetian Lagoon.

Castello della Regina Caterina Cornaro is only open during performances at the **Teatro Duse** located within the structure that served as the queen's abode from 1489-1509. Within the castle are the Torre Civica and the smaller Torre Reata.

> **Panoramic View:** Scenic views of the Asolan landscape can be had from the castle's courtyard that overlooks the countryside.

Chiesa di Sant'Anna. Travel out of the center along Via Canova then onto Via S. Caterina to find a small 16th-century church with an adjacent cemetery that houses the tomb of Eleonora Duse and Freya Stark.

> **Historic Interest:** Excavations have uncovered remains of ancient thermal baths from the Roman period under the Piazza Brugnoli. On the northeast side of the piazza are remains of the Roman aqueduct *La Bot*.

Duomo (Piazzetta S. Pio X 192, ☎ 0423-952376). Asolo's 18th-century cathedral off the Piazza Maggiore houses two beautiful altarpieces of the *Assumption*, one by Lorenzo Lotto and the other by Jacopo da Ponte.

Villa Barbaro (Via Cornuda 7, Maser, ☎ 0423-92300; Mar-Oct, Sat and Sun, 3-6 pm; Nov-Feb, Sat and Sun, 2:30-5 pm; €5). In the small agricultural village of Maser, only a few miles from Asolo, stands one of Andrea Palladio's great

Treviso

works, Villa Barbaro, built circa 1560 for the Venetian brothers, Daniele and Marcantonio Barbaro. This country residence is embellished with frescoes by  Paolo Veronese and contains works by Giambattista Zelotti.

Panoramic View: Follow Via Canova past the porticoed buildings and through the narrow Porta di S. Caterina. When you reach the Church of Santa Caterina on the corner of Via S. Caterina continue straight on Foresto del Casonetto. Just a few steps up on the left is a low stone wall and opening onto the beautiful scenery at the foot of Monte Grappa.

Adventures

Golf

 Asolo Golf Club (Via Ronche, Cavaso del Tomba, ☎ 0423-942000). The graceful Asolan hills are the ideal setting for this challenging 18-hole golf course. Open year-round, the club features a driving range, clubhouse, fitness and spa facilities, a putting green and a restaurant.

On Foot

 Exploring Asolo: A good place to start a walking tour of this sleepy town is at the **Porta Loreggia**, one of the town's gates. Follow the road as Via Forestuzzo turns into **Via Browning**, a lovely porticoed street whose buildings contain many fine shops.

Ascending the hill, you will find yourself in the town's main square, **Piazza Garibaldi** (commonly referred to as Piazza Maggiore), lined with a few cafés. The Duomo and the Loggia della Ragione are to the left.

After visiting the **Duomo** and the **Museo Civico**, located in the **Loggia della Ragione** (see *Sightseeing*), follow Via Cornaro past them until you arrive at **Queen Caterina Cornaro's castle**. Turn onto the **Piazza d'Annunzio** (see *Dining Out* for a good restaurant located here) after visiting the castle's courtyard, and then turn right again onto Via Dante. Continue to follow this road as it turns into Via Collegio past the main square. The large **Villa Scotti-Pasini** sits on the right above the Piazza Brugnoli and the ancient Roman aqueduct.

Keep left on the road as it ascends slightly and just up the road from here you will exit the walls through **Porta del Colmarion**, the only gate still in its medieval form.

Follow the cobblestone way that runs along the walls and finally ends at the **Rocca**, where there is a beautiful panoramic view of the countryside.

Porta del Colmarion

Descending Monte Ricco, retrace your steps, but instead of re-entering the walls at the Porta di Colmarion, continue outside the walls along Via Colmarion until you reach **Foresto del Casonetto**. Turn left here for pretty views of the countryside. Follow the road as it turns into Via Canova and passes the famous **Hotel Villa Cipriani** (once owned by Robert Browning), before re-entering the walls at the **Porta S. Caterina**.

Follow the arcaded street slightly uphill on Via Canova past several elegant boutiques, including the **Tessoria Asolana** (see *Shopping*) until you reach the town center.

Festivities

Palio della Regina takes place the third Sunday of Sept each year when Asolo celebrates her ancient Queen of Cyprus, Caterina Cornaro. The Middle Ages come alive in Asolo's streets with period costumes, traditional food, entertainment and amusing competitions between Asolo's *contrade* (districts).

Dining Out

Ristorante Locanda Due Mori (Piazza D'Annunzio 5, ☎ 0423-952256; closed Wed; €€). Soak in one of the best views of the Asolan hills from **Due Mori's** panoramic terrace while dining on seasonal dishes. Their menu changes frequently but always includes a wide selection of grilled meats (their specialty) and homemade pastas. The *agnolloti alle erbe spontanee* (pasta filled with herbs) is a good choice. If you like asparagus, try the traditional spring dish, white asparagus served with eggs. Copper pots hang from the ceiling of the indoor dining room. There are three guest rooms that are available upon request.

Hostaria Ristorante Ca'Derton (Piazza D'Annunzio 11, ☎ 0423-529648; 12:30-2 pm and 8-10 pm; closed Sun evening and Mon; major credit cards accepted; €€€). For generations cooking has been a tradition in Nino's family and with the help of his wife Antonietta and children, he's keeping the tradition alive. He's the chef and owner here. Nino's interpretations of classic Veneto dishes showcase the zone's finest seasonal products in dishes like asparagus soup, artichoke flan with cheese sauce and roasted wild duck with orange sauce. Their large selection of homemade desserts is too tempting to pass up. Italian and international wines and distilled liquors keep Nino's cellar well-stocked and if you're up for a wine tasting or interested in purchasing a bottle, stop into their enoteca.

Villa Razzolini Loredan (Via Schiavonesca Marosticana 15, ☎ 0423-951088, www.villarazzolini.it; closed Mon evening and Tue; €€-€€€). Once owned by the noble Razzolini family, the 17th-century Villa Razzolini Loredan, surrounded by an expansive park, is one of the better known restaurants in the Asolan hills. This is the site of many formal events

DINING PRICE CHART	
Price per person for an entrée	
€	Under €5
€€	€5-€12
€€€	€13-€20
€€€€	€21-€30
€€€€€	Over €30

and several times each year the chef orchestrates dinners to showcase seasonal products complemented by fine local wines.

Al Morer (Via Risorgimento, ☎ 0423-55060, www.almorer.it; Fri and Sat, from 7 pm on, Sun, 12-2:30 pm and 7 pm; €€). This family-operated *agriturismo*, in business since 1991, is just outside Asolo's exit gate on the road to SS248 and is a good place to sample locally made products. Try their Merlot, accompanied by homemade salami, or in spring sample their cherries. If you arrive in time for a meal, the *pollo in umido* (chicken prepared with fresh tomato sauce and cooked slowly in the oven) is good.

Accommodations

Hotel Duse (Via R. Browning 190, ☎ 0423-55241, www.hotelduse. com; closed two weeks in Jan; major credit cards accepted; €€€). In Asolo's historic center, just across from Piazza Garibaldi and the cathedral, stands the quaint Hotel Duse, named after the great Italian actress. There are eight doubles equipped with a mini-bar, air conditioning, telephone and television, but the

Eleanora Duse

most spacious rooms, with pretty views of the piazza, are 103, 203 and 303. The sloped, wood-beamed ceilings enhance the atmosphere of the junior suite on the top floor that sleeps five and is ideal for a family. Breakfast is an additional €6 per person.

Treviso

Hotel Villa Cipriani (Via Canova 298, ☎ 0423-523411, www.starwood.com/italy; handicap-accessible rooms; major credit cards accepted; €€€€). A stay at this charming, exclusive 16th-century villa (one of Italy's finest sleeps) will surely feel like a dream, from its romantic gardens on the Asolan hillside to its elegant rooms, handsomely

HOTEL PRICE CHART	
Based on a double room for two	
€	Under €50
€€	€50-€80
€€€	€81-€120
€€€€	€121-€190
€€€€€	Over €190

decorated with old prints and 19th-century antiques. Now owned by the Starwood chain, this graceful Palladian-style villa was once the property of Robert Browning, and has been visited by many celebrities, including Aristotle Onassis. Its restaurant is highly acclaimed and the hotel's sophistication and fine service are unsurpassed.

Casasolano (Via Sottocastello 18, ☎ 0423-55754, www.casasolana.it; €€). Not far from Queen Cornaro's castle and Asolo's historic center, Stefania and Arturo welcome guests into their 19th-century Venetian farmhouse. Renovated in 2002, the three rooms named after women who left their mark on the town – Caterina Cornaro, Eleonora Duse and Freya Stark – are tastefully furnished and have large modern bathrooms. If you're arriving by train, ask to have transportation arranged from the nearest railway station. Bicycles are available for guests to discover the Asolan countryside.

VOCABULARY	
Telaio	loom
Seta	silk
Tessuto	cloth, fabric
Ricamo	embroidery
Arazzo	tapestry
Tessile	textile
Merletto	lace

Shopping

Asolo has a long tradition of lace, embroidery and woven crafts and there are several shops around town where you can purchase these.

Scuola Asolana Antico Ricamo (Via Canova 333, ☎ 0423-952906; 10 am-2 pm and 3:30-6:30 pm; major credit cards accepted). The history of this school of tapestry dates back to the late 1800s when the son of Robert and Elizabeth Barrett Browning, Pen, founded a school of lace. By 1920 the school passed into the hands of Lucia Bonaffons Casale, who made profound changes and adapted antique embroidery styles to modern tastes. Over the years the school has changed hands several times and today Anna Milani carries on this Asolan tradition in a small shop where she continues to produce refined embroidery.

Tessoria Asolana (Via Canova 317, ☎ 0423-952062; open mornings only). The Tessoria Asolana, one of Italy's oldest textile mills, from 1840, preserves the Asolan tradition of textile weaving. Visitors can see delicate silk fabrics woven on ancient wooden looms, though the finished products are quite pricey.

Markets

The weekly **general market** is held in the historic center on Saturday mornings.

The **antique market**, one of the Veneto's finest, takes place in the historic center the second Sunday of each month (except July and August).

Nightlife & Entertainment

 Teatro Duse (Castello, ☎ 0423-952361). This theater, in Queen Cornaro's castle, is named after Eleonara Duse, a famous Italian actress in the 19th and 20th centuries. It is the seat of many important cultural events year-round. Stop into the tourist information center or check www.asolo.it for a list of upcoming events.

Tourist Office

IAT
Piazza Garibaldi 73
☎ 0423-529046
Closed Mon afternoon

Website

www.asolo.it

■ Montebelluna

This small town west of the Montello hill, where the last bloody battles of World War I took place, is the world capital of mountain footwear production and there are many factories and shops located in this zone.

Getting There

By Car: Montebelluna is along **SS248**, the road that travels from Bassano and Asolo toward the Piave River.

By Bus: Several **La Marca** bus lines pass through Montebelluna daily, including the Treviso-Bassano line, which runs every one to two hours, and the Treviso-Valdobbiadene line, which runs one to two times per hour.

By Train: There is a train station in Montebelluna on Viale Stazione. Trains arrive approximately once or twice each hour from Treviso and the trip is 30 minutes.

By Plane: Venice's Marco Polo is the region's primary airport with numerous international and domestic flights daily. An alternative airport is **San Giuseppe**, only three km from Treviso's center, but it offers fewer flights daily and only connects to select destinations. www.trevisoairport.it

Sightseeing

Museo dello Scarpone (Villa Zuccareda-Binetti, ☎ 0423-303282; Tue-Sat, 9 am-noon and 3-6 pm, Sun, 9 am-noon and 3-7 pm; closed Mon; €3). This 16th-century villa was owned by the Zuccareda family in the 1800s and served as a command center for the Italian forces during World War I. The villa's rooms are devoted to Montebelluna's mountain footwear industry and there is an interesting display of boots here, including snowshoes from the 1800s and boots from the First World War. This display illustrates the evolution of mountain footwear and exhibits Montebelluna's contribution to the footwear industry. There is also a display of tools used in footwear production over the years, as well as the more recent production of snowboard bindings, cycling shoes and soccer shoes. Many international footwear companies have established themselves in

Montebelluna, including Benetton, HTM, Rossignol, Nike and Invicta.

Villa Pisani (Via A. Anassillide, ☎ 0423-23048). In the mid-17th century the Correr family commissioned the construction of the villa with Montello in the background, which was later inherited by the Pisani family, who owned some 50 villas. The inside is used by various associations but the grounds are open to the public.

Shopping

The **general market** held each Wednesday morning is centuries-old and, once considered the most important marketplace in the hills and pre-Alps zone, merchants would come with their filled carts to vie for the best spot in the marketplace.

Tourist Office

Pro Loco
Piazza Aldo Moro, 1/A
☎ 0423-23827

■ Castelfranco Veneto

The well-preserved walls of Castelfranco Veneto, built circa 1199 to defend the city from the Paduans and other enemies, enclose a quiet medieval town that was the birthplace of the painter Giorgione (1478-1510), who left a remarkable impact on High Renaissance art. The city was fortified due to its strategic position that guaranteed good control over important roads. A moat and pretty garden with walkways surround the walls and a large statue of Giorgione sits on the northern corner outside the walls.

Getting There

By Car: Castelfranco Veneto is easy to reach, located on **SS53** approximately 25 km west of Treviso and 12 km from Cittadella. Cars may enter into Castelfranco's walls through the Porta di Musile from the direction of Vicenza or the entrance at the Piazza Giorgione. Historically, the town's main entrance gate was at the tower,

Treviso

but it is now open only to pedestrian traffic. The main thoroughfare in town is Via F.M. Preti. The best option for visitors arriving by car is to park in Piazza Giorgione, outside the walls and explore the small center on foot.

 By Bus: Castelfranco's main bus stop is in Piazza Giorgione. Buses travel between Castelfranco Veneto and Treviso approximately once per hour.

 By Train: Castelfranco's train station is an important one in the region, with direct trains running frequently to Padua, Vicenza, Treviso and Venice. It is approximately 20 minutes from Treviso, 30 from Padua and 50 from Venice.

 By Plane: Venice's Marco Polo is the region's primary airport with numerous international and domestic flights daily. An alternative airport is **San Giuseppe**, only three km from Treviso's center, but it offers fewer flights daily and only connects to select destinations. www.trevisoairport.it

Sightseeing

 Duomo di San Liberale (Piazza San Liberale; 9 am-noon and 3-6 pm; free admission). The 18th-century cathedral in Castelfranco's historic center, designed by Francesco Maria Preti, contains Giorgione's altarpiece, *The Madonna and Child with Saints Francis and Liberale,* right, commissioned in the early 16th century. This great treasure, along with frescoes by Veronese, Zelotti and paintings by Palma the Younger, adorn the cathedral.

Casa di Giorgione (Piazzetta San Liberale, ☎ 0423-491240; 9 am-noon and 3-6 pm; closed Mon; €1; guided visits by

appointment only). This small Romanesque-Gothic house, said to have been the home of Giorgione, houses a museum dedicated to the life of the celebrated painter. A frieze on the first floor was almost certainly frescoed by Giorgione, who was a student of Giovanni Bellini and influenced Titian.

Villa Emo Capodilista (Via Stazione 5, Fanzolo di Vedelago, ☎ 0423-476334; Apr-Oct, Mon-Sat, 3-7 pm, Sun, 10 am-12:30 pm and 3-7 pm; Nov-Mar, weekends only, 2-6 pm; closed mid-Dec to mid-Jan; €5.50). This 16th-century work by Andrea Palladio stands in the countryside only miles from Castelfranco Veneto and is considered one of Palladio's most classical designs. Zelotti's frescoes adorn the villa's interior.

Parco della Villa Revedin Bolasco (Borgo Treviso 73, ☎ 337-805304; spring and fall, Tue and Thurs, 10 am-12:30 pm and 3-5:30 pm, Sat and Sun, 10 am-12:30 pm and 2:30-5:30; summer, Tue and Thurs, 10 am-12:30 pm and 3-7:30, Sat and Sun, 10 am-1 pm and 3:30-7:30 pm; €3). This 19th-century villa built by Giovan Battista Meduna (on the site of Vincenzo Scamozzi's 17th-century structure) is not open to the public, but its picturesque gardens are. One of the region's most delightful romantic gardens, it encompasses a lake, statues and an arena that was once a riding stable.

> **Sidetrip:** Pope Pio X, canonized in 1949, was born just outside of Castelfranco Veneto in the small village of Riese Pio X (along the road from Montebelluna to Castelfranco), where his boyhood home is open to visitors. **Museo e Casa Natale di San Pio X** (Piazza Pio X 1, Riese Pio X, ☎ 0423-483929; Tue, 2:30-7 pm, Wed-Sun, 9 am-noon and 2:30-7 pm; free admission).

Treviso

Adventures

Festivities

 Festa del Radicchio Variegato, held the Sunday prior to Christmas, is a celebration of the "eatable flower of Castelfranco." This member of the chicory family is highlighted through tastings and agricultural displays.

Dining Out

 The *radicchio variegato*, also known as *il fiore che si mangia* (edible flower), is a varied white and green chicory with flecks of red that is ready beginning in November. Evidence suggests that it is derived from an 18th-century cross between the red radicchio of Treviso and the wide-leaved endive scarola.

Fregollota is a dessert from Castelfranco Veneto prepared with almonds. The name comes from the dialect word *fregola* (crumb), for its crumbly texture.

Barbesin (Via Montebelluna 41/B, ☎ 0423-490446, www.barbesin.it; 12-2:30 pm and 7:30-10:30 pm; closed Wed night, Thurs and several weeks in August and Sept; reservations recommended; major credit cards accepted; €€€). The elegant dining rooms are a true reflection of the fine local cuisine you can expect to find at Barbesin, one of Castelfranco's exceptional eateries. Locals come here for the chef's modern interpretation of traditional Veneto dishes that highlight seasonal products. Their menu changes weekly but the *tagliata di manzo* (prime cut of beef), served with roasted potatoes, is a classic dish found year-round at Barbesin. Risotto dishes are another specialty, prepared with seasonal ingredients such as radicchio and asparagus. The fixed-price midday menu is an excellent choice and, for €18, includes a first and second course with wine. In summer, request a table in the garden. The *insalatina di radicchio con salmone marinato* (radicchio salad with marinated salmon) is a very good choice for an appetizer. Located just minutes from the historic center on the corner of SS53 and the road leading to Vedelago, it attracts a business crowd at lunchtime. The restaurant also features an *enoteca* where it is possible to request a wine tasting or purchase regional wines.

Tamburello (Via Pozzi, San Floriano di Castelfranco, ☎ 0423-487101; closed Mon; €€€). Only a few km from the heart of town in S. Floriano, this spot is known for meat cooked on the spit and the grill. The restaurant's warm, friendly atmosphere is rustic and, in summer, enjoy outdoor dining in a quiet wooded garden. They have a good selection of fresh local cheeses.

Accommodations

Hotel Ca' delle Rose (Via Montebelluna 41, ☎ 0423-420374, www.cadellerose.it; €€). This small 18-room hotel is operated by the owners of the adjacent Barbesin restaurant. Rooms are simple but comfortable and all have television, air conditioning and bathrooms. Breakfast is €5 per person but parking is free of charge.

Hotel alla Torre (Piazzetta Trento-Trieste 7, ☎ 0423-498707, www.hotelallatorre.it; handicap-accessible rooms; breakfast included; major credit cards accepted; €€€). Alla Torre is an elegant hotel with all of the creature comforts needed for a relaxing stay. Rooms are modestly furnished and certain ones are situated with a nice view of the city walls. The location is convenient and free parking is available.

Shopping

The **general market** is held twice weekly on Tuesday and Friday mornings in the **Piazza Giorgione** just outside the town's walls.

Nightlife & Entertainment

Teatro Accademico (Via Garibaldi, ☎ 0423-494500). Castelfranco's 18th-century theater designed by Francesco Maria Preti hosts musical, operatic and theatrical events year-round. Stop into the information office to inquire about events that coincide with your stay.

Tourist Office

Pro Loco
Via F.M. Preti 66
☎ 0423-495000

Websites

www.castelfrancoonline.it
www.comune.castelfranco-veneto.tv.it

■ Prosecco Country

Conegliano and Valdobbiadene and the 15 communities connecting the two, are world-famous as the capital of Prosecco
D.O.C., a topaz-colored spumante. The sunny territory is a
kaleidoscope of wine cellars, villages and vineyards and its
location equidistant from sea and mountains has a positive
impact on the climate and growing conditions. Prosecco vines,
grown in pergolas on steep south-facing slopes, date back to
the early 19th century, though some say its origins can be
traced to the Roman era.

Conegliano, the birthplace of painter Giambattista Cima
(Cima da Conegliano), is famous for its winemaking school,
which is Italy's oldest. Via XX Settembre is the main thoroughfare in town and Conegliano's 14th-century walls stretch
up to the hilltop castle that looks down over the zone.

Valdobbiadene (derived from *Vallis Duplavis* meaning Valley of the Piave) was invaded by German and Austrian troops
during World War I and townspeople were evacuated due to
the heavy bombing. After the war, cultivation of vineyards
began to spread rapidly and, today, Valdobbiadene is the core
of Prosecco production and among Italy's most valuable wine
towns.

Just outside of the wine production zone in the northern part
of the province sits **Vittorio Veneto**. There are two distinctive districts of the town – Serravalle and Ceneda – that were
joined to form Vittorio Veneto in 1866 and named after the
first King of Italy, Vittorio Emanuele II.

Getting There

 By Car: Vittorio Veneto can be easily accessed from the north by taking **SS51**. From Venice and points south on **A27**, exit at Vittorio Veneto Sud. To reach Valdobbiadene from Treviso, take **SP348** and exit at Fener. To reach Conegliano, take the **A27** from Venice and points south and exit at Conegliano. Or from Treviso, take **SS13** to Conegliano. From the north take **SS51** to **A27** and exit at Conegliano.

 By Bus: There is one **La Marca** bus line that travels from Treviso to Vittorio Veneto, one from Treviso to Valdobbiadene and another from Vittorio Veneto to Conegliano. The Valdobbiadene-Conegliano bus runs every one to two hours and passes through many of the principle towns of the Prosecco zone. It's a good way to explore the zone without your own vehicle.

 By Train: Trains run from both Treviso and Venice to Vittorio Veneto and Conegliano. The nearest station to Valdobbiadene is at Alano-Fener (five km away) and can be reached from Venice or Treviso. Conegliano is on the Udine-Venezia and Calalzo-Venezia lines and there are frequent trains to Treviso (about 20 minutes) and to Venice (a 50-minute trip).

 By Plane: Venice's Marco Polo is the region's primary airport with numerous international and domestic flights daily. An alternative airport is **San Giuseppe**, only three km from Treviso's center, but it offers fewer flights daily and only connects to select destinations. www.trevisoairport.it

Getting Around

While the towns of the Prosecco zone are all relatively small, they are separated by vineyard-clad hills and not easy to travel between on foot. The **La Marca** buses service this area, but the most convenient way to explore is by car. This is the best way to stop at the many wineries, monuments, restaurants and inns along the Prosecco road, in order to truly appreciate the area.

Treviso

Sightseeing

 Casa di Giambattista Cima (Via Cima 24, Conegliano, ☎ 0438-21660 or 0423-411026; call ahead to schedule a visit; €1). Once the home of the painter Giambattista Cima, it now houses several reproductions of his artwork as well as other objects found when the house was restored.

Duomo (Via XX Settembre, Conegliano, ☎ 0438-22606; 9 am-noon and 3-6 pm). This 14th-century cathedral contains Cima's 1493 *La Madonna in Trono e Santi*, shown at right; its exterior was frescoed in the 16th century.

Sala dei Battuti (Via XX Settembre, Conegliano, ☎ 0438-22606; Sat, 10 am-noon, Sun, 3-6 pm; €2). It is worth paying a visit to the *Sala dei Battuti* while in town to see the 15th-century frescoes by Girolamo da Treviso and Jacopo da Montagnana.

Museo Civico del Castello (Piazzale San Leonardo, Conegliano, ☎ 0438-22871; Apr-Sept, 10 am-12:30 pm and 3:30-7 pm, Oct-Mar, 10 am-noon and 3-6:30 pm; closed Mon; €2). Located in the old castle tower, this civic museum houses frescoes by Pordenone, along with many other local artifacts. The view over the surrounding hills is beautiful from the charming courtyard.

Museo della Battaglia (Piazza Giovanni Paolo I, Vittorio Veneto, ☎ 0438-57695; winter, 9:30 am-12:30 pm and 2-5 pm; summer, 10 am-12:30 pm and 3-7 pm; €3). This museum was established in honor of the Battle of Vittorio in 1918, the last battle of the Italian army in World War I. The entrance ticket here allows access to the **Museo del Cenedese** (Piazza Flaminio, ☎ 0438-57103; winter, 9:30 am-12:30 pm and 2-5 pm; summer, 10-12:30 am and 3:30-7 pm). It is in the Loggia del Cenedese and covers local history. The ticket also is good for **San Lorenzo dei Battuti** (Piazza Vecellio, Vittorio Veneto), with a beautiful fresco cycle from the 15th century.

Adventures

Driving

 Strada del Vino Prosecco is a 47-km route that winds through the hills of the Treviso province connecting Conegliano with Valdobbiadene and passing through Costa, Rua, S. Pietro di Feletto, Refrontolo, Pieve di Soligo, Solighetto, Farra, Col S. Martino, Guia, Santo Stefano and San Pietro di Barbozza. Along this wine trail, there are many charming villages, country inns, wine cellars, ancient castles, villas and war monuments that make up the splendid patchwork of countryside famous for its production of Prosecco. The rolling slopes are covered with boundless vineyards and brimming with charm, history and culture; magnificent panoramas can be spotted every step along the route. Spring is the best time to visit, when the zone comes alive with festivals and exhibitions. Stop off at any of the wineries (a few have been suggested in this book) to sample wine, tour the vineyards or purchase a few bottles.

> **Route:** Begin in front of the castle in Conegliano and follow the road down toward Costa, where you'll begin to see picturesque, vineyard-clad hills. Stay on this road, and follow signs in the direction of Valdobbiadene. Sunday is a quieter day to drive through the Prosecco zone, but many of the wine cellars will be closed, so call in advance.

The route from Conegliano to Valdobbiadene without stops takes approximately one hour.

 A great place to hit a few wineries is in the hillside town of Guia, with a large concentration of *cantine*.

VOCABULARY

Cantina . . . . wine cellar

D.O.C. . . . . Denomination of Controlled Origin

Degustazione . . . . tasting

Bicchiere . . . . glass

Vigneti . . . . vineyards

Azienda . . . . business

Vite . . . . grapevine

Spumante . . . . sparkling wine

Amabile . . . . sweetish

Vendemmia . . . . harvest

Frizzante . . . . sparkling

Botti . . . . barrels

Grappoli . . . . bunches

With Wine

 Prosecco is Italy's second-rated spumante and the D.O.C. (Denomination of Controlled Origin) label ensures that the grape selection, processing, bottling and marketing are controlled, in order to achieve the highest quality products.

Prosecco D.O.C. is produced in several varieties. There are two types of *Prosecco D.O.C. di Conegliano-Valdobbiadene Spumante,* the sparkling Prosecco. These are *Brut* (good for fish and vegetable antipasti, seafood and fish dishes) and *Extra Dry* (an aperitif that complements light soups, seafood dishes, cheeses and pasta).

The *Prosecco di Conegliano-Valdobbiadene Frizzante* is a semi-sparkling wine that makes a wonderful aperitif, and the *Prosecco di Conegliano-Valdobbiadene Tranquillo* is excellent with fish and appetizers.

The *Prosecco di Valdobbiadene Superiore di Cartizze*, a superior quality sparkling wine produced in a small hilly zone rich in lime, sand and clay, is an excellent accompaniment for desserts.

There are approximately 20 towns in the hills of Treviso that produce the wines of the *Colli di Conegliano*. The variety of wines includes *Colli di Conegliano Bianco, Colli di Conegliano Rosso, Refrontolo Passito D.O.C.* and the *Torchiato di Fregona D.O.C.*

> **Did You Know?** The *Bellini*, one of Italy's most popular cocktails, was invented at Harry's Bar in Venice in the mid-20th century, combining Prosecco Spumante with white peach nectar. Named after the great Renaissance artist Giovanni Bellini, this was a favorite drink of Hemingway.

Wine Schools

La Scuola Enologica di Conegliano - G.B. Cerletti (Via XXVIII Apre 20, Conegliano, ☎ 0438-62185, www.scuolaenologica.it). Conegliano's wine school, founded in 1876, has a modern wine cellar and a large vineyard where the one time director, Professor Luigi Manzoni, invented the well-known "Incrocio Manzoni." The school produces many wines, from Prosecco to the Incrocio Manzoni Bianco. Although its primary mission is didactic, they also produce wine and it's possible to taste and purchase wines upon request. A variety of wine-related events take place at the school, such as the *Calici di Vini* in June and *Conegliano con Gusto* in November, where you can taste wine and other products of the territory.

Wineries

Cantina Adamo Canel (Via Castelletto 73, Col San Martino, ☎ 0438-898112, www.canel.it). This winery has its seat in an aristocratic villa from the 1800s – owned by four siblings, Annamaria, Fausto, Tiziano and Vicenzo Canel, who devotedly carry on the family tradition handed down to them by their father Adamo. Tastings and tours in the restored farmhouse can be arranged upon request and typically include salami, local cheeses and three types of Prosecco, for €5. Dinners can also be arranged with advance notice. Adamo Canel is located along the wine route in Col S. Martino before you reach Valdobbiadene. After turning right off the main road continue down the long driveway and the villa will be in front with the farmhouse on the left.

Mionetto (Via Colderove 2, Valdobbiadene, ☎ 0423-9707, www.mionetto.it; Tue-Sat, 9 am-12:30 pm and 2:30-7 pm; closed Sun and Mon). Since 1887 Mionetto has had a genuine passion for wine production and has grown to be one of the best-known producers of Prosecco. On the American market since the late 1990s, it is now considered a brand leader. The Prosecco D.O.C. Spumante, Moscato and Cartizze are among its popular products. If you stop in for a tasting, be sure to try the *bibanesi* (snacks).

Ca' Salina (Via S. Stefano 2, Valdobbiadene, ☎ 0423-975296, www.casalinaprosecco.it; major credit cards accepted). Gregorio, Neva and children take great pride in their family winemaking tradition and sell their products in their *azienda*, where it is also possible to taste wines and visit the cantina and vineyards. Call ahead.

Val D'Oca (S. Giovanni in Valdobbiadene, ☎ 0423-982070, www.valdoca.com). This is a large producer of Prosecco; wine tastings and tours can be arranged upon request.

On Bikes

 Team ViVi Bike (Via Buozzi 2, Vittorio Veneto, ☎ 0423-552301, www.vivibike.net). Explore Treviso's pre-Alpine zone on a bike with the experts at Team ViVi Bike. These qualified guides who are intimately familiar with the zone have developed a series of itineraries geared to different skill levels, ages and interests. There are half-day and full-day excursions, as well as biking holiday packages. Some popular itineraries include *La Vallata*, *Canova Tour* and the two-day *Prealpi Road Tour*. Most bike excursions include sections on both surfaced and unsurfaced roads. All routes begin and end in Vittorio Veneto and can be arranged with an English-speaking guide. A sample half-day ride for five-10 people is €10 per person (this increases for smaller groups). Program participants are provided a bicycle, helmet, technical help and guides. Inquire about bicycle rentals and personalized itineraries.

On Foot

 Molinetto della Croda (Via Molinetto 40, Refrontolo, ☎ 0438-978199, www.molinettodellacroda.it). Evidence suggests that this mill dates (at least in part)

back to the 1600s. Bought and restored by the town in the 1990s, it is now the seat of cultural shows and exhibits, including art collections by local artists, model boats and nativity scenes. There are signs for the mill along the Prosecco road in Refrontolo that lead back to the parking lot. From here, you'll find nature paths behind the waterfall that are accessible to visitors at the mill.

Festivities

 Mostra Nazionale degli Spumanti (www.mostranazionalespumanti.it) takes place the first half of Sept each year in the Villa dei Cedri in Valdobbiadene and is an opportunity to learn about Italian Spumante firsthand from the experts. For more details about scheduled wine and food pairing events and art exhibitions, check the website.

Primavera del Prosecco takes place from March until June in the Prosecco zone with a series of Prosecco exhibitions. A variety of associations in the province collaborate to organize this event that highlights products from numerous regional producers. Prestigious prizes are awarded for a variety of categories.

Festa dell'Uva (www.damacastellana.it) takes place on the fourth weekend of September in Conegliano. This is a chance to taste approximately 200 different wines from the zone, enjoy performances in the town square and take part in a traditional dinner along Via XX Settembre.

Family Adventures

Castelbrando (Via Brandolini 29, Cison di Valmarino; information, ☎ 0438-976091; hotel, ☎ 0438-9761 or 0438-976093, www.castelbrando. it). In the foothills of the Venetian pre-Alps, the immense 12th-century Castelbrando is one of Italy's largest and has played host to several dig-

Treviso

nitaries and luminaries in recent years. Featuring a hotel and congress center, a spa facility with a Roman bath, several restaurants, bars, museums, theaters, shops and art galleries, the castle offers visitors a wide selection of activities and services for a medieval holiday. The entertaining *medieval dinner* takes place the last Friday of each month with traditional dishes and entertainment, and is a great activity for families (reserve in advance). Guided visits to the castle can be arranged and the **Museo delle Arme** is also interesting for children. If the weather is nice and you'd like to explore the castle's surroundings, several recreation paths are accessible from the top level of the castle. If you're interested in sampling a glass of locally produced Prosecco, stop into the enoteca **La Cantina di Ottone** (be sure to take a look at the ancient Roman oven from the late Imperial period). The primary way to access the castle is by funicular, located in the parking lot below (€1).

Tour Operators

Vichival Tour (Via Pira 76, Valdobbiadene, ☎ 0423-976322, www.vichival.it). Vichival Tour offers a variety of tours throughout the province of Treviso, and their Prosecco itineraries expose travelers to the finest elements of the Prosecco zone through their two- or three-day trips specializing in gastronomy and culture. Itineraries are frequently scheduled to coincide with local events such as the *Primavera del Prosecco* and the *Mostra Nazionale degli Spumanti*. Package prices include lodging at three-star hotels, guides, winery visits, select meals and admission to some sites.

Dining Out

Da Gigetto (Via A. De Gasperi 4, Miane, ☎ 0438-960020; closed Mon night and Tue; closed Aug and two weeks in Jan; reservations necessary; major credit cards accepted; €€€-€€€€). This elegant restaurant in the pre-Alps of Treviso is one of the most highly acclaimed in the region and will add the perfect touch to your tour of the Prosecco zone. The warm, refined atmosphere alone justifies the price of this restaurant, but it's the polished traditional dishes that will leave you raving about your meal for months to come. The Trevisian kitchen makes full use of the finest seasonal ingredients in a range of dishes, including *sopa coada* (pigeon and bread soup), one of their specialties. For an antipasto, try the crostini with duck liver pâté. All of their desserts are homemade, but the *pan zuppa con crema alla vaniglia* (prepared with vanilla pastry cream) is one of the best. The extensive wine list surpasses most in the region and your dinner at Da Gigetto wouldn't be complete without a tour of the wine cellar where they store some of the finest (and priciest) vintages and aged balsamic vinegars. Wine tastings can be arranged as well.

Tre Panoce (Via Vecchia Trevigiana 50, Conegliano, ☎ 0438-60071; 12-2:30 pm and 8-10 pm; closed Sun night and Mon; closed Aug and two weeks in Jan; €€€). In the heart of the Prosecco zone in a 16th-century building is Tre Panoce, one of Italy's *Ristoranti di Buon Ricordo* (see page 39). Armando Zanotto, praised for his culinary creativity and passion, is a highly acclaimed chef in the Veneto and author of several regional cookbooks where many of his prized recipes can be found. Try the *insalata di carciofi e asparagi crudi con pollastra* (asparagus and artichoke salad) and the *spaghetti cotti nel prosecco* (spaghetti in Prosecco). Their wine list displays an excellent range of labels from the zone.

Locanda da Condo (Via Fontana 134, Col S. Martino, ☎ 0438-898106, www.locandadacondo.it; 12-2 pm and 8-10 pm; closed Tue night and Wed, as well as all of July; major credit cards accepted; €€). Proprietor Erico Canel spent many years dreaming about a career in the medical profession, but instead chose to follow in the footsteps of his restaurateur parents, a decision which has given him great pleasure over the years. Since the 1920s, when his grandfather established this restaurant, locals have enjoyed traditional Trevisian specialties served in a casual atmosphere. Condo, a name derived from Canel's father, Giocondo, changes its menu daily, always adhering to Trevisian traditions. The

DINING PRICE CHART	
Price per person for an entrée	
€	Under €5
€€	€5-€12
€€€	€13-€20
€€€€	€21-€30
€€€€€	Over €30

pipe alla salsiccia e rosmarino (pasta prepared with sausage and rosemary) is very good, as is the *salame al cioccolato*. There are three dining rooms decorated with lace-draped lamps, old prints and checkered tablecloths. The taverna room with the fireplace is cozy, but my favorite is the *Sala della Storia* (history room) with oversized maps of Central Europe from the early 20th century covering the walls.

Accommodations

Hotels

 Relais Le Betulle (Via Costa Alta 56, Conegliano, ☎ 0438-21001, www.relaislebetulle.com; major credit cards accepted; €€€). Just a few minutes drive outside of Conegliano's center along the wine road is this relais, open since early 2004. Rooms are spacious and comfortable; #401-405 look out onto the vineyards. It features a wellness center, tearoom and a wine bar where guests can sample a glass of Prosecco.

Hotel Diana (Via Roma 49, Valdobbiadene, ☎ 0423-976222, www.hoteldiana.org; major credit cards accepted; €€). Centrally located in Valdobbiadene's small town center and surrounded by Prosecco-producing hills, Diana's rooms are modern and standard, though they lack the charm that many smaller establishments in the area have.

Flora Hotel (Viale Trento e Trieste 28, Vittorio Veneto, ☎ 0438-53625; €€). Refurbished in 2004, the Flora is a simple hotel near Vittorio Veneto's train station and a good choice for travelers arriving by train.

Agriturismi

Vigneto Vecio (Via Grave 8, S. Stefano di Valdobbiadene, ☎ 0423-900338, www.vignetovecio.it; closed Jan, Sept and Oct; €€). This is set on a slope below the Strada del Vino Prosecco outside of Valdobbiadene. The Miotto family takes great pride in their *agriturismo*, welcoming guests into the cozy rooms of the renovated hayloft. Breakfasts are hearty and feature homemade marmalades and salami. On weekends, its kitchen serves bean soup, meats on a spit and Trevisian specialties accompanied by Prosecco from the family's vineyards. Finding a table on a Sunday can be tough, so

Above: Squero di San Trovaso, 17th-century shipyard
Below: Doge's Palace & the bell tower in St. Mark's Square

Above: The Arsenale in Venice's Castello district
Below: View across the Grand Canal to the daily Rialto market

arrive early. Wines from their vineyards are available for purchase. The kitchen is open Friday and Saturday evenings and Sunday all day. This makes a good base for exploring the Strada del Vino Prosecco.

HOTEL PRICE CHART	
Based on a double room for two	
€	Under €50
€€	€50-€80
€€€	€81-€120
€€€€	€121-€190
€€€€€	Over €190

Agritur La Bella (Via Ligonto 45, ☎ 0423-970309; lodging open every day, kitchen open Thurs-Sun; major credit cards accepted; €€). Quietly situated in an old farmhouse in the Follina Valley, this *agriturismo's* setting and accommodations hold true to its name. The pleasant wood-beamed rooms have private bathrooms and air conditioning. The kitchen is well-known among locals for its trout-based menu and meats cooked on the spit.

Bed & Breakfasts

Il Faè B&B (Via Faè 1, San Pietro di Feletto, ☎ 0438-787117, www.ilfae.com; €€€). The owners of Il Faè make certain that all guests are exposed to genuine hospitality and local traditions during their stay. Il Faè offers an escape into country living, with its two villas that can be rented by the week, or (as individual rooms) by the night. The houses are set on a large property with a swimming pool and guests can arrange for cooking classes and wine tastings on-site, as well as guided bike and walking tours. If you're interested in a romantic getaway, request the suite with a Jacuzzi. Be sure to sample a glass of their Prosecco.

Shopping

The **general market** takes place in Valdobbiadene's center on Monday morning.

Conegliano's **weekly market** takes place on Friday mornings in the town center.

In Vittorio Veneto, the market is along Via Cavour, Via Martiri della Libertà, Piazza Minucci and Piazza Flaminio each Monday morning.

The **antique market** in Vittorio Veneto is held the first Sunday of the month.

Treviso

Tourist Offices

IAT
Piazza Marconi 1
Valdobbiadene
☎ 0423-976975

IAT
Viale della Vittoria 110
Vittorio Veneto
☎ 0438-57243

IAT
Via XX Settembre 61
Conegliano
☎ 0438-21230

Websites

www.comune.vittorio-veneto.tv.it

www.comune.valdobbiadene.tv.it

www.conegliano.com

www.conegliano2000.it

www.prosecco.it

www.primaveraprosecco.it

■ Monte Grappa & Environs

Serving as the front line defense against Austrian troops during World War I, the battleground of Monte Grappa witnessed the devastation of battles lost and finally the glorious victory when the Austrians retreated in Oct of 1918. Located where the provinces of Treviso, Belluno and Vicenza meet, at 1,776 m/5,825 feet above sea level, Monte Grappa is the highest peak in its group in the Veneto pre-Alp region between the Brenta and Piave Rivers.

At the foot of *Grappa* (as its referred to among locals) are several small towns, including **Borso del Grappa**, world-famous for its ideal hang-gliding and paragliding; **Crespano del Grappa**, with its 18th-century cathedral containing works by Antonio Canova; **Possagno**, the birthplace of Antonio Canova; and **Paderno del Grappa**, whose hiking paths that depart from the profound valley, **Valle San Liberale**, are among the most traveled in the zone. A bit farther south from these towns but still within their zone is **San Zenone degli Ezzelini**, a beautiful town once under the dominion of the mighty Ezzelini family.

Getting There

 By Car: Borso del Grappa, Crespano del Grappa, Paderno del Grappa, Possagno and roads leading to the peak of Monte Grappa can all be easily accessed and are located along **SP26**, also known as *Via Molinetto* and *Stradale Provinciale Pedemontale di Grappa* (on the northern outskirts of Bassano del Grappa). San Zenone degli Ezzelini is on **SP248** east of Bassano del Grappa.

 By Bus: There is a **La Marca** bus that travels between Treviso and Bassano, stopping in San Zenone degli Ezzelini.

 By Train: The nearest main train station to Monte Grappa is Bassano del Grappa, which is well connected with most of the principal cities in the region.

 By Plane: Venice's Marco Polo is the region's primary airport with numerous international and domestic flights daily. An alternative airport is **San Giuseppe**, only three km from Treviso's center, but it offers fewer flights daily and only connects to select destinations. www.trevisoairport.it

Treviso

Getting Around

The best way to travel between these towns is by car, especially if your plans include visiting Cima Grappa (Monte Grappa's peak).

Sightseeing

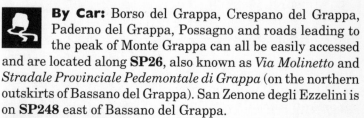 **Tempio Canoviano** (Via Stradone del Tempio, Possagno, ☎ 339-6548000; summer, 9 am-noon and 3-6 pm; winter, 9 am-noon and 2-5 pm; free admission). Antonio Canova (1757-1822) incorporated three primary architectural elements in this neoclassical building at the foot of *Col Draga* to symbolize the three main phases of

civilization – Greek, Roman and Christian (the colonnade from the Athens Parthenon, the round body from Rome's Pantheon and the apsidal chapel). Designed between 1804 and 1818, the temple's hallways and staircases are located within the eight-meter/26-foot thick walls of this immense structure and its floor is white and red marble from the Piave. Several important works by Palma the Younger, Pordenone and Antonio Canova are housed within the temple, including Canova's altarpiece, the *Deposizione*. Canova died before the frieze and typanum were complete, but his students completed the frieze using his models. Construction began in 1819 with help from the community and it was likely funded almost entirely by Canova.

Daedalus and Icarus, Canova, 1778

 Ask the caretaker if you can visit the magnificent dome, one of the temple's most stunning features.

Venere Vincitrice, Canova, 1808

Museo Gipsoteca Canoviana (Piazza Canova 74, Possagno, ☎ 0423-544323, www.museocanova.it; Tue-Sun, 9 am-noon and 3-6 pm; €4). The Museo Gipsoteca Canoviana houses sketches, plaster casts, marble statues and several incomplete works by Antonio Canova. Attached to the Gipsoteca is Canova's home, containing many objects and mementos from his life. Guided visits can be arranged, but are often free the first Sunday of each month.

Santuario della Madonna del Monte (San Zenone degli Ezzelini). Better known among locals as *La Chiesetta Rossa* (Little Red Church), this 19th-century church dedicated to the Madonna stands on the remains of the 13th-century **Complesso del Castello di Ezzelino**. Once encircled by high walls, only a tower of the Ezzelino castle remains today. The **Chiesa del Castellano** (castle's church), which once stood next to the castle, was modified several times, but only the chapel and crypt remain. A restaurant exists on the grounds of the complex today. **Driving Directions:** From SP248 in San Zenone degli Ezzelini, turn in the town center toward Crespano del Grappa and follow signs – it is hard to miss the church atop a hill. From here, you will have some of the most scenic views of the area, looking out to the Montello and Grappa.

Monte Grappa still bears the tragic scars left by the three major battles fought here during World War I, the last fought by the *Armata del Grappa* in Oct of 1918. On the peak of Monte Grappa stands a circular tiered memorial (open 7 am-dusk, free admission), built in 1935 to honor the fallen soldiers from World War I. A memorial was later built here to commemorate the fallen soldiers from World War II as well. At the top of the monument sits the votive chapel, the **Sanctuary of the Madonnina del Grappa**, which contains the statue of the *Madonnina del Grappa*, an important relic for Italian troops. Also here is the tomb of Generale G. Giardino, the Commander of the 4th Army, Armata del Grappa, who wished to be laid to rest with his soldiers. The **Galleria Vittorio Emanuele III** (recently closed to tourists for safety reasons), consists of tunnels beneath the mountain summit planned by Colonel Gavotti during World War I to strengthen the troops' ability to defend Grappa (these took 10 months to complete and are nearly five km long). The main tunnel's many branches have artillery posts and observatories. Also here is the **Caserma Milano**, military barracks used by soldiers during the war, that now houses a museum (☎ 0423-544840; daily, 8 am-noon and 1:30-5 pm; free admission, guided tours possible). It contains weapons, photos and other artifacts from World War I as well as a video about Monte Grappa's role in the Great War. The Casa Armata del

Grappa now serves as the **Rifugio Bassano**, with a bar and restaurant (☎ 0423-53101; open year-round, 8 am-11 pm).

Adventures

Driving

 Cima Grappa Drive (45 minutes). Follow SS141, the main access road leading up to Monte Grappa and the memorial. The beginning part of the road is steep, with many switchbacks, and eventually opens to picturesque mountain meadows with grazing cattle during the summer months. The well-maintained road is open year-round, but takes steady nerves to travel in inclement weather and can be a slow-go on weekends. To reach SP141 from Bassano, take SS47 or SP248 to Romano D'Ezzelino.

On Foot

 Cima Grappa Hike (CAI 151; full-day hike, thee-four hours up, three hours down). From Bassano del Grappa, head toward Paderno del Grappa on SP26. In Paderno del Grappa, turn left, following the signs for Valle San Liberale. Continue to follow Valle San Liberale signs for several km, winding through small towns and countryside, eventually reaching a parking lot with a small restaurant where the road ends.

CAUTION Although it is classified as an easy trail it requires proper hiking footwear. There are certain narrow, steep sections of the trail that can prove tricky so use caution. Wear hiking boots, bring water, snacks and inclement weather gear since temperatures cool off at the top and rain may roll in.

Follow the roughly paved road to the left of the restaurant until you arrive at the trailhead, where several unpaved trails (indicated by red and white trail markers) begin. Take trail CAI 151, which leads to Cima Grappa, parts of which were a World War I access route to Monte Grappa. The lower section winds through densely wooded forests with switchbacks.

Tip: Be sure to follow signs for CAI 151 Cima Grappa for the entire route.

Eventually the terrain transitions to a rocky pre-Dolomite landscape with steep ravines and magnificent panoramic views of the Pedemontana zone. The trail again changes to sparsely wooded meadows, where in summer herds of cows graze. CAI 151 crosses over and sometimes follows short stretches of asphalt road. Keep an eye out for *stelle Alpine* (Edelweiss), one of the most revered mountain flowers. Take as many photos as you'd like but don't pick them as they are protected by law.

 Keep in mind that Via Attrezzata is an iron way trail that is the most direct route to Grappa but is reserved for experts, requiring harnesses and helmets. Remain on CAI 151.

The trail culminates at the base of **Rifugio Bassano** (☎ 0423-53101; open year-round, 8 am-11 pm). It is right by the World War I monument, the **Galleria Vittorio Emanuele III** and the museum (see *Sightseeing*). If Mother Nature cooperates, you'll be rewarded with a view of the Venetian Lagoon. When you're ready to head back, the best way down is retracing your steps. Allow about an hour for exploring the monument.

Inside Advice: The best times of year for this trail are late spring through early fall. This is a popular trail with locals and it's highly trafficked in summer months.

In Air

 Paragliding and hang-gliding enthusiasts from around the world are attracted to Monte Grappa for its ideal conditions, created by good thermal currents, its natural structures for take-off and good landing zones. There are several different take-off and landing areas in the zone and the use of them depends on a variety of factors, including paragliding vs. hang-gliding, wind and weather conditions and the season. On a pleasant day, bril-

Treviso

liantly colored paragliders and hang-gliders cloud the sky near Monte Grappa. While solo flights are reserved only for licensed pilots, there are a few pilots licensed by the **Federazione Italiana Volo Libero** who accompany clients on *voli biposto* (two-seater paragliding flights) that generally last from 10 to 30 minutes. All departures for flights are from Piazza al Paradiso in Semonzo del Grappa.

Monte Grappa Air Park (Piazza al Paradiso 7, Semonzo di Borso del Grappa, ☎ 0423-910445 or 329-1597944, airpark@libero.it; Tue-Sun, 9 am-noon and 3-6 pm). The International Paragliding Center's English-speaking instructor, Andreas Breuer, has been flying for almost two decades and is an expert paraglider with another school in Dresden, Germany. Year-round paragliding flights are possible, weather-permitting. The center includes a school for pilots, a shop selling paragliding gear and a shuttle service to launch sites. Request to have your piloted flight videotaped if you're interested. The approximate rate for a piloted flight is €80. Call ahead or e-mail for details.

> **Did You Know?** In 2004 the Paragliding World Cup was held on Monte Grappa and Monte Avena.

On Wheels

 Montegrappaquad (Via Marti 1, Romano d'Ezzelino, ☎ 349-2973532, mgquad@virgilio.it). A thrilling way to explore the beautiful terrain on the slopes of Monte Grappa is with guided half-day quad excursions that travel along the old World War I roads and stop at *malghe* (mountain dairies) for a sampling of mountain cheeses and other local products. These tours (with a minimum of three people) typically cost €55 per person on a double and €90 for a single, and include helmets and tastings of local products along the route. Open year-round, advanced booking is required for this popular activity.

Premier Cicli (Via G. Rossini 12, S. Zenone degli Ezzelini, ☎ 0423-968244; 8 am-noon, 2:30-7 pm; closed Sun). During summer months only, Premier Cicli rents bicycles and organizes excursions in the nearby zone. Bike rentals are typically €10 for six hours, and guided excursions usually cost €20 per person. The shop is on a side street just off SP248 (coming from Bassano) before reaching San Zenone's church square.

The **Italian Cycling Center** (In the US, ☎ 215-232-6772; in Italy, Locanda Montegrappa, ☎ 0423-561113, www.italiancycling.com). The primary focus of this center, based at Locanda Montegrappa from May-Sept, is cycling adventures in the Pedemontana zone. The team of cyclists from Pennsylvania offers reasonably priced, challenging rides through the mountains, valleys, flatlands and rolling hills of the zone. They tailor rides to accommodate different skill levels. The experienced guides offer touring rides, fitness rides and themed rides and events. Cyclists interested in racing can participate in weekend races with a local club. Cyclists may choose how many days they'd like to participate and must arrive with their own bicycle. Program fees include accommodations at one of Locanda Montegrappa's establishments (see *Accommodations*) and participants also have access to the team mechanic and masseuse.

On Horseback

 La Staffa (Via Rovai 6, San Zenone degli Ezzelini, ☎ 0423-968555; closed Mon). La Staffa specializes in accelerated weeklong horseback riding courses for beginners but also offers a series of great excursions on horseback into the Veneto countryside. The proprietor Fabrizio guides day, evening, weekend and weeklong horseback riding adventures. Each month La Staffa offers different themed adventures in the Veneto from the Adriatic to the mountains. They highlight local panoramas, gastronomy, culture and history. The trek to Venetian villas is one of their more popular excursions. The average fee is €20 per person per hour (€70 for a full day) but this varies based on the itinerary. Spring and autumn are the most popular times of year for excursions. The center is off SP248 on the road toward Crespano del Grappa. Inquire about the guest rooms if you're interested in spending a few days here.

In Water

 Conca Verde (Via Molinetto 45, Borso del Grappa, ☎ 0423-561220; summer only). After an active day in the mountains, relax poolside at one of Conca Verde's pools or take your family there for a fun day at the water park.

On Snow

Grappapark (Rifugio Scarpon, ☎ 0424-559060 or 340-057050, www.grappapark.it; winter, Sat and Sun 9:30 am-5:30 pm, Mon 11 am-5 pm). This new snowboard park on Monte Grappa, opened by the Romani brothers, Daniele and Paolo, is the first of its kind in the area entirely dedicated to snowboarding. Snowboarders of every age and skill level can enjoy a full day (€15-18) or a half-day (9 am-12 pm) on the park's various slopes.

Dining Out

Locanda Montegrappa (Via Montegrappa 2, ☎ 0423-561113, www.locandamontegrappa.it; major credit cards accepted; €€). Although Locanda offers travelers a bit of almost everything, the key attraction even for locals is its kitchen, inspired by proprietor Silvia's grandmother, Amelia. At the foot of Monte Grappa, this family-owned restaurant and inn is a local favorite year-round but a particular favorite among active mountain travelers during the summer months. Its two main dining rooms are tastefully decorated with copper pots and local ceramics and its unpretentious atmosphere makes this a great place to enjoy a relaxed meal after a long day. Ask to be seated in the front dining room opposite the bar or in the terrace room out front for a more intimate meal, but if tables here are full or you have a large group, the dining area behind the kitchen allows for easy access to the antipasti bar. You can ask the friendly wait staff to prepare a mixed antipasti plate, but I prefer to visit the antipasti bar myself to sample the large array of warm and cold antipasti that are the highlight of owner Silvia's kitchen. The *bigoli con anatra* (pasta with duck sauce) and risotto dishes prepared with seasonal ingredients are popular choices for a first course and the *tagliata di manzo* (a prime cut of beef) served with a choice of roasted potatoes and greens is one of their specialties. Don't leave without sampling a *sorbetto*, their famous refreshing digestive drink. I've enjoyed many dinners at Locanda and each time I look at my bill I'm amazed at the value.

Baita Camol (Via Giardino, Camol/Borso del Grappa, ☎ 0423-567910; closed November and two weeks in Dec; open weekends and holidays only). At 1,200 m/3.936 feet above sea level along the road from Borso del Grappa to the mountain's summit, Baita Camol is a convenient stopover for mountain travelers passing through Campo Croce and is easily accessible by either foot or car. With its large fireplace, rustic furnishings and an impressive tree growing through one of the three dining rooms, Baita Camol is most famous for *formaggio fuso*, a second-course dish prepared with a variety of baked cheeses. Be sure to try one of their homemade berry liquors as a digestive after the meal. Since this locale is open only on weekends and is popular with the local folk, call ahead to reserve a table.

Ristorante alla Torre (Via Castellaro 25, San Zenone, ☎ 0423-567086, www.allatorre.it; 12-3 pm and 7:30-10; closed Tue all day and Wed for lunch; €€€). Just outside San Zenone's center, Ristorante alla Torre enjoys a privileged hilltop position with scenic views of the surrounding hills. It has several dining rooms, as well as a panoramic outdoor terrace, but if the weather keeps you indoors, request a table in the medieval dining room. The chef uses the freshest seasonal ingredients in dishes such as *pappardelle ai porcini* (pasta with mushrooms) and *grigliata mista di pesce* (a mix of grilled fish). Ask to see their list of cheeses. Built on the remains of the Ezzelini castle, the restaurant frequently hosts *cene medievali* (medieval banquets).

Accommodations

Hotels

 Locanda Montegrappa (Via Montegrappa 2, ☎ 0423-561113, www.locandamontegrappa.it; major credit cards accepted; €€). Once a small trattoria, Locanda Montegrappa stands on the slopes of Monte Grappa and has flourished over the years, expanding into a restaurant, hotel, and residence to meet the diverse needs of its active travelers. Locanda's hotel has 13 simply furnished rooms with en-suite bathrooms but, for guests considering a longer stay, traveling in groups or who prefer more privacy, there are other options. The **Residence Silvia** offers 21 mini-apartments with a kitchen. **Garni The House** has six rooms and sleeps 22 people. The 30-room **Sporting Star**

Hotel has two pools, a wellness center, a restaurant and bar and all modern amenities. Silvia and her friendly staff enjoy getting to know their adventure travelers, many of whom return year after year. The staff has a good rapport with many local establishments and provides assistance in scheduling paragliding, bicycle excursions, horseback riding, shopping trips to many nearby factory stores, wine tasting events at nearby wineries and excursions on foot. Whether or not you choose to stay in one of their rooms, don't miss a dinner at their restaurant (see *Dining Out*).

Hotel San Giacomo (Piazza Martiri 13-13/A, Paderno del Grappa, ☎ 0423-930366, www.hotelsangiacomo.com; major credit cards accepted; €€€). Hotel San Giacomo offers all of the standard comforts of a modern hotel with its 30 tastefully furnished rooms. In Paderno del Grappa, it makes a good base for adventure travel in the Pedemontana zone. Breakfasts are served in a room on the hotel's top floor.

Bed & Breakfasts

Locanda alla Posta (Via Viei 13, Borso del Grappa, ☎ 0423-910363, www.locandaallaposta.it; breakfast included; €€). Established by the Bonato family in 1911, Locanda alla Posta has some of the Grappa zone's most attractively decorated rooms. The well-furnished rooms are spacious and bright and have large modern bathrooms and TVs. They don't have air conditioning, but you're not likely to need it here because of the hotel's position near the mountains. The congeniality of the establishment's owners makes for a pleasant stay. This is a great value – almost a steal for the level of comfort and hospitality here – and you really feel at home in the rooms. It is possible to dine here if you ask the owners in advance.

Tilly's Bed and Breakfast (Via Casale 87, Semonzo del Grappa, ☎ 0423-561418, www.tillys.it; breakfast included; €€). Used as quarters by troops during World Wars I and II, this bed and breakfast (near one of the paragliding landing zones) is today a choice for active travelers who come to the zone, particularly for paragliding and hang-gliding. There are eight rooms with common bathrooms in this no-frills establishment, but it is a good value for budget-conscious travelers.

Tilly's Fly Bar is a popular hangout for active travelers in the evening.

Agriturismi

Agriturismo Ca' Roer (Via Vallorgana 1, San Zenone degli Ezzelini, ☎ 0423-53042; €€). Located between the Asolan hills and Monte Grappa, this *agriturismo* is open year-round and offers guests the choice of two attractively decorated apartments with antique furnishings from the Rovero family, wood-beamed ceilings, a kitchen, bedrooms and bathrooms. If you're in the mood to cozy up next to a fireplace, be sure to request the one with a *caminetto*.

Shopping

The main weekly market in the zone takes place on Sunday mornings in Crespano del Grappa's town center.

Tourist Offices

Consorzio Turistico
"Vivere il Grappa"
Piazza al Paradiso 11
Semonzo del Grappa
☎ 0423-910526
Closed in August

Websites

www.montegrappa.org
www.cmgrappa.gov.it

Treviso

VOCABULARY	
Parapendio	paragliding
Deltaplano	hang-gliding
Maneggio	horseback riding
Escursionismo	hiking, trekking
Via Ferrate	"iron way," walking route with iron hand-grips for climbing
Attrezzato	equipped
Attrezzatura	equipment, gear

Venice Sights

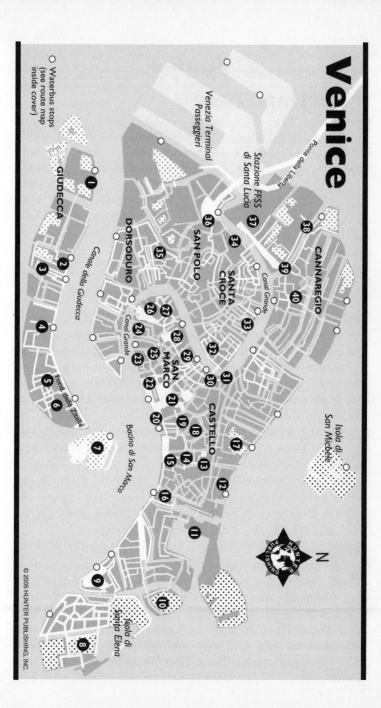

Venice

Venezia Terminal
Passeggieri

Stazione FFSS
di Santa Lucia

Ponte della Libertà

CANNAREGIO

SAN POLO

SANTA
CROCE

DORSODURO

Canal Grande

Canal Grande

SAN
MARCO

CASTELLO

GIUDECCA

Canale della Giudecca

Fond delle Zitelle

Bacino di San Marco

Isola di
San Michele

Isola di
Santa Elena

○ Waterbus stops
  (see route map
  inside cover)

N

HUNTER PUBLISHING

© 2005 HUNTER PUBLISHING, INC.

Venice

■ Getting There

By Car: Take the A4 (Milano-Venezia) motorway from Verona, Vicenza or Padua or the **A27** motorway from Belluno to Venice. Venice can also be reached by taking any of the state roads, including the **SS11** from Padua and the **SS13** from Treviso.

Parking: As you approach Venice via the Ponte della Libertà (Liberty Bridge), you can either park at one of the garages or lots on Piazzale Roma, or continue to Tronchetto Island and park there. These lots cost €10-20 for a 24-hour period. Another option is parking near the railway station in Mestre and taking the train into Venice, but, while parking may cost slightly less, remember that you will pay for a train ticket.

By Train: Venice is linked to cities throughout Europe by Eurostar, Intercity and express trains. Venice's railway station – Venezia Santa Lucia – is in Venice's Cannaregio district. If you arrive by train, do not make the common mistake of disembarking at the Venezia-Mestre railway station immediately prior to the Venezia-Santa Lucia station. www.trenitalia.com.

By Plane: Aeroporto Marco Polo (☎ 041-2606111, www.veniceairport.com). Less than 10 miles north of Venice, the Marco Polo Airport is one of Italy's largest, with many international and domestic flights arriving and departing daily. Travelers have a number of options to reach Venice from the airport. **Taxis** (☎ 041-936222) depart outside of arrivals and take approximately 15 minutes to reach Venice's Piazzale Roma. They typically cost €20 to €30. The 30-minute trip to Venice by private **water taxi** is without a doubt the most expensive way to go, even if it is the most comfortable. The blue **ATVO buses** (www.atvo.it) depart the airport outside of arrivals and provide a 20-minute direct connection to Piazzale Roma. Buses leave every half-hour and cost about €3 per person (including luggage). There is also another direct ATVO bus to the railway station in Mestre. The public orange **ACTV buses** (www.actv.it) depart outside of arrivals and make several stops on the 30-minute route to Piazzale Roma. While they only cost about €1, you'll have to purchase an additional ticket for each piece of luggage you're transporting. **Alilaguna Boats** (www.alilaguna.it) provide a comfortable and convenient way of arriving in Venice by boat and are less expensive than private taxis. There are two main lines of this public water taxi service that run hourly to Venice. The Red Line goes to Murano, Lido, Arsenale, San Marco and the Zattere; the Blue Line goes to Fondamenta Nuove and San Marco. It costs approximately €10 to travel between Venice and the airport and passengers may carry one suitcase and one handbag each.

Car Rental: If you choose to rent a car when you arrive, there are several rental agencies at the airport, including: **Avis** (☎ 041-5415030), **Sixt** (☎ 041-5415570) and **Europcar** (☎ 041-5415654). There are also rental agencies at Venice's Piazzale Roma: **Hertz** (☎ 041-5283524) and **Avis** (☎ 041-5225825).

■ Getting Around

On Foot: Other than by boat, this is virtually the only other way to make your way around Venice, so remember to pack a comfortable pair of walking shoes. There are only three (soon to be four) bridges that span the Grand Canal and, if you're exploring Venice on foot, you'll find yourself crossing at least one of these sooner or later: **Ponte degli Scalzi**, **Ponte di Rialto** and **Ponte dell'Accademia**.

> **Did You Know?** Plans are in the works for a new bridge (the fourth one spanning the Grand Canal) linking Piazzale Roma to the railway station. Designed by Spanish architect Santiago Calatrava, this is known as the Calatrava Bridge project.

By Vaporetto: Venice's network of public transportation in the lagoon is operated by ACTV (www.actv.it) and consists of *vaporetti,* which took their name from the one-time steam-powered boats that they replaced. There are many routes along Venice's Grand Canal and through its lagoon, but the primary ones are lines #1 and #82 that travel between the railway station and San Marco regularly. This scenic route typically takes 30 minutes and makes several key stops on the Grand Canal, including at the Rialto and the Accademia. A variety of tickets (including one-way, three-day and one-week passes) can be purchased at the ticket booths near the docks and at some tobacco shops prior to boarding. If you purchase a ticket directly from a ticket booth at the dock, it may be validated already. If not, be sure to validate it prior to boarding.

> **Important Notes:** Vaporetto stops usually have two platforms, one for boats traveling in each direction. Several boats stop at one dock and some may have limited service, so be sure the boat is heading where you want before boarding. Vaporetto routes are often altered during events like Carnevale, Vogalonga and the Regatta Storica. Note that routes can change frequently without notice. Pick up an ACTV map at a tourist office.

By Traghetto: Traghetti are *gondole da parada*, or gondolas that ferry back and forth across the Grand Canal. This is a quick, convenient way to cross the Grand Canal and passengers typically make this traghetto ride standing up. Traghetto crossings are located between: the railway station and Fondamenta San Simeon Piccolo; San Marcuola and Fondaco dei Turchi; Santa Sofia and the Rialto Market; San Tomà and San Angelo; San Samuele and San Barnaba; Santa Maria del Giglio and Calle del Traghetto and between Dogana de Mar and San Marco/Calle Vallaresso.

By Gondola: This quintessential method of transportation, known as *charterage gondole* in Venice, ranks high on my list of "must do's" in this city. Gondola rides are, however, more of a leisurely tourist activity than a practical way of traveling

between two points and the prices reflect that. Gondola fares are regulated by the *Istituzione per la Conservazione della Gondola* (☎ 041-5285075, www.gondola-venezia.it) and a 50-minute ride for a maximum of six people costs €62. If you want a gondola ride between 8 pm and 8 am, tack another €15.45 onto that fare. Request an additional 25 minutes and the price increases by another €31 (€38.75 after hours).

By Water Taxi: Private water taxi service aboard *motoscafi* (motor boats) will cost you a pretty penny in Venice, but they are certainly the most comfortable way to get around and for some, worth every cent. The main water taxi stops are at Piazzale Roma, the railway station, the Rialto and San Marco. The primary companies that offer water taxi service are **Consorzio Motoscafi Venezia** (☎ 041-5222303), **Cooperativa Serenissima** (☎ 041-5221265) and **Venezia Taxi** (☎ 041-723112). Look for the yellow registration sticker in the water taxi's window to ensure that you're boarding a registered taxi.

> **Tip:** Do not embark on a gondola or water-taxi trip without first agreeing on the fare or you may be in for a big surprise when it's time to open your wallet.

HANDICAP ACCESSIBILITY

Venice can pose a unique challenge to handicapped travelers, particularly because the city is composed of many small islands interconnected with bridges that do not typically have ramps or lifts for wheelchair access. There are a few bridges in Venice that are accessible to wheelchairs (a key from the tourist office is needed to access the chair lift), and the most useful resource is the map that **Informa Handicap Venezia** puts out high-

Venice

lighting the bridges and zones within the city that can be accessed by travelers in wheelchairs (ask for this at the tourist office). Many of the vaporetti are also wheelchair-accessible. Informa Handicap Venezia (www.comune.venezia.it/informahandicap, ☎ 041-2748144).

 Exploring its labyrinths of canals and alleys is part of the charm of discovering Venice. But, in a city where getting lost is the rule, not the exception, this can prove frustrating to some travelers who are pressed for time. A good map is an indispensable resource. The most detailed one that I found is the *Terre di Venezia* map sold at the tourist information office in the train station for €2.50. Don't underestimate the value of a good map in this city!

Tour Operators

Avventure Bellissime (San Marco 2442/A, ☎ 041-5208616, www.tours-italy.com). Although this company has grown to offer tours throughout Italy, their tours were originally based in Venice and the Veneto region where they continue to offer several interesting walking, boat and wine tours daily in English. Among their most popular tours are *The Original Venice Walk*, *The Grand Canal Boat Tour*, *Venice Ghost Walk*, *Cannaregio and the Jewish Ghetto* and the *Doge's Palace Walking Tour*. Most tours last for two hours and begin at €20 per person.

Venice's tourist offices (☎ 041-5298711) organize various guided visits to Venice, including *Gondola Serenades* (40-minute gondola ride with musical accompaniment, €35), guided two-hour walking tours of the city in English daily (€27) and combination walking and gondola sightseeing tours daily in English (€35). Contact the tourist offices for details.

Cumulative Tickets

The **Venice Card** (☎ 041-2424, www.venicecard.it, 8 am-7:30 pm) is a cumulative ticket that allows usage of public transportation, public restrooms and museums. The junior card (under 30 years old) and senior cards (30 and over) can be purchased for one, three or seven days. The blue card gives access to public transportation and public toilets, while the orange card allows access to public transportation, public toilets and many museums. Venice Cards can be purchased online or by calling the ticket office at least 48 hours in advance and can be picked up at various locations throughout the city. A one-day senior blue card is €14 and an orange card is €28. The ticket also gives discounts at some bars, restaurants, shops and events.

The **Museum Pass** is a cumulative ticket that allows entrance to all of the *Musei Civici Veneziani* (www.museiciviciveneziani.it). These include the **Museums of St. Mark's Square** (Doge's Palace, Museo Correr, Museo Archeologico Nazionale, Monumental Rooms of the Biblioteca Nazionale Marciana), **Museums of 18th-Century Culture** (Ca' Rezzonico, Palazzo Mocenigo, Casa Goldoni), **Island Museums** (Glass Museum, Lace Museum, Ca' Pesaro). This costs €15.50 and is valid for three months. The **Museum Cards** allow entrance into a group of museums: the Museums of St. Mark's Square is €11; Museums of 18th-Century Culture is €8; Island Museums and Museums of Modern Art is €6. Both the Museum Pass and the Museum Card can be purchased at any of the above museums. **Note:** Single tickets are only available for some of the above museums and where a single ticket is not available, a Museum Pass or Museum Card must be purchased.

Chorus: Associazione Chiese di Venezia (www.chorusvenezia.org, Single Church Admission, €2.50, Chorus Pass, €8). Chorus, the non-profit organization whose focus is the ongoing restoration of 15 of Venice's churches, offers a cumulative ticket that can be purchased and used at all of the 15 churches: Santa Maria del Giglio, Santo Stefano, Santa Maria Formosa, Santa Maria dei Miracoli, San Giovanni Elemosinario, San Polo, Santa Maria Gloriosa dei

Frari, San Giacomo dall'Orio, San Stae, Sant'Alvise, Madonna dell'Orto, San Pietro di Castello, Santissimo Redentore, Santa Maria del Rosario (Gesuati) and San Sebastiano.

■ Adventures

Traveling

Venice Simplon-Orient Express (www.orient-express. com). In the *dolce vita* days, there was little more fashionable than a cross-continental voyage on the Orient Express. First inaugurated with a journey from Paris to Romania in 1883, the Orient Express became one of the most celebrated and glamorous methods of travel, particularly in its heyday in the 1920s and 1930s.

Today, the Venice Simplon-Orient Express continues its luxurious passage through dramatic landscapes between Venice and several European cities, including London, Paris, Rome, Budapest, Bucharest, Prague and Istanbul. The legendary train's carriages each have their own interesting history and have always been opulently furnished. Guests are served sumptuous cuisine prepared by French chefs complemented by fine wines.

Go Barging (www.gobarging.com). One the newest additions to Go Barging's fleet of hotel barges is the six-passenger luxury Dutch vessel, *La Dolce Vita*, aboard which passengers can enjoy a weeklong cruise in sheer style around Venice, the Venetian Lagoon and the nearby Brenta Riviera. Fares begin at €2,000 per person and include three gourmet meals daily and shore excursions.

■ Festivities

Carnevale (February, www.carnevale.venezia.it). Venice's Carnevale festivities are among the world's most famous. Carnevale, or *carne levare* (take away the meat) festivities, date back to the 11th century but became increasingly popular in medieval times and reached their peak during the Renaissance when Venetians began their celebrations the day after Christmas. The period leading up to Lent was traditionally a time for lavish excesses, when the common people donned masks and costumes and intermingled with the nobles, all social divisions aside.

When the Venetian Republic fell to Napoleon in the late 18th century, Carnevale festivities were brought to an end, and not officially revived until 1979. Today, Venice's Carnevale period lasts for 10 days prior to Lent, culminating on Shrove Tuesday and is marked by pageantry, masquerade balls, performances, concerts and great fun. Many mask shops around Venice rent and sell costumes, but if you're planning on attending, reserve your costumes well in advance.

> **Tip:** Upcoming Carnevale dates are: February 21-28, 2006 and February 13-20, 2007.

COSTUME RENTALS

Tragicomica (San Polo 2800, Calle dei Nomboli, ☎ 041-721102, www.tragicomica.it, 10 am-7 pm daily); **Ca' del Sol** (Castello 4964, Fondamenta Osmarin, ☎ 041-5285549, www.cadelsolmaschere. com); **Atelier Marega** (Dorsoduro 3046/a, Campo San Rocco; Dorsoduro 2940/b, S. Tomà Calle Larga, ☎ 041-5221634 and 041-717966, www. marega.it).

Su e Zo per i Ponti (a Sunday in March). This annual non-competitive walk begins near the Ponte della Paglia and winds its way through Venice's historic center, ending in Piazza San Marco.

Festa della Sensa (second Sunday of May each year). This festival originated circa 1000 AD as a rather simple celebration for the Venetian fleet's victory over pirates from Dalmatia. Over time it evolved into a lively celebration of Venice's marriage to the sea on the Sunday following the Ascension, with a ring traditionally cast into the sea from a ceremonial boat.

La Vogalonga (May, www.vogalonga.it). All manner of rowing boats participate in this 30-km, non-competitive boat race in Venice's lagoon, a Venetian tradition that originated in 1974 when a group of rowers decided to honor the Venetian rowing tradition.

Festa del Redentore (third weekend of July each year). When a plague devastated Venice in 1576, the Senate decided to build a church in honor of Christ the Redeemer (*Redentore*), with an annual procession to give thanks for being delivered from the plague. Now, on the third Saturday evening of July each year, a bridge of illuminated boats connects the Zattere in Dorsoduro to the Redentore Church on Giudecca and festivities culminate with a fireworks display.

La Mostra Internazionale del Cinema (late Aug to Sept each year, www.labiennale.org). Established as part of Venice's cultural organization, La Biennale in 1932, Venice's Film Festival has become one of the film industry's most important events. The excitement is centered on the Lido where distinguished celebrities gather for film screenings and gala events, while paparazzi and cinema buffs bear the sometimes-oppressive heat and crowds to catch a glimpse (and if they're lucky, an autograph). Most film screenings are held at theaters in the Palazzo del Cinema and some are open to the public.

Regatta Storica (first Sunday of Sept each year). First held in honor of the arrival of Caterina Cornaro, Queen of Cyprus, this historical regatta on the Grand Canal has become one of Venice's grandest celebrations. Festivities begin with a procession in 16th-century costume and feature themed gondola races with many elaborate ceremonial gondolas, traditional food and entertainment.

Venice Marathon (Oct, www.venicemarathon.it). This scenic marathon route begins near Villa Pisana in Stra and travels along the Brenta Riviera into the heart of historic Venice, ending on Castello's quayside Riva dei Sette Martiri.

La Biennale (www.labiennale.org). Venice's cultural organization, La Biennale was established in 1893 and held its first International Art Exhibition in 1895. Since then, the Biennale has come to represent the visual arts, architecture, music, cinema and dance and organizes exhibitions in each, including the Mostra Internazionale del Cinema (Venice Film Festival). Several venues in the city are used for the exhibitions, including the Giardini Biennale in Castello.

■ Food & Drink

 Venetian cuisine features a wide range of fish and seafood-based dishes that showcase fresh ingredients from the lagoon like *peoci/cozze* (mussels), *seppie* (cuttlefish), *capesante* (scallops), *calamari* (squid), *capelunghe* (razor clams), *moleche* (soft-shelled crabs) and *vongole* (clams).

Some popular fish-based dishes include *broeto* (fish-based soup prepared with a mix of the freshest fish), *sarde in saor* (sardines marinated in vinegar, onions and pine nuts), *frittura mista* (mixed fried fish), *bigoli in salsa* (pasta prepared with a fried sardine sauce), seafood risotto and assorted grilled fish served with polenta. One of the more popular non-fish dishes is *fegato alla veneziana*, liver prepared with vinegar and onions.

Venice's traditional dishes also consist of a variety of fresh vegetables cultivated on nearby lagoon islands, including Sant'Erasmo and Malamocco. Some of the best produce includes baby artichokes, zucchini flowers, peas, asparagus and tomatoes.

Typical Venetian desserts include *frittelle* or *fritole* (sweet fritters filled with pastry cream or zabaglione served during Carnevale season), *bussolai* (biscuits from Burano), *galani/crostoli* (fried ribbons of pastry dough dusted with sugar) and *zaleti* (cookies made with cornmeal and raisins). You'll notice that many pastry shops around Venice also carry *krapfen* (doughnuts) and *strudel*, delicious sweets that reflect the 19th-century Austrian influence on the city.

Among Venice's signature drinks are the *Bellini* (first invented at Harry's Bar) with Prosecco and peach nectar, and the *sgroppino*, a sorbet-like drink made with Prosecco, lemon vodka and lemon gelato.

■ Accommodations

 Associazione Veneziana Albergatori: If you arrive in Venice without accommodations, stop into one of the Venetian Hoteliers Association offices and they will assist you in finding a suitable place to stay (www.veneziasi.it). Offices are located at the Marco Polo Airport (☎ 041-5415133), the Santa Lucia Railway Station (☎ 041-715288) and the city garage at Piazzale Roma (☎ 041-5231397).

If you prefer to rent an apartment or private home, there are several companies that specialize in **property rentals**, including: www.venrent.com, www.venicerentals.com and www.venicerealestate.it.

■ Nightlife & Entertainment

 Following is a list of useful websites that list detailed information regarding theatrical, musical and dance performances in Venice:

- www.teatroincampo.it
- www.virtuosidivenezia.com
- www.imusiciveneziani.com
- www.collegiumducale.com
- www.musicinvenice.com.

■ Sports

 AC Venezia (www.veneziacalcio.it): Venice's professional soccer team plays at the Stadio P.L. Penzo on Castello's Sant'Elena Island. Tickets can be purchased up to five days prior to the match at the official head-quarters of the team (Via Ceccherini 19, Mestre, ☎ 041-2380700) or two hours before the match at the stadium box office. Home games typically begin at 3 pm and the stadium can be reached by taking line #1 from the train station or Piazzale Roma to the Sant'Elena stop.

■ Shopping
What to Buy

Venice is well known around the world for its centuries-old production of glassware, concentrated on the northern lagoon island of Murano. You'll find many glass shops around Venice and Murano, ranging from the kitsch to the upscale.

In addition to glassware, there are numerous workshops and boutiques throughout town that sell handcrafted masks. There are also a great number of stationery shops that sell handmade paper and stationery supplies, and several shops that sell high quality refined lace from the island of Burano.

General Markets

Erberia – Venice's main fruit and vegetable market is held in San Polo's Rialto district Mon-Sat from 7 am until noon.

Pescheria – Venice's fish market takes place in San Polo's Rialto district Tue-Sat from 5 am until noon.

PUBLICATIONS

Un Ospite di Venezia (www.aguestinvenice.com): Free bilingual guide distributed monthly in many of Venice's hotels. Highlights cultural news, events, sightseeing and transportation information in Venice.

LEO Bussola: Free bilingual magazine available in Venice's tourist offices. Includes detailed sightsee-

Venice

ing information, museum hours and exhibitions, concerts and cultural news.

Venezia da Vivere (www.veneziadavivere.it): This seasonal guide highlights Venice's nightlife from wine bars and restaurants to piano bars and discotheques. Put out by Venice's tourist office. You can pick up a copy at many bars and shops around town.

Tourist Offices	
IAT Piazzale Roma Garage ASM ☎ 041-5298711	IAT Venice Pavilion - Ex Giardini ☎ 041-5298711
IAT Santa Lucia Railway Station ☎ 041-5298711	IAT Marco Polo Airport – Arrivals ☎ 041-5298711
IAT San Marco 71/f ☎ 041-5298711	IAT Lido di Venezia, Gran Viale 6/a ☎ 041-5265711 June-Sept only

■ Websites

www.aguestinvenice.com

www.turismovenezia.it

www.hellovenezia.it

www.promovenezia.it

www.venicebanana.com

www.veneziacultura.it

www.veniceonline.it

www.meetingvenice.it

www.veniceby.com

■ Venetian Vocabulary

Aqua alta – High water sometimes strikes Venice at the peak of high tide due to a combination of meteorological, astronomical and geographical factors, typically during fall and winter months, flooding squares and streets. The city's aqua alta plan is in effect between Sept 15 and Apr 30 and maps are posted around the city indicating the best pedestrian routes. In the event of an imminent high tide, sirens are sounded in the city so that residents, shop owners and visitors can prepare. A good pair of rubber boots or galoshes comes in handy and many shops around town sell these.

Bacaro – Osteria/wine bar where locals meet for a drink and snack, often standing up.

Bellini – A *Harry's Bar* invention named for the Venetian painter Giovanni Bellini, this is a blend of white peach nectar and Prosecco.

Calle – Another term for street.

Campo / campiello – A square.

Canalazzo – Venetian term for the Grand Canal.

Canottieri – Oarsmen.

Carpaccio – Another *Harry's Bar* invention, this was named for the Renaissance painter Vittore Carpaccio (who was famous for his use of deep reds) and consists of paper-thin slices of raw beef served with a vinaigrette and sometimes a bed of greens and Parmesan shavings.

Cicheti – Tapas-like dishes and fingerfoods that can consist of anything from *francobolli* to *polpettine* (meatballs) and *sarde in saor* (sardines marinated in a sweet and sour sauce).

Doge – The Venetian Republic's ruling magistrate.

Fondaco / fondego – Warehouse.

Fondamenta – Walkway beside a canal.

Francobollo – Literally postage stamp, but can also refer to a piece of *tramezzino* (sandwich), often served as a snack.

Merletto / pizzo – Lace.

Ombra – Venetian term for a glass of wine. The history of this word probably dates back to the days when vendors sold wine in Piazza San Marco and had to move their carts into the

Venice

shade, or *ombra*, to keep the wine from spoiling in the sunlight.

Passerèlla – Gangway/plank used by pedestrians in high water to walk around the city.

Rio – Canal.

Rio terà – Street that was formerly a canal.

Ruga – Street lined with shops.

Scole – Synagogues.

Scuole – Confraternities, charitable organizations.

Sestiere – District.

Squero – Gondola yard.

Vetràio – Glass blower.

Vetro – Glass.

Vogare – To row.

Voga alla Veneta – Venetian-style rowing.

IMPORTANT NOTES

■ **Street addresses** are rarely provided in Venice when asking for a location. Instead, you're more likely to see postal addresses such as *San Marco 4299* or *Dorsoduro 701*. Where possible, I've included both the postal address and the street address to simplify your task of hunting down museums, hotels and restaurants around Venice. Another point of confusion for many is the varied spellings of streets. Strada Nuova is the same as Strada Nova, and Fondamenta Nuove is the same as Fondamente Nuova.

■ One of the biggest mistakes travelers make when they come to Venice is bringing along an excess amount of **luggage** that they then have to drag (quite inconveniently) around town. Even if you're planning to take a water taxi instead of walking around town with your luggage, you may be charged ridiculous fees for each additional piece you have. If you arrive in Venice for the day and don't want to carry your luggage around the city, there are baggage deposits at the Piazzale Roma car park and at the railway station that charge a fee based on the number of bags.

■ Everything arrives in Venice by **boat**, from vegetables to appliances and Venice has a boat for everything. Postal boats, ambulance boats, funeral boats, sanitation boats and police boats are only a few types you're likely to spot on the Grand Canal and in the lagoon.

■ After the 1966 floods devastated Venice and threatened many of its masterpieces, several organizations were founded in an effort to protect and restore the city's works of art, including **Save Venice** (www.savevenice.org). Today Save Venice is extremely active in preserving Venice's treasures.

■ The characteristic wooden **gondola** has come to be a symbol for Venice, but few realize how highly technical and involved the gondola trade is. The asymmetrical gondola itself is produced using eight different types of wood and about 280 different parts that each serves a different structural or ornamental purpose. Although the gondola has evolved over the years, every effort has been made to preserve the traditional craft. Only a handful of *squerariòli* (gondola carpenters) remain in Venice today but, beyond these, there are also *remèri* (carpenters) who make the oars and oarlocks, *ottonài* and *fonderie* who make the brass seahorses and other metal ornamentation, *fràvi* (blacksmiths) who make the bow iron and ferro, *intagiadòri* who engrave parts of the gondola, *indoradòri* who apply gold leaf to the ornamental parts, *tapessièri* who add the upholstery and cushions, *baretèri* who make the gondolier's caps, *caleghèri* who make the gondolier's shoes and *sartòri* (tailors) who make his

Venice

clothing. After all of this, gondolas generally sell for upwards of €30,000 each.

■ The organization called **El Felze** (San Marco 430, ☎ 041-5200331, www.elfelze.com) takes its name from the removable cabin that was once commonly placed in the middle of the gondola to protect its passengers from the weather, represents craftsmen from all aspects of the gondola industry and aims to promote and support the history and tradition of the gondola.

■ Santa Croce

Although this district (named after the church and monastery that once existed here) is just across the canal from the railway station, tourists bypass the majority of Santa Croce's small squares and narrow alleys while following signs for the Rialto and San Marco, keeping it tranquil and unhurried.

Campo San Giacomo dall'Orio is a small, modest square named after its church, where you'll find locals chatting on benches and in cafés and children playing together.

Sightseeing

 Fondaco dei Turchi (Santa Croce 1730, Fondaco dei Turchi, ☎ 041-2750206, www.museiciviciveneziani.it; Sat and Sun, 10 am-4 pm, free admission). Constructed as a private residence on the Grand Canal in the 13th century and later purchased by the Duke of Ferrara in 1381, this palace's name derives from one of its most important functions when it was used by Turkish merchants as a commerce and living center from the 17th to 19th centuries. Since 1923 the fondaco has housed

the **Museum of Natural History**. Although the museum was undergoing restoration work at time of publication, two of its exhibits are open to the public – one an aquarium that reproduces part of the lagoon ecosystem, and the other a dinosaur fossil exhibit. The best place to truly appreciate the magnificent exterior of the Fondaco dei Turchi is from across the canal.

Ca' Pesaro (Santa Croce 2070, Fondamenta Ca' Pesaro, San Stae, information ☎ 041-5240662, ticket office ☎ 041-5240695, www.museiciviciveneziani.it; Nov-Mar,

10 am-5 pm, Apr-Oct, 10 am-6 pm; closed Mon; ticket office closes one hour prior to closing time; Museum Pass or Museum Card; €5.50). Some consider this grand structure designed by Baldassare Longhena to be the most important Baroque palazzo in Venice. Today it houses the **Museo d'Arte Moderna** with its collection of 19th- and 20th-century paintings and sculptures by Klimt, Chagall, Kandinsky, Klee, Matisse, De Chirico and Moore.

Palazzo Mocenigo (Santa Croce 1992, ☎ 041-721798, www.museiciviciveneziani; Nov-Mar, 10 am-4 pm, Apr-Oct, 10 am-5 pm; closed Mon; ticket office closes 30 minutes prior to closing time; Museum Pass or Museum Card; €4). With seven doges in the family, the patrician Mocenigo family had an unmistakable influence on Venetian society and the elegantly frescoed interior of their Grand Canal residence reflects that. The palace now houses a textiles and clothing museum, **Museo di Palazzo Mocenigo Centro Studi di Storia del Tessuto e del Costume**.

Dining Out

Vecio Fritolin (Santa Croce 2262, Calle della Regina, ☎ 041-5222881, www.veciofritolin.it; 12-2:30 pm and

7-10:30 pm; closed Sun evening and Mon; major credit cards accepted; €€€). From gondoliers to businessmen, locals return to the Vecio Fritolin day after day for an *ombra de vin,* Irina's home-cooked dishes and her pleasant smile. The old Venetian tradition of fry shops has faded over the decades leaving il Vecio Fritolin the only one in town. And, although they don't serve fish-to-go in *scartosso* (a paper cone) the way they once did, Irina and daughter Barbara bounce between the kitchen and dining rooms serving fresh fish dishes with a smile (and no apparent sense of time either). Their homemade pasta is featured in dishes like *spaghetti con scampi e pomodorini piccanti* (spaghetti with a spicy shrimp and cherry tomato sauce) and *bavette* with porcini mushrooms and shrimp tossed with fresh parsley. As if to remind patrons that they are in fact dining in a fry shop, the chef is a bit heavy-handed on the oil, but overall their dishes are quite good and prepared with fresh ingredients from the daily market. To top off the meal, Irina keeps a wide selection of wines on hand, in addition to grappas and liquors.

La Zucca (Santa Croce 1762, Campo San Giacomo dell'Orio/Rio del Megio, ☎ 041-5241570, www.lazucca.it; 12:30-2:30 pm, 7-10:30 pm; closed Sun one week in Dec and one week in Aug; €€). Far from the flurry of tourists and souvenir hagglers, this informal osteria adjacent to a narrow canal near Campo San Giacomo specializes in creative vegetable-based dishes and an interesting use of non-traditional ingredients like curry and yogurt. Try the *flan di zucca con ricotta stagionata* (pumpkin flan with aged ricotta cheese) or, if you find their side dishes as irresistible as I did, order several of them (tapas-style) like the savory *tortino di patate, porcini e radicchio* (potato, mushroom and radicchio quiche) and the *piatto di formaggi con miele di castagno* (cheese plate with chestnut honey). While this is not a vegetarian restaurant, they certainly do put vegetables to the best use. But don't be put off by the veggies if you're a meat-lover – there are

DINING PRICE CHART	
Price per person for an entrée	
€	Under €5
€€	€5-€12
€€€	€13-€20
€€€€	€21-€30
€€€€€	Over €30

plenty of hearty dishes, including roasted rabbit with olives and pine nuts. Just be sure not to provoke your dining companions if you're seated in the room behind the kitchen – the canal-side door beside the table may be too tempting for some!

Al Prosecco (Santa Croce 1503, Campo San Giacomo dall'Orio, ☎ 041-5240222; 8:30 am-9 pm; closed Sun; €-€€). The draw is the *ombra*, but it's hard to resist a sampling of one of their fresh fish dishes, a *panino* or a light snack. Locals stop into this small wine bar daily for a spritz or a glass of wine from their hefty wine list and each day brings a new featured wine and Prosecco.

Accommodations

Hotel San Cassiano - Ca' Favretto (Santa Croce 2232, Calle della Rosa, ☎ 041-5241768, www.sancassiano.it;

breakfast included, handicap accessible, water-taxi stop; major credit cards accepted; €€€). The 14th-century red stucco palazzo named after its one-time resident, 19th-century realist painter Giacomo Favretto, is beautifully positioned on the Grand Canal opposite the impressive Ca' D'Oro. Before becoming a *pensione* in 1951, many noble families resided in this palazzo, whose rooms are equally as grand as its elegant foyer marked by tapestries and oversized Murano chandeliers. Six of the hotel's Venetian-style rooms have balconies facing onto the canal (thus the most expensive rates), including the prettiest one, #322. You'll enjoy an espresso and fresh pastries each morning in the lovely breakfast room, with a small terrace overlooking the canal.

HOTEL PRICE CHART	
Based on a double room for two	
€	Under €50
€€	€50-€80
€€€	€81-€120
€€€€	€121-€190
€€€€€	Over €190

Hotel ai due Fanali (Santa Croce 946, Campo San Simeone Profeta, ☎ 041-718490, www.aiduefanali.com; breakfast included; major credit cards accepted; €€€). Room-size aside, this hotel is a real find. And, if you're here during low season, it's a real bargain too, with room rates slashed more than 50%. Located in a tranquil square in part of what was once the school of San Simeon Grande, ai due Fanali is a pleasant hotel with 16 spotless rooms that feature high ceilings and newly renovated bathrooms. When you book, request a room with views of the Grand Canal.

Shopping

Alberto Sarria (Santa Croce 1807, S. Stae, ☎ 041-717907; San Polo 777, Ruga Rialto, ☎ 041-5207278, www.masksvenice.com). This is my all-time favorite mask shop in Venice and, even though the owners have another shop closer to the Ponte Rialto, I prefer the *laboratorio* in the Santa Croce district, where visitors can watch the artisans handcrafting lovely (and often pricey) masks. This shop carries a fine selection of handmade traditional Venetian masks, including Commedia dell'Arte masks and those from Fellini's *Casanova*. Some of their more unusual masks have acrylic, watercolor and hand-sketched scenes of Venice on them. In addition to masks, the artisans craft marionettes and watercolors. If you're interested in learning to design a mask of your own, call to request a personal lesson or purchase one of their plain white masks and try mask-making at home.

 For Kids: Gardens and parks are hard to come by in Venice, but the English-style **Giardino Papadopoli** is only a five-minute walk from the train station. While it's not the quietest park, it is a good place for the kids to play or to sit with a sandwich and a map.

■ San Polo

The name of this small district refers to the 15th-century church at its heart, **Chiesa di San Polo**, surrounded by a square of the same name. Made famous by the assassination of the Florentine Lorenzo de' Medici that took place here in the 16th century, **Campo San Polo** was a lively public gathering place for many years and the site of bullfights, races and masquerade balls. Today, the square is a quiet spot where locals meet on park benches to share the day's gossip and small children entertain one another.

Northeast of the square in the more populated Rialto zone of the district, the majestic **Ponte Rialto** spans the Grand Canal. Venice's oldest bridge was initially constructed out of wood in the 12th century, but the present version is a 16th-century design by Antonio da Ponte.

If you're able to navigate your way through hordes of tourists crawling over the bridge, you'll enjoy superb views of the canal in both directions. Beyond the souvenir market stalls are the centuries-old *pescheria* (fish) and *erberia* (fruit and vegetable) markets that traditionally served as a commercial hub where goods were unloaded from barges and traded.

Tip: The **Riva del Vin** (also called the *Fondamenta del Vin*) is one of the few promenades along the Grand Canal where you can enjoy a canal-side stroll and drink. But this is one of the more highly trafficked spots in the city so don't expect your walk to be intimate. And you may be pestered by persuasive (and downright annoying) gondoliers who just happen to have an empty gondola with your name all over it!

Sightseeing

 Scuola di San Rocco (San Polo 3052, Campo San Rocco, ☎ 041-5234864; Apr-Oct, 9 am-5:30 pm, Nov-Mar, 10 am-4 pm; ticket office closes 30 minutes prior to closing time; €5.50). Founded in 1478 as a charitable institution and named in honor of San Rocco, the 16th-century building houses a much-celebrated fresco cycle by  Jacopo Tintoretto that is likely his largest. Frescoes adorning the *scuola*'s walls and ceilings were painted by Tintoretto in the 1580s and gloriously depict scenes from the Old and the New Testaments.

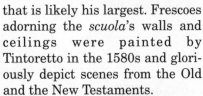

Santa Maria Gloriosa dei Frari (Campo dei Frari, San Polo, Mon-Sat, 9 am-6 pm, Sun, 1-6 pm; closed Sun in July-Aug; Chorus Pass, €2.50). Known among locals as *I Frari*, the 14th-century Gothic church is one of  Venice's largest and its brick bell tower is one of the city's tallest. The church's main altarpiece, *Assumption of the Virgin* by Tiziano (Titian – detail above) along with Giovanni Bellini's *Triptych of the Madonna and Saints*, are among the church's finest works of art. Canova's monumental tomb is here and Tiziano and a few doges are buried here. Don't miss Donatello's wooden statue of St. John the Baptist (left), the rood screen and the frescoes above the main doorway. The church is frequently the site of concerts.

Adventures

Cultural Adventures

Tragicomica (San Polo 2800, Calle dei Nomboli, ☎ 041-721102, www.tragicomica.it; 10 am-7 pm daily). Where better to learn about Venice's centuries-old tradition of **mask-making** than from the *maschereri* (mask-makers) themselves. Tragicomica has been crafting traditional Venetian masks, Commedia dell'Arte masks and various decorative masks for years and their master artisans offer courses that give participants the chance to try their hand at the craft. If you're planning a visit during Carnival and need a costume, they have a handsome selection of costumes (for sale and rent) and masks appropriate for even Venice's most fashionable balls.

Dining Out

Antica Trattoria Poste Vecie (San Polo 1608, Rialto Pescheria, ☎ 041-721822, www.postevecie.com; closed Tue; reservations needed for dinner; major credit cards accepted; €€€). The letters on the walls of Venice's oldest trattoria date back to the 1500s, reminding patrons of the trattoria's past life as Venice's post office. Since discovering its new identity nearly 200 years ago, this osteria – a hop from Venice's fish market over a small bridge – has served homemade pasta and primarily fish-based dishes, including their year-round special *orata alle poste vecie* (orata baked with small tomatoes, olives and porcini mushrooms). If the weather is pleasant, request a table in the lovely garden room. According to some accounts, this was the first place to cook with spices from the Orient once merchants introduced them.

Cantina do Mori (San Polo 429, Rialto, ☎ 041-5225401, 8:30 am-8:30 pm; closed Sun; €). Locals love this place for its wines and *cicheti* (tapas-like fingerfoods) and if you haven't yet had the traditional *bacaro* (osteria or wine bar) experience, this could be a great place for it. Open since 1462, Do Mori is one of Venice's oldest *bacari* and you get the impres-

Venice

sion that the place has aged like the fine wine it serves. Small and rustic, it's a place where you sip your wine and sample the *cicheti* on foot (no tables here) but you won't be sorry. This is one of the city's most popular haunts.

Accommodations

 Albergo Guerrato (San Polo 240/a, Rialto, Calle drio la Scimia, ☎ 041-5227131, hguerrat@tin.it; breakfast included; €€). Brothers-in-law Piero and Roberto manage this comfortable hotel in a converted convent near the Rialto market. You'll have to climb to the second floor to reach the hotel's reception, where you'll find yourself in a richly decorated hall with antique furniture. Some of the rooms' nicer features are hand-painted headboards and modern bathrooms. Rooms #3, #5 and #7 have views of the *mercato*. The newer rooms on the top floor have high-beamed ceilings and look out onto Venice's rooftops. At publication time, they had plans to install double-paned glass in all of the rooms, which should make sleeping during the morning market a bit easier. If you prefer more privacy, the hoteliers also rent three apartments, one here and two near San Marco.

Locanda Sturion (San Polo 679, Calle del Sturion, ☎ 041-5236243, www.locandasturion.com; breakfast included; major credit cards accepted; €€€). Assuming you're not opposed to climbing an absurd number of steps up a steep stairway to reach the hotel's reception, this moderate hotel could be a good choice. Built in the 13th century by the doge to accommodate visiting merchants bringing their goods to the nearby Rialto market, it served this purpose for centuries until it was converted into a private noble residence in the 18th century. When it reopened in the 1950s as a hotel, they clearly didn't have the resources (or the need) to install an elevator, and that doesn't appear to have changed. Of course, we sympathize with building codes and architectural restraints on historical buildings, but an elevator would certainly make this easier.

All rooms have been well restored, even if they are somewhat overdone and ornate with coordinated wallpaper, bedding and upholstery. The largest rooms opening onto the canal are #1 and #2 and they are comfortable enough for families. All rooms have nice baths. There is one room on the lower level for those who can't manage the stairs.

Nightlife & Entertainment

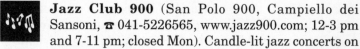

Jazz Club 900 (San Polo 900, Campiello dei Sansoni, ☎ 041-5226565, www.jazz900.com; 12-3 pm and 7-11 pm; closed Mon). Candle-lit jazz concerts on Wednesday evenings from October-April draw locals and tourists. Jazz greats from around the world have played here. The club is decorated with old instruments and black and white photos of jazz greats. Some food is served.

Shopping

Alberto Sarria (See *Shopping* in *Santa Croce*, page 208). This small mask shop is a branch of the larger one in the Santa Croce district where they also make the masks.

■ Cannaregio

It is uncertain whether this district's name derives from the reed (*canna*) beds that exist here or from its Canal Regio but, with the exception of the railway station and a few nearby streets, the zone is largely unexplored by travelers.

Constructed on the site of a former church, the **Santa Lucia railway station** is the point of arrival for thousands of visitors, who typically head straight for the vaporetto stop opposite the station, or cross the highly trafficked **Scalzi Bridge** on a mission to San Marco.

Stretching from the base of the Scalzi Bridge northeast toward the Campo S. Geramia, the **Lista di Spagna** is a lively tourist thoroughfare marked by souvenir stalls, pastry shops and a handful of overpriced (albeit convenient) hotels.

But beyond this lies the heart of a humble district where Tintoretto, Titian and Marco Polo once lived, music drifts from open windows above storefronts and laundry is hung out to dry across alleyways.

Locals head to the outdoor fruit and vegetable market on the bustling **Rio Terà S. Leonardo** each morning. Just north of the market is the world's first *ghetto* (a name that derives from the *geti* or foundries that once existed here) where Venice's Jewish population lived for centuries.

The colorful, unhurried parts of the district stretch from the Fondamenta dei Ormesini and Fondamenta della Misericordia to the Sacca della Misericordia (a man-made basin). Cannaregio's broad quayside, **Fondamenta Nuove** is the departure point for ferries to the northern lagoon islands.

Sightseeing

 Chiesa degli Scalzi (Fondamenta degli Scalzi, Cannaregio; no entrance fee). Most travelers pass this Baroque church (also known as Santa Maria di Nazareth) at the foot of the Scalzi Bridge, but few enter what Baldassarre Longhena designed for the Barefooted Carmelites in the 17th century. The church's Carrara marble façade is the only one of its kind in the city and the church once housed beautiful frescoes by Tiepolo, largely destroyed when a bomb struck during World War I.

Ca' d'Oro (Cannaregio 3933, ☎ 041-5238790; Mon, 8:15 am-2 pm, Tue-Sun, 8:15 am-7:15 pm; ticket office closes 30 minutes prior to closing; €5). The sumptuous 15th-century Ca' d'Oro, a Gothic palace whose façade was once embellished with gold, houses the **Galleria Franchetti**. On display in the museum are tapestries, antique furnishings and paintings, including the splendid *San Sebastiano* by Andrea Mantegna and *Transito della Vergine* by Carpaccio.

Madonna dell'Orto (Fondamenta Madonna dell'Orto, Cannaregio; Mon-Sat, 10 am-5 pm, Sun, 1-5 pm; closed Sun in July and Aug; Chorus Pass, €2.50). Several of Tintoretto's magnificent works adorn the 14th-century Gothic church of Madonna dell'Orto, named after a miraculous statue of the Virgin and child found nearby in a garden (*orto*). Hidden away in his parish church, Tintoretto's paintings include the *Presentation of the Virgin at the Temple* and the *Last Judgment*.

THE GHETTO

During the 16th century, the Venetian Republic decided to mandate that all Jews live in a confined area now known as the *Ghetto Vecchio*. Jews who had previously immigrated from Spain and Portugal as well as several Eastern countries since at least the 11th century, were permitted to practice their religion and many *scole* (synagogues) were built in the ghetto for worship. Jews were restricted as to the types of jobs they held, with many engaging only in money lending, pawn-shop businesses, textile-trades and medicine. By law they were required to wear a yellow patch or scarf identifying them as Jewish and the ghetto was guarded by Christians during the night. When Napoleon arrived at the end of the 18th century, he brought an end to the segregation of the Jews. Today, the district is marked by quiet and humble neighborhoods. The Campo del Ghetto Nuovo consists of holocaust monuments, a Hebrew museum (see below), a children's Hebrew school and a few bookstores.

Museo Ebraico di Venezia (Cannaregio 2902/b, Campo del Ghetto Nuovo, ☎ 041-715359; June-Sept, 10 am-7 pm, Oct-May, 10 am-4:30 pm; closed Sat and on Jewish holidays; museum €3, museum and synagogue tour €8, cemetery guided visit €8). Venice's Hebrew Museum contains a collection of objects from as far back as the 17th century that reflect religious and social Jewish life. The museum offers guided visits to the synagogues in English at half past each hour. There is also a bookshop and kosher eatery here.

Ca' Vendramin Calergi - Casino Municipale (Cannaregio 2040, ☎ 041-5232544). A prime piece of real estate along the Grand Canal, the Renaissance palace Ca' Vendramin Calergi was built in the 16th century by Mauro Codussi and served as the home to several noble families. Tour the apartments where Richard Wagner lived (and died in 1883) on Saturday at 10:30 am; call to reserve on Friday, 10 am-noon. Today the palace houses the city's casino.

Venice

Adventures

Gondola Building

Squero Canaletto (Cannaregio 6301, Rio dei Mendicanti, ☎ 041-2413963, www.squero.com; tours Tue and Fri, 10:30 am; adults €25, children under 12 €5). Dubbed by locals as *l'Americano della Gondola*, Thomas Price established the Squero Canaletto (named after the 18th-century painter who depicted this very gondola yard in one of his paintings) in 2003. One of Venice's oldest gondola yards, it is on a side street off the Fondamenta Nuove. When Price first came to the city on a fellowship in 1996 with the mission of preserving the craft and tradition of gondola building, he was a twenty-something with a college degree and a few years experience working in a boatyard in Maine. During an apprenticeship with a local gondola builder, Price learned the techniques and traditions of the trade and began building his own, many of which he has sold for tourism purposes in the United States. Today, Squero Canaletto is the site of a twice-a-week, hour-long tour where Price or his assistant Mathias explain the evolution and construction of a gondola and the traditional methods they adhere to in the construction process. If your interest is piqued, consider enrolling in a gondola workshop with their *Centro Internazionale per la Costruzione di Imbarcazioni Tradizionali*. Thomas Price offers demonstration workshops in Italian, English and German and, while it's impossible to master gondola-building during a weeklong course, their workshops expose you to the various phases of gondola construction and teach the history and role of the gondola in Venetian society. The course is offered between May and Oct and costs approximately €500.

Art Courses

Scuola Internazionale di Grafica (Cannaregio 1798, Calle Seconda del Cristo, ☎ 041-721950, www.scuolagrafica.it). This established international school of graphic arts offers a wide range of courses at various levels for painting, drawing and graphics and web design. Most of their courses take place over a period of several months, but they also offer one- and two-week summer workshops. Even if you won't be in the area long enough to enroll in a course, stop into the small school's gallery to view an interesting collection of works by international artists. To reach the school, follow the Calle del Cristo to the Calle Seconda del Cristo.

Dining Out

Fiaschetteria Toscana (Cannaregio 5719, Salizzada San Giovanni Grisostomo, ☎ 041-5285281, 12:30-2:30 pm and 7:30-10:30 pm; closed Mon for lunch and Tue all day; closed July; major credit cards accepted; €€€€). This restaurant's association with Tuscany goes no further than its name, which reflects its past life as a Tuscan wine storehouse. Thanks to Albino and Mariuccia Busatto and their son Stefano, the cuisine reflects strictly Venetian traditions and ingredients, unified with a touch of creativity. Inside the kitchen of Venice's only *Ristorante del Buon Ricordo* (see page 39), the chefs prepare risotto, frittura and other specialties based on the daily market-based menu.

The pasta is homemade and some of their best dishes include *fegato veneziana* (Venetian-style liver prepared with onions) and *frittura di pesce senza respina con verdure fresche* (a mixed fried fish platter served with fresh vegetables). More than 500 wines and 50 cheeses (during winter) crown their already rich menu.

Torrefazione Caffè Costarica (Cannaregio 1337, Rio Terà S. Leonardo, ☎ 041-716371, 8 am-1 pm and 3:30-7:30 pm; closed Sun; €). Open since 1962, this caffè has been a popular place for locals to stop for a coffee and to purchase fresh roasted beans. Several antique coffee grinders are on display along with sacks of coffee beans.

Brek (Cannaregio 124, Lista di Spagna, ☎ 041-2440158, €-€€). See *Dining Out* in Padua, page 88.

Pasticceria dal Mas (Cannaregio 150/a, Lista di Spagna, 7:30 am-9 pm, ☎ 041-715101; closed Tue; €). Among their delectable desserts are several Austrian-inspired pastries, including the *kranz al cioccolato* (a chocolate pastry twist) and *strudel*. Try the homemade *torrone* (nougat).

Gam Gam (Cannaregio 1122, Sottoportego del Ghetto Vecchio, ☎ 041-715284; Sun-Thurs, noon-10 pm, Fri, noon-3:30 pm; €€). Venice's only strictly Kosher restaurant, near the entrance to the Ghetto Vecchio, Gam Gam serves many Israeli and Italian dishes, several of which may have originated in the Ghetto. The menu changes frequently and includes a wide range of dishes from falafel to pasta and fish.

Accommodations

Palazzo Foscari (Cannaregio 4200/1, Campo Santa Sofia, ☎ 041-5297611, www.hotelfoscaripalace.com; breakfast included; handicap-accessible; water-taxi stop; major credit cards accepted; €€€-€€€€). One of Venice's newer hotels, Palazzo Foscari is on the Grand Canal near the S. Sofia traghetto (water-taxi) stop. Among its 23 rooms are two doubles and two suites with views of the Grand Canal, but expect to pay more for these. The overall feeling is contemporary but the décor seems somewhat inconsistent.

Antico Doge (Cannaregio 5643, Campo SS. Apostoli, ☎ 041-2411570, www.anticodoge.com; breakfast included; handicap-accessible rooms; major credit cards accepted; €€€). The one-time residence of the 14th-century Doge Marin Falier now hosts the decidedly elegant Antico Doge, a remarkable value, particularly during low season. Antique pieces, canopy beds and dam-

asks evoke old-world charm while Jacuzzis (in some rooms) and all modern amenities cater to needs of discerning guests. Each room is decorated differently and some have balconies.

Grand Hotel dei Dogi (Cannaregio 3500, Fondamenta Madonna dell'Orto, ☎ 041-2208111, www.boscolohotels.com; water-taxi stop; major credit cards accepted; €€€). The palatial Grand Hotel dei Dogi is sheltered from Venice's hustle and bustle by a pretty neoclassical garden where guests can dine outdoors at Il Giardino de Luca during summer. Owned by the Boscolo hotel group, this exclusive hotel has several suites, including the Presidential Suite, in addition to its standard rooms.

Budget Accommodations

Bernardi-Semenzato (Cannaregio 4366, Calle de l'Oca, SS. Apostoli, ☎ 041-5227257; breakfast included; major credit cards accepted; €€). I guarantee that by the time you find this hotel you'll be thoroughly confused by the street that it sits on. Only in Venice can a street wind its way in several directions, all the while keeping the same name. But, even if it's not easy to find this 15-room hotel off the Strada Nuova, the Bernardi-Semenzato is one of Venice's better budget options worth looking for. There are two attached rooms that are ideal for a family and most rooms are fairly spacious and simply furnished.

Ostello Santa Fosca (Cannaregio 2372, Fondamenta Diedo, ☎ 041-715733, www.santafosca.it; check-in 5-8 pm; major credit cards accepted; €). In a peaceful setting not far from the Rio Terà Maddalena, this hostel offers no-frills accommodations for next to nothing by this city's standards. This is by far one of the best deals you'll find, but the 12:30 am curfew may not agree with night owls.

Nightlife & Entertainment

Casino Municipale – Ca' Vendramin Calergi (Cannaregio 2040; slot machines 2:45 pm-2:30 am, game tables 3:30 pm-2:30 am; must be 18 years or older to enter). The Renaissance palace Ca' Vendramin Calergi houses the city's famous Casino Municipale where visitors come to try their luck at the slot machines and game tables.

Casanova Disco Music Club (Cannaregio 158/a, Lista di Spagna, ☎ 041-2750199, www.casanova.it). A short walk from the railway station, Casanova is an Internet lounge and bar by day and Venice's popular *discoteca* by night where students and the young tourist crowd gather.

Shopping

Ferro Battuto Artistico - De Rossi (Cannaregio 4311, Strada Nuova, ☎ 041-5222436; Cannaregio 5045/F-5068, Fondamenta Nuove, ☎ 041-5200077). For more than 50 years the De Rossi family has been handcrafting iron and glass lanterns, and their shops carry a dizzying selection of lanterns, chandeliers, candelabras, sconces and other iron objects that range in price from a few euros to several thousand.

Tà Kalà (Cannaregio 4391/C, Strada Nuova near Campo SS. Apostoli, Cannaregio, ☎ 041-5222837). This small shop on the bustling Strada Nuova has an eclectic selection of Venetian products, including unique handmade Murano glass, jewelry and decorative masks made with pastels. In addition, the shop carries interesting holograms from around the world.

Al Ponte del Ghetto Vecchio (Cannaregio 1190, Ghetto Vecchio; Mon-Fri, 10 am-1 pm and 3-7 pm; major credit cards accepted). This rare and used bookshop in the heart of the Jewish quarter carries books about Judaism and Venice in Italian and English.

Internet Points

Friendly Cyber Lounge (Cannaregio 149, Lista di Spagna, ☎ 041-2758217, www.ve-nice.com; 9 am-midnight; major credit cards accepted). This small lounge offers Internet, fax, webcam, printing and CD burning services. Internet fees are €4.50 for 30 minutes and €8 for one hour.

■ San Marco

Long before the tourists arrived, Venice's *sestiere* of San Marco was the city's lively center – its religious, commercial and political hub from where the Venetian Republic gloriously reigned for centuries.

Once called the world's most beautiful drawing room by Napoleon, Piazza San Marco is Venice's most impressive piazza (and its only one for that matter, since other squares in this city are merely *campi*).

Above: St. Mark's Basilica

Below: Carnevale costumes in Venice

Carnevale

But explore beyond the realm of the shimmering Piazza's grand monuments and museums and you won't be disappointed. From the famed theater *La Fenice* and the Riva del Carbon near the Ponte Rialto to the low-key church squares and bustling shopping districts, San Marco is an animated quarter.

Today, this highly trafficked district is one of colorful contrasts, where elegant boutiques and kitsch souvenir shops are neighbors, sophisticated ladies sport rubber boots to greet the *aqua alta* and travelers rub elbows with celebrities at exclusive cafés and masquerade balls.

Sightseeing

 Basilica di San Marco (Piazza San Marco, San Marco, ☎ 041-5225697, www.basilicasanmarco.it; Oct-Mar, Mon-Sat, 9:45 am-4:45 pm, Sun, 2-4 pm; Apr-Sept, Mon-Sat, 9:45 am-5 pm, Sun, 2-5 pm; last entrance is 30 minutes prior to closing time; Basilica, free admission; Pala d'Oro, €1.50; Tesoro, €2; free guided visits with advanced booking at www.alata.it). Shortly after St. Mark's body was smuggled to Venice from Alexandria, Egypt in 828, the first church of St. Mark the Evangelist was consecrated in his honor. By 1094, a new church was built on the foundations of the earlier one and was consecrated when St.

Mark's body was placed in a tomb beneath the high altar. Modeled after a basilica in Constantinople, Venice's sumptuous basilica known as the *Chiesa d'Oro* was constructed on a Greek cross plan with five cupolas, an impressive example of Byzantine architecture.

Over the course of many centuries, modifications were made to the original church, with columns, statues and mosaics added to enhance its opulence. The best time to visit the basilica is around midday when more than 9,600 square yards of

golden mosaics adorning the vaults, walls and cupolas are resplendent. The Byzantine mosaics depict stories from the Old and New Testaments and the lives of Christ, the Virgin Mary and St. Mark. Be sure to visit the *Pala d'Oro*, the gilded altarpiece sumptuously ornamented with pearls and precious gems, and the *Tesoro*, where treasures from Constantinople and other relics are on display. **Free guided tours** with a Biblical reading related to the basilica's mosaics are held between Apr and Oct, Mon-Sat at 11 am. See the schedule in the basilica entrance for tours in English.

Basilica di San Marco - Galleria e Museo (Piazza San Marco, San Marco, ☎ 041-5225205, www.basilica sanmarco.it; Apr-Sept, 9:45 am-5 pm; Oct-Mar, 9:45 am-4:45 pm; €3). Established in the late 19th century, the basilica museum's collection consists of liturgical vestments, fragments of mosaics, wool tapestries depicting episodes of the Passion of Christ and Persian carpets, but the crowning jewel is the *quadriga*, the four original bronze

horses brought from Constantinople to Venice. The museum allows visitors access to the Loggia dei Cavalli where you can look out onto the Piazza San Marco.

Campanile (Piazza San Marco, San Marco, ☎ 041-5224064; Oct-Mar, 9:45 am-4 pm; Apr-June, 9:30 am-5 pm; July-Sept,

9:45 am-8 pm; €6). The city's tallest bell tower was originally constructed in the 12th century, then rebuilt in the 16th century with a loggia by Jacopo Sansovino and rebuilt again after collapsing in 1902. The brick tower that once served as a lighthouse opens onto some of the most breathtaking views of the city and surrounding lagoon.

Palazzo Ducale (Piazza San Marco 1, San Marco, ☎ 041-2715911, www.museiciviciveneziani.it; Apr-Oct, 9 am-7 pm; Nov-Mar, 9 am-5 pm; ticket office closes one hour prior to closing time, Museum Pass or Museum Card). Built between the 14th and 16th centuries on the foundations of a ninth-century fortress, the Gothic-style Doge's Palace served as the doge's residence and seat of political power for the Venetian Republic until the fall of *La Serenissima* in the late 18th century. The palace's salons are richly decorated with gilded stuccowork, sculptures and frescoes by many of Venice's masters, including Tintoretto, Veronese, Titian, Bellini, Palma il Giovane and Tiepolo. Don't miss the two magnificent stairways, *Scala dei Giganti* and the *Scala d'Oro*.

> **Author's Tip:** For a behind-the-scenes look at the prison cell that Casanova escaped from, hidden passages, torture chambers and the doge's apartments, sign up for the *Secret Itinerary Tour* (☎ 041-5209070) at least two days in advance. English language tours are at 9:55, 10:45 and 11:35 am and cost €12.50 per person.

Museo Correr (San Marco 52, Piazza San Marco, Ala Napoleonica, Monumental Staircase, ☎ 041-2405211, www.museiciviciveneziani.it; Apr-Oct, 9 am-7 pm; Nov-Mar, 9 am-5 pm; ticket office closes one hour prior to closing time; Museum Pass or Museum Card). In the Napoleonic Wing of St. Mark's Square, the Museo Correr was established in honor of Teodoro Correr, who left a sizeable collection to the city in 1830. The museum includes neo-classical rooms with sculptures by Antonio Canova, an art gallery with paintings by Venetian masters like Lorenzo Veneziano, the Bellini family and Carpaccio, as well as many documents, prints, drawings and photographs that shed light on Venice's history.

Venice

Torre dell'Orologio (Piazza San Marco, San Marco, ☎ 041-5224951, www.museiciviciveneziani, Museum Pass or Museum Card). On the north side of Piazza San Marco, two bronze Moors strike the hour atop Venice's famous 15th-century clock tower. Just above the archway leading to the Mercerie shopping district is the complex clock mechanism in gold and blue enamel.

Palazzo Contarini dal Bovolo (San Marco 4299, Corte dei Risi o del Bovolo; Apr-Oct, 10 am-6 pm daily; Nov-Mar, Sat and Sun, 10 am-4 pm; during Carnevale and the Christmas season open daily 10 am-6 pm; €3). In Venetian dialect, *bovolo* means snail shell, which is what the spiral staircase built in the late 15th century on the exterior of the palace looks like. Climb the stairs of the cylindrical staircase above the courtyard for a magnificent view over San Marco's rooftops.

Museo Fortuny (San Marco 3780, San Beneto, ☎ 041-5200995, www.museiciviciveneziani, Museum Pass or Museum Card, €4). The eccentric Spaniard Mariano Fortuny converted the Gothic palazzo (once owned by the noble Pesaro family) into his residence and workshop for photography, textiles, set-design and painting. The 15th-century palazzo now houses a museum with a collection of his works. At publication time the museum was closed for restoration.

Dining Out

Ristorante da Ivo (San Marco 1809, Ramo dei Fuseri, ☎ 041-5285004, open until midnight; closed Sun; reservations needed; major credit cards accepted; €€€€€). The exceptional cuisine almost justifies da Ivo's over-the-top prices where you can easily splash out a pretty penny without realizing it. For starters try the *fichi con gamberoni* (figs and shrimp), and then move on to one of their grilled meat or fish dishes like the *tonno con pancette e funghi* (tuna with ham and mushrooms) or the classic Tuscan favorite *fiorentina* (a grilled prime cut of beef). You'll need reservations if you expect a table to be awaiting you in their intimate, candle-lit dining room.

Caffè Florian (Piazza San Marco, San Marco, ☎ 041-5205641, www.caffeflorian.com; closed Wed; €€€€). When Floriano Francescani first opened the doors of this café in 1720 onto what Napoleon called one of the world's most beautiful drawing rooms, it was known as *Venezia Trionfante*. Over time, the café's regulars dubbed it the *Florian* after its owner, and the name eventually caught on. Artists, intellectuals, politicians and writers living in or visiting Venice regularly came here. Today, a coffee at Florian can easily run you between €5 and €14 (especially if one of their specialty coffees appeals to you, like the *Caffè dell'Imperatore* prepared with zabaglione and crema di latte liqueurs). If you absolutely must experience Florian, I've found their toasts and panini to be a fair deal, but they also serve a variety of salads and desserts. When the orchestra is serenading, be prepared for an additional €5 per person to be tacked onto your bill.

Gran Caffè Ristorante Quadri (Piazza San Marco 120, San Marco, ☎ 041-5289299, www.quadrivenice.com; open 9 am-12:30 am; lunch 12:15-2:45; dinner 7:30-10:30 pm; €€€€). With the help of his Greek-born wife Naxina, the entrepreneurial Giorgio Quadri purchased a small coffee shop in 1775 and was responsible for helping develop the Venetians' taste for coffee. Over time the caffè became a fashionable hangout for illustrious patrons like Stendhal, Byron, Proust and even Wagner, who took his coffee here religiously each morning. A romantic feeling pervades Quadri's dining rooms, from its creamy green and yellow hued walls and elegant frescoes to its tables delicately set with fine china. Quadri's menu includes pastries and toasts in addition to its coffees and aperitifs, and you'll pay an extra €4.40 per person when the orchestra is playing.

DINING PRICE CHART	
Price per person for an entrée	
€	Under €5
€€	€5-€12
€€€	€13-€20
€€€€	€21-€30
€€€€€	Over €30

Venice

Harry's Bar (San Marco 1323, Calle Vallaresso, ☎ 041-5285777, www.cipriani.com; major credit cards accepted; €€€€). When Giuseppe Cipriani opened this bar in 1931 with the support of his American financier friend, Harry Pickering, he unknowingly created one of the world's most popular watering holes, attracting the likes of Hemingway, Welles and Onassis. As you make your way through the narrow entrance beside the bar you may be surprised to find that it is hardly anything to write home about (by its looks in any case). Still, there is little doubt that this popular haunt effortlessly delivers sophistication and panache along with the finest cocktails (albeit the priciest) from its signature *Bellini* (a marvelous blend of Prosecco and white peach nectar) to its martinis, making it revered by locals in addition to curious tourists. Pop upstairs, where you can enjoy a fine Venetian meal, beginning with none other than Harry's famous *carpaccio*.

Hostaria da Zorzi (San Marco 4359, Calle dei Fuseri, ☎ 041-5208816; closed Sun; major credit cards accepted; €€). Da Zorzi's frequently changing menu reflects the kitchen's focus on good Venetian fare, showcasing dishes like *bigoli in salsa* (a type of pasta) and *pesce spada ai ferri* (grilled swordfish) Their fixed-price menu at midday is a good value and includes a first- and second-course entrée. The dining rooms upstairs are the coziest.

Vino Vino (San Marco 2007/A, Calle della Veste, ☎ 041-2417688, www.anticomartini.com; 10:30 am-midnight; closed Tue; €-€€). The fantastic selection of wines is the draw at this wine bar adjacent to the restaurant Antico Martini, with more than 350 available by the glass or the bottle. Their daily menu is presented on a chalkboard and consists of reliably well-prepared local specialties like *sarde en saor* (sardines in sweet and sour sauce), *insalata di polipo* and *polpettine con funghi* (mini-meatballs with mushrooms). Although their hours are continuous, try to arrive along with (or slightly ahead of) the crowds, because they've been known to run low on food early in the afternoon. For a late-night, post-theater drink, drop into their **Piano Bar Martini Scala** (San Marco 1980, Campo S. Fantin, ☎ 041-5224121, www.anticomartini.com; 10 pm-3:30 am; closed Tue and

July-Aug; €€), an elegant upscale bar around the corner, with live music.

Accommodations

 Gritti Palace (San Marco 2467, Campo S. Maria del Giglio, ☎ 041-794611; water-taxi stop; major credit cards accepted; €€€€€) One of Venice's premier hotels, the late 15th-century Gritti Palace once served as residence to the Vatican's Venetian ambassadors and later hosted  many illustrious guests, including Queen Elizabeth and the Princess of Monaco. Canal-front rooms account for the Gritti's steepest room rates, but the grand views across to the Dogana are unsurpassed. The Gritti's opulent rooms are steeped in luxury and a sunset meal on the canal-side terrace will put a lovely touch on your stay here.

La Fenice et des Artistes (San Marco 1936, Campiello della Fenice, ☎ 041-5232333, www.fenicehotels.it; breakfast included; major credit cards accepted; €€€). On the doorstep of Venice's famed theater, this charming hotel has been a popular stop for artists, many of whom have left their paintings to adorn the hotel's walls. The hotel lobby separates its new wing (to its left) from its old wing (to its right) and just beyond is a small garden where guests can enjoy breakfast during summer. The size and comfort level of the rooms varies as much as the views, with some overlooking the square and theater, some the garden and others a canal. Rooms 354 and 355 share a lovely terrace and are ideal for small families, but if these are booked there are a few other rooms that are similarly connected. If you're traveling solo, request the attic

HOTEL PRICE CHART	
Based on a double room for two	
€	Under €50
€€	€50-€80
€€€	€81-€120
€€€€	€121-€190
€€€€€	Over €190

Venice

room, a cozy one with abundant closet space that is often the choice of traveling artists. This hotel rates high in terms of character, but outdated furnishings and uncomfortable mattresses make certain rooms less desirable.

Hotel Flora (San Marco 2283/A, Calle Bergamaschi, ☎ 041-5205844, www.hotelflora.it; breakfast included; €€€). This family-run hotel a short walk from Piazza San Marco just off the Calle Larga XXII Marzo is a lovely moderate hotel with a pretty garden behind the lobby. Two rooms on the ground floor accommodate guests who'd rather not climb the stairs and the family-size rooms that accommodate up to four people are among the Flora's prettiest.

Novecento (San Marco 2683/84, Calle del Dose, Campo San Maurizio, ☎ 041-2413765, www.locandanovecento.it; €€€). This small boutique hotel's nine rooms are attractively furnished, each in its own unique style with furniture from the 1900s. The courtyard is an ideal place to take breakfast on a sunny Venetian morning. If charm is high on your list, Novecento should be too. *Molto carino.*

Budget Accommodations

Domus Ciliota (San Marco 2976, Calle delle Muneghe, S. Stefano, ☎ 041-5204888, www.ciliota.it; breakfast included; major credit cards accepted; €€). Situated in a 15th-century Augustinian monastery, the Domus Ciliota is part of a religious institution and welcomes guests in modern, well-kept rooms. The non-smoking accommodations are simple, with private bathrooms and, although there is a midnight curfew, it isn't always strictly enforced.

Nightlife & Entertainment

Gran Teatro La Fenice (San Marco 1965, Campo San Fantin, www.teatrolafenice.it). After the second fire in its history burned Venice's famed Gran Teatro La Fenice to the ground, it was rebuilt and officially reopened in 2004. One of the world's most celebrated theaters, La Fenice hosts opera, theater, ballet and musical performances. Tickets may be purchased at the HelloVenezia box office on the Tronchetto (☎ 041-2424) or online.

Interpreti Veneziani (San Marco 2862, Chiesa San Vidal, San Marco, ☎ 041-2770561, www.interpretiveneziani.com). Since 1987 this group of soloists and ensemble musicians has been performing classical concerts in Venice's Chiesa San Vidal to rave reviews. Interpreti Veneziani performs year-round and concert tickets are available online.

Devil's Forest Pub (San Marco 5185, Campo San Bartolomeo, ☎ 041-5200623, 8:15 am-1 am; closed Sun; €). This lively pub is a great spot to meet people from around the world, particularly if you're looking to meet up with fellow English-speaking folk. Beer, music and some food.

Shopping

Venice's prime shopping is concentrated in the San Marco district, whose many shopping zones contain everything from haute couture boutiques to kitschy souvenir shops. The **Mercerie dell'Orologio**, **Mercerie S. Zulian** and **Mercerie S. Salvador** meander through the San Marco district between the Piazza San Marco and the Rialto bridge, luring passersby with all manner of shops. To the west of the Piazza is the bustling **Frezzeria**, a lively restaurant- and shop-lined street. San Marco's exclusive shopping culminates in **Calle Larga XXII Marzo**, Venice's upscale district boasting top-name boutiques.

Frette (San Marco 2070/A, Calle Larga XXII Marzo, ☎ 041-5224914, www.frette.com, Mon-Sat, 10 am-7:30 pm, Sun, 10:30 am-6:30 pm). Frette carries an exclusive selection of refined bed linens and loungewear in addition to accessories for the home. A wonderful place to splurge if you like this sort of thing.

Venetia Studium (San Marco 2425, Calle Larga XXII Marzo, San Marco, ☎ 041-5236953, www.venetiastudium.com; major credit cards accepted). You'll come across several of these shops around town, best known for their exclusive production of Fortuny lamps (named after the 20th-century stage-designer).

La Pietra Filosofale (San Marco 1735, Frezzeria, ☎ 041-5285885; 9:30 am-1 pm and 3-7:30 pm; major credit cards accepted). This small workshop fashions Commedia

Venice

dell'Arte masks for the theater; the artisans' material of choice is *cuio* (leather) for its durability.

> **Photo Op:** The most sublime times to visit Piazza San Marco are early in the morning before the crowds arrive and at dusk on a clear evening.

■ Castello

One of the earliest territories to be settled when barbarian invasions drove the earliest inhabitants from the mainland, Castello was historically important for its shipbuilding zone, the Arsenale – once a powerhouse that supplied the maritime Venetian Republic with wartime and merchant vessels.

A flurry of tourists keep the **Riva degli Schiavoni** one of Castello's most familiar (and trafficked) zones, as they stroll the broad quayside promenade in search of upscale hotels, kitsch souvenir shops and vaporetto and water-taxi stops.

From the **Ponte della Paglia** (Bridge of Straw), look toward the 17th-century **Ponte dei Sospiri** (Bridge of Sighs) leading from the Doge's Palace to the prison cells. Continuing eastward along the promenade, the crowds thin out, revealing Castello's quiet, unhurried nature.

The **Giardini Biennale** make up Venice's largest parkland and have been the site of the Biennale (See *Festivities*, page 196) for many years. Venture out a bit farther from the Biennale and you'll find the residential district of S. Elena, where streets are wider, laundry is hung between buildings and locals carry groceries.

> **Tip:** Although rarely explored by travelers, Via Garibaldi is a lively street and one of Venice's widest, lined with markets and flower shops. Continue down the Riva degli Schiavoni until you reach Via Garibaldi and follow it to the Viale Garibaldi which leads through a small park.

Sightseeing

 Palazzo Querini-Stampalia (Castello 5252, ☎ 041-2711411, www.querinistampalia.it, Tue-Thurs and Sun, 10 am-6 pm, Fri and Sat, 10 am-10 pm; closed Mon; €6). The one-time residence of the influential Querini Stampalia family, this 16th-century palace now houses a noteworthy museum with original neoclassical and 17th-century furniture, porcelain, sculptures and a sizeable picture gallery with paintings by some of Venice's great 14th- to 16th-century artists, including Giovanni Bellini, Giambattista Tiepolo and Palma il Giovane.

Chiesa Santa Maria Formosa (Campo Santa Maria Formosa; Mon-Sat, 10 am-5 pm, Sun, 1-5 pm; closed Sun in July and Aug; Chorus Pass, €2.50). Built by Mauro Codussi in the 15th century in a Latin cross plan, Santa Maria Formosa was erected on the foundations of a seventh-century church. Marked by two facades and a Baroque-style bell tower, the church houses several great works, including the *St. Barbara polyptych* by Palma il Vecchio (detail above).

Museo Storico Navale di Venezia (Castello 2148, ☎ 041-5200276; Mon-Fri, 8:45 am-1:30 pm; Sat, 8:45 am-1 pm; closed Sun; €1.55). Established after World War I, this museum documents Venice's naval history from its days as Maritime Republic through modern times. In addition to uniforms, nautical instruments and various mementos from Venice's shipbuilding industry, the museum has a large model collection that includes WWII battleships, submarines and frigates. The highlight by far is the model of the historical vessel, the *Bucintoro,* a ceremonial barge used by the doge when he would throw a ring from the boat into the lagoon to symbolize Venice's marriage to the sea.

Chiesa Santi Giovanni e Paolo (Castello 6363, Campo dei Santi Giovanni e Paolo, Castello, ☎ 041-5237510; Mon-Sat, 9:30 am-noon and 2:30-6 pm; Sun, 3-6 pm, €2). Centered in a lovely square in the company of the equestrian statue of Bartolomeo Colleoni, the church of Saints John and Paul was considered by the Venetian Republic to be its official church after St. Mark's Basilica. Predominantly Gothic in its style, the 14th-century church is something of a pantheon for its tombs of more than 20 doges and prominent figures from the Republic. Known among locals as San Zanipolo, this luminous church contains a polyptych by Bellini and has a splendid altarpiece canvas by Lorenzo Lotto.

Adventures

Cultural Adventures

Ca' del Sol (Castello 4964, Fondamenta Osmarin, ☎ 041-5285549, www.cadelsolmaschere.com). Since 1986 when a group of artisans decided to contribute to revitalizing Venice's Carnival traditions, Ca' del Sol has been producing elaborate masks and costumes for both Carnival and for the theater. Their master artisans conduct five-day

(three hours a day) mask-making workshops where participants are taught a variety of techniques and guided in the development of their own masks. If your plans put you in Venice for Carnival, call ahead to reserve a costume

from their large selection of 18th-century costumes (€80-350) or consider purchasing one.

Dining Out

Hostaria da Franz (Castello 754, Fondamenta San Giuseppe, Castello, ☎ 041-5220861, www. hostariadafranz.com, €€€). This small osteria facing a tranquil canal behind Venice's Giardini Biennale takes its name from an Austrian soldier who married a local Venetian woman and opened a bar here in the early 1900s. His daughter later converted it to an osteria and it remained as such until 1984 when Gianfranco Gasparini purchased it and turned it into one of Venice's finer restaurants. In their small dining room, Gasparini serves a primarily fish-based menu crowned by dishes like the antipasto *tartarra di tonno con la salsa avocado* (tuna tartare with an avocado sauce), *maltagliati alle capesante e zucchine* (pan-seared scallops with zucchini over noodles) and the *tagliata di tonno* (tuna fillet served with oil and rosemary accompanied by a purée of radicchio or celery). Gasparini caters to non-fish lovers with a few signature dishes, including the *filetto di branzino alle erbette* (beef marinated with lemon and orange juice, pan-seared with oil and served with marjoram, basil, thyme, mint and other seasonal herbs). For dessert, don't miss da Franz's decadent twist on the Trevisian specialty *tiramisu*, prepared with lemon in lieu of cocoa. Da Franz's wine list focuses on wines from Italy, France, California and Chile, and you can spend upwards of €800, depending on what you choose.

Al Mascaron (Castello 5225, Calle Longa Santa Maria Formosa, ☎ 041-5225995; Mon-Sat, 12-3 pm and 7-11 pm; closed Sun; €€). Old sketches and photos cover the walls of this informal (not inexpensive) *bacaro / osteria*. This is a popular stop for an *ombra* and *cicheti* (wine and fingerfoods), but their selection of well-prepared Venetian dishes like *sarde en saor* (sardines in sweet and sour sauce) keep the tables full at lunchtime. Remember to bring enough euros to pay for your meal since credit cards are not accepted here.

Accommodations

Hotel Danieli (Castello 4196, Riva degli Schiavoni, ☎ 041-5226480 or 041-2961111, www.starwood. com/italy; major credit cards accepted; €€€€€). Even if you can't quite justify spending upwards of €600 on a room for one night, a visit to Venice's enchanting Hotel Danieli is obligatory, if only to catch a glimpse of the glorious entrance hall. For good reason this hotel has long been considered to be one of Venice's most enchanting sleeps and it rates

Venice

high on my list for its elegance and value (relatively speaking of course). The golden-arcaded staircase is the focal point of the opulent entrance foyer and only hints at the Danieli's luxurious accommodations and its rich history. It was here that illustrious guests like Proust, Dickens, Wagner and Ruskin stayed in one of the city's most romantic ambiances. This one-time palatial residence of Doge Dandolo has an aristocratic air about it, from its Murano chandeliers and damasks to its sumptuous banquet rooms and grand views of the lagoon.

Metropole (Castello 4149, Riva Schiavoni, ☎ 041-5205044, www.hotelmetropole.com; breakfast included; water-taxi stop; major credit cards accepted; €€€€). A stay at Venice's discreetly elegant Metropole is nothing short of memorable, particularly if you splurge for a room with lagoon views. The hotel is made lovelier by its geraniums pouring from window boxes, opera tunes piped into its lobby, and antique furnishings. The

Metropole's history is rich, from serving as a music school for Antonio Vivaldi in the 18th century and later as a hospital for the Red Cross during World War II. The Metropole is less expensive than several other ritzy hotels along this quayside, particularly during low season.

Liassidi Palace (Castello 3405, Ponte dei Greci 3405, ☎ 041-5205658, www.liassidipalacehotel.com; handicap-accessible rooms; water-taxi stop; major credit cards accepted; €€€€). This hotel infuses contemporary comfort with its rich Baroque ambiance and the result is a delightful spot with 26 rooms and suites that have all been caringly decorated with a good sense for style. Open since 2003, the hotel's more modest doubles are a great deal during off-season compared to many other Venice sleeps in the same category.

La Residenza (Castello 3608, Campo Bandiera e Moro, ☎ 041-5285315, www.venicelaresidenza.com; breakfast included; major credit cards accepted; €€). Don't be deceived by the rather humble appearance of the square that unfolds in front of La Residenza. Renovated in 2001, La Residenza occupies an authentic Venetian palazzo and gives you the opportunity to experience a night in a Venetian palace without breaking the bank. When you climb the stairs to the second floor reception, you're greeted in an airy hall with rich stuccowork, frescoes and antique furnishings. Half of the 14 rooms have a view of the campo and are decidedly less ornate than the entrance foyer, but agreeably simple and spacious.

Shopping

Itaca Art Studio (Castello 5267/a, Calle delle Bande, ☎ 041-5203207, www.itacavenezia.it; major credit cards accepted). Tucked into a side street near the Campo S. Maria Formosa, this closet-sized art shop showcases works by Monica Martin and is truly an understatement. Off the path of most travelers, the gallery is at the top of my list of favorites in this city for Monica's vibrantly animated watercolors. If you have a few euros to spare at the end of your trip (in the ballpark of €1,000!), ask to see her Picasso-like contemporary oil paintings. Her prints and abstract etchings are priced lower and most of her work can be purchased with or without her hand-painted frames.

■ Dorsoduro

Dorsoduro, Venice's southern-most district, is a colorful mélange of celebrated art collections, unfussy fishermen's homes and palatial monuments.

Venice

The copper statue of Fortuna atop a bronze globe crowns the 17th-century **Punta della Dogana** (customs house) where Dorsoduro's easternmost territory juts out into the San Marco basin. The splendid church of Santa Maria della Salute dominates its Grand Canal side, while on its opposite side begins the **Zattere**, a wide promenade established in the 16th century along the Giudecca Canal to unload timber from rafts (*zattere*) arriving from the Dolomite region's Cadore zone.

Two highly regarded art galleries are situated along Grand Canal-front property: the Galleria dell'Accademia and Peggy Guggenheim's collection in the Palazzo dei Leoni.

Farther into the district is one of Venice's more fascinating elements, **Squero di San Trovaso**, a small 17th-century shipyard where passersby can watch workers construct and repair gondolas in their open workshop. One of the few still in existence in Venice today, this workshop includes a small wooden house typical of the Cadore zone in Belluno where the boatyard workers (many of whom came from Cadore) once lived.

The quarter's lively day-to-day activities are centered in **Campo Santa Margherita's** cafés and market stalls and in **Campo San Barnaba** where, near the Ponte dei Pugni, a colorful market barge is filled daily with crates of fruits and vegetables.

> **Did you know?** Ponte dei Pugni (Bridge of Punches) is named for a dispute between two Venetian families who fought on this bridge.

Sightseeing

 Accademia (Dorsoduro 1050, Campo della Carità, ☎ 041-5222247, www.gallerieaccademia.org; Tue-Sun, 8:15 am-7:15 pm, Mon, 8:15 am-2 pm; ticket office closes 30 minutes prior to museum closing; €6.50). Regarded as one of Europe's most exceptional art galleries, and the world's most extensive collection of Italian art from the 14th-18th centuries, Venice's Accademia boasts remarkable works by many of the artistic geniuses who left their imprint on the city during that period, including Giorgione, Bellini, Carpaccio, Tiziano, Veronese, Tintoretto and Tiepolo. Inquire at the ticket office about guided tours offered on Fri, Sat and Sun.

Santa Maria della Salute (Campo Salute, Dorsoduro, ☎ 041-5225558; 9 am-noon and 3-6 pm; free admission). Both Longhena and Massari have been credited for their involvement in the construction of this Baroque church built on Dorsoduro's eastern end in the 17th century to give thanks for the city's deliverance from a devastating plague. Dedicated to the Virgin of Good Health, the sumptuous white Istrian stone exterior dramatically contrasts with a rather understated octagonal interior. Among the works contained within the luminous church are several by Tintoretto and Tiziano. Each year on November 21 the church is the site of a pilgrimage in which Venetians give thanks for having been spared from a plague.

Palazzo Venier dei Leoni (Dorsoduro 701, San Gregorio, ☎ 041-2405411; 10 am-6 pm; closed Tue; guided visits, ☎ 041-2405400; €10). Peggy Guggenheim's personal collection of 20th-century art is housed within her former resi-

dence, the Palazzo Venier dei Leoni, an enviably prime piece of real estate on the Grand Canal. For rea-

sons unknown, the 18th-century palace purchased by Guggenheim in 1948 was never completed, hence its distinctively contrasting low facade. The American-born patron of the arts adopted Venice as her home later in life where she continued to expand her impressive personal collection of masterpieces from the Cubist,

Futurist, Metaphysical, European Abstract, Surrealist, and American Abstract Expressionist schools. The works featured in her collection are by 20th-century artists, including Picasso, Duchamp, Dalì, Kandinsky and Ernst. The museum is occasionally the site of temporary exhibits.

Scuola Grande dei Carmini (Dorsoduro 2617, Campo Carmini, ☎ 041-5289420; Apr-Oct, Mon-Sat, 9 am-6 pm, Sun, 9 am-4 pm; Nov-Mar, daily 9 am-4 pm; €5). The 75,000-member Carmelite confraternity of Santa Maria del Carmelo commissioned Longhena to design this chapter-house beside the Santa Maria dei Carmini church in the 17th century and later commissioned Tiepolo to paint nine canvases in the upper hall's Sala Capitolare, an undertaking that was begun in 1740 and took several years to complete. Be sure to pick up one of the mirrors to better appreciate the sheer depth and beauty of Tiepolo's cycle.

Ca' Rezzonico (Dorsoduro 3136, Fondamenta Rezzonico, ☎ 041-2410100, www.museiciviciveneziani.it; Nov-Mar, 10 am-5 pm; Apr-Oct, 10 am-6 pm; closed Tue; ticket office closes one hour prior to closing; Museum Pass or Museum Card; €6.50). Initiated in the 17th century by Baldassare Longhena and later completed on his plans by Giorgio Massari for the patrician Rezzonico family, Ca' Rezzonico now houses the **Museo del Settecento Veneziano**, a fascinating collection of 18th-century paintings and decorative art, including works by Tiepolo (below),

Tintoretto and Canaletto in addition to tapestries, porcelain and period furnishings. Robert Browning's son, Pen, acquired the palazzo in 1880 and, while the elder Browning was on an extended stay at the Ca' Rezzonico, he fell ill and died.

Adventures

Gondola Workshops

Tramontin (Dorsoduro 1542, Fondamenta Ognissanti, ☎ 041-5237762, www.tramontingondole.it; 8 am-noon and 2:30-6 pm; closed three weeks in Aug). Gondola construction is a well-respected trade not only in Venice but throughout the world for the delicate balance of various wood types, and the precision of design. There are only five workshops that still exist in Venice today carrying on this tradition, and the 120-year-old Tramontin workshop is among them, producing an average of only two or three gondolas each year (it takes several months to produce just one). Guided visits can be arranged Mon-Fri for €55 for a group and on Saturday and Sunday for €140 (tack on an additional €55 if you need an English interpreter); Roberto Tramontin explains a bit about the gondola's history, various phases of construction and the types of wood used.

Saverio Pastor (Dorsoduro 341, Fondamenta Soranzo, ☎ 041-5225699, www.forcole.com; closed Aug; call ahead to arrange a visit). Carved from walnut wood into an elbow-shaped object that the gondola's oar rests in, *forcole* (oarlocks) make the art of Venetian rowing and the maneuvering of the gondola possible. Schedule a visit at Saverio Pastor's workshop near the Madonna della Salute church to learn about this age-old craft and to see Pastor's *forcole* and *remi* (oars) that are used for different types of boats. During your visit request to see a few of his oarlock models (there are 40).

Mask Making

Ca' Macana (3172 Dorsoduro, ☎ 041-2776142, www.camacana.com). Among Venice's lovelier mask shops, Ca' Macana received considerable public attention after fashioning the masks for Tom Cruise, Leonardo Di Caprio and Nicole Kidman's characters in Stanley

Kubrick's 1999 film *Eyes Wide Shut*. Similar to many other mask shops, Ca' Macana was founded in the 1980s as Venice began its revival of the old Carnival traditions that had been dormant for several centuries. The *laboratorio* offers five-day intensive mask-making courses, 2½-hour abbreviated courses and 45-minute lectures on the history and evolution of Venice's long tradition of mask making. Advanced booking is required.

Language Courses

Istituto Venezia (Dorsoduro 3116/a, Campo Santa Margherita, ☎ 041-5224331, www.istitutovenezia.com). One of the few established language schools in Venice, Istituto Venezia offers intensive language courses for beginning through advanced students. Courses last a minimum of two weeks and, while enrolled in the program, students are encouraged to participate in various cultural activities to help enrich their experience.

On Water

Canottieri Bucintoro (Dorsoduro 15, Zattere, ☎ 041-5205630, www.bucintoro.org). Take a *vogare* lesson from Venice's master rowers at Bucintoro and you'll be on your way to participating in the next *Regatta Storica*. Well, maybe not quite that soon, but you'll certainly have a great time while learning the basics of rowing. The Bucintoro club offers weeklong rowing courses for anyone interested in learning one of Venice's historic sports.

Dining Out

 Ai Gondolieri (Dorsoduro 366, San Vio, ☎ 041-5286396, www.aigondolieri.com; 12-3 pm and 7-10 pm; closed Tue and during July and Aug for lunch; reservations recommended for dinner; €€€-€€€€). In a city where fish-based dishes are the rule, you may be surprised to dine in a restaurant where fish is nowhere to be found on its menu and meat is the specialty. The chef prepares some recognizable classic Venetian dishes, but with so many other exciting options, why stick to what you know? Start off with the antipasto *insalata di speck d'anatra* (duck salad prepared with balsamic vinegar) and then consider the grilled lamb or the *filetto al Barolo* (filet of beef prepared with wine from Piemonte). Truffles and mushrooms are widely used when in season here even in the *dolci*. Don't leave without sampling one of their decadent homemade desserts like the *crocantino di riso soffiato*

DINING PRICE CHART	
Price per person for an entrée	
€	Under €5
€€	€5-€12
€€€	€13-€20
€€€€	€21-€30
€€€€€	Over €30

alla gianduia con tartufo bianco, made with hazelnuts and white truffles. The restaurant takes its name from the gondoliers who once made a habit of passing in front of its window and requesting an *ombra* (wine). The restaurant's wine list features a copious selection of Italian wines and the friendly staff will be happy to guide you in making a selection.

Lineadombra (Dorsoduro 19, Ponte dell'Umilità 19, ☎ 041-2411881; noon-3 pm and 7-11 pm; dinner reservations needed; €€€). One of Venice's hippest eateries, far from the intensity of crowds, closed for several years and when it reopened in 2004, its new vibe made it worthy of attention. Trendy as it seems, you'll still find classic Venetian dishes on its menu prepared with market-fresh ingredients, including *en saor*. Their rendition of this sweet and sour dish is prepared with the market's freshest fish (cuttlefish, scampi or rospo) rather than the traditional *sarde* (sardines). The *fegato di vitello all Veneziana* is served with figs and polenta and their homemade ravioli are filled with ever-changing ingredients, including *ricotta e spinaci alle verdure*. My favorite tables are the alcove table for two in the backroom and the low Asian-inspired bench table for a small group opposite the bar. There were plans for another room upstairs which should make getting a table here that much easier. Call ahead if you have a table preference and especially if you plan on having dinner here.

Antica Locanda Montin (Dorsoduro 1147, S. Trovaso, Fondamenta Eremite, ☎ 041-5227151, www.locandamontin. com; closed Wed; major credit cards accepted; €€€). The star-studded list of patrons includes everyone from former President Jimmy Carter to Ezra Pound and Brad Pitt, but

Venice

you'd hardly notice any pretentious airs or stuffiness at this small restaurant open since the late 1800s. On a quiet canal in the Dorsoduro quarter, this family-operated *locanda* is a low-key eatery and a favorite among visitors who return for its warm atmosphere and remarkable classic dishes. The menu changes frequently, but if you see the *filetto di branzino con pomodorini e olive* (bass with tomatoes and olives) that's a good bet. When the weather is nice, Montin's best tables are on the terrace. Indoors, paintings by artists who once stayed here adorn the walls. In addition to the restaurant, there are 12 comfortable guest rooms upstairs.

Osteria da Codroma (Dorsoduro 2540, Fondamenta Briati, ☎ 041-5246789; 8 am-midnight; closed Sun; €€). Stop into da Codroma for a quick lunch or an evening snack of *cicheti* (fingerfoods), *panini* or *tramezzini* (sandwiches). Pasta and veggie dishes satisfy larger appetites.

Gelateria Nico (Dorsoduro 922, Fondamenta alle Zattere, ☎ 041-5225293; €). My itinerary put me on the Zattere outside of Nico early one morning where I stood for all of 30 seconds contemplating the sinfulness of consuming ice cream in lieu of breakfast, before the temptation proved too strong and I found myself at a small table, spoon in hand, staring down at Nico's first serving of *giandiuotto* for the day. This downright decadent dessert is a fusion of hazelnuts and chocolate, prepared with a block of hazelnut and chocolate ice cream and topped with homemade whipped cream and toasted hazelnuts from Piemonte. It's one dessert not to be missed.

Accommodations

Pensione Accademia Villa Maravege (Dorsoduro 1058, ☎ 041-5237846, www.pensioneaccademia.it; breakfast included; water-taxi stop; €€-€€€). Move away from the congested areas near San Marco and the Rialto bridge and you'll be rewarded with delightful accommodations at the Villa Maravege that seem more mainland than they do Venetian. Step off your private water-taxi into the 17th-century villa's courtyard and you'll hardly feel as though you're in the heart of such a large city. Surrounded by its own gardens in a quiet area, the understatedly elegant villa, where the 1955 film *Summertime* starring Katherine Hepburn was filmed, will soon feel like your own private villa. There are four rooms on the ground floor that can be accessed through the garden, while the superior rooms are located off the *piano nobile*. Standard doubles have a canal view, while the more stylish superior

HOTEL PRICE CHART	
Based on a double room for two	
€	Under €50
€€	€50-€80
€€€	€81-€120
€€€€	€121-€190
€€€€€	Over €190

rooms face the attractive garden. Rooms are bright and cheery, featuring spacious, modern baths. Sitting rooms are elegant and in nice weather you can take breakfast on the terrace. If stairs won't work for you, request one of the two ground-floor rooms since they don't have an elevator here. There are only 27 rooms and, if you don't book well in advance, you're not likely to find one waiting for you. On the doorstep of both the Accademia and the Grand Canal, you're never far from the excitement, even though you'll feel worlds away.

Hotel Galleria (Dorsoduro 878/a, Accademia, ☎ 041-5232489, www.hotelgalleria.it; breakfast included; €€). Budget accommodations are hard to come by in this notoriously overpriced city, but the unfussy Hotel Galleria, ensconced in a 17th-century palazzo, does a good job of delivering above-average accommodations at a rate that won't have you scraping for your next meal. The hotel's nine rooms vary in size and all but three have their own private bathrooms. The décor is in the typical Venetian style and their best room is #8, a spacious one with pretty canal views. Breakfast is served in the privacy of your own room.

La Calcina (Zattere 780, Dorsoduro, ☎ 041-5206466, www.lacalcina.com; breakfast included; major credit cards accepted; €€). Overlooking the Giudecca Canal, this one-time *locanda* hosted John Ruskin in 1876 and has been owned by the same family since the 1940s. The Calcina's last major renovation was in the late 1990s and, although hallways are on the dark side, most rooms and bathrooms are fairly modern. The cheeriest rooms overlook the canal and you'll be comfortably welcomed by the friendly staff. If canal views are what

Venice

you're after but you're on a budget, €20-30 extra will do the trick here. If you prefer more private accommodations, inquire about their suites and apartments located throughout the city.

Shopping

Atelier Marega (Dorsoduro 3046/a, Campo San Rocco; Dorsoduro 2940/b, S. Tomà Calle Larga, ☎ 041-5221634 and 041-717966, www.marega.it). If you're thinking about attending one of Venice's masked balls and you need a costume, you'll find a good selection to rent at Atelier Marega, in addition to hand-made masks.

 **Capriccio** (Dorsoduro 880/A/D, ☎ 041-5209097, www.capriccio.it). This small shop sells interesting and unusual handmade Murano glass objects. If you're in the market for a Murano glass lamp, they carry a good selection here.

Genninger Studio (Dorsoduro 2793/A, Calle del Traghetto, ☎ 041-5225565, www.genningerstudio.com). This lovely studio near the Ca' Rezzonico Museum features Leslie Ann Genninger's collection of custom glass jewelry, sculptures and Byzantine-inspired lighting.

■ The Lagoon Islands

Murano

Ever since 1291 when Venice's glass factories were moved to the northern lagoon island of Murano in an effort to reduce the fire hazard that they posed to the city, glass production has continued to evolve into one of the city's finest contributions.

Although it is not certain exactly when glass production began in Venice, we do know that its flourishing probably had a great deal to do with the Republic's involvement in trade with the East. By the 13th and 14th centuries, the Republic had regulated the practices of the glassmaking guild through a series of laws addressing everything from the production to the sale and taxing of glass. At one time Venice's glass-blowing secrets were so heavily guarded that it was illegal for glassmakers to leave Murano for fear of treason.

Today visitors to the lagoon's most visited island arrive at the La Colonna ferry stop where they are greeted by a flurry of people with fliers advertising glass factories. As you begin your exploration of Murano's nine less hurried islets, stop into any of the factory showrooms along **Fondamenta dei Vetrai** for free demonstrations and visits to their workshops and showrooms.

Getting There

The quickest way to reach Murano is via the **Laguna Nord ferry** (41/42) that leaves from Cannaregio's Fondamenta Nuove.

Sightseeing

Museo del Vetro (Fondamenta Giustinian 8, Murano, ☎ 041-739586, www.museicivicivenezia ni.it; Nov-Mar, 10 am-4 pm; Apr-Oct, 10 am-5 pm; closed Wed; ticket office closes one hour prior to closing time; Museum Pass or Museum Card, €4). A large historical collection of Murano glass is on display in the island's glass museum and merits a visit for its

interesting chronological collection of glassware that dates back as far as the first century AD. The exhibit begins in the ground floor's archaeological room with a collection of free-blown and mould-blown glass cups, bowls, urns, beakers

and jewelry from the first to third centuries AD. Upstairs, exhibits chronicle the science and craft of glassmaking, highlighting various stages of the process, *ferri da lavori* (tools) and techniques that have evolved over the centuries. Noteworthy are the three oversized Murano glass chandeliers hanging from the frescoed ceiling in the room upstairs and the room's late 19th-century mosaic portraits. Exhibit descriptions are written in both Italian and English.

Basilica dei Santi Maria & Donato (Mon-Sat, 9 am-noon and 2-6 pm, Sun, 2-6 pm). Erected on the foundations of a seventh-century church, Murano's Byzantine basilica dates back to the 12th century and is worth visiting for its ornamental mosaic floor from the year 1140.

Adventures

Glass Production

Mazzega (Fondamenta Da Mula 147, Murano, ☎ 041-736888, www.mazzega.it; Mon-Fri, 9 am-5 pm). Founded in the late 1800s, this is one of Murano's largest glass factories that supplied some of the mosaics for the Vatican in Rome. From lamps and tableware to decorative pieces and sculpture, all objects are produced by hand in a process that can be seen during a guided visit (with advanced scheduling). During your tour, ask to see the photo of one of the world's largest chandeliers, made by Mazzega in the 1990s for an Indonesian family. This upscale factory focuses on special production and, unlike some of Murano's other factories, it is

not open for large group tours. Mazzega's artisans will produce custom pieces (for a hefty fee of course) if you have something in mind. Over the years the factory has hosted many illustrious guests, including Brooke Shields and Barbara Bush. Mazzega's designs reflect their adherence to tradition and classic styles as well as their sense for evolving designs and tastes.

Venini (Fondamenta Vetrai 47, Murano, ☎ 041-2737204). Since it was established in 1921, Venini has become one of Murano's premier glass factories and has achieved international acclaim for its glass, much of which is on display in museums around the world. In addition to its showroom in

Murano, there is another near Piazza San Marco in Piazzetta Leoncini, where you can discover Venini's largely contemporary collections.

Shopping

Manin 56 (Fondamenta Manin 56, Murano, ☎ 041-5275392; 11 am-6 pm; closed Jan). As you move deeper into the island away from the touristy ferry stops, you'll find several lovely boutiques like this one, named for its address. Manin 56 primarily showcases contemporary pieces by a handful of designers, its most popular being one of Murano's oldest, Salviati. In the 19th century, Salviati specialized in engraving and embellishing pieces with gold. Today their sleek collections include Murano glass chandeliers hanging from the frescoed ceiling in the *portego* (portico) room.

Burano

The lively fishing village of Burano is a riot of rich and subtle colors, from the ocher, tangerine, lilac and azure houses that line its canals to the creamy handcrafted lace in boutique windows.

Generations of fishermen and lace-makers have made a peaceful life for themselves on this small island, best known for its centuries-old art that is kept alive today by only a handful of skilled artisans. The vibrant town is a much-loved spot for painters.

> **Did you know?** Burano's expensive *punto di aria* lace dates back to the 16th century and requires the intricate weaving of extremely fine thread.

Getting There

The boat ride from Murano to Burano takes about 25 minutes and, since both of these islands are in the northern lagoon, it is convenient to visit them together using a **Laguna Nord ferry** ticket. If you prefer to bypass Murano, take the LN line from Fondamenta Nuove and don't disembark until you reach Burano (35 minutes).

Venice

Sightseeing

Museo del Merletto (Piazza B. Galuppi 187, Burano, ☎ 041-730034, www.museiciviciveneziani.it; Nov-Mar, 10 am-4 pm; Apr-Oct, 10 am-5 pm; closed Tue; ticket office closes one hour prior to closing time; Museum Pass or Museum Card; €4). Since the latter part of the 20th century, Burano's old school of lace has

housed a small museum with a collection of lace that documents its highly treasured craft of lace making as far back as the 16th century.

Dining Out

Da Romano (Via S.M.D. 221, Burano, ☎ 041-730030, www.daromano.it; 12-2:30 pm and 6:30-9 pm; closed Sun night and Tue, and from mid-Dec to early Feb; €€€). Da Romano's walls are just as colorful as Burano's painted houses, with paintings by artists (former patrons) left to create a collage. Since it first opened as a trattoria in the late 1800s, this family-run restaurant has hosted many legendary guests, including Sinclair Lewis, Ezra Pound and Katherine Hepburn. Various fish-based dishes are its claim to fame and their *risotto di pesce* and *risotto di frutte di mare* are standards. Fried, grilled, boiled, roasted, sautéed or raw, da Romano's fish recipes are the reason so many return.

Shopping

Two lovely shops that sell refined Burano lace are **Emilia** (Piazza Galuppi 205, Burano, ☎ 041-735299, www.emiliaburano.it) and **La Perla** (Via Galuppi 287, ☎ 041-730009; Via Galuppi 474, ☎ 041-735442; Via Terranova 28, Burano). The shops sell remarkably handcrafted tablecloths, bed linens and lingerie and if you're lucky you may find an artisan at work when you visit.

Torcello

When barbarians invaded the mainland in the fifth and sixth centuries, inhabitants from the nearby Roman town of Altino fled to the northern lagoon's island of Torcello for protection. It flourished over time and became a prosperous residential center, particularly between the seventh and 10th centuries.

Malaria and Venice's subsequent growth eventually turned Torcello into a ghost town, but not without leaving behind a few impressive monuments that convey a telling story about its past. The island's population never returned, and today only a handful of people call Torcello home, making it a low-key place.

Getting There

 It's a 15-minute ferry ride on the **Laguna Nord** route from Burano to Torcello. If you're coming directly from Fondamenta Nuove instead, the ride will take about 45 minutes.

Sightseeing

 Santa Maria dell'Assunta (Torcello, ☎ 041-2702464; Mar-Oct, 10:30 am-5:30 pm; Nov-Feb, 10 am-5 pm; ticket office closes 30 minutes prior to closing; Cathedral, €2, Bell tower, €3). Torcello's early 11th-century cathedral was built on the foundations of the lagoon's most ancient monument, a cathedral dating back to 639 AD. Its shimmering Byzantine mosaics are a sharp contrast to this lonely island and justify the trip out here. Adjacent is the 11th-century **Church of Santa Fosca**.

> **Don't Miss:** The large stone throne referred to as the **Trono di Attila**. While it could very well have been the throne of the King of the Huns, it was more likely that of a bishop or a magistrate.

Museo di Torcello (Palazzo del Consiglio, Torcello, ☎ 041-730761, www.provincia.venezia.it/museotorcello; Nov-Feb, 10 am-5 pm; Mar-Oct, 10:30 am-5:30 pm; closed Mon; ticket office closes 30 minutes prior to closing time; museum, €3, museum and basilica, €5.50, museum, basilica and bell tower, €8). Torcello's museum chronicles the island's history in a series of interesting collections and consists of an archaeological section and a medieval and modern section. The museum's collection includes bronze pieces and pottery dating back to Greek and Roman antiquity, documents and public records that reflect life on the island and other features that chronicle Torcello's history and relationship with Venice.

Lido

The once-unoccupied strip of land shielding Venice and its lagoon from the forces of the Adriatic, this was transformed into Venice's chic seaside resort in the 19th and 20th centuries and has lured the international jet set ever since.

Characterized by tree-lined avenues and Art Deco villas, the Lido is perhaps better known nowadays for its annual film festival than for its beaches that in fact gave the world the international term for beach – *lido*.

It's a straight shot from the ferry stop down Lido's main thoroughfare, **Gran Viale Santa Maria Elisabetta**, to the Marconi promenade and seaside where you'll find several privately operated beach facilities. If you need a break from camera-toting tourists on mainland Venice, all you'll need to bring is a bathing suit and these beach facilities will supply the rest, from cabanas, chaise lounges, umbrellas and bathrooms, to bars and various other services (for a fee of course).

Getting There

 It is about a 15-minute boat ride from the San Zaccaria station near San Marco to the Lido.

Getting Around

It is relatively easy to get around the central zones of the Lido on foot, but, if you want to explore more of the island, consider taking one of the Lido's buses (Lido is the only island in the lagoon with car traffic) or renting a bicycle from one of the rental shops along S. Maria Elisabetta.

Accommodations

 Hotel des Bains (Lungomare Marconi 17, Lido, ☎ 041-5265921, www.sheraton.com/desbains; open Apr-Oct; major credit cards accepted; €€€€€).

Since this Belle Epoque hotel opened its doors in July of 1900, paparazzi have been drawn here by its élite clientele, from aristocrats to movie stars. Designed by two Venetians, the Art Nouveau structure preserves its essence of bygone days and offers guests refined hospitality in an exclusive atmosphere. After its renovation in 1905-06, the Des Bains grew to be one of Italy's largest seaside resorts and was easily one of the most popular in post-war Europe.

 Did You Know? The early 20th-century German writer Thomas Mann used the Des Bains as inspiration for his tale *Death in Venice*, which was subsequently filmed here.

Westin Excelsior Palace (Lungomare Marconi 41, Lido, ☎ 041-5260201, www.starwood.com/luxury, open Apr-Oct only; major credit cards accepted; €€€€€). When 30,000 people came for the grand opening of the Excelsior in 1907, it was destined to become an upscale summer resort for the international jet set. The high society hotel's guest list has included such illustrious guests as Winston Churchill, along with scores of others who have arrived for Venice's annual film festival. The Moorish-style hotel is the epitome of luxury on the Lido, characterized by expertly manicured gardens, extravagant suites and premier restaurants serving fine international cuisine.

Did you know? The first International Film Festival was inaugurated as part of Venice's Biennale on Aug 6th, 1932 with the film *Doctor Jekyll and Mr. Hyde*. The Palazzo Cinema was built in 1937.

Venice

Giudecca

During the 16th century, Michelangelo is said to have spent several years in exile on Venice's largest lagoon island. Sadly, Giudecca is overlooked by many tourists who never explore beyond the realm of the city's six main districts but those who do are amply rewarded by the fabulous views across the canal to Venice and its colorful residential neighborhoods.

The island is also characterized by several factories, including the Mulino Stucky, and a women's prison where inmates are given the task of tending a garden, harvesting products and turning them into soaps, creams, deodorants and shampoos.

Getting There

 It takes about 30 minutes to travel by ferry to Giudecca from the railway station heading in the direction of San Marco and about 10 minutes from San Zaccaria to Giudecca. If your plans include a visit to the Redentore, it is most convenient to get off at the Redentore stop.

Author's Tip: If you're fond of Palladian architecture, disembark from the ferry at **S. Giorgio Maggiore** before reaching Giudecca (coming from S. Marco) and explore Palladio's 16th-century church. The interior of this classically-inspired structure is rather stark but made luminous by two stunning Tintoretto paintings that sit on either side of altar. For great views across to Piazza San Marco and the lagoon, take the elevator to the top of the bell tower (€3). You won't pay admission to this church, but it's worth shelling out €.50 to illuminate a few of the church's paintings.

Sightseeing

 Il Redentore (Campo del Redentore, Giudecca, ☎ 041-5231415; Mon-Sat, 10 am-5 pm, Sun, 1-5 pm; closed Sun in July and Aug; €2). One of Palladio's two classical masterpieces in Venice, and one of his comparatively few pieces of religious architecture, the 16th-century Redentore Church was built to celebrate Venice's liberation from the plague. Its luminous interior contains an altar in Baroque style and noteworthy works by Palma il Giovane, Jacopo da Bassano and Veronese.

Adventures

Cooking Courses

Laboratory of Venetian Cuisine - Cipriani (Giudecca 10, ☎ 041-5207744, www.hotelcipriani.com). Led by the Cipriani's head chef, Renato Piccolotto, the Laboratory of Venetian Cuisine focuses on researching and teaching about traditional Venetian recipes. Several times each year, formal cooking courses are organized at the Cipriani where, through cooking demonstrations, participants learn to prepare meals Cipriani-style. The cooking program typically lasts six days and includes five nights accommodation at the Cipriani, formal dinners, cocktail parties, outings, and sometimes a visit to a wine cellar. This is an exclusive program, but worth noting that it is decidedly not hands-on.

Accommodations

Cipriani (Giudecca 10, ☎ 041-5207744, www.hotelcipriani.com; breakfast included; private water-taxi launch; major credit cards accepted; €€€€€). A luxurious atmosphere pervades Giudecca's dramatic Cipriani, where the most decadent treatments are applied to every aspect of a guest's stay. Founded by Giuseppe Cipriani

in 1958, the Cipriani sits on private, secluded grounds at the eastern tip of the Giudecca, in a world of its own. The polished service and sheer elegance of the Cipriani's rooms make for a memorable stay, whether your room is facing the lagoon, the gardens or the pool. In addition to rooms within the main hotel, the Cipriani's 15th-century Palazzo Vendramin and the Palazzetto Nani Barbaro offer guests decadent suites with enviable views, one with a private garden. The Cipriani also features an Olympic-size pool, health club and tennis courts and its restaurant on the Zitelle, speaks for itself. Their regular cultural programs are very popular, including the cooking courses (see *Adventures* above).

 Venice can get downright ugly when the weather doesn't cooperate, but the effects of the wind and torrential rain are far more dramatic when you're on one of its smaller, less-protected islands that are less accustomed to tourists and therefore do less to accommodate them. When I say Giudecca and S. Giorgio Maggiore are better visited in calm weather, I can't emphasize that enough.

Riviera del Brenta

As the Venetian Republic began to sense a decline in trade with the Orient due to the opening of new trade routes, it recognized the value of expanding its influence on the mainland. By the 14th and 15th centuries, it began acquiring territories on the mainland in order to shift its investments and secure itself both politically and economically.

In doing so they stimulated agricultural development in these mainland territories and with that came a wave of construction of agricultural estates, primarily along the Brenta Canal that flows between the cultural centers of Padua and Venice. Their location along the canal facilitated both transportation and communication.

Over time, the concept of functional estates evolved into holiday residences and Venetian patricians began commissioning famous architects like Palladio, Scamozzi, Longhena and

Frigimelica to construct lavish villas along the banks of the Brenta between the 15th and 18th centuries that were embellished with sumptuous frescoes, statues, fountains and gardens.

And so was born *villegiatura*, the period between June and November when noble Venetians fled to the countryside and engaged in lavish parties, entertainment, and a variety of excesses that preceded Venice's 18th-century decline.

A great many of the villas still exist today between Malcontenta and Stra, several of which are open to the public. While they can be reached by car, the most scenic way of discovering the Brenta Riviera and its villas is by boat.

■ Getting There & Getting Around

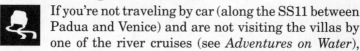

If you're not traveling by car (along the SS11 between Padua and Venice) and are not visiting the villas by one of the river cruises (see *Adventures on Water*), ACTV provincial buses depart from Venice's Piazzale Roma twice each hour and stop at most of the Brenta Riviera's towns, where you can reach the villas included in the Village Tour below.

■ Adventures

The Villa Tour

Villa Foscari "La Malcontenta" (Via dei Turisti, Malcontenta di Mira, ☎ 041-5470012; Apr-Oct, Tue and Sat, 9 am-noon; €7). As the story goes, Villa Foscari, dubbed *La Malcontenta* (The Unhappy), derived its name from a noblewoman who was once confined here as punishment for her restless nature. Considered by many to be among Palladio's finest country works, La Malcontenta was built for Nicolò and Alvise Foscari and later frescoed by Giambattista Zelotti and Battista Franco. The villa still belongs to descendents of the original owners and its grounds and *piano nobile* are open to the public.

 Available from Apr-Oct, the **Pass Ville** is a single ticket that allows entry into five of the Brenta's grandest villas: Villa Pisani, Villa Widmann, Barchessa Valmarana, Barchessa Alessandri and Barchessa Villa Foscarini Rossi. The Villa Pass is available at the villas themselves and at Venice's tourist offices for €19.

Villa Widmann Foscari Rezzonico (Via Nazionale 420, Mira Porte, ☎ 041-424973; Nov-Feb, Sat and Sun, 10 am-5 pm; Mar-Oct, Tues-Sun, 10 am-6 pm; Pass Ville; €5). Originally begun in the early 18th century, this villa was not completed in its French-influenced Rococo style until later that century. Especially worth noting is the sumptuously frescoed main salon, probably the work of the 18th-century painter Giuseppe Angeli.

Villa Pisani (Via Doge Pisani 7, Stra, ☎ 049-502270; Apr-Sept, Tues-Sun, 9 am-6 pm; Oct-Mar, Tues-Sun, 9 am-4 pm; Pass Ville; Park and museum, €5, Park only, €2.50). One of the Riviera's most stately villas, the Villa Pisani was commissioned by the Pisani family on the occasion of their rise to fame in the 18th century. The villa was begun by Gerolamo Frigimelica and later taken over by Francesco Maria Preti, and its great hall was frescoed  by Giandomenico Tiepolo. If the weather permits, take a leisurely stroll through the extensive gardens and the labyrinth that Gabriele D'Annunzio referred to in one of his works.

Villa Foscarini Rossi (Via Doge Pisani 1, Stra, ☎ 049-9801091, www.villafoscarini.it; Apr-Oct, Mon-Fri, 9 am-12:30 pm and 2:30-6 pm, Sat, 9:30 am-12:30 pm and 2-6 pm, Sun, 10 am-6:45 pm; Nov-Mar, Mon-Fri, 9 am-12:30 pm and 2:30-6 pm; closed in Aug; Pass Ville; €5). In

the early 17th century the patrician Foscarini family commissioned Vincenzo Scamozzi to build a country estate which was later altered by Giuseppe Jappelli in a more neoclassical style. The villa, with its interesting shoe museum, and the guesthouse with its richly frescoed salon, are both open to the public and used regularly for concerts, weddings and other events.

Barchessa Valmarana (Via Valmaran 11, Mira, ☎ 041-424754, www.villavalmarana.net; Mar-Oct, 9:30 am-noon and 2:30-6 pm; closed Mon, Nov-Feb; call to schedule a visit; Pass Ville; €6). This 17th-century country house is a popular stop on the river cruises and one of the most famous along the Brenta. Although once part of a larger villa complex that no longer exists, the Barchessa was formerly a guest house and is worth visiting for its beautifully frescoed hall (likely the work of a student of Tiepolo) and its period furnishings.

On Water

Il Burchiello (Via Orlandini 3, Padua, ☎ 049-8763044, www.ilburchiello.it). For years the Burchiello has been one of the most popular ways to explore the Brenta's villas between Venice

and Stra. Boats depart Venice (Tue, Thurs and Sat) at the Pietà Dock along Riva degli Schiavoni where the full-day tour commences and the group sets off for the Villa Foscari La Malcontenta. The boat travels past more than 50 villas during its Brenta tour and stops at the Barchessa Valmarana di Mira, the Villa Pisani and for lunch in Oriago. The full-day tour ends at approximately 6:30 pm and passengers may return to Venice on their own, by bus or train. The Brenta tours take place between Mar and Oct and cost approximately €62.

■ Accommodations

 Villa Margherita (Via Nazionale 416, Mira Porte, ☎ 041-4265800, www.villa-margherita.com, €€€€). Top off your discovery of villa life along the Brenta Riviera with a memorable stay at the elegant 16th-century Villa Margherita. Once the home of a noble Venetian family, grandeur continues to pervade this charming villa where guests are catered to with polished hospitality. Begin your day in the cheery breakfast room and, after exploring the Riviera, return to the villa and relax in the gardens. Just a short walk from the villa is the bus stop where buses run frequently to Venice.

Villa Colloredo (Via Brusaura 24, Sambruson di Dolo, ☎ 348-2102337, www.villacolloredo.it, €€€€). Experience a taste of villa life in the countryside outside of Dolo Mirano, in the 18th-century Villa Colloredo. Set on lovely grounds, the villa's four spacious apartments are tastefully furnished and offer guests the opportunity for an independent, low-key holiday in the countryside. Between Venice and Padua, the villa is convenient for exploring the major cities as well as the Brenta's many villas. Apartments are typically rented for one week from Saturday to Saturday but, depending on the season and availability, it may be possible to book for a minimum of three nights. Credit cards are not accepted but cash and travelers checks are.

■ Tourist Office

APT - Riviera del Brenta
Villa Widmann Foscari
Mira
☎ 041-424973

Veneto's Beach Towns – Bibione, Caorle & Jesolo

Bibione, Caorle and Jesolo are among the Adriatic Coast's most popular beach towns between Venice and Trieste. Although they are all great places to enjoy the sun and the sand and have a developed tourism industry with a wide range of accommodations, restaurants, sports facilities and activities, they each offer unique attractions.

Bibione, one of the youngest beach towns outside of Venice, is best known for its modern thermal center, constructed after thermal waters were discovered here in the 20th century.

To Bibione's south sits the old fishing port of **Caorle** that, in addition to its attractive beaches, is particularly appealing for its colorful historical center and *casoni* (traditional fishermen's huts).

The last and most established of the three seaside resort towns is **Lido di Jesolo**, an ancient Roman town whose tourism dates back at least as far as the 1800s. With 15 km of beaches, Jesolo offers the most extensive accommodations, restaurants, and sports and leisure facilities.

■ Getting There

By Car: The best way to reach Bibione is by exiting the **A4** motorway at **Portogruaro** or **Latisana** and following signs. To reach Caorle exit the **A4** at **Santo Stino di Livenza**. To reach Jesolo from the west, exit the **A4** at the **Aeroporto Tessera/Jesolo** exit.

By Bus: The regional **ATVO** buses run frequently between Piazzale Roma in Venice to Bibione, Caorle and Jesolo.

By Train: The nearest train station to Bibione and Caorle is **Portogruaro** which is on the Venezia-Trieste railway line. The stations closest to Jesolo are in **Mestre** and **San Donà di Piave**. It is possible to connect to the towns by bus from the train stations.

By Plane: The nearest airport to the coastal towns with domestic and international flights daily is Venice's **Marco Polo**. From here visitors have the option of continuing on by train or by bus. For details: www.veniceairport.it.

■ Sightseeing

I Casoni

 Although many of Caorle's fishermen once lived in this fishing village, for the most part they now only work and eat in the small *casoni* (characteristic straw huts). The best time to visit is around midday when the fishermen are preparing their lunch – grilling the fresh catch of the day and cooking polenta. To get there, pass Duilio restaurant on the left and turn right at the light onto Palangon. Follow the unpaved narrow road and park toward the end.

Beaches

 While seaside hotels in Bibione, Caorle and Jesolo have private beaches where guests are provided lounge chairs and umbrellas, there are also public beach facilities with beach bars, umbrella and lounge chair rentals, bathrooms and other services. Many of the beaches have promenades that are perfect for strolling but off-limits to bicycles.

■ Adventures

For the Soul

 Bibione Thermae (Via delle Colonie 3, Bibione, ☎ 0431-441111, www.bibioneterme.it; 8 am-12:30 pm and 2:30-6 pm; closed Jan; major credit cards accepted). Discovered in the 20th century, Bibione's thermal waters emerge from a hydrothermal basin at about 52°C/125°F and are acknowledged for their therapeutic properties. Bibione's state-of-the-art complex was established to offer curative and rehabilitative spa treatments and programs, including mud therapy, saunas, Turkish baths and hydromassages, as well as general aesthetic treatments and fitness programs. There are two hotels in the complex, but this is also a great place to come just for the day. In addition to the spa facilities, there is an outdoor and indoor pool. Tickets for the thermal center can be purchased for the day, depending on the services you're interested in. Note that the hours of the various services and facilities within the complex vary.

■ Dining Out

 Duilio (Via Strada Nuova 19, Caorle, ☎ 0421-81087; closed Mon in winter and for the month of Jan; major credit cards accepted; €€€-€€€€). Since Duilio first opened its doors in 1959, this nautical-themed restaurant has been well known for its expertly prepared fish-based dishes. Colored lanterns, fishing nets, an old wine press and a *bragozzo* (a hand-painted antique fishing boat from Caorle) decorate Duilio's dining room, where *polenta e seppoline* (their *Buon Ricordo* dish) and *risotto alla onda di mare* are among the most popular dishes served. For dessert try the *frutta dorata Duilio* (caramelized fresh fruit). Duilio's wine list features predominantly Italian wines and their in-house sommelier will be happy to help you choose the wine that best complements your dish. Request a table outdoors in summer; at publication time they had plans to open a greenhouse room.

Da Tituta (Viale Panama 2, Caorle, ☎ 0421-210022; major credit cards accepted; €€-€€€). You may have to stop and ask for directions to reach Da Tituta, just outside of Caorle's historic center, but seafood lovers will agree that it is worth the effort. There isn't much in the way of seafood that you won't find on the menu here and you can count on it to be excellent. I usually begin with a *misto* of hot and cold seafood antipasti. For a *primo*, try the tagliatelle in a red lobster sauce or the seafood *broeto* (soup) served with polenta. Then, for a second course, request the *piatto misto grigliato,* a mix of fresh grilled fish served with white polenta, or try their grilled *capelunghe* (razor neck clams). Don't hesitate to order their table wine and try their *sorbetto*. If you plan to dine here on a Sun, arrive ahead of the crowds. Meals are so relaxed that the last lunch guests walk out the door just before the early dinner guests arrive.

■ Accommodations

 Savoy Beach Hotel (Corso Europa 51, Bibione, ☎ 0431-437317; handicap-accessible rooms; breakfast included; major credit cards accepted; €€€). The Savoy Beach is a contemporary seaside hotel next to Bibione's thermal center and an ideal place to retreat for a few days any time of year. All of the Savoy's rooms are spacious, with private balconies, many facing the Adriatic. Elevators and a tunnel provide guests with direct access to Bibione's thermal center from their hotel floor, and each room has its own cabin with an umbrella and lounge chair on the beach. Unlike many other seaside hotels, the Savoy is open year-round.

Villa dei Dogi (Via Cadore 5, Caorle, ☎ 0421-88125, www.villadeidogi.it; €€). Outside of Caorle's center on the bank of the Livenza River, this lovely villa that once belonged to Venice's doges is set back from a main road surrounded by pretty gardens. Accommodations are comfortable and a cut above what you'll find in the historic center, but you'll need a car for this to be a convenient option.

Stellamare (Via del Mare 8, Caorle, ☎ 0421-81203, www.hotelstellamare.com; €€). On the seaside promenade a short walk from Caorle's historic center, the Stellamare is a newly renovated hotel with comfortable, modern rooms. Many have sea views and there are several conjoined rooms that are ideal for families.

■ Shopping

The **general market** is on Saturday mornings in Caorle.

An **antique market** takes place in Jesolo the second Saturday of each month.

■ Tourist Offices

APT - Bibione
Via Maia 37
Bibione
☎ 0431-442111

APT - Caorle
Calle delle Liburniche 16

Caorle
☎ 0421-81085
APT - Jesolo
Piazza Brescia 13
Lido di Jesolo
☎ 0421-370601

■ Websites

www.bibionecaorle.it
www.jesolo.it
www.venetiancoast.com

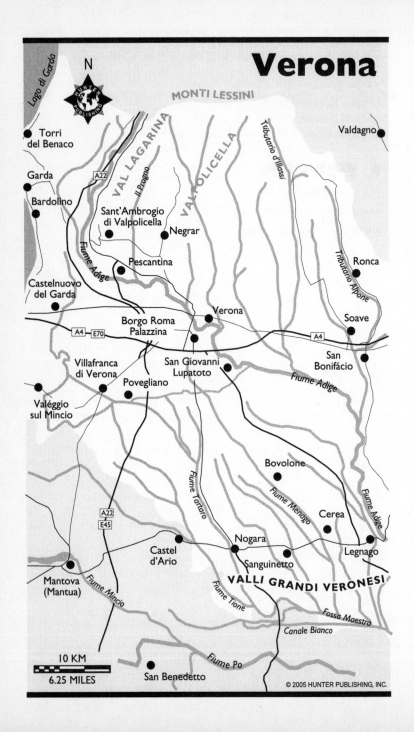

Province of Verona

Despite Verona's status as a forward-thinking cosmopolitan province, the vast ruins, castles, churches and fortifications anchored throughout the territory provide a solid reminder of its significance to the Holy Roman Empire, the Scaligeri dynasty and the Venetian Republic over the centuries.

On the western side of the Veneto region, Verona is an extremely diverse province that is divided into several zones: Lake Garda and the Olive Riviera, Monte Baldo, the Lessini Mountains, Valpolicella, Est Veronese, Bassa Veronese and, of course, the city of Verona.

As the province's capital and the region's second-largest city, Verona is a tourist hot spot that was once a key base in the Roman Empire's northward expansion.

The province has developed a distinctive, sophisticated character and among its greatest contributions to the Italian economy are its D.O.C. wines, olive oil, agricultural products and tourism.

■ Verona

As one of the most prosperous cities in northern Italy and the second-most visited in the Veneto, Verona's streets exhibit an interesting mélange of Roman, medieval, Renaissance and Venetian influences. And with unmistakably firm roots in classical tradition, the city that underwent significant urban development following World War II has a cosmopolitan identity that its high-fashion stores and impeccably dressed businessmen reflect.

At the crossroads of two important Roman roads, Verona served as a critical strategic and commercial center for many centuries. It began as a colony of the Roman Empire in the first century BC and was joined with the Empire in 49 BC. The arena, one of the world's best-preserved Roman amphitheaters, was built to accommodate upwards of 20,000 spectators and, along with the Roman theater and the city's gates, Verona maintains its Roman identity today.

Over the centuries many ruling families and factions came to Verona and in the 12th century it was a free commune. Catastrophe struck in the form of a major earthquake in the 12th century, badly damaging many of the city's important monuments, including the Arena. By the early 13th century, Ezzelino da Romano came to power in Verona where he ruled until 1259. Shortly thereafter, the powerful Scaligeri dynasty (not always popular but eventually remembered for bringing peace to the city) came to rule Verona until the late 14th century.

Great cultural and artistic developments took place during the Scaligeri rule, particularly under Cangrande I, who hosted Dante Alighieri at his court in the early 14th century and Dante dedicated a canticle of the *Divina Commedia's Paradiso* to Cangrande. Judging from the names of the family's mighty rulers, such as Cangrande (Big Dog) and Mastino I (Mastiff), you might expect their symbol to reflect their peculiar obsession with canines. Instead, when you're exploring Verona, keep your eyes open for the *scala* (ladder) that is their trademark.

After the Scaligeri, Verona came under the rule of many other parties, including the Republic of Venice when the city served as an important connection along a trade route between Venice with Genoa. Later, the French and Austrians dominated Verona before it finally joined the Kingdom of Italy in 1866.

A magical city in its own right, Verona is more than Roman ruins, noble palaces and Gothic and Renaissance buildings. Thanks to Luigi da Porta and William Shakespeare, the author and the playwright who eternalized the city in their tales of Romeo and Juliet, Verona retains a certain mystique that attracts so many each year.

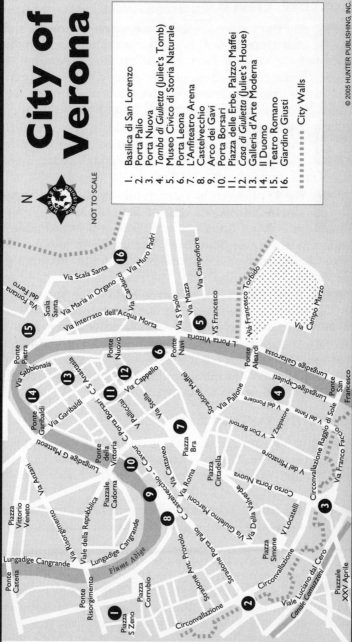

City of Verona

N

NOT TO SCALE

1. Basilica di San Lorenzo
2. Porta Palio
3. Porta Nuova
4. *Tomba di Giulietta* (Juliet's Tomb)
5. Museo Civico di Storia Naturale
6. Porta Leona
7. L'Anfiteatro Arena
8. Castelvecchio
9. Arco dei Gavi
10. Porta Borsari
11. Piazza delle Erbe, Palzzo Maffei
12. *Casa di Giulietta* (Juliet's House)
13. Galleria d'Arte Moderna
14. Il Duomo
15. Teatro Romano
16. Giardino Giusti

▪▪▪▪▪▪▪ City Walls

© 2005 HUNTER PUBLISHING, INC.

Verona

Getting There

 By Car: Verona is easily accessible via the **A4** highway from Lake Garda, Vicenza, Padua and Venice. Exit **Verona Sud** and follow indications for the *centro*. Coming from points north or south of Verona, take **A22** and exit at **Verona Nord**. Verona is about 55 miles from Padua, 75 miles from Venice and 37 miles from Vicenza.

 By Bus: The principle bus station in Verona is at the **Porta Nuova railway station** and buses travel frequently to Verona from Lake Garda, Vicenza, Padua and Venice. www.aptv.it

 By Train: Verona's main railway station is Verona **Porta Nuova**, which is on both the Milano-Venezia and Roma-Brennero lines. The trip from Padua to Verona is about one hour, from Vicenza 35-45 minutes and from Venice between 1½ and 2¼ hours from Peschiera del Garda.

 By Plane: Venice's **Marco Polo** is the Veneto's primary airport with numerous international and domestic flights daily. An alternative airport approximately 10 km southwest of Verona is **Valerio Catullo di Verona-Villafranca**, but it offers fewer flights daily and only connects to select destinations. (Information, 6 am-midnight, ☎ 045-8095666, www.veronaairport.com).

Getting Around

 On Foot: The best way to cover all of Verona's nooks is on foot. There is so much to discover and, since bus and car traffic is restricted in the historic center, bring your best pair of walking shoes.

 By Bike: Bicycles can be rented from June through Sept on the corner of Via Roma and Piazza Bra.

 By Taxi: Radio Taxi Verona (☎ 045-532666, www.radiotaxiverona.it, 24-hour service). Taxis can be found at the Verona Porta Nuova railway station as well as in Piazza Bra, Piazza Erbe, Piazza S. Zeno and

Above: The canal during Carnevale
Below: Boats in port on Lake Garda

Above: Soave

Below: Port and lakeside promenade in Peschiera del Garda

Above: Lake Garda (Archivio Provincia di Verona)

Below: The Funivia (cable car) from Malcesine on Lake Garda leads to the top of Monte Baldo (Archivio Provincia di Verona)

Above: Performance of Aida *at Verona's Arena (Archivio Provincia di Verona)*

Below: Verona's Roman Arena (Archivio Provincia di Verona)

Piazza S. Giorgio. Radio Taxi also offers service to Valerio Catullo Airport and taxi service for the disabled.

 By Car: There are several zones within Verona's historic center that have traffic restrictions and can only be accessed by cars at specific times of day (with certain exceptions for local residents and visitors going directly to hotels). Consequently, navigating the streets of Verona by car can be a challenge and it is advisable to park in one of the many lots or garages, including **Parking Arena** on Via Bentegodi and **Gran Garage Touring** in Piazza Cittadella. There are also several park-and-rides outside the historic center. Cars can be rented at Verona's Porta Nuova railway station from **Avis** (☎ 045-8000663), **Hertz** (☎ 045-8000832) and **Europcar** (☎ 045-592759).

 By Bus: Although Verona can be traversed on foot, if you prefer a bus, lines 70/71 and 72/73 make several stops throughout the historic center (including the Arena) and are a good way to get around town. These buses pass stops on their route approximately every 10 minutes from early in the morning until the evening. The AMT city buses are orange and tickets should be purchased at newsstands or tobacconists prior to boarding.

Another way to get around town (especially on a rainy day) is the **Verona tour bus, Romeo** (Romeo@servizi.amt.it), a service available only from June-Sept that tours the city in approximately an hour and a half. Headsets are available for a guided tour, and you can purchase tickets on the bus or in the tobacco store Rossini located in Piazza Bra 62/B. The bus departs the western end of Piazza Bra, Tue-Sun, 10 am, 11:30, 1 pm and 3:30. The tour is €15 for adults. On Saturday, the 3:30 tour combines a walking tour with an English- and German-speaking guide on board for €20.

Adventures on Foot/Sightseeing

Exploring Roman Verona

Allow 45-60 minutes to walk the route, plus additional time to see the sites.

One of the most obvious and central locations to begin a tour of Roman Verona is at the **Anfiteatro Arena** (Piazza Bra,

☎ 045-8003204, www.arena.it; Tue-Sun, 8:30 am-7:30 pm, Mon, 1:30-7:30 pm; during opera season, 9 am-3:30 pm, €3.10, free admission with VeronaCard). This is undoubtedly one of the best-preserved monuments from the Roman Era and is most commonly referred to as the *Arena*. The elliptical

structure is said to be Europe's third-largest amphitheater after those in Rome and Naples; it was here that many gladiators fought to their deaths. Since 1913 it has been the home of Verona's summer opera season.

After visiting the arena, walk around to its back until you reach the **Mura di Gallieno** (in Piazza Mura Gallieno), remains of the third-century wall named after the Roman Emperor Gallieno that once extended along Via Leoncino to Porta Leona.

From here, follow Via Leoncino until you reach Via Cappello and turn left. Here you'll find ruins of the base of a tower and a mid-first-century gate.

Just a few steps ahead on the right are ruins of the **Porta dei Leoni** gate, one of the main entrances to the city. Above its middle column is an inscription indicating that the gate was built when Verona was already a municipality (with sidewalks, streets and sewers).

Continue along via Capello to **Piazza delle Erbe**, which once served as a Roman forum and is today a large market square. Walk toward the opposite end of the square where there stands a column with the winged lion of St. Mark. Turn right onto Corso S. Anastasia and follow it until you reach the church of S. Anastasia.

Turn left here onto Via Massalongo and then right onto Via Ponte Pietra. Follow this road until it ends in a small piazza where you'll find a panoramic view of the Ponte Pietra and Teatro Romano.

From here retrace your steps back to Via Ponte Pietra and follow it to the **Ponte Pietra**, a first-century stone bridge that was restored by the Scaligeri, destroyed during World War II and then rebuilt using some of the original material.

Cross the bridge and turn right onto Via Rigaste Redentore. Just up the road on the left is the **Teatro Romano e Museo Archeologico** (Rigaste Redentore 2, ☎ 045-8000360; Tue-Sun, 8:30 am-7:30 pm, Mon, 1:30-7:30 pm; ticket office closes at 6:45 pm; €2.60, free admission with VeronaCard). Built at the beginning of the first century AD, its remains were discovered in the 19th century. Since 1948 the theater has been the seat of

Estate Teatrale Veronese and many theatrical events take place, including Shakespearian plays as well as dance performances and the jazz festival. The museum houses Greek, Roman and Etruscan artifacts.

Retrace your footsteps back over the bridge and toward Piazza delle Erbe along Corso S. Anastasia, which turns into Corso Porto Borsari. Just ahead is the **Porta Borsari**, originally called *Porta di Giove* (Jupiter's Gate). This first-century AD construction was the city's other main gate and there are now several shops and cafés surrounding it.

Verona

Past the old Roman gate, the road turns into **Corso Cavour**, which once served as an important Roman road.

Up ahead on the right you'll come to a square with the **Archi Gavi**, originally constructed nearby in the first century to honor the wealthy Gavia family, but rebuilt in the 20th century after its 18th-century destruction by French troops.

Continue up the road and turn left onto Via Roma, which leads back to Roman Arena where the tour ends.

Scaligeri Verona

Allow 45-60 minutes to walk the route and additional time to see the sites.

 The VeronaCard can be purchased at various museums, monuments, churches and some tobacconists. It is possible to purchase a one-day card for €8 that allows free use of city buses and free access to the city's museums, monuments and churches. For visitors planning to spend more than a day in Verona, consider purchasing a three-day pass for €12. This is a great value and an inexpensive way to see the city.

Beginning in Piazza Bra, follow Via Roma to the **Castelvecchio**, constructed along the river during the second half of the 14th century toward the end of their reign by the Scaligeri. Used almost exclusively for military purposes over the centuries, it houses the **Museo di Castelvecchio** (Corso Castelvecchio 2, ☎ 045-594734; Tue-Sun, 8:30 am-7:30 pm, Mon, 1:30-7:30 pm; ticket office closes at 6:45 pm; guided tours can be arranged; €3.10; free admission with VeronaCard). It exhibits a large collection of 14th- to 18th-century Veronese art, including works by Bonsignori, Bellini,

Virgin & Child (Francesco Bonsignori, 1455-1519)

Veronese, Mantegna and Tintoretto. On the ground floor there is a large equestrian statue of Cangrande, circa 1335. Once known as San Martino in Aquaro, the castle was constructed between 1354 and 1356 by Cangrande II della Scala. While visiting the castle, cross the fortified bridge for panoramic views of the castle and the city.

From the castle, continue on Corso Cavour as it turns into Corso Porta Borsari and Corso S. Anastasia until you reach **St. Anastasia's Church** (Piazza S. Anastasia; Mar-Oct, Mon-Sat, 9 am-6 pm, Sun, 1-6 pm; Nov-Feb, Mon-Sat, 10 am-4 pm; closed Mon; free admission with VeronaCard). Constructed by Dominican Friars between the 14th and 15th centuries, Verona's largest church houses several important frescoes, including Pisanello's *San Giorgio e la Principessa* and an important Gothic fresco by Altichiero (right).

Verona

From here, return to Via S. Anastasia until reaching Via Cavalletto and turn left, then right toward the Piazza Signori. Here sits the **S. Maria Antica** church and the **Arche Scaligeri**, a Veronese-Gothic steepled tomb on the church's grounds. Among those buried here is Cangrande I (Big Dog). At Via Arche Scaligeri 4 you'll find a plaque indicating the **Casa di Romeo**, Romeo's legendary house (now a restaurant) and from here turn back to Piazza Signori.

Piazza Signori, unlike mercantile Piazza delle Erbe, was part of the prince's palace and used for ceremonies and events. Located here is the **Loggia del Consiglio** (a Renaissance building), the **Palazzo di Scaligeri**, the **Palazzo del Commune** (also known as Palazzo della Ragione) with its **Cortile Mercato Vecchio** and **Scala della Ragione** and the **Torre dei Lamberti** (Cortile Mercato Vecchio, ☎ 045-8032726; Tue-Sun, 8:30 am-7:30 pm, Mon, 1:30-7:30 pm; ticket office closes at 7 pm; €2.10 by elevator, €1.50 on foot; free admission with VeronaCard).

Continue out of the Piazza Signori into Piazza delle Erbe and turn left onto Via Cappello; just ahead on the left is the entrance to the courtyard and entrance to **Casa di Giulietta** (Via Cappello 23, ☎ 045-8034303; Tue-Sun, 8:30 am-7:30 pm, Mon, 1:30-7:30 pm; ticket office closes at 6:45 pm; €3.10, free admission with VeronaCard). Legend has it that the heroine of the Shakespearian tragedy once lived here in what has become one of Verona's most symbolic places, but in fact there is no proof that the Capuleti family lived here. Many say that touching Juliet's bronze statue in the courtyard will bring luck in love, but you'll have to find out for yourself.

Tourist Trap: While a trip to Verona might not be complete without a visit to Juliet's house, unless you go at an off-hour, the courtyard is usually mobbed with crowds and has been vandalized with graffiti over the years, making it rather unattractive.

After visiting the house, exit the courtyard, turn right and then left onto the famous shopping street **Via Mazzini** and follow it until you reach Piazza Bra.

Continue through Piazza Bra and walk around the Arena until you reach Via Pallone. Turn right onto Via Pontiere. Up ahead on the left is a courtyard with the **Tomba di Giulietta e Museo degli Affreschi** (Via del Pontiere 35, ☎ 045-8000361; Tue-Sun, 8:30 am-7:30 pm, Mon, 1:30-7:30 pm; ticket office closes at 6:45 pm; €2.60; free admission with VeronaCard). See Juliet's tomb and a museum of frescoes in the medieval cloisters of a Capuchin monastery. The church is where they were supposedly married and access to the gardens here is free. Just as the authenticity of the lovers has been debated, so has the validity of this tomb. This is where the tour concludes.

Sacred Verona

Associazione Chiese Vive (Corte S. Elena, Piazza Duomo 35, ☎ 045-592813, www.chieseverona.it; Mon-Fri, 9 am-12:30 pm). Visiting any one of the following churches costs €2, but the cumulative ticket that allows entrance into all of them is €5. Churches are strictly off-limits during religious services.

Basicila di San Zeno (Piazza S. Zeno, Mar-Oct, Mon-Sat, 8:30 am-6 pm, Sun, 1-6 pm; Nov-Feb, Tue-Sat, 10 am-1 pm and 1:30-4 pm, Sun, 1-5 pm; closed Mon; free admission with VeronaCard). The majority of this Romanesque basilica, dedicated to Verona's patron saint San Zeno, who was said to have converted  Verona to Christianity in the fourth century, dates back to the 12th century. The ornate church's red and white striped exterior is characterized by bands of red brick and white stone and at the church's west entrance are bronze paneled doors depicting scenes from the Bible and the life of San Zeno. Within the church pay special attention to the crypt of San Zeno, Andrea Mantegna's 15th-century altarpiece *Madonna and Saints* (below) and the rose window, referred to as the Wheel of Fortune.

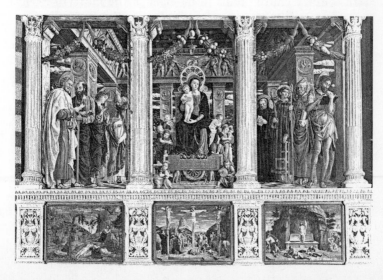

Verona

Church of San Lorenzo (Corso Cavour; Mar-Oct, Mon-Sat, 10 am-6 pm, Sun, 1-6 pm; Nov-Feb, Tue-Sat, 10 am-1 pm and 1:30-4 pm; closed Mon; free admission with VeronaCard). Evidence suggests that a sixth-century Christian church once stood on the site of this Romanesque church built in 1117.

Church of Santa Anastasia (Piazza S. Anastasia; Mar-Oct, Mon-Sat, 9 am-6 pm, Sun, 1-6 pm; Nov-Feb, Tue-Sat, 10 am-1 pm and 1:30-4 pm, Sun, 1-5 pm; closed Mon; free admission with VeronaCard). Verona's largest church is a Gothic construction designed by Dominican friars and erected between the 13th and 16th centuries. Its distinguishing features are the 12 large Verona Red marble columns and its unfinished facade. Be sure to look for the water font of the *gobbo* (hunchback). Some say that touching a humpback on his hump brings good fortune.

Church of San Fermo Maggiore (Stradone S. Fermo; Mar-Oct, Mon-Sat, 10 am-6 pm, Sun, 1-6 pm; Nov-Feb, Tue-Sat, 10 am-1 pm and 1:30-4 pm, Sun, 1-5 pm; closed Mon; fee admission with VeronaCard). This  11th-century church built in memory of the martyrs Fermo and Rustico has cloisters on two levels, the lower Romanesque (shown above) and the upper Gothic. Its vaulted wooden ceiling is beautiful.

Duomo (Piazza Duomo, Mar-Oct, Mon-Sat, 10 am-5:30 pm, Sun, 1:30-5:30 pm; Nov-Feb, Tue-Sat, 10 am-1 pm and 1:30-4 pm, Sun, 1-5 pm; closed Mon; free admission with VeronaCard). One of the most striking pieces of art housed in Verona's cathedral is Titian's 16th-century altarpiece, the *Assumption*.

Other Sites

Scavi Scaligeri (Cortile del Tribunale, Piazza Viviani 5, ☎ 045-8077504; exhibitions, 10 am-7 pm; ticket office closes at 6:30 pm; closed Mon; ticket prices and hours vary; reduced admission with VeronaCard). Visit the remains of a fifth-century Roman building.

Giardino Giusti (Via Giardino Giusti 2, ☎ 045-8034029, spring and summer, 9 am-8 pm; fall and winter, 9 am-7 pm, €5). The terraced gardens were designed for the 16th-century Giusti Palace and contain marvelous fountains, grottoes, mythological statues, a labyrinth, and Cyprus trees. This tranquil garden is perfect for an afternoon stroll.

Museo Lapidario Maffeiano (Piazza Bra 28, ☎ 045-590087; Tue-Sun, 8:30 am-2 pm, Mon, 1:30-7:30 pm; ticket office closes at 7 pm; €2.10; free admission with VeronaCard). This museum houses Greek, Roman and medieval epigraphs collected by an 18th-century Veronese scholar.

Museo Civico di Storia Naturale (Lungadige Porta Vittoria 9, ☎ 045-8079400, www.museostorianaturaleverona.it; Mon-Thurs and Sat, 9 am-7 pm, Sun, 2-7 pm; closed Fri; €2.10; free admission with VeronaCard). Since 1962 Verona's natural history museum has exhibited a great collection of botanical, geological and historic artifacts.

Adventures

On Water

Verona dall'Adige-Equipe d'Acqua Viva Verona (Via Confortini 7, ☎ 347-8892498, www.adigerafting.it). Set out on the Adige River in a raft and tour Verona's fascinating sites from a different perspective. Excursions from Feb through Nov depart from the Diga del Chievo and the Ponte Catena. Evening excursions are possible and all excursions are organized with a minimum of six participants (€18 per person). Lifejackets, helmets and paddles are provided and excursions should be scheduled several days in advance.

> **Panoramic view:** For one of the best views of Verona, follow Via Castel S. Pietro up to the S. Pietro hilltop across the Adige River from Verona's historic center.

Cultural Adventures

Idea Verona (Stradone Provolo 16, ☎ 045-8015352, www.ideaverona.com). Want to enhance your trip by speaking to someone other than your English-speaking hotel clerk? Consider a few intensive Italian courses at Idea Verona located within the Istituto Salesiano Don Bosco near Castelvecchio and learn to read more than a restaurant menu during your stay in Italy. Since 1998, professional instructors have been immersing students in Italian language and culture in courses that typically last for four weeks but can be arranged for fewer depending on participant's needs and schedule. Courses focus on vocabulary, grammar, conversation and culture and are appropriate for students at every level. And if a one-on-one crash-course is what you have in mind, inquire about the school's individual lessons. Classes typically have five or six students (12 is the maximum during high seasons) and enrollment entitles students to use the school's computer and music rooms, take free guided tours of Verona and other cultural courses. Instructors arrange cooking classes in a nearby villa, as well as fresco, opera, literature, and art history courses. The friendly staff also assists students in arranging lodging with families or in nearby apartments, hotels or bed and breakfasts.

Lingua IT (Via Anfiteatro 10, ☎ 045-597975, www.linguait.it; 9 am-noon and 4-6 pm; closed mid-Dec through mid-Jan). Located behind the amphitheater, this small language school offers intensive language courses and individual lessons to beginner through advanced students. The multilingual instructors conduct courses solely in Italian and possess several years of classroom experience. The institute also offers students the option of enrolling in other cultural classes such as music, history, art and cooking and arranges frequent guided tours of other towns in Northern Italy. At time of publication the school had plans for expansion.

 For Kids: If you're in search of a playground to bring some fun into your little one's sightseeing day, try the **Campo Giochi Per Bambini**, a playground just across Castelvecchio's bridge.

With Wine

 L'Enoteca – Istituto Enologico Italiano (Via Sottoriva 7/B, ☎ 045-590366, www.enotecaverona. com; 9:30 am-12:30 pm and 3:30-7:30 pm; closed Mon morning and Sun; major credit cards accepted). Verona's oldest and largest enoteca is in a 17th-century palazzo and has an expansive medieval wine cellar with nearly 2,000 wines. Once used as a warehouse for goods being transported via the Adige, it was later a refuge during World War II bombing raids. The enoteca organizes one or two wine tastings each month and individual tastings may also be scheduled on request. One of their oldest vintages is a Cognac from 1802 valued at nearly €20,000 dollars. Tastings consisting of three wines cost between €15 and €20, depending on the wines. Signor Bixio has owned this enoteca since 1978 and, in addition to the tastings, sells many wines and other locally produced gourmet products. Each week the enoteca typically showcases a different wine and offers clients a free tasting. Even if you're only stopping in to purchase a bottle, request a tour of the wine cellar.

Festivities

Schermi d'Amore

This cinema festival takes place each spring in Verona and showcases love in film. Contact the tourist information center for a schedule of events.

Dining Out

 Popular Veronese dishes include *gnocchi*, *pastissada de caval* (horsemeat stew), *il bollito con la peara* (boiled meat with pepper sauce) and *pandoro* (a Christmas cake).

Ristorante 12 Apostoli (Corticella S. Marco 3, ☎ 045-596999; 12:30-2:30 and 7:30-10:30; closed Sun night, Mon and last two weeks of June; €€€€). You may have to search a bit for this historic restaurant whose roots date back to 1750, but discovering it is your prize. Named after a group of 12 business people who once met in this locanda to conduct business, this restaurant was founded in a building erected

above the ruins of a Roman road and Roman temples, and the foundation of a 13th-century noble family's home built with pieces of the arena after an earthquake (all discovered in the 1980s during renovation work). The elegant medieval-style dining rooms have frescoed, vaulted ceilings and a posh atmosphere, but don't get too comfortable here before requesting to start your meal with an aperitif in the cantina where you can tour the ruins. History and ambience aside, this restaurant is one of Italy's restaurants of *Buon Ricordo* for good reason (see page 39). The kitchen puts a delicately creative spin on traditional recipes like *tortelli al branzino con salso al finocchio* (pasta with a fennel sauce) in order to appeal to today's tastes. Since the early 1900s the Gioco family has owned 12 Apostoli and has been honored with prestigious awards for the work of its fine chefs.

Antica Bottega del Vino (Via Scudo di Francia 3, ☎ 045-8004535; closed Tue, 9:30 am-3 pm and 6 pm-midnight; €€-€€€). On a side street off Via Mazzini, this place dating back to 1890 once catered to many famous poets, painters and journalists and today draws everyone from students and businessmen to tourists. Its kitchen serves mainly traditional favorites, particularly grilled meats and polenta dishes and homemade pastas. And while the food is good, it shouldn't come as a surprise that, with a name like Bottega del Vino, what they all really come for is the wine, particularly Amarones and Barolos. Crowds last well into the night here and if you're looking for somewhere to sink into a glass of wine among the locals, this is the place.

Cesare Club Sottoriva (Via Sottorive 42, ☎ 045-8002255; 12-2:30 pm, 7:30-10 pm; closed Sun; reservations recommended; €€€). You'd hardly expect such an elegant dining experience tucked into a small alley off Sottoriva, but that is exactly what you'll find here. Upon entering, the narrow uninviting hallway might throw you off, but reserve your judgments. This small restaurant is in a lucky position along the Adige River and has a limited number of tables split between the panoramic room overlooking the river and an intimate room with a fireplace. You'll only find fish on the menu here, but if you aren't opposed to that, you'll find it to be very good.

Many of their fine dishes feature lobster and shrimp so be prepared to spend a bit for your meal here.

Ristorante Arche (Via Arche Scaligere 6, ☎ 045-8007415, 12:30-2:30 pm and 8-10 pm; closed Mon for lunch and Sun, as well as three weeks in Jan; €€€). Since 1879, four generations of the Gioco family have been bringing refined tastes to Verona and Chef Giancarlo Gioco carries on the tradition started by his great grandfather in this historic establishment beside Romeo's house. Originally a tavern, then an inn, the building's history likely dates to the 15th century and it has been frequented by luminaries like Gabriele D'Annunzio, Maria Callas and Ernest Hemingway (where didn't he dine?). The elegant restaurant's specialty is fish and, with its fine linens, professional service, old-fashioned recipes and historical charm, this is not a place to grab a quick bite and run. Bring your friends and your appetite and savor a delightful meal in good company.

Osteria Giullietta & Romeo (Corso S. Anastasia 27, ☎ 045-8009177, 12:30-2:30 pm, 6:30-10:30 pm; closed Sun and Mon at lunchtime, as well as two weeks in June; €€). The family-operated osteria-enotecca named for the famed lovers serves traditional Verona dishes at fair prices. Their menu consists of classic dishes such as *bigoli ai torchi all acciuga con uvetta e pinoli* (pasta with anchovies, grapes and pine nuts) and *pastissada de caval* (horsemeat stew) but they also cater to less exotic tastes with an international menu featuring *pappardelle al pesto* (ribbon pasta with pesto sauce) There are nearly 300 Italian and French wines to choose from and desserts are homemade. The dining rooms are small and the upstairs room is decorated with black and white photos of Verona.

Caffè Rialto (Via Diaz 2, ☎ 045-8012845, www.grupporialto.it; summer, 7 am-2 am; winter, 7 am-midnight; closed Mon; €€). Part of a group of Verona eateries, this small pizzeria and restaurant behind the Arena has a large selection of pizzas and first and second courses. It's particularly popular with the theater crowd after performances at the Arena and has continuous hours that make it perfect for dining at off-peak time.

Brek Ristorante (Piazza Bra, see *Padua*, page 88)

Accommodations

Expect to spend more on accommodations in Verona than in many other cities in the Veneto. If you're concerned about getting the biggest bang for your buck and you don't mind taking a train or bus into town daily, consider staying in one of the smaller towns in the Veronese countryside where you're more likely to find quaint rooms and good hospitality at a lower price.

Due Torri Hotel Baglioni (Piazza Sant'Anastasia 4, ☎ 045-595044, www.baglionihotels.com; major credit cards accepted; €€€€€). The most discerning travelers will appreciate the imposing grand foyer marked by ceiling frescoes, lush velvet couches, fresh floral arrangements and red Verona marble columns from the 1300s. This charming hotel in the historic center was once a 14th-century Scaligeri palazzo called *Dell'Aquila*. It is by far one of Verona's finest sleeps, and over the years has hosted many illustrious visitors, including Mozart, Goethe, Wagner, Pavarotti and Sting. The exclusive rooms in this prestigious establishment are richly decorated with period furnishings. Its **Ristorante All'Aquila** features 18th-century porcelain from Japan and China and a 19th-century bronze statue by Gregolli di Torini.

Hotel Accademia (Via Scala 12, ☎ 045-596222, www.accademiavr.it; breakfast included; major credit cards accepted; €€€€). The elegantly furnished rooms and fine hospitality make the Accademia an excellent choice. It may be a good value during off-peak season, but is rather over-priced during high season (although its prime location off Verona's high-fashion shopping street, Via Mazzini, may justify the price for some). There are several suites for guests in need of extra comfort but even the standard rooms are spacious and tastefully decorated. At time of publication the hotel was readying rooms to accommodate disabled guests.

Hotel Torcolo (Vicolo Listone 3, ☎ 045-8007512, www.hoteltorcolo.it; €€€). This is one of the city's most sought-after hotels primarily for its hospitable staff, convenient location and inexpensive rooms. On a side street near the Piazza Bra, Silvia Polmari and Diana Castellani have run the small 19-room establishment for years. The small foyer seems a bit outdated, but the rooms are quite comfortable, albeit simple, each tastefully decorated and with en suite bathrooms. It is in the heart of the action in Verona and can get a bit noisy even in the evenings, but overall this is one of the better values in town. Breakfast is available (though not included) and is served in an indoor room and outdoors on the street-side terrace. The ladies are very helpful and speak English well, always offering useful travel advice to guests. If you're traveling solo, there are singles as well.

Hotel Trieste (Corso Porta Nuova 57, ☎ 045-596022, www.hotel-trieste.it; breakfast included; major credit cards accepted; €€€-€€€€). A family-run establishment since the mid-20th century, Hotel Trieste is a lovely hotel centrally located near both Verona's train station and the Piazza Bra. The multilingual staff is very friendly. The six floors are designated either smoking (with marble flooring) or non-smoking (with carpeting) and rooms have private balconies (even if many do overlook the main road) and safes. Some of the rooms are dark, though rooms on the top floor have been newly renovated and are quite airy, with sloped ceilings and large bathrooms. The continental breakfast buffet is a good spread. If you come by car, the hotel has its own parking garage. **Another bonus:** They have their own bicycles for guests to take around town free of charge.

Hotel Bologna (Piazzetta Scalette Rubiani 3, ☎ 045-8006830, www.hotelbologna.vr.it; breakfast included; €€€-€€€€). While the rooms at this hotel are quite plain, both the location and the service are very good. Only a few steps from the arena in a building dating back to the 1200s, the hotel has a few rooms (110, 230 and 350) that have a view of Piazza Bra and the arena. The hotel's restaurant is popular with the late-night theater crowd.

Hotel De'Capuleti (Via del Pontiere 26, ☎ 045-8000154; breakfast included; major credit cards accepted; €€€€). Part of the Best Western chain, De'Capuleti is near Juliet's tomb, just outside the historic center. All rooms are standard with en suite bathrooms and modern amenities.

Budget Accommodations

Villa Francescatti (Salita Fontana del Ferro, ☎ 045-590360; €). In a 16th-century villa that hardly appears to be a youth hostel, though it is one, the Villa Francescatti offers budget-conscious travelers a fair option in a city where hotel prices swell, particularly during summer months. The basic rooms vary in size and linens and lockers are provided to each guest. Beware that the 11:30 pm curfew is enforced and the bathrooms with communal showers leave something to be desired.

Shopping

Verona hosts some of the world's most exclusive designers and its classy urban boutiques are located primarily along Via Mazzini on the north end of Piazza Bra. The buildings on this road are very pretty and, even if you're only window-shopping, it's a nice street to stroll along. The upscale boutiques here include Louis Vuitton, Bulgari, Swarovski and Cartier. Corso Porta Borsari is also quite famous for its fashionable shops.

Shops are generally open from 9 am-12:30 pm and reopen from 3:30-7:30 pm daily, but this can vary. Remember that they are typically closed on Monday morning.

> **Tip:** If you plan to shop during your stay in Verona, stop into the tourist office and request the *Guida allo Shopping in Centro Storico*, a helpful guide that lists shops in Verona and even includes a discount card that is accepted at many retailers around town.

A **general market** takes place in Piazza delle Erbe, Monday through Saturday, but Verona's most expansive market is at the Stadio Bentegodi (the soccer stadium) on Saturday mornings.

An antique, arts and crafts market takes place in Piazza San Zeno the third Saturday of each month.

Nightlife & Entertainment

 Opera Festival at the Arena (Via Dietro Anfiteatro 6/B, ☎ 045-8005151, www.arena.it; box office, Mon-Fri, 9 am-noon and 3:15-5:45 pm, Sun, 9 am-noon; opera season box office hours, performance days, 10 am-9 pm, no performance, 10 am-5:45 pm). *Aida* and several other operas are performed in the ancient Roman arena each summer. This opera season began in 1913 with a performance of *Aida* in honor of the 100th anniversary of Verdi's birth. Now several other Verdi works are also performed here and tickets typically range from €70 to €150. Many restaurants near the Arena remain open very late to accommodate theatergoers after performances.

Teatro Camploy (Via Cantarane 32, ☎ 045-8008184; ticket sales on evenings of performances only). Most performances at the Teatro Camploy are amateur and local theater and take place during the winter season.

Teatro Filarmonico (Via dei Mutilati, ☎ 045-8002880, www.arena.it; Mon-Fri, 9 am-noon and 3:15-5:45 pm, Sat, 9 am-noon; performance days, ticket office open from 3:15 pm until performance begins; on days of matinee performances, office opens at 2:30 pm; closed Mon after performances). Construction on the theater began in the early part of the 18th century and, although it was destroyed during World War II, it was rebuilt to its original design and now hosts classical concerts, opera and jazz performances from Oct through May.

Teatro Romano (Rigaste Redentore 2, ☎ 0458-066485, www.estateteatraleveronese.it; ticket office, Palazzo Barbieri, Via Leoncino 61, Mon-Sat and performance days, 10:30 am-1 pm and 4-7 pm). Near the Adige River, the Teatro Romano hosts Verona's Estate Teatrale Veronese from June through Aug each year. This summer theater program includes a Shakespeare festival, a jazz festival and many dance performances.

Teatro Filippini (Vicolo Dietro Campanile Filippini, ☎ 045-592709). This theater showcases primarily children's and family theater. Performances include fairy tales, puppet shows and short plays, taking place on weekday mornings and Sunday afternoons.

Sports

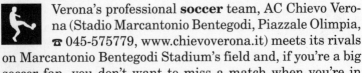 Verona's professional **soccer** team, AC Chievo Verona (Stadio Marcantonio Bentegodi, Piazzale Olimpia, ☎ 045-575779, www.chievoverona.it) meets its rivals on Marcantonio Bentegodi Stadium's field and, if you're a big soccer fan, you don't want to miss a match when you're in town. Check the website or contact the tourist information center for details.

Nightclubs

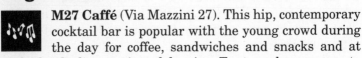 **M27 Caffé** (Via Mazzini 27). This hip, contemporary cocktail bar is popular with the young crowd during the day for coffee, sandwiches and snacks and at night for the live music and dancing. Try to make your way to the upstairs room where there are sofas and tables and an outdoor terrace.

Internet Access Points

Internet Train
Via Roma 17A
(between Piazza Bra and Castelvecchio)

Lui e Lei Gelateria
Via Leoni 4/F
(near the Porta Leona)

Internet Bar
Via Redentore 9/B
(near the Teatro Romano)

Tourist Offices

IAT
Via degli Alpini 9
Verona
☎ 045-8068680

IAT
Piazzale XXV Apre (at Verona's train station)
Verona
☎ 045-8003638

Websites

www.verona-apt.net

www.verona.net

www.veronashopping.it

www.tourism.verona.it

www.veronaitalia.it

www.veronatuttintorno.it

www.visitverona.it

■ Soave

The charming fortified town of Soave, between the Valle d'Illasi and the Val d'Alpone, is surrounded by verdant hills that are world-famous for their production of Soave D.O.C. wine and it's dominated by a well-preserved 10th-century castle.

The name *Soave* most likely derives from *a* reference to the Swabian people who settled in the area in approximately 568 with the Longobards, but evidence (including coins and crockery) suggests that long before then Soave was a village during the Roman period. It is probable that centuries ago, the Postumian Way (SS11 that runs alongside the A4) was a significant access road used for military purposes. The town's strategic location made it long contested and over the centuries Soave came to be ruled by many prominent families. During the rule of the Venetian Republic, the town experienced great prosperity.

Perched on a hillside among vineyards, Soave's intact walls with 24 towers enclose the town center, marked by narrow streets, wineries, Gothic buildings and several palazzi, including **Palazzo di Giustizia** (that once served as the law courts) and **Palazzo del Capitano**.

Evidence of grape cultivation in this zone dates back to ancient times and Soave's wine has become internationally recognized.

A *Bandiera Arancione* town (see below), Soave makes for a pleasant side-trip from Verona or Vicenza and is a delightful place to sample local wines, experience the charm of a sleepy medieval town and enjoy a break from a hectic itinerary.

The ***Associazione Paesi Bandiera Arancione*** unites communities around cultural, historical, gastronomic and environmental factors and promotes tourism in these small towns. The Veneto's Bandiera Arancione towns are: Arquà Petrarca, Mel, Montagnana, Portobuffolé and Soave.

Getting There

 By Car: Soave is on the **A4** highway approximately 20 km east of Verona and 30 km west of Vicenza. It is also accessible from Venice and Padua via the A4 motorway.

 By Bus: To reach Soave from Verona by bus, take the Verona-San Bonifacio line, which runs daily several times each hour and takes approximately 45 minutes.

 By Train: The nearest train station to Soave is in San Bonifacio, along the Milano-Venezia line. From both Verona and Vicenza to San Bonifacio the train ride is 15-20 minutes, from Padua it is generally 35-45 minutes and from Venice just over one hour. From San Bonifacio's railway station, APTV buses run several times each hour to Soave and take less than 10 minutes.

 By Plane: Venice's **Marco Polo** is the Veneto's primary airport, with numerous international and domestic flights daily. An alternative airport approximately 10 km southwest of Verona is **Valerio Catullo di Verona-Villafranca**, but it offers fewer flights daily and only connects to select destinations. (Information, 6 am-midnight, ☎ 045-8095666, www.veronaairport.com).

Getting Around

Soave is a small, sleepy village that is easy to travel on foot. Park outside of Soave's walls in one of the lots and explore the narrow streets on foot.

Sightseeing

 Castello Scaligero (Via Castello Scaligero, ☎ 045-7680036; summer, 9 am-noon and 3-6:30 pm; winter, 9 am-noon and 2-4 pm; closed Mon). One of the best-preserved medieval fortifications in the Veneto region, the Soave castle dates back to the early 10th century, and over the centuries passed into the hands of many promi-nent ruling families, including the Scaligeri, who enlarged the castle in the 13th century. This medieval castle's walls cascade down the hillside and enclose the small town center. The castle features a draw-bridge at the entrance, several rooms decorated in period fur-nishings and a small study with several paintings of Dante and other illustrious figures.

> **Tip:** Don't forget to walk to the top of the *mastio* (the large tower) for beautiful views of the Monti Lessini. The walk up to the castle from Piazza Antenna takes about five minutes and is somewhat steep. It is possible to park at the top just outside of the walls instead of parking in the town center and walking up to the castle.

Adventures

Driving

 La Strada del Vino Soave (The White Wine Road) winds through the vineyard-clad territory north of Soave and passes many wineries, churches, villas and castles that call to mind the history and culture of the ancient land. Beginning at Soave's northern gate, travel west along Route 37, passing through San Vittore and Colognola ai Colli at the beginning of the Illasi valley. From here, follow signs to San Pietro di Lavagno and then on toward Illasi and to Costeggiola, Castelcerino and Costalunga. Then travel to

Ronca and back towards Monteforte D'Alpone before returning to Soave. Vineyards, cherry trees and olive trees mark the
lovely scenery. Signs mark the wine route, but if you have
extra time, explore some of the smaller roads off the main
wine route.

Tourist Trap: Caldiero's
Terme di Giunone, an old
Roman bath center near
Soave, is still open to the
public, but it has not been as well maintained
as many of the other thermal bath centers in
the Veneto region. This was once an important thermal bath but is disappointing and
probably not worth the side trip.

With Wine

Soave and its surrounding territory form one of
Italy's major wine production zones, world-famous
for its production of *Soave Classico*, *Soave D.O.C.* and
Recioto di Soave D.O.C.G. The Soave area encompasses
numerous towns, including Soave, Monteforte d'Alpone, San
Martino, Mezzane, Colognola ai Colli, Illasi and Ronca. The
principal grape variety (one of Italy's oldest) is *Garganega*,
but the *Trebbiano di Soave* grape is also frequently used. The
title *Classico* is reserved for products made from grapes that
have been harvested and vinified in the municipalities of
Soave and Monteforte d'Alpone.

Coffele (Via Roma 5, Soave, ☎ 045-7680007, www.coffele.it;
9 am-12:30 pm and 2-7 pm; closed Sun; call prior to visiting on
Sat). In the early 1970s Giovanna Visco, heir to the noble
Visco family's wine estate that had dissolved several years
earlier, decided to leave the teaching profession along with
her husband, Giuseppe Coffele, to revive her family's tradition. In the 1800s the Visco family established an important
wine estate in the zone that Giovanna and Giuseppe, along
with their two children Alberto and Chiara, take great pride
in. One of Soave's premier wineries, Coffele produces approximately 100,000 bottles each year, including *Soave Classico*,
Ca Visco and *Recioto di Soave* wines made from primarily

Garganega grapes. Their wines are exported to Germany, Switzerland, Holland, Belgium, Norway, Sweden, Great Britain, the USA, Australia and Hong Kong. Wine tastings can be arranged upon request, but Signor Coffele, who spends much of his time tending his grapes, is particularly happy to take visitors for a tour of his vineyards in Castelcerino (seven km north of Soave) to demonstrate the relationship between art and science in the process. Wine tastings generally cost €6 per person for three wines and €12 when served with cheese. They often take place at the large banquet table in the main hall but if you're fortunate enough to arrive on a pleasant day, the Coffele family may invite you into their garden that sits just below Soave's castle (one of the prettiest settings in town) for wine tastings. If not for the award-winning wine alone, stop in to chat with the friendly owners who take great pride in their winemaking tradition and are interested in imparting their knowledge to visitors.

Cantina del Castello (Corte Pittora 5, Soave, ☎ 045-7680093, www.cantinacastello.it; Mon-Fri, 8:30 am-12:30 pm, 2:30-6:30 pm, Sat, 8:30-12:30 pm; closed Sun). The Cantina del Castello in Soave's historic center is housed in what is believed to have been the 13th-century palace of the Sanbonifacio Counts. The winery produces approximately 120,000 bottles of *Soave Classico* each year, including *Brut di Soave Classico*, *Soave Classico*, *Cru di Soave Classico*, *Recioto di Soave Classico* and *Grappa*. Their wines are exported to the US, Japan, Germany, England, Belgium, Holland and Norway and their most characteristic wines include the *Soave Classico D.O.C.* and the *Pressoni D.O.C.* The approximate cost of a wine tasting consisting of four wines is €8 per person. The tour and tasting last 1½ hours and should be scheduled in advance. Request an English-speaking guide when scheduling your visit.

Pieropan (Via Camuzzoni 3, Soave, ☎ 045-6190171, www.pieropan.it; Mon-Fri, 8:30 am-12:30 pm and 2:30-6 pm, Sat, 9 am-12:30 pm; closed Sun and two weeks in Aug). Founded in 1890 by Dr. Leonildo Pieropan, the tradition of vine cultivation and wine making has been in the Pieropan family for three generations and today his grandson and his family carry on this practice, always employing innovative methods. The winery has developed extraordinarily over the decades and now produces nearly 350,000 bottles annually, many of which are exported to the USA, Germany, Belgium, Luxembourg, Denmark, Japan, Australia and Russia. Their most characteristic wines include the *Soave Classico*, *Calvarino* and *La Rocca*. The winery is within Soave's walls just a few steps from Piazza Antenna, but visitors should call ahead to arrange a tasting and tour. A guided visit and a tasting consisting of four wines is typically €7, and English-speaking guides can be arranged on request.

Festivities

 Since 1929, Soave has been celebrating **La Festa dell'Uva**, a cultural and folkloric event that takes place the third week of September each year and showcases the *Garganega* grape and products that derive from it.

La Festa Medievale del Vino Bianco di Soave takes place the third weekend of May annually and is a medieval celebration with a procession in period costume, wine tastings and a variety of cultural festivities.

Dining Out

 Lo Scudo Soave Ristorante (Via San Matteo 46, Soave, ☎ 045-7680766; 12-2 pm and 8-10 pm; closed Sun evening and Mon; €€€). Operated by a mother and son team, Lo Scudo specializes in local dishes and is one of Soave's more elegant spots to enjoy a fine meal. Since 1988, this one-time 16th-century abbey just out of Soave's Porta Verona has housed a restaurant popular with locals and tourists for its classic dishes that showcase the finest seasonal products. The menu changes frequently and some of their most requested dishes include the *risotto con rosmarino e Monte Veronese* (rice with rosemary and Monte Veronese cheese) and *canelloni ai carcofi e noci con fonduta di formaggi allo zafferano* (pasta filled with artichokes and nuts with a saffron cheese sauce). For dessert, try their *sfogliattine di mele con la salsa arancia* (pastry with apples and an orange sauce). The indoor dining rooms are lovely (albeit small) with marble floors and a refined atmosphere, but if the weather permits, request a table *al fresco* where you can savor Chef Giovanni's dishes.

Enoteca Il Drago (Piazza Antenna, Soave, ☎ 045-7680670; €€). This enoteca in the heart of town is a popular spot for an informal lunch or an evening meal. Located in an old palazzo, the interior has a medieval style, with its large stained glass windows and booth seating. Outdoors, the terrace looks out onto Piazza Antenna, Soave's main square. The menu offers a good selection of *bruschetta* (toasted bread rubbed with garlic and topped with tomatoes) and, if you like radicchio, try the *bruschetta* with Monte Veronese cheese and red radicchio.

> *E' il vino della giovinezza e dell'amore, non sarebbe piu adatto per me, carico di anni e amatore discreto come sono. Ma io bevo in omaggio al passato: se non mi ridà i miei venti anni, me ne ravviva il ricordo.*

It is the wine of youth and of love, no longer suited for me, burdened as I am with years and discrete lovers. But I drink in homage to the past; it will not give me back 20 years, but it will revive the memory.

~ Gabriele D'Annunzio, on Soave wine

Accommodations

Hotels

Hotel Roxy Plaza (Via San Matteo 4, ☎ 045-6190660, www.hotelroxyplaza.it; breakfast included; pet-friendly; major credit cards accepted; €€€). Just beyond the old castle's walls, the Roxy Plaza (open since 1999) offers guests non-smoking, spacious rooms with hardwood floors and modern furnishings. If your budget permits, there are four junior suites entitled "Giulietta e Romeo" with a pretty view of the castle. Guests may use the hotel's bicycles to explore the town and, upon request, the staff will organize tours of nearby wineries.

Relais Villabella (Via Villabella 72, San Bonifacio, ☎ 045-6101777; breakfast included; major credit cards accepted; €€€). Just a few miles beyond Soave's historic center is a renovated 17th- to 18th-century country house with spacious and elegantly appointed accommodations, a pool in the garden and all modern amenities. Consider a stay here in lieu of an over-priced Verona sleep. The train ride is only 15-minutes from Verona, the setting is peaceful, and you're only a hop from some of the best wineries in Soave.

Shopping

The weekly **general market** in Soave takes place Tuesday morning on Via Roma and Via Camuzzoni.

Soave hosts an **antique market** the third Sunday of each month.

Tourist Offices

IAT
Piazza Antenna 2
Soave
☎ 045-6190773

Websites

www.turismo.estveronese.it

www.comunesoave.it

www.ilsoave.com

■ South of Garda

Custoza, Villafranca & Valeggio sul Mincio

The territory that encompasses Valeggio sul Mincio, Villafranca di Verona and Custoza dates back to ancient times and was a critical battleground at many stages throughout history due to its strategic location.

A few miles south of Lake Garda, but still very much a part of its culture and character is Valeggio sul Mincio, most noted for its refined cuisine that shares its origins with both the Veneto and Lombardy regions.

The castles in both Valeggio and Villafranca, as well as those in several other villages in the zone, were ruled by the Scaligeri during the Middle Ages, and centuries later they still attest to the highly strengthened defense systems.

The small village of Custoza just northwest of Villafranca has a long tradition of vine cultivation and wine making and is famous for its production of the *Bianco di Custoza D.O.C.*

Getting There

 By Car: The best way to reach Valeggio sul Mincio from Verona and points east is by taking the **A4** highway to the **Peschiera del Garda exit** and following signs for Valeggio sul Mincio. To reach Villafranca, Custoza and Sommacompagna, **exit A4** at **Sommacompagna** and follow signs.

 By Bus: The **Verona-Pozzolengo line** originates at Verona's railway station and makes stops in Villafranca, Custoza and Valeggio every one to two hours on weekdays.

 By Train: The two nearest train stations are in Villafranca and Peschiera del Garda. It takes approximately 15 minutes to reach Villafranca from Verona, 1½ hours from Padua and two hours from Venice. The Villafranca station (on the Mantova-Verona line) is about 12 km from Valeggio sul Mincio, and the Peschiera del Garda station is about 13 km from Valeggio sul Mincio. It takes just over an hour from Padua to reach Peschiera del Garda, 15 minutes from Verona and approximately two hours from Venice.

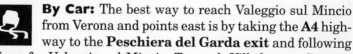 **By Plane:** Venice's **Marco Polo** is the Veneto's primary airport with numerous international and domestic flights daily. An alternative airport that is approximately 10 km southwest of Verona is **Valerio Catullo di Verona-Villafranca** but it offers fewer flights daily and only connects to select destinations (6 am-midnight, ☎ 045-8095666, www.veronaairport.com).

Sightseeing

 Museo Nicolis (Viale Postumia, Villafranca, ☎ 045-6303289, www.museonicolis.com; Tue-Sun, 10 am-6 pm; €5.50). The Museo Nicolis features an interesting collection of automobiles, motorcycles and bicycles that chronicle the evolution of transportation technology. The museum exhibits many unique automobiles, including the Pia Motorcar (1884), the first vehicle built with a gas engine, and the Alfa Romeo RL (1923), the company's first model. From luxury vehicles to cars that made historic journeys, the contemporary museum illustrates an interesting history that motor enthusiasts will enjoy.

Castello Scaligero (Villafranca). Construction on this medieval fortification likely began in the early 13th century, but it wasn't until the 14th century under Scaligeri rule that the 16-km *Serraglio* defense walls were added,

leading from Villafranca's castle to those at Nogarole Rocca and Valeggio sul Mincio. Although only sections of this wall still remain today, Villafranca's castle itself is in good condition and is occasionally used during summer for concerts and outdoor cinema events. The **Museo del Risorgimento** (Sat, 4-6 pm, Sunday, 3-6:30 pm) is in the castle and contains relics from the Italian wars of independence, including sabres, helmets and weaponry. It is possible to visit the castle's tower on Sunday (winter, 3-5 pm; summer, 5-7 pm; €2).

The wide **Ponte Visconteo**, the remains of an ancient fortification, stretches across the Mincio River and can be traversed by car or on foot. From here you'll have a nice view of **Valeggio's Castello Scaligero**, (the only military fortress under control of Giangaleazzo Visconti) and the surrounding countryside.

Adventures

On Foot

Parco Giardino Sigurtà (Valeggio sul Mincio, ☎ 045-6371033, www.sigurta.it; Mar-Nov, 9 am-6 pm, €8.50). Once the gardens of the 17th-century *Villa*

Maffei (designed by a student of Palladio) that served as Napoleon III's headquarters in 1859, the Parco Giardino Sigurtà is just south of Lake Garda and can be explored on foot, by a mini-train that travels the seven-km "Magic Route," by bicycle or by golf cart (all for an additional fee). The expansive park features two itineraries (the red and the yellow) that wind through the park's water gardens, tropical fish ponds, herb gardens, box-trees, statues and olive trees. Its pretty grounds make for a peaceful afternoon out, and there are several bars and picnic areas where you can enjoy lunch.

Family Adventures

Picoverde (Via Ossario 19, Custoza, ☎ 045-516025, www.picoverde.it; summer, 10 am-7 pm, weekdays, €9, weekends, €12). Cool off at the Picoverde Water Park – only a few miles south of Lake Garda and a short drive from Verona. From the park's hilltop perch overlooking the Custoza zone, families can enjoy a day of fun activities – the water lagoon for kids, the large pool, water slides, tennis courts, a playground and water aerobics classes. There are lounge chairs and umbrellas, a restaurant, pizzeria, snack bar and first aid services.

With Wine

Cantina di Custoza (Via Staffalo 1, Custoza, ☎ 045-516200, www.cantinadicustoza.it; 8:30 am-12:30 pm and 3-7 pm). Founded in 1968, the cantina's vineyards are primarily on the low rolling hills south of Lake Garda. Call ahead to request a tasting if time permits; otherwise stop in to purchase a bottle from the large *punto di vendita* (point of sale/shop) where locals fill their oversized jugs from large wine pumps (that look similar to gas pumps).

> **Tip:** *Bianco di Custoza D.O.C.* is a light-bodied, straw-colored white wine produced in a concentrated zone south of Lake Garda using primarily Trebbiano Toscano, Garganega, Tocai Friulano, Malvasia Toscana, Riesling Italico and Cortese grape varieties. It is a dry, fragrant wine and is particularly good served with fish and cheese.

Verona

Festivities

 Festa del Nodo d'Amore takes place on the third Tuesday of June each year, along Valeggio's Visconteo Bridge. Nearly 3,000 people gather for a large *cena* (dinner) to celebrate local cuisine, including Valeggio's characteristic *tortellini*, known more commonly here as *nodi d'amore* (knots of love).

Golf

Golf Club Verona (Ca' del Sale 15, Sommacampagna, ☎ 045-510060, www.golfverona. com). This 18-hole course west of Verona offers year-round golf in a gentle country landscape. Featured here are a clubhouse located in a renovated farmhouse, a restaurant, bar and proshop. Many agree that the 13th hole is the course's most challenging.

Dining Out

Valeggio sul Mincio's location near the border of the Mantua province has had a significant impact on the local gastronomy that fuses elements from both the Veneto and Lombardy regions. Valeggio sul Mincio's classic dish is *tortellini* (*nodi d'amore*), pasta prepared from a light dough and filled with meat, pumpkin, artichokes, ricotta, spinach and other fresh ingredients, then served either in a *brodo* (broth) or topped with butter and sage.

Villafranca's characteristic dessert, *sfogliatine* (puff-pastry made with *aqua di fiume* liquor), has been an important element of the town's gastronomic heritage for years and is sold at pastry shops around town.

Antica Locanda Mincio (Via Michelangelo Buonarotti 12, Borghetto, Valeggio sul Mincio, ☎ 045-7950059, www.anticalocandamincio.it; 8:30 am-4 pm and 6 pm-midnight; closed Wed evening and Thurs; €€). When he was in command of the Italian Army more than two centuries ago, Napoleon reportedly stopped at this locanda. But with its history dating back to the 1600s, he was not the only illustrious figure to have set foot in the restaurant. Located near the Villaggio il Borghetto, it is well known for trout dishes as well as *agnolotti* (a type of tortellini) prepared from an antique recipe. The indoor rooms are warmly decorated, but on a nice day ask for a table on the terrace overlooking the river.

Fantoni (Corso Vittorio Emanuele 165, Villafranca, ☎ 045-7900304; €). Villafranca's broad avenue leading from the castle hosts several cafés and *pasticcerie* but none are as celebrated as Fantoni (1842). In the café's early days its pastry chef Fantoni was well known for his inventive desserts, and was apparently a friend to many legendaries, including the poet d'Annunzio who visited his shop. Fantoni's most famous dessert is a Villafranca favorite, *sfogliatine*. From the looks of it, the dark café doesn't seem special, but its pastries are excellent.

Accommodations

Apartments

 Villaggio il Borghetto (Via Raffaello Sanzio 14/A, Borghetto di Valeggio sul Mincio, ☎ 045-7952040, www.borghetto.it; reception, 9:45 am-12:45 pm and 3-7 pm; €€€€). Along the shores of the Mincio River, this vacation village in six antique *mulini* (mills) overlooking the Ponte Visconteo is clearly something special. If you're in the market for a romantic getaway, or simply prefer your overnight stay touched with class, consider one of the Villagio's 12 suites that can be booked daily or weekly.

Each charmingly decorated suite has its own special attributes, including hardwood floors, beamed ceilings, exposed stone walls, and kitchenettes. Certain suites also feature fireplaces, terraces and lofts. My personal favorites are *La Cascata*, the most requested suite, with views of the waterfall and Ponte Visconteo, or *Le Rocche,* with a classy dark-wood kitchenette and an upstairs loft particularly suitable for children. *La Mansarda* is one of the more spacious suites, while *Il Camino* features an old fireplace in the kitchen area. Each suite comes equipped with a private bathroom, television, air conditioning and hairdryers; some have sleeper sofas that accommodate an additional two guests (there is an extra fee for more than two people per room).

Housekeeping and room service are available and meals delivered to suites come from the **Café Mulino** and the **Enoteca Divinosteria**, both located within the village.

Villagio il Borghetto also features the ice cream shop, **Borgo Antico Gelateria**, and several small shops geared to visitors. The mill's paddle wheels, probably dating back several centuries, still function and enhance the romantic atmosphere of the village. If you have your bike in tow, ask at the reception for guidance on how to reach the nearby bicycling path that leads to Lake Garda. Budget-conscious travelers may find this to be one thing worth splurging on; if not, at least stop by to walk around the village and admire the attractive scenery.

Shopping

La GrandeMela Shopping Land (Lugnano di Sona, ☎ 045-6081815; Mon, 2-10 pm, Tue-Thurs and Sat, 9 am-9 pm, Fri, 9 am-10 pm, closed Sun; www.lagrandemela.it). If you're interested in experiencing a European-style mall, you need a rainy day escape from Lake Garda, want to purchase some high-fashion Italian merchandise before your return trip or if you're just interested in grabbing a bite at McDonalds, stop into La GrandeMela Shopping Land. Included in this shopping center are stores such as **Sisley**, **Stefanel**, **Benetton**, **Sergio Tacchini**, **Swatch**, **Foot Locker**, **Mandarina Duck**, **Warner Brothers**, **Walt Disney** and **Toys Center**. Additionally, there are several eateries, a cinema complex, an entertainment center and a bowling alley.

The **antique market in Villafranca** takes place along Corso Vittorio Emanuele the second Sunday of each month.

Valeggio sul Mincio's antique market is the fourth Sunday of each month in the town center.

The **general market in Villafranca** is held on Wednesday in the town center and in **Valeggio sul Mincio** on Saturday mornings.

Tourist Office

Pro Loco
Piazza Carlo Alberto
Valeggio sul Mincio
☎ 045-7951880

Websites

www.villafranca.it

www.comune.villafranca.vr.it

www.valeggio.com

■ Lago di Garda

Italy's largest lake and one of its most visited vacation spots, Lake Garda is between the Alps and the Pianura Padana (Padana plains) with the Trentino region bordering it to the north, the Lombardy region to its west and the Veneto region to the east.

Lake Garda has an unusually mild climate and its northern zone is frequently compared to Nordic fjords, while its southern area is more similar to a Mediterranean environment. The eastern shore, known as the *Riviera degli Olivi*, or the Olive Riviera, was named for the large-scale olive cultivation there.

The Olive Riviera extends for about 32 miles from the most narrow northern points, where it is bordered by spectacular mountains, to the widest southern shore, bordered by gently sloping vineyard-covered hills.

Many Scaligeri castles and fortifications built to defend the family dynasty in the 13th and 14th centuries, along with Romanesque churches and Venetian-style villas, add a fascinating dimension to the beautiful landscape of olive and lemon groves, oleanders, palm trees and vineyards.

The lake is an attractive destination for those in search of both active and relaxing vacations, with most resorts open from April until October.

Regular breezes from the north provide ideal conditions for wind and water sports, including paragliding, windsurfing, sailing, yachting and fishing. The nearby hills and Monte Baldo are perfect for mountain biking, trekking and horseback riding.

The Olive Riviera is also a gastronomically rich region thanks to the wines and extra virgin olive oil, fish from the lake and many seasonal products locally grown in the Alpine environment of Mount Baldo, the hills and the plains.

Verona

The Riviera may seem far-removed from the hustle and bustle of city life, but is only a stone's throw away from northern Italy's metropolitan areas.

Getting There & Getting Around

 By Car: Exit either the **A4** (Milano-Venezia) motorway at **Peschiera del Garda**, or the **A22** (Brennero-Modena) motorway at **Affi** and follow signs toward the Riviera's towns.

 By Boat: (Piazza Matteotti, Desenzano, ☎ 030-9149511, www.navigazionelaghi.it). The ferry (*traghetto*) service between Torri del Benaco and Maderno transports passengers and vehicles and takes approximately 30 minutes. The ferry service between Malcesine and Limone also carries vehicles and takes approximately 25 minutes. Motorboats and hydrofoils travel between Desenzano and Riva del Garda year-round, making many stops, including Peschiera del Garda, Lazise, Bardolino, Garda, Torri del Benaco and Malcesine on the eastern shore of the lake and Gardone, Salo and Maderno on the western shore.

 By Bus: APTV (www.aptv.it) buses 62 and 64 travel between the Verona Porta Nuova railway station and Riva del Garda, stopping in Peschiera del Garda, Lazise, Bardolino, Garda, Torri del Benaco and Malcesine (including the Gardaland and CanevaWorld theme parks). Buses run about once hourly in both directions.

 By Train: The railway station in Peschiera del Garda is the principle station serving the Veneto side of Lake Garda. Peschiera sits on the Venezia-Milano line and trains depart frequently for this station from Verona Porta Nuova, the province's main railway station. Peschiera del Garda is approximately 15 minutes by train from Verona. For more information: www.trenitalia.com.

 By Plane: Venice's **Marco Polo** is the Veneto's primary airport with numerous international and domestic flights daily. An alternative airport that is approximately 10 km southwest of Verona is **Valerio Catullo di Verona-Villafranca** but it offers fewer flights daily and only connects to select destinations (6 am-midnight, ☎ 045-8095666, www.veronaairport.com). Shuttle buses run regularly from the airport to the Verona railway station where travelers can take a quick train ride to the lake.

Tour Operators

For tours around the Garda zone and all of the Veneto, **LagoTourist** (Via Capitanato 2/3, Malcesine, ☎ 045-7400512; Piazza della Chiese 20, Garda, ☎ 045-7255722, www.lagotourist.it) organizes themed excursions, sports and theater events, cooking and wine courses and a wide variety of activities for travelers.

> **Tip:** Despite the large crowds, the best time to visit the lake is April through October. You'll find many restaurants, hotels, shops and sports outfitters closed during other periods, which can be disappointing, unless your plans only include taking in the scenery.

Adventures

Family Adventures

 The surest way to enjoy your vacation is to plan activities the whole family can enjoy. And unless your six-year-old is an art historian in the making, a museum-heavy itinerary may not be much appreciated. Luckily, Lake Garda is a family vacation spot with plenty of theme parks, sports activities and entertainment to make for a memorable vacation.

On Water

 The opportunities for water sports are endless in the Garda zone, from windsurfing and sailing to diving and water skiing and, depending on what you're looking for, certain towns are better equipped than others.

On Foot

 There are many designated walking paths along the Riviera, with some that lead into the countryside, others high above the lake. The lakeside promenades in several of the Riviera's towns are pleasant to stroll along, but if you're up for something more challenging, stop into one of the tourist offices, particularly in Malcesine and San Zeno di Montagna, for maps and advice.

On Bikes

 The diverse topography along Garda's Riviera makes it a great place for cyclists, mountain bikers and recreational bikers of all skill and interest levels, where you can enjoy pedaling for hours. From paved roads, dirt paths, uphill slopes and paths through vineyards and chestnut groves, there are routes for everyone and a number of shops that rent bikes, organize excursions and provide maps and tips.

Beaches

 Most of the Riviera's beaches are pebbled, narrow and quite crowded in summer months. Keep in mind that the beaches are on a lake, not the ocean, and are considerably smaller than what you may be accustomed to.

Food & Drink

 Lake Garda's cuisine is highly regarded for its diversity. It benefits from ingredients grown around Mount Baldo (chestnuts, truffles, honey and mushrooms), the rich agriculture from the hills around Verona (grapes, kiwi, asparagus and peaches), the premium extra virgin olive oil from the Olive Riviera and Lake Garda's fresh fish (trout, carp, eel and other lake fish).

Fishing has long been one of the most important trades along the Riviera and this had a significant impact on the development of its cuisine. Lake fish are most frequently prepared without heavy sauces and you're likely to find fish that are *lessata* (poached), *al cartoccio* (in foil), *ai ferri* (grilled) and *fritte* (fried).

Several popular fish dishes you can expect to find on the Veronese lakeshore include *risotto con la tinca* (rice prepared with tench, a type of fish), *le aole fritte* (small fried fish that are munched like French fries) and *lavarello alla griglia* (grilled lake trout).

Garda's extra virgin olive oil ranks among Italy's best, due in part to the gentle climate and low acidity of the oil.

Many world-famous wines are produced locally, including Bardolino and Valpolicella that both complement and are used to prepare many local dishes.

Accommodations

 Lake Garda is one of the top holiday destinations not only in Italy, but all of Europe, and there are an abundance of accommodations to choose from along the Riviera, whether you are planning a visit for a day, week or summer.

There is certainly no shortage of hotels along the Olive Riviera, the majority of which are two- and three-star rated that cater to families and couples, with entertainment, sports activities and half- and full-board options.

Camping is also extremely popular in most Riviera towns, but if you didn't pack your tent or arrive with your trailer, many sites rent bungalows and trailers. Campsites and tourist villages offer an economical option to families and many have large facilities with swimming pools, supermarkets, game rooms, bars, sports tournaments, planned excursions and evening entertainment. Additionally, apartments are ideal for visitors who plan to spend a week or longer in the Garda zone.

Shopping

The best products to shop for along the Riviera are locally produced olive oil, wine, cheese and honey and, although many shops sell these items, the local weekly markets are a great place to sample and purchase a variety of products. These markets typically take place mornings in the historic city centers and also sell fresh produce, clothing, leather goods and household items.

General Markets

Mondays – Peschiera, Torri del Benaco

Tuesdays – Castelnuovo

Wednesdays – Lazise

Thursdays – Bardolino

Fridays – Garda

Saturdays – Malcesine

Antique Markets

Bardolino – Third Sunday each month

Torri del Benaco – Wednesday evenings in summer only

Nightlife

Once the summer sun sets over the Lombardian coast of Garda, the night heats up on the Riviera. Discos, piano bars and clubs have live entertainment in the summer months along the Riviera. Many large hotels also organize entertainment and, in the summer, there are a variety of concerts and theatrical performances. Check with local tourist offices for a schedule of events.

Tourist Offices	
IAT Peschiera del Garda Piazzale Betteloni 15 Peschiera del Garda ☎ 045-7551673	IAT Valpolicella Viale Ingelheim 7/9 San Pietro in Cariano ☎ 045-7701920
IAT Lazise Via Fontana 14 Lazise ☎ 045-7580114	IAT Torri del Benaco Via F.lli Lavanda ☎ 045-7225120 Apr-Sept only
IAT Bardolino Piazzale Aldo Moro, Bardolino, ☎ 045-7210078	IAT Malcesine Via Capitanato 6/8 ☎ 045-7400044
IAT Garda Via Don Gnocchi 25/27 Garda ☎ 045-6270384	IAT Monte Baldo Via Ca' Montagna San Zeno di Montagna ☎ 045-7285076, Seasonal

Websites

www.lagodigardamagazine.com

www.gardaworld.com

www.gardainforma.com

www.malcesinepiu.it

www.gardalake.it

www.gardacamp.com

www.peschieraweb.it

www.aptgardaveneto.com

Peschiera del Garda

At the southernmost point of the lake where the Mincio River flows out of Lake Garda sits Peschiera del Garda, one of the lake's largest ports and a strategically important town for its ability to control navigation between river and lake.

Peschiera's history stretches back to Roman times when it was known as *Arilica*, and it was later important to many, including the Scaligeri and the Venetians who began construction of its bastion walls in the 16th century.

The walls fortifying Peschiera were built in stages over the centuries and added to by Napoleon and the Austrians. Its harbor, built in the 1860s by the Austrians during the Italian Wars of Independence, is a great departure point for many activities such as sailing, boating and water-skiing.

Peschiera's historic center is quaint and, although the cafés, boutiques and ice cream parlors that characterize its lanes attract primarily tourists, it doesn't have the kitsch touristy atmosphere that some of Garda's other resort towns do.

Sightseeing

 Santuario Madonna del Frassino (Piazza Madonna del Frassino 3, Peschiera del Garda, ☎ 045-7550500 or 045-7552244; summer, 6:30 am-noon and 3-7:30 pm; winter, 6:30 am-noon and 2:30-5:30 pm; free admission). Constructed on the very spot where the Virgin is said to have appeared to a farmer in 1510, this early 16th-century construction draws pilgrims from around the globe. The church contains fine paintings by Paolo Farinati and Zeno di Verona. Adjacent to the sanctuary, the **Casa Francescana di Accoglienza** (where the friars who run the sanctuary live) offers visitors lodging in simple rooms.

Abitato Romano di Peschiera. Evidence of Roman inhabitation still exists today near the old Scaligeri castle in Peschiera del Garda. Remains of a Roman village dating back to the first to fourth-century AD were discovered in 1974 and can be seen off the Piazza F. di Savoia.

Beaches

 There are three pebble beaches within Peschiera's town limits and, although they are small by most standards, they are among the eastern lakeshore's best. **Lido Cappucini** is just outside of Peschiera's center along the promenade. There is a small park here, a few bars and a place to rent paddleboats and lounge chairs. **Spiaggia Fornaci** is a small beach just a bit past **Lido Cappucini** along the promenade and there are pretty views of the lake from here. **Ai Pioppi** can be reached from Lungolago G. Garibaldi and borders the lake on the other side of the Mincio River. There is a large marina, here along with restaurants and an attractive promenade.

Adventures

By Car

 La Gardesana. This 163-km scenic route hugging the coast of Lake Garda is a great way to enjoy the picturesque views of the lake from both the Veronese and the Lombardian shores. Start off in Peschiera del Garda and follow the main road around the lake. Stop off along the route to enjoy the dramatic scenery as it transforms from Mediterranean to Alpine, visit historic sites and sample Garda's signature cuisine.

 This route is highly trafficked during the summer months and, although it can normally be traveled in a few hours, it will take longer when tourists are in town.

On Foot

 Beginning at Punta Marina, Peschiera's main harbor, follow the lakeside promenade southward along the tree-lined lakeshore. From Lungolago G.

Mazzini, the promenade continues through small pebble beaches and is an easy stroll.

On Bikes

 Articoli da Campeggio e Spiaggia (Via Venezia 7, Peschiera del Garda, ☎ 349-4678006; 9 am-8 pm, Easter-Sept only). Bicycles are one of the best modes of transportation around Lake Garda, especially in summer when traffic slows everything to a halt. This small shop rents bicycles for €11 per day (€3 per hour) and also sells beach and camping equipment. Call ahead or arrive first thing in the morning to reserve a bicycle.

On Water

 One of the best ways to experience Lake Garda is by boat and **Peschiera Boat Rental** (☎ 349-7906599) and **Il Pentagono** (☎ 045-6402526), both located in Peschiera's main harbor, make that possible. Four- to six-person motorboats can be rented from one hour up to a full day. Don't want to navigate the lake on your own? Sign up for a guided excursion on Lake Garda and Peschiera del Garda's canals. Pentagono also arranges fishing excursions and canoeing lessons and has additional departures from the Porta Brescia and Ai Pioppi.

Garda Diving – Associazione Sportiva (Camping S. Benedetto, Via Bergamini 14, Peschiera del Garda, ☎ 339-3119080, info@gardadiving.com). Consider exploring the depths of Garda with Garda Diving, located in the S. Benedetto camping village. Divers have the option of daytime, evening, half-day or full-day guided dives with certified instructors. The facility rents everything from masks to fins and also offers diving instruction.

Family Adventures

 Parco Natura Viva (Localita Figara 40, Bussolengo, ☎ 045-7170113, www.parconaturaviva.it; Mar-May and Oct, 9 am-4 pm; June, July and Sept, 9 am-5 pm; Aug, 9 am-6 pm; Nov, 9 am-4 pm, closed Wed; closed Dec and Jan; Parco Safari, €9, Parco Faunistico, €9, combined ticket, €15). Consider an African Safari in lieu of your Italian holiday? At Parco Natura Viva's safari park, you can enjoy both! Visit the safari park by bus or car and see giraffes, zebras, antelopes, lions and tigers up-close. Watch hippos and rhinoceroses cool off in the lake and, if you'd like an English-speaking guide to narrate your adventure, call in advance to request one. Then, head over to the Parco Faunistico and see red pandas, snow leopards and other fascinating animals from around the world in recreated natural habitats. Don't miss the dinosaur park's models and exhibits and the aquarium, with its interesting species of fish, reptiles and amphibians.

Gardaland (Castelnuovo del Garda, ☎ 045-6449777, www.gardaland.it; Apr-mid June, last two weeks in Sept and weekends in Oct, 9:30 am-6 pm; mid-June through mid-Sept, 9 am-midnight; €23). The kids don't have to be along to justify a visit to Italy's number one theme park, Gardaland. More than 40 attractions and several restaurants and shops are contained within the park's four villages and, with several roller coasters and water rides, there is enough fun to keep even the adults satisfied. Medieval shows, pirate ships, a double loop coaster, Magic Mountain, Space Vertigo free fall, and a trip through ancient Egypt with the La Valle Del Re – Gardaland promises a fun-filled day for visitors of all ages. There is bus service during summer months for visitors arriving at the Peschiera del Garda railway station. The main entrance to the park is on the Gardesana (SS 249) between Peschiera del Garda and Lazise.

Cultural Adventures

Alba (Via Marconi 20, Bussolengo, ☎ 045-6755270, www.albascuola.it). Just outside of Peschiera del Garda, this language institute offers Italian language, art, history, cultural and conversation courses. Instructors accommodate students' schedules and interests by offering individual lessons, intensive courses and day and evening courses. One of their highlight programs is a course for six- to 12-year-old children.

Dining Out

 La Plume Grill & Pizza (Viale Risorgimento 1, Peschiera del Garda, ☎ 045-7550584; 6 pm-2 am; €€). This upbeat lakeside eatery with – surprise – a good selection of grilled and fried fish, may be a tourist favorite, but it is excellent. The *gamberoni alla griglia* and their *insalatoni* (large salads) are quite good and their kids' menu will keep the little ones happy.

Al Canal (Via Fontana 3/5, Peschiera del Garda, ☎ 045-7552770; 12-2 pm and 6:30-11 pm; closed Wed; €€). On one of Peschiera's pretty canals, this osteria/pizzeria offers a large selection of pizzas and local dishes and many of its tables overlook the canal. In July and August the kitchen remains open daily.

Accommodations

Hotels

 Hotel San Marco (Lungolago Mazzini 15, Peschiera del Garda, ☎ 045-7550077; www.hotelsanmarco.tv; breakfast included; major credit cards accepted; €€-€€€). Several of the rooms in this small hotel just outside of Peschiera's historic center enjoy pretty views of the lake, though their décor is understated and rather bland. The on-site restaurant is only open during spring and summer months.

Camping

Bella Italia (Via Bella Italia 2, Peschiera del Garda, ☎ 045-6400688, www.camping-bellaitalia.it; €-€€). On Garda's lakeshore, Bella Italia is one of Garda's best-rated and most popular campsites for its expansive, well-maintained facilities and wide range of activities. This tourist village offers guests the option of staying in bungalows, apartments, tents and RVs. Tennis and volleyball courts, several pools, markets, bicycle rentals and eateries are located on-site and a path leads from the village to the pebble beach. Sports activities, including water aerobics, archery and windsurfing, are organized for guests of all ages. In high season (July-Aug) rentals are by the week only.

Camping Cappuccini (Via Arrigo Boito 2, Peschiera di Garda, ☎ 045-7551592, www.camp-cappuccini.com; €-€€). If you're looking to cut costs but not fun, consider a stay at the Cappuccini tourist village. Guests are accommodated in bungalows, apartments and RVs, can access the village's pools, eateries and markets and have a wide range of on-site activities to partake in daily.

Nightlife & Entertainment

 Café Momus (Viale Risorgimento 1/A, Peschiera del Garda, www.cafe-momus.it; Wed-Sun, 6 pm-3 am). Owner Maurizio livened Peschiera's night scene when he opened the hip Café Momus in 2004. This spirited hot spot with a picturesque terrace overlooking Garda draws crowds from Wed to Sun (except from Oct-Dec when it's open only Fri and Sat evenings). Music varies from hip-hop to Brazilian and Cuban and Friday nights usually attract the youngest crowds. In addition to cocktails, wine and mixed drinks, the bar also serves panini, salumi and cheese plates, as well as desserts.

Lazise

An ancient Scaligeri stronghold on the southeastern shore of Lake Garda, the harbor town of Lazise was one of Italy's first free communes more than 1,000 years ago and served as an essential fortified port on Lake Garda for many years. The 14th-century castle and the ring of walls surrounding Lazise's center illustrate the might and influence of the Scaligeri dynasty during the Middle Ages. Another important historic building is the **Dogana Veneta**, or Venetian Customs and Excise house, in Lazise's port. Once used as an arsenal, the Republic of Venice later used it to control its commerce on Garda and today it serves as a congress center and site for many concerts and events.

Tourism began to develop significantly in this lakeside town during the 1950s and today Lazise is one of the preferred holiday destinations on the Riviera degli Olivi. Many of the town's narrow, medieval streets are closed to traffic and lined with craft shops, boutiques, enotecas and eateries, some of which keep their doors open late in the evening during summer months. Although Lazise is more touristy than Peschiera del Garda, it manages to retain a quaint atmosphere that some of the resort towns farther up the coast lack.

Sightseeing

Chiesa di S. Nicolo. This 12th-century Romanesque church has served as a warehouse, theater, barracks and movie theater and, since the 20th cen-

tury, a war memorial chapel. The church houses frescoes from
the 1300s.

Adventures

Family Adventures

Caneva World Resort (Via Fossalta 1, Lazise,
www.canevaworld.it) includes the **Movie Studios
Park** (☎ 045-6969800, www.moviestudios.it;
Apr-Oct, 10 am-6 pm, July and Aug, 10 am-11 pm; €16). And
it also has the **Aqua Paradise Park** (☎ 045-6969700,
www.aquaparadise.it; May-Sept, 10 am-7 pm; €18). The family will enjoy discovering the world of cinema at the Movie
Studios Park, with a studio tour, a special effects show or the
popular Stuntmen Academy Show. Over at the waterpark,
slides, pools, a pirate ship, a fishing village and more provide
a half-day or more of entertainment. But don't let the fun stop
there. Entertainment continues into the evening at the **Rock
Star Café** (☎ 045-6969888, 6 pm-2 am, open year-round) a
rock n'roll themed family restaurant, and the **Medieval
Times Restaurant and Show** (☎ 045-6969777, Apr-Oct,
show times vary on weekday and weekend evenings, reservations necessary).

On Water

**Da Gianni - Giovanni Olivetti Noleggio
Motoscafi** (Zappo 65, Lazise, ☎ 349-4067366). This
water taxi service departs from Porto Vecchio in
Lazise and offers chartered excursions on Lake Garda.

On Bikes

Cicli Degani (Piazzetta Beccherie 13, Lazise,
☎ 045-6470173, deganimotor@libero.it; open daily
from Easter-Oct, 9 am-10 pm; major credit cards
accepted). If you're considering exploring the Garda zone by
bike, Cicli Degani has a large stock of street and mountain
bicycles for rent and charges reasonable prices. City bike
rentals cost approximately €3 per hour, €9 for a day and €45
for one week. If you're interested in guided excursions, check
the board outside the shop for upcoming excursions and
events.

Los Locos (Via Casara di Sotto 20, Lazise, ☎ 045-7581349). This bike shop rents mountain, city and road bikes and will assist customers in arranging guided excursions of the Garda zone. Rentals begin at €11 for a half-day, €22 for a full day and €110 for one week.

Adventures for the Soul

 Parco Termale del Garda (Villa dei Cedri, Piazza di Sopra 4, Cola di Lazise, ☎ 045-6490382, www.villadeicedri.com; Mon-Thurs and Sun, 9 am-1 am, Fri and Sat, 9 am-2:30 am). Garda's thermal park, on the grounds of the neoclassical 18th-century **Villa dei Cedri**, is an ideal place to unwind after an intense day of hiking, cycling or sunbathing. In addition to the hydrating baths, massage services, and a thermal lake, visitors may dine in the **Ristorante Villa Moscardo** and find lodging at the residence's apartments (See *Accommodations*).

Festivities

 In July and Aug each year, **Lazise Notte Classica** brings evenings of classical music and theatrical performances to Lazise's historic center. Check with the tourist information center for an event listing.

Dining Out

Ristorante Kambusa (Calle Prima 20, Lazise, ☎ 045-7580158; 12-2 pm and 7-10:30 pm; closed Mon except for summer; €€€). If you're lucky enough to snag a table at this lakeside favorite, don't miss their exceptional grilled fish. And if you can't decide between fish and pasta, the *bigoli alla tinca* is one of the chef's specialties. The dining room has a warm atmosphere but it is small so reserve your table in advance.

Osteria Antica Corte (Via F.F. Scolari 18/A, Lazise; 10 am-2 pm and 6 pm-2 am; closed Tue; €€). Although this *osteria* is particularly popular in the evening for drinks and music, they also serve plates of salami and *bruschette* (toast with garlic and tomato) topped with seasonal ingredients. If it's a warm evening, grab a table outdoors; otherwise find one upstairs under the exposed beam ceilings.

Accommodations

 Hotel Benacus (Via Roma 10, Lazise, ☎ 045-7580124, www.hotel-benacus.com; breakfast included; €€€). Conveniently situated just outside of Lazise's historic center on a side street near the lake, Benacus is a pleasant hotel and, if you can see past the slightly outdated furnishings, it is a very good value for the area. Many of the rooms have been renovated and have tile floors and new bathrooms. The downside is that they only accept credit cards after a minimum three-night stay.

Alternative Accommodations

La Residenza di Villa dei Cedri (Villa dei Cedri, Piazza di Sopra 4, Cola di Lazise, ☎ 045-7590988, www.villadeicedri.com; €€€€€). The beautiful grounds of the Garda Thermal Park encompass several villas and country houses, including the Residenza di Villa dei Cedri, carefully restored for guests who prefer the privacy and sophistication of an apartment. The modern apartments are spacious and tastefully furnished, have their own kitchenettes and come equipped with air conditioning, television and a safe. The real treat that makes a stay here worth the steep price is that each apartment includes its own thermal room with a Jacuzzi, filled by mineral water from the thermal wells.

Bardolino

Once a prehistoric fishing community, the lakeside resort town of Bardolino is best known for its wine of the same name that has gained increasing recognition in recent years. Approaching Bardolino from the south, you'll notice that the landscape begins to transform here, and there is more of an Alpine sense with the mountains coming into view. The historic center with its long promenade is better than it appears from the main road, though still not quite as charming as some of the southern Riviera towns.

Adventures

Bicycle Rentals

 Leave the car behind and hop on a bicycle at **Ercospazi** (Via B. Cavour 30, Bardolino, ☎ 045-6211422, www.ercospazi.com, 9 am-7 pm) or **Bici Center by Ezio Cardi** (Via Marconi 60, Bardolino, ☎ 045-7211053). Bike and scooter rentals start at €16 and €38 respectively per day.

Culinary Adventure

Museo dell'Olio d'Oliva (Via Peschiera 54, Cisano di Bardolino, ☎ 045-6229047, www.museum.it; Mon-Sat, 9 am-12:30 pm and 2:30-7 pm, Sun, 9 am-12:30 pm; closed Sun in Jan and Feb and holidays, free admission). The olive oil museum just outside of Bardolino on SS249 celebrates the history of an important cultural aspect and displays the olive oil production process, with many pieces of equipment that have been used over the years, including an old lever press, millstones, screw presses and a reconstruction of a 19th-century water-powered oil press. Stop into the shop to taste freshly pressed oil and purchase extra virgin olive oils, as well as other products made with olives from the zone.

With Wine

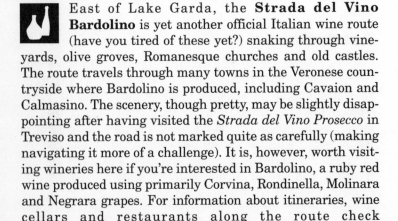 East of Lake Garda, the **Strada del Vino Bardolino** is yet another official Italian wine route (have you tired of these yet?) snaking through vineyards, olive groves, Romanesque churches and old castles. The route travels through many towns in the Veronese countryside where Bardolino is produced, including Cavaion and Calmasino. The scenery, though pretty, may be slightly disappointing after having visited the *Strada del Vino Prosecco* in Treviso and the road is not marked quite as carefully (making navigating it more of a challenge). It is, however, worth visiting wineries here if you're interested in Bardolino, a ruby red wine produced using primarily Corvina, Rondinella, Molinara and Negrara grapes. For information about itineraries, wine cellars and restaurants along the route check www.stradadelbardolino.com.

Museo del Vino - Cantina Zeni (Via Costabella 9, Bardolino, ☎ 045-6228331, www.museodelvino.it; open

Above: Marostica

Below: Ponte Vecchio (Ponte degli Alpini) in Bassano

Ceramics on display outside a shop in Bassano del Grappa

The Grotto di Oliero, near Bassano (courtesy of Ivan Tears)

Above: Valbrenta at dusk (courtesy of Ivan Team)

Below: Rafting on the Brenta River (courtesy of Ivan Team)

mid-Mar through late Oct, 9 am-1 pm and 2-6 pm; Nov to mid-Mar, only the shop is open; free admission). Founded by the Zeni brothers of Bardolino, the Cantina Zeni's Wine Museum exhibits various tools used in wine production and depicts the process through many photos and exhibits. From the vineyard management systems to a 17th-century plow and 14th-century press, the wine museum at the Zeni winery offers a glimpse into the art and science of wine making and the techniques employed in Bardolino's viniculture industry over the centuries. Wine tastings are organized from June through Sept on Mon, Tue and Wed evenings; depending on the featured wines, tastings typically cost €18 for 10 wines served with grissini (breadsticks) and cheese. Weather-permitting, tastings take place outdoors in the gazebo but, unfortunately, at publication time the winery only offered tastings in Italian and German. Tastings other times upon request only.

● **Wine Festivals**

The first weekend of Oct each year, Bardolino hosts the **Festa dell'Uva e del Vino Bardolino Classico**, a manifestation that celebrates Bardolino Classico wine. The festival includes many wine tastings, regional foods, entertainment and informational events and local wineries are on hand selling a large selection of their products.

Each May Bardolino hosts the **Chiaretto Bardolino Wine Festival** in the town center. Local producers of Chiaretto are present for wine tastings, demonstrations, informational sessions and to sell their products.

Accommodations

 Hotel alla Riviera (Via Lungolago Lenotti 11, Bardolino, ☎ 045-6212600, www.allariviera.it; open Palm Sunday through mid-Oct; breakfast included; major credit cards accepted; € *and* €€€). Rumor has it that this 19th-century villa, once the summer home (and scandalous retreat) of a wanton count, was hotly contested during his unraveling marriage and ultimately sold. Since 1939, the Mezzetto family has operated a pleasant hotel in this antique villa on Bardolino's promenade. All rooms have en-suite baths, and several have a view of the lake. There are also five spacious suites with living rooms and balconies. Upon booking you'll likely notice a discrepancy in prices as rooms in the main building are three-star and the simpler rooms in the annex are one-star.

Nightlife

 Orange Disco Garden (Via Monsurei, Bardolino, ☎ 045-6212711, www.orangedisco.it; May-Sept, 9 pm-4 am; closed Mon, Tue and Thurs). You'll quickly realize where Bardolino's hippest dance club gets its name. This orange-inspired dance club is one of the town's hottest spots, drawing not just tourists, but locals as well for dance and (with reservations only) dinner too. Partiers can roam between the indoor and outdoor bars and dance floors to the sounds of house, R&B and hip-hop. Relax in rattan chairs with a drink in hand and enjoy the semi-tropical garden.

Garda

Many wonder what came first – the town or the lake? In fact, this medieval fishing village (historically one of Lake Garda's most important communities), lent its name to the lake, a word that likely derives from the German word *warte*, meaning fortress.

Garda's historic center, smaller and noticeably less charming than its neighbors to the south, has a tree-lined lakeside promenade and side streets with a variety of boutiques and shops catering to tourists. The kitsch atmosphere is more noticeable here than in many other more refined towns farther south. An overwhelming majority of the hotels are overpriced two-stars and few restaurants here are worth mentioning. That said, Garda is still worth a quick stopover if you're driving along the Riviera for a few water sports, some pretty views and, perhaps most importantly the Punta San Vigilio.

Adventures

Just north of Garda's city center is **Punta San Vigilio** (Località San Vigilio, ☎ 045-7256688, www.punta-sanvigilio.it), an enchanting harbor formed where Mount Luppia dives into the lake. The cypress-lined avenue lures visitors toward the Punta San Vigilio, with its 16th-century **Villa Guarienti**, designed by Sanmicheli and surrounded by olive groves, cypress trees and beautiful gardens. This romantic panoramic spot is the perfect place to watch the sunset and has a hotel, **Albergo San Vigilio**, a restaurant and a harbor. Be sure to see the **11th-century olive tree**, the **citrus groves** and **Mermaid Bay Park** (10 am-8 pm, entrance fee), an olive grove leading down to a small beach where there are picnic tables, a playground, a volleyball court, ice cream shop, a beach and shower facilities. A visit here will make it clear why this has been a much-loved retreat among celebrities like Lawrence Olivier, Vivien Leigh and Sir Winston Churchill.

On Wheels

 Velocifero (Via Don Gnocchi 36, ☎ 347-8944605, www.velocifero.com; open Easter-Sept daily, 9 am-7 pm). Even if they are on the pricier side when it comes to bike rentals, Velocifero has the largest selection of well-maintained mountain, road and city bikes in the area and accommodates customers by delivering bicycles to hotels upon request and arranging for guided excursions. If you prefer navigating the zone on four wheels but still want the excitement, consider renting a *Smart*, the ultimate little mini-car that makes traveling (and parking) a cinch and is one of Velocifero's hottest rentals. The shop is located just outside of the town center on the road leading to Costermano.

In Water

 Tinka Diving Center (Via San Bartolomeo 18, Garda, ☎ 338-7765558 or 340-6464825, www.tinka-diving.it). The Tinka Diving Center rents equipment and its certified dive instructors teach beginner to advanced level courses, including Discover Scuba, Scuba Diving and Advanced Open Water Diver. Consult the dive center for rates as they vary depending on the number of guides, equipment rentals and locations of the dives.

Festivities

 Natale tra gli Olivi is Garda's Christmas celebration that takes place from the end of November through January 6th each year in the Piazza del Municipio. Many vendors sell locally produced goods and holi-

Verona

day products. Various entertainment events are organized as well.

Sardellata al Pal del Vo, Garda's sardine festival held at the beginning of July, celebrates the ancient trade of fishing with many events, including a moonlight dinner on fishing boats.

Dining Out

 Giardino delle Rane (Hotel Astoria, Via Lungolago, Garda, ☎ 045-7255278, www.ilgiardinodellerane.com). This "Frog Garden" restaurant on the lake promenade draws more tourists for its relaxed atmosphere than for its food, but that doesn't mean you won't eat well here as long as you stick to something simple. Try the *pizza marinara* (hold the cheese, double the garlic and tomato sauce) or an *insalatone* (large salad). Children like the frog theme here and there are several kid-friendly dishes to satisfy small appetites. The best tables are on the terrace out front.

Accommodations

 Hotel Villa Mulino (Via Don Gnocchi 20, Garda, ☎ 045-7255055, www.villamulino.com; €€€). The old mill wheel in the lobby gave the name to this establishment that is a particular favorite with German visitors, many of whom opt for the half- and full-board packages. The hotel is centrally located and within easy walking distance of Bardolino's promenade. Rooms and bathrooms are on the small side, and in general this is a much better deal if you eat breakfast elsewhere.

Valpolicella Zone

The rich and fertile Valpolicella zone bordered to its north by Trentino and to its west by the Adige River, has been inhabited since Roman times and consists of three major valleys: Negrar, Fumane and Marano. The zone embraces several towns, including Marano, Fumane, Sant'Ambrogio and San Pietro Incariano. In addition to the fine Valpolicella, Amarone and Recioto wines that have been produced for many years in this zone, precious marble and stone are quarried here, including Verona Red and Prun, used as far back as Roman times to construct edifices, including Verona's Arena. Valpolicella's small towns make for a great half- or full-day excursion from Lake Garda or Verona, and wine lovers may enjoy spending even more time soaking in, not just the aesthetic charm of the area, but also the fine cuisine and drink served in restaurants, wineries and inns.

Adventures

On Foot

Giardino di Pojega (Negrar di Valpolicella, ☎ 045-7210028, www.guerrieri-rizzardi.com, Apr 1-Oct 31, Thurs 3-7 pm; call to schedule group tastings and guided tours; €7). In the 18th century the Veronese count Antonio Rizzardi commissioned Luigi Trezza to design a garden on his family's land that incorporated both Italian and English design elements. This garden, Giardino di Pojega, found among Valpolicella's vineyards beside the Guerrieri-Rizzardi's wine cellars, is a peaceful place to explore on a sunny afternoon. Guided tours and wine tastings can be arranged with advance notice.

Parco delle Cascate (Via Bacilieri 1, Molina, ☎ 045-7720185, www.cascatemolina.it, Apr-Sept, 9 am-7:30 pm daily, Oct-Mar, weekends only 9:30 am-4 pm; €3.50). The waterfall park in Molina, a tiny village that derives its name from the numerous mills that once characterized the area, is a 20- or 30-minute car ride from Negrar through winding steep mountain roads passing through red marble quarries and a good place to get out and enjoy nature. When you arrive in town, follow the parking signs and then signs for the information center/ticket booth, where you can pick up a map with the three itineraries. The official entrance to the park is below town in the valley where different trails depart. The three trails (the green, the red and the black) wind past several waterfalls, ruins of an old mill, picnic areas and scenic view points and each one helps visitors discover nature, history and archaeology.

The *Percorso della Salute is* a fitness trail winding through Gargagnago in the heart of the Valpolicella zone, and is a good way to explore the area on foot, particularly in spring and fall when it is the most scenic and makes for a fairly easy walk. A large sign in Gargagnago's church square marks the beginning of the well-marked trail, and throughout the route you'll find several signs suggesting exercises.

With Wine

 Valpolicella (www.valpolicella.it) wines are produced in three zones east of Lake Garda: Valpolicella Classico is the westernmost zone, Valpolicella Valpantena the central, and Valpolicella farthest east. Valpolicella, Valpolicella Superiore, Recioto and Amarone are produced using primarily Corvina, Rondinella, Molinara, Negrara and Rossignola grapes. Valpolicella Classico is ruby red, dry and somewhat sweet, Recioto is a garnet red, delicate and either sweet or dry and good with desserts, and Amarone, violet red is dry, and good with red meat and game. Valpolicella Superiore is aged at least one year.

Corteforte (Via Osan 45, Fumane, ☎ 045-6839104, www.corteforte.com, €€€). If you're interested in learning about Valpolicella wine and have time for only one stop in the zone, I highly recommend paying Barbara Cerutti and her one-time lawyer husband a visit at their winery in Fumane. In the early 1990s, Barbara decided to turn her passion for wine into a lucrative business and since then, hasn't looked back. More than a decade later, her winery produces award-winning wines that garner praise from the best in the business and are exported to the United States, Ireland and Australia (Amarone being their most popular seller on the US market). The Corteforte estate, built in the early 15th century, changed hands several times before finally being purchased by the Ceruttis and only one of its original towers remains standing. Call ahead to schedule tours of the surrounding vineyards followed by tastings (can be arranged in English). Often, tastings are held outdoors on the family's private terrace and feature a minimum of three wines accompanied by salumi (coldcuts made from pork) and cheese from the Lessini zone for approximately €10. And if you're anything like me, after a chat with Barbara you won't want to leave the winery – and you don't have to. The owners enjoy the company of visitors so much that they don't want them to leave – so they've converted a tower and another country house on their property to comfortable guest rooms. Within the ancient romantic tower are four medieval-style rooms with en suite bathrooms and a rooftop sunbathing terrace (a popular choice with couples). Along with the cantina and tastings room in the main building are two mini-apartments that offer a lot of privacy and are ideal for families. For the ultimate privacy, however, request the *casette*, a small house in the midst of Corteforte's vineyards. The Cerutti family values warm hospitality and treats each guest with the same kindness and warmth as their own family members.

> **Tip:** If you don't take kindly to dogs, let the owners know and they'll be sure to keep them out of your way.

Tommasi Viticoltori (Via Ronchetto 2, Pedemonte di Valpolicella, ☎ 045-7701266, www.tommasiwine.it). With the majority of its vineyards located in the Valpolicella Classico zone in Sant'Ambrogio di Valpolicella and San Pietro in Cariano, Tommasi winery has been refining its wines for over a century. One of Valpolicella's biggest names, Tommasi's wines are exported to countries throughout the globe in Europe, North and South America, Asia, and Africa.

Dining Out

Enoteca della Valpolicella (Via Osan 45, Fumane, ☎ 045-6839146, 12-2:30 pm and 7-11 pm; closed Sun evening and Mon; major credit cards accepted; €€€). This enoteca on the grounds of the Corteforte winery is one of the best known in the zone and its cantina features nearly 75 of Valpolicella's producers (not to mention many more other Italian wines), making it a perfect place for a wine tasting. The chef specializes in excellent regional cuisine and his most popular dishes include *stracotta di manzo al Amarone* (beef marinated with wine and vegetables and slow cooked).

Al Ritrovo (Via San Vito 16, San Vito di Negrar, ☎ 045-7501216; €€). If you're in the mood for home cooking and you're in the neighborhood you won't be disappointed at Al Ritrovo, a popular restaurant (especially on Sun) decorated with antique cooking utensils and farm tools. Several of the pasta dishes, including the hearty *bigoli al anatra* (thick pasta prepared with a duck sauce) are served in parmesean crisp shells. The pasta and dolce here are homemade and, if that's not enough reason to stop in, then its location near many of Valpolicella's cantine, should be.

Accommodations

Corteforte (Via Osan 45, Fumane, ☎ 045-6839104, www.corteforte.com; €€€). See *Wine Adventures*.

La Magioca Relais (Via Moron 3, Negrar, ☎ 045-6000167, www.magioca.it; breakfast included; major credit cards accepted; €€€€-€€€€€). Few places are as exclusive and tranquil as this stone inn, set on beautiful sprawling landscape with a small 13th-century Romanesque church dedicated to Santa Maria. At the turn of the century, Matteo Marighi and his mother keyed in on a need for a sophisticated retreat and converted a private residence into an elegant bed and breakfast. The six luxurious rooms (one suite, two junior suites and three doubles) overlook the gardens and are decked out in fine linens and fresh cut flowers. *La Suite* and *La Camera dell'Amarone* both feature a hydro massage bath, and all rooms have television, air conditioning, telephones and either a shower, bath or Jacuzzi. Families are welcome here, particularly in the *Greta*, a junior suite with enough room for children. One of my favorite rooms, *La Camera del Mosaico*, enjoys a lot of bright sunlight but what gives it its name is what makes it so unique – the mosaic tile bathtub. If you're after romance, *La Suite* has a large bathroom, fireplace and canopy bed to put you in an indulgent

mood. Weather permitting, breakfast is served in the garden where guests are also invited to relax on lounge chairs and in the hot tub. This is the perfect base for exploring Valpolicella's wineries (inquire about renting a Smart Car), and, only kilometers from Verona and Garda, it is also a wonderful choice for those who don't want to worry about overpriced, charmless hotel rooms. Don't leave without sampling their homemade confections.

> **Tip:** The Mosaico and Amarone rooms are most requested, so plan far in advance if you have either of the two in mind.

Serego Alighieri (Gargagnago di Valpolicella, ☎ 045-7703622, www.seregoalighieri.it; breakfast included; €€€€). In the mid-14th century, Pietro Alighieri, son of the famed poet Dante, purchased the Casal dei Ronchi, an estate in Gargagnago where his father spent time in exile writing the *Paradiso* section of his *Divina Commedia*. Today, more than 600 years later, the estate still remains in the hands of the legendary poet's descendants who have carried forward the long tradition of viniculture and agriculture, producing wine, jam, olive oil, balsamic vinegar, honey and liquor with the help of the distributor Masi. Located on the estate's grounds is the **La Foresteria** residence. The eight apartments are spacious and equipped with kitchenettes and modern amenities, although some guests may find the rooms on the dark side. The residence also includes a cantina and tastings rooms as well as a kitchen where cooking classes are held upon request.

The wine cellar and shop are open to the public daily from 10 am-6 pm except for Sunday. Their off-season rates are more reasonable.

Verona

La Meridiana (Via Osan, Fumane, ☎ 045-6839146; €€).
Tucked in the heart of wine country, you'd never know that
the rooms in this restored 1800s country house exist, hidden
in a pretty courtyard across the street from the Enoteca della
Valpolicella. And one of the only ways to score a room here is
by calling the enoteca or stopping in to talk to its owners.
Open since 2002, the small inn welcomes guests in its six
tastefully furnished rooms, all new and comfortable. Room 4
has a terrace, 5 and 6 have sloped ceilings and 1 and 2 have
private entrances but share a bathroom. The latter two are
perfect for a family of four, with a double bed in one and two
single beds in the other. Breakfast is served at the neighboring enoteca and, though not included, is a delicious spread for
€10 featuring homemade cakes and marmalades.

■ Torri del Benaco

It's remarkable how traveling a few short miles along the
Olive Riviera can transport you from purely Mediterranean
scenery to a semi-Nordic landscape, but this transformation
that seems so unlikely is precisely what characterizes central
and northern lakeside towns, particularly Torri del Benaco,
where the lake narrows and the slopes of Monte Baldo act as
the canvas for a colorful harbor marked by olive trees and
fishing boats.

As in many other harbor towns on the Riviera, toward the end
of the 14th century the Scaligeri family built a castle in Torri
del Benaco upon Roman foundations in an effort to protect the
harbor from enemy invasion. The charming historic center,
more refined than Garda's and Bardolino's, is marked by
many clothing and ceramic shops and a handful of good restaurants and cafés.

> **Historic Interest:** The cultivation of citrus
> fruit in Torri del Benaco became important in
> the 17-18th centuries and there were likely as
> many as eight lemon groves, one of which still
> remains in use in Torri's castle. Torri is one of
> the few places in the Garda zone where lemon
> cultivation has survived.

Sightseeing

 Museo del Castello Scaligero (Viale Fratelli Lavanda 2, Torri del Benaco, ☎ 045-6296111; Apr-May and Oct, Tue-Sun, 9:30 am-12:30 pm and 2:30-6 pm, Mon, 9:30 am-12:30 pm; June-Sept, 9:30 am-1 pm and 4:30-7:30 pm, €3). Erected in the 14th century by the Scaligeri clan, the various *sale* in Torri's castle exhibit Torri's colorful history from the fishing trade and the craft of boat

 building that were such vital aspects to olive and citrus cultivation. There are many interesting things to see, including a reconstructed olive press with its stone parts

dating back to Roman times, antique fishing nets, a flat-bottomed gondola and the 18th-century citrus grove. During summer months, the castle hosts outdoor cinema evenings.

Verona

Adventures

Hotel Continental (Via Gardesana, Località S. Felice, Torri del Benaco, ☎ 045-7225966; hotel open Mar-Oct). From late May through Oct this is THE one-stop shop for water, wind and other sports activities in the area. You'd be hard-pressed to find an adventure on the lake that they can't arrange and with choices like windsurfing, wakeboarding, canoeing, diving, beach volleyball and free climbing, you're more likely to tire out before exhausting all possibilities here. Bicycles and cars can be hired at the hotel (**Velocifero** has a seat here – see *Garda*). **Stube del Giardino delle Rane** (see *Bardolino*) also has a location here. **Directional Info:** The hotel is located along the Gardesana road just north of Torri heading toward Malcesine.

On Horseback

 Centro Ippico Rossar (Via Montarion 16, Castion di Costermano, ☎ 045-6279020, www.rossar.it). Since 1978, this equestrian center near the Ca' degli Ulivi Golf Club has been exposing visitors to some of the prettiest lake and mountain scenery accessible on horseback by way of their excursions to Monte Baldo, Lake Garda and the Adige River. Hour-long lessons cost approximately €20 and two-hour lessons, including an excursion cost roughly €35. Other excursion fees depend on the length and scope of the excursion.

> **Romantic Adventure:** It doesn't have to be an anniversary or birthday to warrant a romantic carriage ride through Garda's territory. Inquire about chauffeured carriage rides in the Garda zone.

Dining Out

 Ristorante Gardesana (Piazza Calderini 20, ☎ 045-7225411, www.hotel-gardesana.com; dinner only: 7-10 pm; closed Tue except from May-Sept; closed Nov-Feb; major credit cards accepted; €€€-€€€€). On the historical hotel's second floor, this refined (if not a bit pricey) restaurant serves some of the Garda region's most outstanding fish dishes. The chef showcases Garda's fish, olive oil and wine in a wide range of traditional Gardesana and Veronese creations and is always crafting new recipes and discovering creative ways of presenting classics. Consider the *battutina di persico in salsa Gardesana* (perch prepared with a scallion and herb sauce) followed by the award-winning *girella di cavedano al burro e timo* (a pancake filled with a lake fish and topped with butter and thyme sauce). Their signature dish, *filetto di lavarello in agrodolce* (pan seared lavarello served with marinated vegetables) is a favorite. Satiated as you may be, it would be a shame to pass up a *dolce* and the *terrina di cioccolato e wasabi con salsa di aranci e amare* (chocolate and wasabi mold with orange sauce) is a good choice that you're unlikely to find elsewhere. Those lucky enough to arrive before the crowds (even locals adore this place), should request the most sought-after tables on the veranda overlooking the port. Somehow, flavors are intensi-fied out here making a meal far more delightful (though that's not to say that the indoor tables aren't elegant too). The extensive wine list features upwards of 300 wines and pres-ents a wide selection of local and international wines to com-plement any meal.

Accommodations

Hotel Gardesana (Piazza Calderini 20, ☎ 045-7225411, www.hotel-gardesana.com; closed Nov-Jan; major credit cards accepted; €€€). This historic landmark hotel located in a 15th-century structure that once served as the Palazzo dei Capitani for the Republic of Venice, has functioned as a hotel since the late 1800s host-ing many illustrious guests, including Spain's King Juan Carlos I, Maria Callas (the legendary soprano) and Vivian Leigh (*Gone With the Wind*). Many of the luminaries who laid their heads on pillows here did so in the hotel's finest room, #123, with a beautiful wooden balcony and an exceptional view of the port. Today's owners take great

care to make sure the service matches the hotel's reputation, and fortunately it does.

Nightlife

Lido Club Night & Day (Viale Marconi 4, Torri del Benaco, ☎ 045-6290405; closed Mon). By day, a beach club. By night, a dance club. Whichever way you look at it though, it's a lot of fun and admission to both is gratis, which makes it even better. Do, however, bring enough euros to pay for your lounge chairs, your meals at the pizzeria and restaurant, and cocktails at the bar when the sun sets.

■ Malcesine & Monte Baldo

At the northern reaches of the Olive Riviera, the colorful resort town of Malcesine is a gateway to both Lake Garda and Monte Baldo and is clearly in touch with both its Mediterranean and Alpine identities.

One of the lake's most visited and well-equipped resort towns, Malcesine's narrow and hilly cobbled streets lead to the small harbor, the Palazzo dei Capitani and the Scaligeri castle, evoking a certain old world charm.

Malcesine's position at the base of Monte Baldo and along the narrowest stretch of the lake where winds are steady, keeping the town cool, makes it an ideal place for water and wind sports such as windsurfing, paragliding and sailing.

Alpine and Mediterranean flora coexist on a mountain that has been known for centuries as the *Hortus Europae* (garden of Europe) and ascending toward Monte Baldo, the most westerly mountain in Veneto's pre-Alps caught between the Adige River and the lake, you'll witness a dramatic transformation of scenery. A landscape initially marked by olive groves changes over to oak and chestnut trees, beech, pine and finally grass pastures with *stelle alpine (edelweiss)*.

Sightseeing

Museo Castello Scaligero di Malcesine (☎ 045-6570333, Apr-Oct daily, 9:30 am-7 pm; Nov-Mar, weekends only; €4). A Longobard fortress once stood on the site of this 13th-14th-century castle that was reconstructed several times over the centuries and changed hands on a few occasions before ending up in the possession of the Scaligeri clan, who transformed it into a castle and residence. In more recent times this castle perched atop a rock was used by Austrians as a military garrison and today it hosts the **Museum of Malcesine**, exhibiting local culture and natural history of Malcesine and Monte Baldo. One of the castle's rooms has been dedicated to the German poet **Johann Wolfgang von Goethe**, who was overwhelmed by Lake Garda's beauty and wrote about it in the 18th century. The view over Lake Garda at the entrance is magnificent and hard to miss.

Orto Botanico di Novezza (Via General Graziani 10, Novezza, Ferrara di Monte Baldo, ☎ 045-6247288; open daily May-Sept, 9 am-6 pm; €2.50). Many rare and protected flowers from the Mediterranean and Alpine environments of Lake Garda can be seen at the botanic garden in Novezza, accessible from the Affi exit off of A22.

Adventures

Funivia Malcesine (☎ 045-7400206; summer, 8 am-7 pm; winter, 8 am-4:30 pm; spring and fall, 8 am-6 pm; closed Nov, Dec and Mar; one-way, €9, round-trip, €14). The quickest and most scenic way of ascending Monte Baldo is by cable car, a 15-minute ride in rotating cabins. Cable cars transport passengers twice hourly to Monte Baldo and those with paraglides and bicycles in tow should check schedules for times equipment is allowed on the funivia and purchase the appropriate ticket. The most scenic part of the ride is from San Michele to Monte Baldo.

On Foot

There are several good hikes around Malcesine and Monte Baldo. Stop into the tourist center for a map.

In Air

If you've ever considered paragliding, Monte Baldo is the perfect place to discover this sport that both youth and adults can enjoy with no prior training. The **Condorfly Scuola di Volo Libero** (www.condorfly.com, info@condorfly.com, ☎ 338-3922412) takes sports enthusiasts for tandem flights. The launch site is not far from the cable car station at the top of Monte Baldo and the landing zone is just north of Malcesine.

On Wheels

Bikexxxxtreme (Malcesine, ☎ 045-7400245, bikexxxxtreme@libero.it, open daily 8 am, May-Oct). Conveniently located at the base of the funivia where customers can hop on a cable car and head for the mountain, this shop rents bikes and arranges bike excursions and holidays. Additionally, the shop offers a shuttle service and will transport bicycles to Monte Baldo where customers can pick them up. Rentals typically cost between €15 and €25 per day depending on the bike and half-day rentals are only possible if enough bikes are available.

> **Tip:** Passengers with bicycles in tow may only use designated cable cars to transport bikes to Monte Baldo.

Cicli Furioli (Piazza Matteotti, Malcesine, ☎ 045-7400089, Mar-Oct, 9 am-1:30 pm and 4-10:30 pm). This small shop in the center of town rents bicycles for €10-20 per day and also arranges guided excursions to places such as Monte Baldo and Torri del Benaco with a maximum of eight people for approximately €90 (for the group). If you'd rather set out on your own, request a trail map when you pick up your bike.

> **Tip:** Bicycles may be picked up the evening prior to a rental at no extra charge to accommodate customers, but bicycles must be reserved in advance. Store hours may change in the event of poor weather.

Fit & Sun Bike Tours (Località Valdimonte 27, Malcesine, ☎ 045-7401359, www.fitandsun.it). Experienced guides from the Italian School of Mountain Biking (SIMB) offer several itineraries to accommodate all interests and incorporate mountain biking while highlighting nature, gastronomy and history of the region. Packages include accommodations, certain meals, entrance fees to sites, baggage transport and boat and funivia tickets where applicable. Their most popular itineraries are *Discovery Garda* (one week), *Twin Garda* (weekend), *Bike Camp* (four-seven days) and *wine and food tours* (two-three days). Independent cyclists may also arrange self-guided itineraries with the assistance of professional SIMB guides.

On Water

Windsurfing & Sailing

Windsurfing and sailing are particularly popular in the northern zone of the lake and **WWWind Square** (Via Gardesana, Località Sottodossi, Malcesine,

☎ 045-7400413, www.wwwind.com) offers sailing and wind-surfing courses for all ages and abilities as well as equipment and boat rentals.

Fitzcarraldo Scuola Vela (Brenzone, ☎ 045-6590178, www.fjsailingschool.com), just south of Malcesine in Brenzone also offers sailing courses for both children and adults that typically last several days at a time.

Diving

 Athos Diving (Via Gardesana 54, Assenza di Brenzone, www.athos-diving.com). Year-round, Athos Diving offers courses, equipment rentals, immersion dives and guided excursions in Lake Garda.

Golf

 Ca' Degli Ulivi Golf Club (Via Ghiandare 2, Marciaga di Costermano, ☎ 045-6279030). Golf enthusiasts will enjoy a few hours on greens at Costermano's 18-hole championship course overlooking Lake Garda. Named for its many olive trees, the course is open year-round and its facilities include a clubhouse, pro-shop, pool and bar.

Beaches

 Between Brenzone and Malcesine, the **lido in Val di Sogno** is one of the Riviera's lovelier beaches with olive trees stretching all the way down to the shore. Even if you're not looking for a beach to lounge on, the mountain backdrop and pathway here make this a nice place for a stroll.

Dining Out

 Enosophia Ristorante (Via Navene 2, Malcesine, ☎ 045-6584286, www.enosophia.it, 7:30-10:30 pm; closed Tue; closed Nov and Feb; major credit cards accepted; €€€). Expect the unexpected to be on the menu at this enoteca/restaurant. With a chef hailing from Japan, specializing in French cuisine and cooking for primarily Italian and German tastes, you'll find a unique selection of Nouveau and traditional dishes on the menu. Such unusual dishes include *gamberoni scottati con salsa di gazpacio* (crayfish in a gazpacho sauce) and *maiale marinato e affumicato con salsa*

all'idea di Zaziki (marinated, smoked pork served with a Greek yogurt sauce). And there is always the orrechiette pasta in a zucchini and speck cream sauce and grilled trout with a caper vinaigrette for those who prefer something simpler. This locale's reputation, however, can be attributed to more than its kitchen. With a large selection of Italian and French wines – nearly 300 – patrons may request wine tastings. The indoor dining rooms are warm and the small courtyard is also lovely. Several nights a week during the summer live music livens up dinner. The budget-conscious will fare best with the fixed price menus – the *Menu di Primavera* (Spring Menu), *Menu del Passatore* (Shepherd's Menu) and *Menu del Gourmet* – that include an antipasto, a first and second course and the service charge for a reasonable €30-40.

Taverna dei Captiani (Via Garibaldi, Malcesine, ☎ 045-7400005, 12-4 pm, 6:30-10:30 pm; €€€). It should come as no surprise that there are more than a few good fish restaurants in this lakeside town, and this is no exception. Aside from the tourist menu, there is also a traditional menu with a fair selection of classically prepared fish dishes. The *lavarello alla griglia* (grilled lake trout) served with a salad was wonderful but not a dish for the squeamish as it is common practice for the waiter to clean the fish in front of you before serving it. If you can't decide between pasta and fish, try the *spaghetti con le sarde* (spaghetti with a sardine sauce). On a sunny afternoon, the restaurant's best tables are in the small courtyard.

Locanda Monte Baldo (S. Michele, Malcesine, ☎ 045-7400612, www.locandamontebaldo.com, €€). If you've worked up an appetite hiking or biking Monte Baldo, consider stopping off at the S. Michele cable car stop on the way down to sample this family-operated restaurant's regional cuisine. Specializing in traditional dishes that include ingredients from the mountain, the chef prepares dishes like rabbit with polenta and mushrooms and dumplings in broth that you're less likely to find in lakeside eateries. If you dine here you

DINING PRICE CHART	
Price per person for an entrée	
€	Under €5
€€	€5-€12
€€€	€13-€20
€€€€	€21-€30
€€€€€	Over €30

MUST find a table on the restaurant's terrace overlooking Lake Garda that affords one of the most scenic views around.

Accommodations

Hotel Dolomiti (Via Monti 1, ☎ 045-7400084, www.dolomitihotel.net; closed Nov-Apr; breakfast included; €€). Centrally located in Malcesine's historic center and within easy walking distance of the port, the castle and the shopping district, this small hotel is a good value in high or low season. Its simple rooms are on the small side and have telephones and bathrooms with showers, but only half of them have air conditioning and television, so remember to request that if you need it. Certain rooms also look out toward the mountains.

> **Tip:** The main road sits just above the town center and if you follow it less than one mile out of town in either direction, the atmosphere is much quieter. Due to the high volume of cars during peak season, traffic into the city is limited and several roads are closed.

Hotel Malcesine (Via Val di Sogno 16, Malcesine, ☎ 045-7400108; closed mid-Oct through Mar; breakfast included; major credit cards accepted; €€€€). Situated directly on the lakefront, this hotel is popular with vacationing Europeans who tend to spend week-long holidays here and take advantage of the half- and full-board options. The hotel has a pool, a beach, and guests can choose between modern rooms with a view of the lake or the mountains.

HOTEL PRICE CHART	
Based on a double room for two	
€	Under €50
€€	€50-€80
€€€	€81-€120
€€€€	€121-€190
€€€€€	Over €190

Historical Interest: Goethe was arrested while sketching the Scaligeri castle in Malcesine. He was suspected of being an Austrian spy.

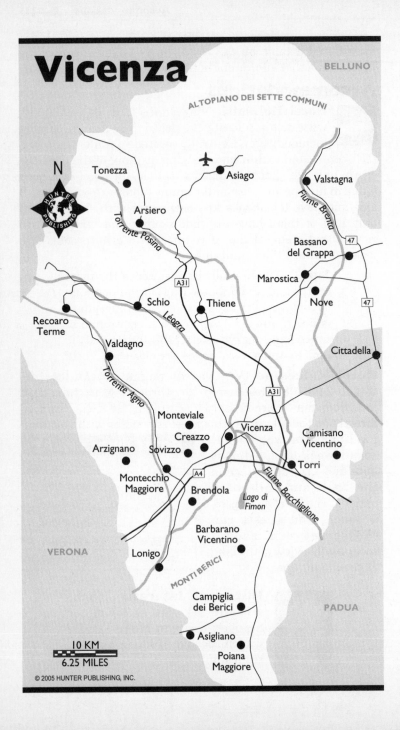

Vicenza

BELLUNO

ALTOPIANO DEI SETTE COMMUNI

N

Tonezza

Asiago

Valstagna

Arsiero

Fiume Brenta

Torrente Posina

Bassano
del Grappa

47

A31

Marostica

Schio

Léogra

Thiene

Nove

47

Recoaro
Terme

Cittadella

Valdagno

A31

Torrente Agno

Monteviale

Vicenza

Camisano
Vicentino

Creazzo

Arzignano

Sovizzo

Torri

Montecchio
Maggiore

A4

Brendola

Fiume Bacchiglione

Lago di
Fimon

VERONA

Barbarano
Vicentino

Lonigo

MONTI BERICI

PADUA

Campiglia
dei Berici

Asigliano

10 KM
6.25 MILES

Poiana
Maggiore

© 2005 HUNTER PUBLISHING, INC.

Province of Vicenza

■ Vicenza

Vicenza is an essential stop on the itineraries of architecture lovers and Palladio's followers, but is unfortunately bypassed by many tourists traveling through the Veneto region who don't realize what it has to offer. This well-kept

secret has made remarkable cultural and economical contributions to the region and merits a visit, if only for a few hours.

Vicenza is an important Renaissance city with an impressive number of buildings dating back to the 1500s, many of them attributed to Andrea Palladio. It was during this period that Andrea di Pietro della Gondola came to Vicenza as a 16 year-old stone mason and through a combination of his own talent and a fine network of mentors, grew to be the great architect who dramatically transformed Vicenza's urban image. Palladio was commissioned to build palazzi for the city's wealthy residents, redesign several buildings which had been badly damaged by the League of Cambrai and to make the city better reflect the influence of the Republic of Venice. His finest works in the city include the Teatro Olimpico, the Basilica Palladiana and the Palazzo Chiericati.

Not only has Vicenza grown in the international spotlight thanks to its famed architect, but over the centuries it has become one of the world's principle centers for gold production, responsible for about half of the gold produced in Italy. Evidence suggests that goldsmiths existed in the city at least as far back as the mid-1300s and today industrial firms and craft industries continue to employ a significant number of locals. Light industry and advanced technology also contribute to Vicenza's healthy economy and Vicenza is considered to be one of Italy's most industrialized cities.

Getting There

 By Car: Vicenza is easily accessible from a few principle highways. From Venice and Padua, take the A4 west to Vicenza; from Milan and Verona, follow the A4 east to Vicenza and follow signs for the *centro*. See *Getting Around*, below, for parking tips.

 By Bus: FTV buses (Viale Milano, ☎ 0444-223111, www.ftv.vi.it) travel between Vicenza and most towns in the province. Buses depart from the bus station on Viale Milano, near the railway station. It takes approximately one hour to reach Vicenza from Padua and, although it is possible to get to Vicenza from Venice by bus, it requires a connection in Padua and the trip is long. The train is a far better option when traveling to Vicenza from Venice.

 By Train: Vicenza's railway station (☎ 0444-326707, www.trenitalia.it) sits on the Milano-Venezia line. It takes approximately 50 minutes to travel to Vicenza from Venice, 30 minutes from Verona and 15-20 minutes from Padua. These trains run several times each hour.

 By Plane: The nearest airport to Vicenza with domestic and international flights daily is **Venice's Marco Polo**, about 50 km from Vicenza. From here visitors have the option of continuing on to Vicenza by train or by bus. For details: www.veniceairport.it.

Getting Around

Note: Due to the American military post in Vicenza, there is a significant American population living in town. Although Vicenza is not a terribly popular tourist destination for non-Europeans, many shop- and restaurant-owners do speak some English.

 On Foot: Vicenza's historical center is fairly small and the easiest way to get around is on foot. There are pedestrian zones and restricted traffic zones that make traveling through the center by car a challenge. Corso Palladio is the city's main pedestrian zone, connecting Piazza Castello and Piazza Matteotti.

 By Bike: If you prefer to explore Vicenza by bicycle, park your car at the Parcheggio dello Stadio on Via Bassano (also known as Parcheggio Bassano) and a bicycle rental is included in your parking ticket. Bicycles may also be rented at **Ostello Olimpico**, the hostel near Piazza Matteotti (Viale Giuriolo 9, ☎ 0444-540222, 7-10 am and 3-10 pm).

 By Bus: Although there are a few places to park in Vicenza's historic center, the best option is parking in one of the parking lots outside of the historic center and traveling to the center by city bus (www.aimvicenza.it). The **AIM** city buses (☎ 0444-394909 or 800-086226, www.aimvicenza.it) travel several routes within Vicenza's city center and its outer limits. The #10 city bus (Park Bassano) travels from the Parcheggio dello Stadio (near the stadium on Via Bassano, open 24 hours) to Piazza Matteotti, Piazza dei Signori, Ospedale Civile and Parcheggio di Viale Cricoli (open 24 hours). The #7 city bus (Park Farini and Park Cairoli) travels from Parcheggio di Via Farini (Via Farini, 6:30 am-9 pm) to Parcheggio di Via Cairoli (Via Cairoli, 5 am-midnight), Piazza San Lorenzo, Piazza Castello and the railway station. The buses travel every 5-10 minutes daily from Mon through Fri between 6:45 am and 8:10 pm to the city center. Parking ticket receipts from any of the *Centro Bus* lots serve as bus tickets on these shuttle buses and it is not necessary to purchase an additional bus ticket.

 Car Rental: If you arrive in Vicenza by train or bus and prefer to explore the province by car, there are several car rental companies in town, including **Avis** (Viale Milano 88, ☎ 0444-321622) and **Budget** (Railway Station, ☎ 0444-545962).

 By Taxi: For taxi service in Vicenza's center, **Radio Taxi** (☎ 0444-920600).

Vicenza

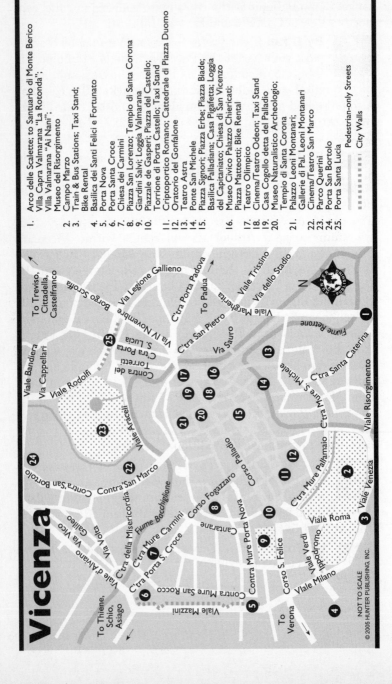

1. Arco delle Scalette; to Santuario di Monte Berico
   Villa Capra Valmarana "La Rotonda";
   Villa Valmarana "Ai Nani";
   Museo del Risorgimento
2. Campo Marzo
3. Train & Bus Stations; Taxi Stand;
   Bike Rental
4. Basilica dei Santi Felici e Fortunato
5. Porta Nova
6. Porta Santa Croce
7. Chiesa dei Carmini
8. Piazza San Lorenzo; Tempio di Santa Corona
9. Giardini Salvi; Loggia Valmarana
10. Piazzale de Gasperi; Piazza del Castello;
    Torrione di Porta Castello; Taxi Stand
11. Criptoportico Romano; Cattedrale di Piazza Duomo
12. Oratorio del Gonfalone
13. Teatro Astra
14. Ponte San Michele
15. Piazza Signori; Piazza Erbe; Piazza Biade;
    Basilica Palladiana; Casa Pigafetta; Loggia
    del Capitaniato; Chiesa di San Vicenzo
16. Museo Civico Palazzo Chiericati;
    Piazza Matteotti; Bike Rental
17. Teatro Olimpico
18. Cinema/Teatro Odeon; Taxi Stand
19. Casa Cogollo detta del Palladio
20. Museo Naturalistico Archeologico;
    Tempio di Santa Corona
21. Palazzo Leoni Montanari;
    Gallerie di Pal. Leoni Montanari
22. Cinema/Teatro San Marco
23. Parco Querini
24. Porta San Bortolo
25. Porta Santa Lucia

          Pedestrian-only Streets
          City Walls

NOT TO SCALE
© 2005 HUNTER PUBLISHING, INC.

Sightseeing

Teatro Olimpico (Piazza Matteotti, Vicenza, ☎ 0444-222800, Sept-June, Tue-Sun, 9 am-5 pm; July and Aug, 9 am-7 pm; closed Mon; ticket office closes 15 minutes prior to closing; admission with cumulative ticket). As a member of the prestigious *Accademia Olimpica*, a group of nobles and artists dedicated to the arts, Andrea Palladio proposed the construction of a theater in 1579 to

stage the academy's theatrical performances and honor classical architecture. He envisioned a theater that would replicate outdoor Greek and Roman theaters and, after much study of ancient theaters, construction began on the theater in 1580 in the courtyard of a 13th-century castle. Although the great architect died shortly after beginning the project, his student Vincenzo Scamozzi saw it through to completion and it has come to be regarded as an urban work of art and one of Palladio's masterpieces. Scamozzi created an impressive wood and stucco set of the Greek city of Thebes for the opening performance of Sophocles' *Oedipus Rex* in 1585 that was never changed. The faux sky above the seating was created to give spectators the impression of being in an outdoor theater.

> **Tip:** Vicenza can be explored in a day or less, but if your itinerary only allows a quick stop in town, be sure to visit the Teatro Olimpico and the pedestrian zones in the historic center.

Vicenza

GREAT VALUE

AUTHOR'S PICK There are several cumulative tickets that allow entrance to the city's main tourist attractions. These include the **Vicenza Musei** (Teatro Olimpico, Pinacoteca di Palazzo Chiericati, Museo Naturalistico Archeologico, €7i), **Musei Full** (Teatro Olimpico, Pinacoteca di Palazzo Chiericati, Museo Naturalistico Archeologico, Museo del Risorgimento e della Resistenza di Villa Guiccioli, €8) and **Musei e Palazzi** (Teatro Olimpico, Pinacoteca di Palazzo Chiericati, Museo Naturalistico Archeologico, Museo del Risorgimento e della Resistenza di Villa Guiccioli, Palazzo Barbaran da Porto, Gallerie di Palazzo Leoni Montanari, €11). The cards are valid for three days and are available for purchase at the Teatro Olimpico.

Museo Civico Palazzo Chiericati (Piazza Matteotti, Vicenza, ☎ 0444-321348; Sept-June, Tue-Sun, 9 am-5 pm; July-Aug, Tue-Sun, 9 am-7 pm; admission with cumulative ticket). This 16th-century construction is considered to be one of Palladio's finest works and is the seat of the Pinacoteca Civica, the art gallery where a large collection of works by Tiepolo, Tintoretto and Veronese is exhibited. At right is *Diana & the Nymphs* by Pittoni.

Did You Know? Many of Vicenza's street names begin with *Contrà*, the dialect term for *Contrada* (District).

Tempio di Santa Corona (Contrà S. Corona, Vicenza, ☎ 0444-321924; Tue-Sun, 8:30 am-noon and 3-6 pm, Mon,

4-6 pm). Constructed in the 13th century to house a thorn from Christ's crown, this Gothic church was the final resting place for Luigi da Porto, the author of the love tale *Giulietta e Romeo* (upon which the Shakespearean play was based). Paolo Veronese's 16th-century *Adoration of the Magi* is one of the church's most splendid works of art.

Museo Naturalistico ed Archaeologico (Contrà S. Corona, Vicenza, ☎ 0444-320440; Sept-June, Tue-Sun, 9 am-5 pm; July and Aug, Tue-Sun, 9 am-7 pm; admission with cumulative ticket). Although this museum does not boast any extraordinary exhibits, if you have time to spare and already possess a cumulative ticket from the Teatro Olimpico and an interest in the natural history and archaeology of the zone, it may be worth a visit.

> **Note:** Locals refer to the historic center's Piazza delle Poste as Contrà Garibaldi and you may hear the two used interchangeably.

Contrà Porti. In spite of its small size, this road is one of Vicenza's most architecturally significant ones for its handful of interesting palazzi, including a few which were designed by Palladio. These include #11, **Palazzo Barbaran da Porto** (see *Cultural Adventures* below) and #21, **Palazzo Iseppo da Porto** (1549-53), whose interior was decorated by Tiepolo in the 18th century.

Corso Palladio is a pretty pedestrian zone and the main thoroughfare in Vicenza's historic center. Walking down the street you'll find several buildings designed by Palladio and his followers, including #167, **Casa Cogollo**. This building, shown at left, was designed by Palladio between 1560 and 1570 but although it is often referred to as Palladio's house, it was most likely not where Palladio lived. Another building attributed to Palladio is **Palazzo Thiene**, which now serves as the Banca Popolare di Vicenza. Buildings along this street reveal the rich architectural importance and history of the city.

Piazza dei Signori. Vicenza's lively Piazza dei Signori just off of Corso Palladio has been an important gathering spot for locals for centuries and was likely once the site of a Roman forum. Several important monuments are located here, including the **Basilica Palladiana**. Contrary to what the first part of its name suggests, this building also known as the **Palazzo della Ragione**, is not a basilica at all. Palladiana does however reflect its architect, Andrea Palladio, who was commissioned to spruce up a Gothic-style building and reconstruct its loggia. The 12th-century **Torre Bissara (Torre di Piazza)** and Palladio's 16th-century **Loggia del Capitaniato** are also located in the piazza.

Casa Pigafetta (Contrà Pigafetta). In a city where Renaissance architecture dominates, this house, shown above, is a fine example of late Gothic architecture. Whether named for Antonio Pigafetta, a sailor who joined Magellan on his circumnavigation of the globe, or for the patrician Matteo Pigafetta who commissioned it, it is particularly worth visiting for its decorative exterior.

The following sites are just outside of Vicenza's historic center and can be reached on foot (about a 15-minute walk), by car or by bus (#8).

Villa La Rotonda (Vicenza, see *Palladio and his Villas,* below)

Villa Valmarana Ai Nani (Vicenza, ☎ 0444-321803; Mar-Oct, Wed, Thurs, Sat and Sun, 10 am-noon, Tue-Sun, 3-6 pm; €). This 17th-century villa, along with its 18th-century stables and *foresteria* (guest house) is located in the countryside outside Vicenza's center near Palladio's villa *La Rotonda*. Its name *ai nani* comes from the dwarf statues

on the wall surrounding the villa. Both Giambattista Tiepolo and his son Giandomenico Tiepolo adorned the interior of the palazzina and the foresteria with magnificent fresco cycles in the 18th century.

Santuario di Monte Berico (Vicenza, ☎ 0444-320998; Mon-Fri, 6:15 am-12:30 pm and 2:30-7:30 pm, Sun and holidays, 6:15 am-8 pm). Originally constructed in the 14th century on the site where a woman had apparitions of the Virgin, this sanctuary was modified several times, first by the architect Lorenzo da Bologna between 1476 and 1480 and later by Giacomo Borella between 1687 and 1703. Veronese's magnificent 16th-century *Supper of St. Gregory the Great* is here.

Panoramic View: There are beautiful views of Vicenza and the Colli Berici from The Santuario Di Monte Berico.

Adventures

Cultural Adventures

 Peccati di Gola (Contrà S. Paolo 25, Vicenza, ☎ 348-5109161, www.peccatidigola.info, t.polo@virgilio.it). The three-hour cooking courses are conducted exclusively in Italian in a private home and begin at 7:30 pm. Some courses consist of only one lesson and cost €50, while others can range from two to eight lessons and cost upwards of €350. Typical courses highlight the *Christmas Menu* and *Fish*. Contact Signora Tiziana Polo for a list of scheduled cooking courses.

Centro Internazionale di Studi di Architettura Andrea Palladio (Palazzo Barbaran da Porto, Contrà Porti 11, Vicenza, ☎ 0444-323014, www.cisapalladio.org; Tue-Sun, 10 am-6 pm). This institute conducts research on the history of architecture and organizes courses, seminars and exhibits that highlight Andrea Palladio and architecture. Visit their website for a schedule of upcoming courses and exhibits. The **Museo Palladio** (Fri-Sun, 6 pm, €5) is also here within the Palazzo Barbaran da Porto, one of Palladio's works of art. This is occasionally the site of various exhibits, thus the entrance fee is subject to change.

Interlingua (Stradella Filippini 27, Vicenza, ☎ 0444-321601, www.interlingua.it) offers small, intensive Italian-language courses for students at all proficiency levels. In addition to immersion courses, the school also offers individual lessons.

Dining Out

 Vicenza's signature dish, *baccalà alla vicentina* (stockfish or dried cod prepared with onions and milk) is a popular dish throughout the Veneto region and has a history dating back to the 15th century. Story has it that when the Venetian merchant Piero Querini and his crew were shipwrecked in the Lofoten Islands off the coast of Norway from 1431 until 1432, they grew to enjoy cod fish which was found in abundance there due to the climatic conditions. When they returned to Italy in 1432 along with a large supply of dried cod, they unknowingly marked the beginning of a Venetian tradition. Although locals had a good supply of fresh fish from nearby Venice, over time they came to like *baccalà* (also known as *stoccafisso* or stockfish). Over the centuries, various dishes were prepared with dried cod, the most famous being *baccalà alla vicentina*, traditionally served with *polenta*. Today Italy continues to import a large amount of its stockfish from the Lofoten Islands.

Antica Casa della Malvasia (Contrà delle Morette 5, Vicenza, ☎ 0444-543704, Wine Bar 10:30 am-3 pm and 5 pm-midnight, Osteria noon-2:30 pm and 7-11:30 pm; closed Sun night and Mon; major credit cards accepted; €€). Named for the ancient road that wine merchants traveled centuries ago, this osteria near the Piazza dei Signori is a favorite with locals for its reliably well-prepared traditional Vicentina dishes and good selection of local wines and grappa. The menu does change frequently to reflect the kitchen's use of seasonal ingredients, but you'll always find a few traditional dishes, including *bigoli di ragu all'anatra* (pasta with duck ragout) and *baccalà alla vicentina* (cod prepared Vicenza-style) on the menu. The atmosphere is warm and inviting and they occasionally host live musical events.

Antico Ristorante Agli Schioppi (Contrà Piazza del Castello 26, Vicenza, ☎ 0444-543701; closed Sat night and Sun; major credit cards accepted; €€). Since the 1800s this restaurant has been serving locals traditional fare such as *fegato di vitello con cipolle* (liver with onions) and *baccalà alla vicentina*. Most pastas and desserts are homemade, and the spicy *bigoli agli schioppi* is a favorite. Most of their 80+ wines are from the Tri-Veneto region (Veneto, Friuli-Venezia Giulia and Trentino-Alto Adige).

If you ask locals where they purchase pastries, most will point you in the direction of **Sorarù** (Piazzetta Palladio, Vicenza, ☎ 0444-320915) and **Pasticceria Venezia** (Contrà Pescaria, Vicenza, 8 am-1 pm and 3-8 pm; closed Mon). The **Enoteca Antica Offelleria la Meneghina** (Contrà Cavour 18, Vicenza, ☎ 0444-323305) is a historical shop founded in 1791 and serves pastries in addition to some local dishes, tramezzini, finger foods, local wines and homemade liquors.

Il Ceppo (Corso Palladio 196, ☎ 0444-544414). This gourmet shop sells locally-produced cheeses and wines, fresh pasta, bread, salumi and other deli meats in addition to hot and cold prepared dishes like seafood salad, *sarde en saor* (sardines in sweet and sour sauce) and *baccalà alla Vicentina*. This is a great place to stop for a lunch on the go. Or, pick up a few items and head to Parco Querini for a picnic.

Brek (Corso Palladio 10/12, Vicenza, ☎ 0444-327829; closed Mon; €-€€). See *Dining Out* in Padua.

Accommodations

Several times each year Vicenza hosts gold trade fairs. Prices indicated here reflect hotel rates the rest of the year – expect prices to climb as much as 50% during the trade fairs. In the case of trade fairs, you'll fare much better seeking accommodations in smaller towns in the province like Marostica or Bassano del Grappa.

Due Mori (Contrà Do Rode 24/26, Vicenza, ☎ 0444-321886, www.hotelduemori.com; handicap-accessible rooms; major credit cards accepted; €€). Due Mori's low rates are attractive to budget-conscious travelers, particularly because they don't equate to scanty accommodations. Although this hotel has been around since the 1800s, renovations have kept it modern and tastefully furnished. Unfortunately, this isn't a convenient option for larger families as their largest room only accommodates three guests.

Hotel Castello (Contrà Piazza del Castello 24, Vicenza, ☎ 0444-323585, www.hotelcastelloitaly.com; breakfast included; major credit cards accepted; €€€). Located in the *centro storico*. You'll have to travel up to the second floor by way of the stairs to reach this small hotel's reception, making it a tough choice for some travelers. Some rooms have been furnished with pieces from a local carpenter's workshop and all but two have en suite baths.

Shopping

The **general market** takes place Tuesaday morning in Vicenza's Piazza dei Signori and Thursday mornings in

Piazza dei Signori, Piazza Biade, Piazza delle Poste, Piazza Duomo, Piazza Castello and Viale Roma.

Vicenza hosts an **antique market** the second Sunday of each month (except July and Aug) in Piazza dei Signori and Piazza Erbe.

Many fine **clothing** and **jewelry** shops are located on Corso Palladio.

The best place in Vicenza to purchase gold jewelry, silver jewelry and items for the home at factory prices is at the *Vezzaro Outlet* (Via Vecchia Ferriera 74, Voice of Gold Building, Vicenza, ☎ 0444-560411, www.vezzaro.com, Mon-Sat, 9 am-12:30 pm and 3-7 pm). Also at **Cash & Gold** (Viale della Scienza 14, Vicenza, ☎ 0444-965947, Mon-Sat, 9 am-1 pm and 3:30-7:30 pm).

> **Note:** The gold industry has been an important aspect of Vicenza's economy for centuries. Three gold trade fairs are held annually: *Vicenza Oro 1* in Jan, *Vicenza Oro 2* in June and *Orogemma* in Sept.

Nightlife & Entertainment

Concerti in Ville is an annual series of classical concerts that take place in villas throughout the province in May and June, including Vicenza's La Rotonda. Contact the tourist office for a performance schedule.

Teatro Olimpico (Piazza Matteotti, Vicenza, Box Office ☎ 0444-222801, Tue-Sat, 9:30 am-2:30 pm; closed Mon and Sun except on performance days). This Palladian theater hosts classical music concerts, classical drama and dance performances. Tickets can be purchased at the theater's box office and are sometimes available the day of a performance.

Local Resources

IAT - Vicenza
Piazza Matteotti 12
Vicenza
☎ 0444-320854

Vicenza

The publication *Informa Città* is Vicenza's monthly guide to cultural and leisure events in the city and is available at the tourist information offices.

Websites

www.vicenzae.org

www.vicenza.com

■ Bassano del Grappa

At the foot of the mountains where the Brenta Valley opens onto the plain sits the ancient market town of Bassano del Grappa, exuding an idyllic mélange of old world charm and cosmopolitan panache.

A possession of the mighty Venetian Republic (as shown by the winged lion of St. Mark in Piazza Libertà), the city enjoyed great prosperity for many years.

Time has been a friend to this luminous city that has aged gracefully and preserves many elements from its history, including the symbolic Palladian bridge, **Ponte degli Alpini**, its famed firewater *grappa* and its ceramic production.

Getting There

By Car: The easiest route to Bassano from Verona and Vicenza is via the **A4** motorway to the **A31** and then exiting at Vicenza Nord. From here follow **SS53** to Cittadella and then **SS47** to Bassano del Grappa. If you're coming from Venice, the easiest route by car is **SS13** north to Treviso, then SS53 west toward Cittadella and finally **SS47** north to Bassano del Grappa. From Padua, follow **SS47** north to Bassano. Unfortunately most of these are two-lane roads that are heavily trafficked during peak hours, but they are the most direct routes.

By Bus: FTV (www.ftv.vi.it) buses run frequently between Vicenza and Bassano del Grappa daily and the **SITA** buses travel to Bassano from Padua. To reach Bassano by bus from Venice there is a SITA bus with a connection in Padua, but the most direct route to Bassano is by train. Bassano del Grappa's main bus station is in Piazzale Trento.

 By Train: Bassano's railway station is on Via Chilesotti. It takes approximately one hour to reach Bassano from Vicenza by train and most trains connect in either Cittadella or Castelfranco Veneto. Direct trains to Bassano from Venice take about 70-85 minutes and from Padua about one hour.

 By Plane: The nearest airport to Bassano del Grappa with domestic and international flights daily is **Venice's Marco Polo**. From here visitors have the option of continuing on to Bassano by train or by bus. For details: www.veniceairport.it.

Getting Around

The best way to travel around Bassano del Grappa is on foot. The city center is small and, although the outskirts sprawl, all of the town's main attractions can be easily reached on foot. If you plan to visit any of the restaurants or lodgings listed in this section that are outside of the town center, you'll need a car to do so but it will be worth venturing beyond city limits for these.

Sightseeing

Ponte degli Alpini. Also known among locals as the *Ponte Vecchio* and the *Ponte di Palladio* (after the great 16th-century architect who designed it) this bridge served for centuries as an important road of communication and has become Bassano's icon. The bridge was likely first built spanning the Brenta River in the 12th century and over the centuries was rebuilt on several occasions after river floods and acts of war demolished it in 1750, 1813 and 1948. The bridge

Vicenza

that stands today is still based on Andrea Palladio's 1569 design and, with the famous Grapperia Nardini on its eastern end, was made famous throughout Italy by a popular song Alpine troops sang during World War II.

> **Panoramic View:** Cross the Ponte degli Alpini to the west side and turn left along the narrow road, following it until you reach a stone wall and the river. Depending on the time of year and the water flowing down from the mountains, you may be able to walk down to the bank of the Brenta and take the classic photo of the bridge.

Viale dei Martiri (Street of the Martyrs). Stretching between Bassano's old castle and the Porta delle Grazie, this road was known as the Contrada delle Grazie until 31 partisans were hung from its trees in 1944 for the whole town to see. According to some accounts, a wall once stood on the north side of the trees but was demolished at the request of wealthy families who wanted a better view of the mountains from their homes along today's Viale dei Martiri.

> **Panoramic View:** Pass the Ostaria Ca' Brando and continue along Via Pusterla through a small tunnel. On the other side of the tunnel you can walk down to the bank of the Brenta. This is a quiet area where you'll seldom see more than a few locals. Bring a book or your lunch and enjoy a different perspective of the bridge than most travelers see.

Museo Civico (Via Museo 12, Bassano del Grappa, ☎ 0424-522235, www.museobassano.it; Tue-Sat, 9 am-6:30 pm, Sun, 3:30-6:30 pm; cumulative ticket for the Museo Civico and the Museo della Ceramica is €4.50). Located in the former monastery of the church of San Francesco, Bassano's civic museum was founded in 1828 and houses several interesting collections, including the world's largest collection of paintings by Jacopo Bassano. Its archeological collection exhibits bronze objects, jewelry and ceramic pieces that date back as far as the Roman age in addition to prints, drawings and engravings that chronicle Bassano's history.

Museo della Ceramica (Palazzo Sturm, Via Ferracina, Bassano del Grappa, ☎ 0424-524933; Tue-Sat, 9 am-12:30 pm and 3:30-6:30 pm, Sun, 10 am-12:30 pm and 3:30-6:30 pm; cumulative ticket for the Museo Civico and Museo della Ceramica is €4.50). The 18th-century Palazzo Sturm along the Brenta's left bank chronicles Bassano's ceramic production from the 16th century to the present. Pieces displayed chronologi-

cally depict the evolution of ceramic styles and techniques and include a collection of pieces by the 18th-century producers Manardi and Antonibon. There are some contemporary ceramics on display as well as pieces found in archaeological excavations. As you walk through you'll notice paintings and frescoes on the walls by Anselmi and Zompini from the 18th century, as well as stucco decorations.

Museo degli Alpini (Taverna degli Alpini, Via Angarano, 8:30 am-8 pm, closed Mon; free admission). This small museum within the Taverna al Ponte contains a collection of photographs, uniforms, weaponry, documents and other objects from the Alpine regiments who fought in both World Wars in the zone.

Torre Civica (Piazza Garibaldi, Nov-Mar, Sat and Sun, 10 am-1 pm and 2-6 pm; Apr-Oct, Tue-Sun, 9:30 am-12:30 pm and 3-7 pm; €2). After a period of restoration, this medieval tower has been reopened to the public. Erected in the 14th century, it once served as a guard tower between the city's two castles and now offers panoramic views of the city and surroundings.

Great Value: A cumulative ticket allows entrance to the Museo Civico, the Museo della Ceramica and the Torre Civica for €6 and is available at the Museo Civico.

Vicenza

Adventures

Cultural Adventure

Discovering Bassano's Firewater

Nardini (Ponte Vecchio 2, Bassano del Grappa, ☎ 0424-227741; Grapperia by the Bridge, 8 am-8 pm; closed Mon from Oct-May; bar near Generale Giardino, 7 pm-midnight on weekends; closed Wed). There is often little distinction in people's minds between the bridge and the grappa – for both the Ponte degli Alpini and the Nardini distillery on the bridge's edge have come to be synonymous with Bassano. It all began back in 1779 when Bortolo Nardini, now somewhat of a local legend, came from the Trentino Valley to establish his distilling business in Bassano. He more than succeeded in his quest and over the years, grappa became the drink of choice for locals and anyone passing through town. The Nardini grapperia served not only as the social heart of town but also as an important gathering place for political groups. Grappa gained particular popularity during the World Wars among soldiers who crossed the strategically important Ponte degli Alpini. Centuries later, after passing into the hands of children and grandchildren many times over, the *aquavitae* (aqua di vita) as it's called, is still being produced and sold in the small grapperia adjacent to the Ponte Vecchio and in the bar near Piazzale Giardino. Although they employ more advanced techniques now in their production process, the product is the same as indicated by Nardini's unchanged label. If you pass by Nardini in the late morning or afternoon, join locals congregating out front and on the bridge for the reddish drink. *Mezzo mezzo* (half and half), as they call it, is a bitter blend of two of Nardini's products and if grappa is too strong for your taste, try this. If it's not too busy when you pay a visit to the distillery, request a tour of the rooms below the grapperia where grappa is stored in large barrels and bottles behind lock and key. You'll enjoy the view of the bridge and the river from down here and, on the stairway down, take notice of the lines indicating where high river levels flooded their cellar over the years.

Poli Museo della Grappa (Via Gamba 6, Ponte Vecchio, Bassano del Grappa, ☎ 0424-524426; 9 am-1 pm and

2:30-7:30 pm; closed Mon morning; free admission). Although this isn't Bassano's most historical distillery, the Poli family continues to produce grappa according to tradition employing old methods and equipment. The museum chronicles the history of grappa distillation and there is also a shop where visitors can purchase Poli's products, including Merlot, Pinot, Moscato, liquorice, herb and berry grappas and liquors.

Festivities

Bassano and its nearby towns host **Opera Estate** (☎ 0424-217815, operafestival@comune.bassano.vi.it) in July and August each year, a festival with a long, varied schedule of outdoor dance and theatrical performances, musical events and opera. Tickets can be purchased at the tourist information center.

White asparagus is to Bassano del Grappa what beer is to Munich and this is no more apparent than at the **Mostra del Asparago Bianco** (Consorzio di Asparago di Bassano, www.asparagodibassano.com), Bassano's annual white asparagus festival in Apr and May. If you have never tasted white asparagus, the festival is the best time to try them at a variety of showcases, tastings, dinners and other events.

Dining Out

Pizzeria La Pace (Via Cartiera 62/A, Rossano Veneto, ☎ 0424-848453; closed Mon; dinner only; €€). The 15-minute drive into Bassano's outskirts is worth the trip for La Pace's out-of-this world pizza. This neighborhood pizzeria specializing in oversized pizzas delivers them hot from the pizza oven to the table on wooden paddles. Several decorated paddles adorn the walls, including a few that have been autographed by Italian celebrities, including the pop-star Jovanotti. Try to plan an early meal here because this place is a local favorite and fills up early. You may not have much of an appetite left after indulging in one of

DINING PRICE CHART	
Price per person for an entrée	
€	Under €5
€€	€5-€12
€€€	€13-€20
€€€€	€21-€30
€€€€€	Over €30

their pizzas, but if they offer you a *digestivo* on the house (as they often do), graciously accept. This kelly green house specialty has a minty flavor and, although its name seems to be a secret, it puts a good finishing touch on your meal.

Belvedere (Viale delle Fosse 1, Bassano del Grappa, ☎ 0424-552187, www.bonotto.it; €€€€). I haven't yet had the opportunity to dine in this restaurant, but it is heralded as one of the area's finest dining establishments and is an excellent place to enjoy expertly prepared traditional dishes.

Birreria Ottone (Via Matteoti 48/50, Bassano del Grappa, ☎ 0424-522206; closed Mon night and Tue; major credit cards accepted; €€). Founded by the Austrian brewer Otto Wipflinger in 1870, this popular beer hall serves a copious selection of German and Austrian beers to accompany its hearty regional and Austrian dishes. Although it is the beer that attracts many patrons, the convivial atmosphere and dishes like *baccalà alla Vicentina* and Wienerschnitzel make this a great choice.

Breseghea (Via delle Statue, Mussolente, ☎ 0424-30407, Fri-Sun; €€). While so many structures throughout Italy have robbed the title *agriturismo*, sometimes using it to wrongly describe a restored country house that has guest rooms and dining facilities with an unfortunate emphasis on neither one, you can count on a genuine agriturismo experience at Breseghea, where they produce nearly all of the products they serve and sell (80%) on their own land. Positioned just outside of Bassano del Grappa, this classic agriturismo is one of the best known in the zone and a popular gathering spot for locals on weekends. The family works hard all week tending their animals and their land to prepare for the weekend when they open their doors with a friendly smile and a great pride in their family's traditions. From Friday until Sunday evening Samantha, her mother Rosa and her sisters entertain everyone from famous clothing designers to the local farm folk who gather together around long tables and take part in a truly homegrown experience. The family prepares traditional specialties using fruits and vegetables from their garden, salumi and meats from their animals, and hearty bread from their wood oven, all complemented by homemade wine from their vineyards. Before leaving, you can purchase a number of their products, including their famous *pane* (bread), *sottoaceti* (pickled garden vegetables) and their *macedonia* of dried fruit soaked in grappa. The faint-hearted should remain in the dining room with their small glass of espresso at the end of the meal (coffee here is served up the old-fashioned way in glasses not cups), but the curious should request a tour of the farm. Visit the cellar where they store their wines and aging salumi, their animal pens, vineyards and slaughter rooms.

Caffè Gelateria Danieli (Piazza Garibaldi, Bassano del Grappa, ☎ 0424-529322; €). Enjoy an ice cream or an espresso on the terrace of one of Bassano's most chic cafés while watching the locals go about their daily routines in the bustling Piazza Garibaldi.

Taverna al Ponte (Ponte Vecchio, Bassano del Grappa, 8:30 am-2 am; closed Mon; €). just across Bassano's historic bridge, this small taverna is a popular local stop for espresso, aperitifs, panini and other quick snacks. Grab one of the few seats on the small balcony overlooking the Brenta River and the opposite side of town.

Bottega del Pane (Piazza Libertà 25, Bassano del Grappa, ☎ 0424-522119). This bread shop on the corner of Piazzetta Monte Vecchio and Piazza Libertà has a great selection of freshly baked breads and, if you're in the area mid-morning, join the locals for a taste of one of their savory *pizzette* (mini-pizzas).

Accommodations

 Villa Ca' Sette (Via Cunizza da Romano 4, Bassano del Grappa, ☎ 0424-383350, www.ca-sette.it; major credit cards accepted; €€€€). If your budget allows you to indulge yourself for one night, why not let Ca' Sette be the place? A

HOTEL PRICE CHART	
Based on a double room for two	
€	Under €50
€€	€50-€80
€€€	€81-€120
€€€€	€121-€190
€€€€€	Over €190

comparable hotel in Venice or Verona would probably cost twice as much as what you'll spend here, and you'll take plea-

Vicenza

sure in every minute of your stay and feel that those extra euros have been well spent. Located just out of Bassano's center in a tranquil country setting, this restored 18th-century villa was once the summer residence of a noble Venetian family and today offers its guests exclusive accommodations in a refined atmosphere. The elegant rooms and suites are in three buildings - the Villa, the Casa Colonica and the Barchessa. While the amenities are unmistakably modern, rooms retain original elements such as exposed stone walls that enhance their appeal and antique quality.

Hotel Belvedere (Piazzale G. Giardino 14, Bassano del Grappa, ☎ 0424-529845, www.bonotto.it; breakfast included; handicap-accessible; major credit cards accepted; €€€) and **Hotel Palladio** (Via Gramschi 2, Bassano del Grappa, ☎ 0424-523777, www.bonotto.it; breakfast included; major credit cards accepted; €€) are both owned by the Bonotto Hotels group and in downtown Bassano. They offer guests all modern amenities. The Belvedere is a notch above the Palladio, offering guests several junior suites and a superb restaurant in a more formal atmosphere.

Al Castello (Piazza Terraglio 19, Bassano del Grappa, ☎ 0424-228665, www.hotelalcastello.it; €€). This small hotel near the Ezzelini castle is a fairly inexpensive lodging option and its rooms are comfortable. Several have nice views of the piazza, including 3, 4, 10 and 11. Breakfast is not included in the rate and you'd fare better stopping for something in town than spending the €6 here.

Residence Nonna Giuseppina (Via Lanzarini 15, Località Sacro Cuore, Romano d'Ezzelino, ☎ 0424-572463, www.nonnagiuseppina.it; major credit cards accepted; €€). The rewards of finding lodging outside of town are no secret. Cheaper rates, fewer crowds and simply more bang for your buck. But the biggest plus for many is crossing over city limits beyond the realm of *turistas* into the land of the locals. In the case of Residence Nonna Giuseppina, you'll only travel a few miles out of Bassano's city center to find this, but the residence's rural setting can change your mood instantly and help you forget for a moment that you're a wandering traveler. The perks here are comfort and affordability, but not at the expense of character or quality. The recently converted country house in the foreground of Monte Grappa offers guests a choice between mini-apartments and rooms, in addition to well-maintained facilities, including a gym, a small pool and nicely manicured gardens. Although it will probably only work if you have a car of your own, it is centrally located just off the SS47 (Valsugana state road) and is a convenient base for exploring the entire Veneto region. This is great for families who want their independence and flexibility.

Shopping

Markets

Bassano del Grappa's **general market** takes place Thursday and Saturday mornings in Piazza Garibaldi, Piazza Libertà and the surrounding streets.

Shops

In addition to the large-scale ceramic production in nearby Nove, Bassano del Grappa has its own history of ceramic production. There are several shops around town that carry a good selection of locally produced ceramics, including **Zeus Ceramiche** (Via Ferracina 1, Bassano del Grappa, ☎ 0424-524339; 10 am-12:30 pm and 3:30-7 pm; closed Mon in winter; major credit cards accepted).

Carteria Tassotti (Via Ferracina 16/18, Bassano del Grappa, ☎ 0424-523013, www.tassotti.it; Mon-Sat, 9:30 am-12:30 pm and 2:30-7:30 pm, Sun, 10 am-12:30 pm and 2:30-7:30 pm; major credit cards accepted). If you're looking for unique souvenirs, this lovely shop near the Ponte degli Alpini carries stationery, prints and office items in addition to books that highlight the local zone. This was the first of the Tassotti shops to open and later ones were opened in Venice, Verona, Florence, Milano and Bologna.

Alessia (Via Ferracina 19, Bassano del Grappa, ☎ 0424-529006; closed Mon morning) is a small boutique that sells fine (and somewhat pricey) children's clothing.

Nightlife & Entertainment

Ca' Brando Ostaria (Via Pusterla 52/54; Tue-Fri, 7 pm-2 am, Sat and Sun, 11:30 am-2 am; €). This small osteria overlooking the Brenta River is a popular local haunt in the evenings, particularly in summer when people take a glass of wine and a cheese and salumi plate outside onto the small terrace.

Caffè Italia (Piazzale Generale Giardino 1, Bassano del Grappa, ☎ 0424-220087; 9 am-1 am; closed Mon; major credit cards accepted; €). This café and wine bar near the Porta delle Grazie serves several renowned local wines, including those from Bassano's *Zonta* winery. The outdoor tables can be rather noisy during the day since the café is on a heavily trafficked road, but despite that it's a great place to enjoy a drink or a small snack any time of day.

Local Resources

IAT – Bassano del Grappa
Largo Corona d'Italia 35
Bassano del Grappa
☎ 0424-524-351

> **Author's Tip:** Bassano's tourist office creates a daily itinerary highlighting sights, markets, concerts and other events taking place in Bassano and its surroundings. The handy itinerary provides details, including addresses and opening hours and is a useful resource that helps tourists make their plans around local holidays, unexpected museum closures, strikes and other events.

Websites

www.turismo.regione.veneto.it

■ Marostica & Nove

Few towns exude such charm and noble grandeur as Marostica, a fortified medieval town at the foot of the Asiago plateau with an enchanting pulse.

Even before entering its gates, most visitors are captivated from afar by the well-preserved rampart walls that cascade down the slopes of the Pausolino hill. Constructed during the

Scaligeri dynasty's 14th-century rule to protect from invasions, the walls enclose a small town that enjoyed relative peace for nearly 400 years. The winged lion of St. Mark perched on a column in the town square calls to mind *La Serenissima*, the Republic of Venice that remained in control until Napoleon invaded in the late 18th century.

Marostica is famous today for its biannual human chess game played in the Piazza Castello and its luscious cherries that ripen in the verdant countryside in late spring.

Getting There

 By Car: To reach Marostica and Nove from Verona, Padua or Venice, take the **A4** (Milano-Venezia) highway to Vicenza and then pick up the **A31** highway. Follow A31 to Dueville and then signs to Marostica. From Bassano del Grappa, follow **SS248** west to Marostica and Nove (about 10 minutes). The best places to park are in the designated lots outside of Marostica's walls.

 By Bus: There is one **FTV** (www.ftv.vi.it) bus line that travels several times daily between Bassano del Grappa and Schio, making stops in both Nove and Marostica. There are also a few other lines that travel between Marostica and Bassano del Grappa and Marostica and Vicenza. Marostica's bus station is on Viale Stazione near the lower castle.

 By Train: The nearest railway station to Marostica and Nove is in Bassano del Grappa. From here, connect to Marostica and Nove by bus.

 By Plane: The nearest major airport to Marostica with domestic and international flights daily is Venice's Marco Polo. From here visitors have the option of continuing on to Marostica by train and bus. For details: www.veniceairport.it.

Getting Around

Marostica is a small town and the best way to get around within the walls is on foot. The easiest way to reach Nove's museum and ceramic shops is by car or by the local bus that travels between Schio and Bassano del Grappa, making stops in Marostica and Nove a few times each day.

Sightseeing

Il Castello Inferiore (Piazza Castello, Marostica, ☎ 0424-72127; Mon-Sat, 10 am-noon and 3-6 pm; Sun, 3:30-6 pm). Constructed in 1320 for Cansignorio della Scala of the mighty Scaligeri clan, Marostica's lower castle was restored many times over the centuries. When the League of Cambrai damaged the town's upper castle, this lower castle in the town square became the Podesta Veneziano in the early 16th century. Today the castle serves as the town hall and merits a visit for the exhibit displaying costumes and weaponry used over the years in the Partita ai Scacchi. Rampart walls connect the lower castle to the **Castello Superiore** (Upper Castle, right), where visitors can walk its walls and discover magnificent views of the zone from its towers.

The Castello Superiore is only a five-minute drive from the town center. From SS248, follow signs for the upper castle (just west of the walls) as the road winds you to the hilltop.

Museo Civico della Ceramica (Piazza De Fabris 5, Nove, ☎ 0424-829807, www.ceramics.it/museo.nove; Tue-Sat, 9 am-1 pm, Sun, 9:30 am-12:30 pm; closed Mon; €3.60). The Palazzo De Fabris houses Nove's ceramics museum that documents the evolution of ceramic production in Nove, Vicenza and the Veneto region from the 1700s to the present. The historical exhibit includes various terracotta, crystal, majolica and porcelain objects and documents the change in production techniques over the centuries. The exhibit also includes various ceramic objects from other regions of Italy and other European countries.

Adventures

On Foot

Sentiero dei Carmini. Marostica's Castello Superiore (Upper Castle) is perched high above the medieval town on Pausolino Hill, from where visitors can enjoy breathtaking views of the territory. The walk is a bit steep, but as long as you arrive better prepared than I did the first time I visited several years ago (with sandals and a sundress), you shouldn't have too much of a problem. Walk beyond the Piazza di Castello on Via S. Antonio toward the hill and follow signs for *Sentiero Panoramico*. Walk up the steps of **La Chiesa del Carmine**, a 17th-century Baroque church built at the foot of the Pausolino hill, and follow the path that from here snakes its way through a landscape dotted with cherry trees to the hilltop. It takes about 30 minutes to reach the top and the reward is a spectacular view of the area.

Festivities

Partita ai Scacchi (www.marostica-scacchi.it). Once upon a time there lived two men, Vieri da Vallonara and Rinaldo D'Angarano, who were deeply enamored with the beautiful Lionara, daughter of Taddeo Parisio (Lord of Marostica's castle). The year was 1454 and the two men challenged one another to a duel to decide which one would marry Lionara. In an effort to maintain peace, the lord suggested a chess match in lieu of the duel. His daughter Lionara was to marry the winner and her sister, Oldrada, would marry the loser. As the tale goes, the match was played in the town square, attended by the lord, his daughter, the noble court and Marostica's townspeople. All lived happily ever after. Today, this legendary duel is re-enacted on the second weekend of September in even-numbered years with great pomp and circumstance. Suited in the finest Renaissance garb, more than 500 townspeople celebrate the majestic legend by playing chess matches on the life-size chess board in the town square (conducted in the dialect of the Venetian Republic) and in processions marked by dancing, music and fireworks. Performances generally take place Friday, Saturday and Sunday evenings at 9 pm and Sunday at 5 pm, lasting approximately two hours. It is best to purchase tickets in advance. Visit the website or contact the tourist office for details.

Sagra delle Ciliegie. Every May Marostica celebrates its annual Cherry Festival, *Sagra delle Ciliegie*, marking cherry season in one of Italy's largest cherry production zones. The production zone for the *ciliegia di Marostica* (Marostica's cherry) reaches Vicenza Salcedo, Fara Vicentino, Breganze, Mason, Molvena, Pianezze, Bassano del Grappa, Schiavon and, of course, Marostica. During this season, stalls line Marostica's town center selling *Roane, Duroni, Sandre* and *Marostegane* cherries from the zone. In a celebration that began in 1933, people gather to sample the year's best cherries and cherry-based products and enjoy local festivities while growers are awarded for their prized cherries. Check with Marostica's tourist office for a schedule of events.

Marostica in Jazz (June-July, www.marosticainjazz.com) takes place each summer in Marostica with jazz concerts, dinners, cooking demonstrations and more. Stop into the tourist office for a schedule of events.

Dining Out

 Ristorante al Castello Superiore (Via Cansignorio della Scala 4, Marostica, ☎ 0424-73315, www.castellosuperiore.it; closed all day Wed and Thurs for lunch; major credit cards accepted; €€€). Consider this delightful restaurant an obligatory stop on your itinerary in Marostica, not only for its remarkable cuisine, but for its privileged position within Marostica's Castello Superiore (Upper Castle). Perched at the top of the Pausolino Hill, some of the restaurant's most desirable tables are on the terrace overlooking the Vicentina landscape below. According to one of the restaurant's accomplished antipasto and pastry chefs, Daniele Tonellotto, the cuisine is *tradizionale ma creativo*. The kitchen utilizes the season's freshest ingredients and, while there may be a few recognizable dishes on the menu, most are creations of their innovative chefs. One of their premier dishes on the autumn menu is *risotto con la zucca e tartufo* (rice prepared with butternut squash and truffles). Their signature dessert, *bacino di Lionara*, pays homage to the beautiful woman in whose honor the first *partita ai scacchi* was played in the 15th century. Don't miss this fantastic tiramisu-like dessert prepared with *frutti di bosco* (berries) in lieu of cocoa.

Accommodations

 Due Mori (Corso Mazzini 73, Marostica, ☎ 0424-471777, www.duemori.com; major credit cards accepted; €€). This small hotel in an 18th-century building within Marostica's walls offers guests more in the way of comfort and style than the standard hotel room. Rooms are modern with hardwood floors, marble bathrooms and some with wood-beamed ceilings. Bicycles are available for guests to explore town and the hotel's modern restaurant **Sotoportego** is a good option for dinner.

Shopping

Markets

Marostica's **weekly market** takes place each Tuesday in the Piazza degli Scacchi and along Viale Stazione.

Ceramics

When the Venetian Republic decided to capitalize on the demand for porcelain and ceramics from foreign markets by developing their own ceramic industry, they took several steps to stimulate ceramic production in towns like Nove. Thanks to Nove's ideal location near the Brenta River (particularly useful for transportation and hydraulic power) it became a burgeoning center for ceramic production. Today, many factories continue to produce ceramics employing traditional methods and there are a large number of ceramic factories, workshops and boutiques in town, particularly along the road from Marostica to Nove.

La Ceramica V.B.C. (Via Molini 45, Nove, ☎ 0424-590312, www.laceramicavbc.com; Mon-Fri 8:30 am-1 pm and 2-7 pm, Sat 8:30 am-1 pm). This factory produces ceramics for many well-known brands, including Lenox, Crate and Barrel and Williams-Sonoma. You'll find some traditional lines in their factory shop, but they also produce contemporary designs, including mosaic-tiled ceramic pieces. English-language guided tours of the factory can be arranged on weekdays by calling Agnese or Andrea at the number above.

Ceramiche Alessi (Via Molino 39, Nove, ☎ 0424-590062; Mon-Fri 8 am-noon and 2-6 pm). Alessi has a good selection of traditional handcrafted ceramics, including fruit baskets, flowerpots and figurines.

Ceramiche Barettoni Già Antonibon (Via Molini 3, Nove, ☎ 0424-590013; Mon-Fri only). This ceramics factory near the Museo Civico dates back to the 17th century and is likely one of Italy's oldest. Guided visits can be arranged with advance notice.

Clothing & Accessories

Surplus (Via Ponticello 34, Molvena, ☎ 0424-411811; closed Sun and Mon morning; major credit cards accepted). You may have a hard time snagging a parking spot at this small clothing shop along the Marosticana road (SS248) but the deals on top-name designers, including the internationally known local designer Diesel, is worth battling the crowds. Be sure to arrive around delivery time (typically 9 am and noon) to find the best selection. Downstairs you'll see several designer labels full-price, but the real deals can be found upstairs. It helps to know your European size before joining the masses. They have another shop in Vicenza, but I haven't been to that one yet.

Local Resources

Pro Marostica
Piazza Castello 1

Marostica
☎ 0424-72127

Websites

www.comune.marostica.vi.it
www.marosticascacchi.it

VOCABULARY	
Scacchi .... chess	
Ciliegie .... cherries	

■ Palladio & his Villas

Andrea di Pietro della Gondola, better known as Andrea Palladio, was born in Padua in 1508 and as a young boy began an apprenticeship with a stone mason. When Palladio moved to Vicenza at the age of 16, he began work that would eventually lead him to be considered one of the greatest architects of all time.

A century before Palladio's time, wealthy Venetians acknowledged the potential effects of the expanding Ottoman Empire and recognized the importance of diversifying their own wealth by developing their power on the mainland. Using fortunes the Republic had amassed from commerce they began commissioning country houses on the mainland and by the mid-16th century, had a sharp focus on agriculture and land development.

It was around this time that Palladio, the architect who had already been commissioned to design several public and private buildings in the city of Vicenza, began to design the rural villas. Although they were primarily destined to be functional agricultural centers, they were also to serve as retreat homes for the nobility.

Celebrated for his classicism and his ability to create a harmonious relationship between villa and land, Palladio left his mark on 24 of the Veneto's 4,000-plus villas. His villas, inspired by Greek and Roman architecture, served as a

Vicenza

remarkable example of rural organization. Elements common to his villas include domes, columns and porticoes.

The impact of Palladio's architecture extends far beyond the borders of the Veneto region, however, significantly influencing Western architecture in both America and Europe. A fine example of Palladian-style architecture in America is Thomas Jefferson's home, Monticello, near Charlottesville, Virginia. Palladio's villas were added to UNESCO's World Heritage List in 1994.

Villa Tour

The Palladian villas are listed below in a relatively logical order beginning with Villa Godi Malinverni near Thiene in the northern zone of the province and ending with Villa Saraceno in the south (deliberately included last for travelers wishing to culminate their villa experience with an overnight stay at a Palladian villa).

Although the majority of Palladio's villas in the province have been included in this tour, several have been omitted because they are either in disrepair or not open to visitors. In planning your personal villa itinerary consider a few factors: your level of interest in Palladian architecture, how much time your itinerary allows in the zone and whether you intend to visit the villa's interiors as well as their exteriors (where appropriate).

Planning a villa tour when all of the villas are open to the public is virtually impossible since their hours are seemingly haphazard. But if you have time for a scenic drive, plan your tour around those you're most interested in visiting and then just enjoy seeing the exterior of others you find closed. Whether you follow all of it or only parts of it, the tour is intended to give you a better appreciation for Palladio's influence on rural society in Vicenza.

Villa Godi Malinverni (Via Palladio 44, Lonedo di Lugo Vicentino, ☎ 0445-860561, www.villagodi.com; Mar-May and Oct-Nov, Tue, Sat and Sun 2-6 pm; June-Sept, Tue, Sat and Sun 3-7 pm; €6). Some evidence suggests that this was in fact Palladio's first country house, designed between 1537 and 1542. Visitors can see the villa's interior, including its

19th-century fossil museum, 19th-century Italian paintings as well as the villa's surrounding park. The villa, shown at right, has been well maintained and its main hall and Venus room are richly decorated with 16th-century frescoes by G.B. Zelotti.

Villa Piovene Porto Godi (Via Palladio 51, Lonedo di Lugo Vicentino, ☎ 0445-860613; exterior open daily, winter, 2:30-5 pm, summer, 2:30-7 pm; €4.50). Just across the way from Villa Godi Malinverni, the Villa Piovene Porto Godi enjoys some of the best views of any of Palladio's villas from its hilltop position.

Only its 19th-century neo-classical park designed by Francesco Muttoni (who is also credited with making later additions to Palladio's original design) is open to visitors.

Vicenza

Villa Caldogno Nordera (Via Pagello, Caldogno, ☎ 0444-905054; Mar-Oct, Fri 3-6 pm and Sat 9 am-12 pm; €3). The 16th-century villa's interior and surrounding gardens are open to visitors. It was probably started in 1542 and not completed until 1567. Though there has been some controversy in attributing it to Palladio, it seems likely that he was responsible for much of its design. Frescoes by G.A. Fasolo and G.B. Zelotti adorn the villa's interior.

Villa Valmarana Bressan (Via Vigardoletto 31, Vigardolo di Monticello Conte Otto, ☎ 0444-595308; Sat and Sun 9 am-noon and 2-6 pm; call ahead to arrange a visit; €3.50). This is one of Palladio's simpler constructions, built relatively early in his career in the 1540s for the Valmarana cousins, Antonio and Giuseppe, just north of Vicenza. Its interior and gardens are open to visitors.

Villa Valmarana Scagnolari Zen (Via Ponte 1, Lisiera di Bolzano Vicentino, ☎ 0444-873121; call ahead to arrange a visit). Palladio was commissioned to redesign a Gothic building in 1563 for Gianfrancesco Valmarana, but the project was stopped several times, resulting in some changes to Palladio's original design. The interior and gardens are open to the public.

Villa Thiene (Via IV Novembre, Quinto Vicentino, ☎ 0444-584224; Mon-Sat 9:30 am-12:30 pm, Tue and Thurs 3-7 pm; free admission). Visit the park and interior of this villa built in the mid-1540s for Marcantonio Thiene.

Villa Chiericati Da Porto Rigo (Via Nazionale 1, Vancimuglio di Grumolo delle Abbadesse, ☎ 0444-387076; last Wed of each month 8-10 am; free admission). Only the grounds of this villa dating back to the 1550s are open to the public.

Villa Almerico Capra Valmarana La Rotonda (Via Rotonda 29, Vicenza, ☎ 0444-321793; Mar-Oct, gardens, Tue-Sun 10 am-noon and 3-6 pm, interior, Wed 10 am-noon and 3-6 pm; €3 for gardens, €6 for interior). Initiated by Palladio between 1556 and 1558 and later completed by his follower Vincenzo Scamozzi in the early 17th century, La Rotonda is often heralded as Palladio's finest architectural achievement and has served as the model for many other structures in Europe and particularly in America's South. The villa is a perfectly symmetrical structure with four identical facades, and its dome reflects Palladio's tendency toward classicism. The villa has been kept in excellent condition and is frequently the site of concerts and other cultural events. Its interior and exterior are open to the public.

Villa Pisani (Via Risaie 1, Bagnolo di Lonigo, ☎ 0444-831104; Apr-Oct; call ahead to arrange a visit; €6).

This villa was likely built in two stages and is considered to be one of Palladio's earlier villas.

Villa Poiana (Via Castello 41, Poiana Maggiore, ☎ 0444-898554; Oct-Mar, Tue-Sun 10 am-12:30 pm and 2-5 pm, Apr-Sept, Tue-Sun 10 am-12:30 pm and 2-6 pm; €4). Not one of Palladio's more impressive structures, this villa was designed by Palladio for Bonifacio Poiana and is open to the public.

Villa Saraceno (Via Finale 8, Agugliaro, ☎ 0444-891371; Apr-Oct, Wed 2-4 pm). Completely restored by the British organization, The Landmark Trust, parts of this 16th-century Palladian villa and its grounds are open to visitors and can be rented for holidays (see below).

Accommodations

Villa Saraceno (Via Finale 8, Agugliaro, ☎ 0444-891371, www.landmarktrust.co.uk). The Landmark Trust is a British organization dedicated to preserving and restoring historic and architecturally unique buildings and turning them into holiday destinations, as they've done with the Villa Saraceno. The villa is available to be rented by the week year-round.

Reading Materials

Andrea Palladio: le Ville (This book was published by the Touring Club Italiano in 2002 and is available at several tourist offices in the province)

I Quattro Libri dell'Architettura by Andrea Palladio

Websites

www.boglewood.com/palladio

www.unesco.org

www.cisapalladio.org

■ Valbrenta

The Brenta River cuts a path between the Asiago Plateau to its west and the Colli Alti to its east, forming a verdant river valley known as the *Valbrenta* (Brenta Valley). The valley encompasses many small villages, including Campolongo sul Brenta, Valstagna, Solagna and San Nazario and, although it has not been discovered by international tourists, it is a Mecca for river sports and outdoor adventures, from white water rafting and cycling to kayaking and hiking.

Getting There & Getting Around

By Car: The best way to access the Valbrenta zone is by car from the SS47 (also known as the Valsugana).

By Train: The closest train stations to the Valbrenta zone are in San Nazario and Bassano del Grappa, but from either station it is difficult to access Valbrenta without a car.

Adventure Outfitters

Ivan Team (Via Oliero di Sotto 85, Valstagna, ☎ 0424-558250, www.ivanteam.com, www.valbrenta.net). Ask almost any local in the zone who Ivan Pontarollo is and you might get the impression he's a celebrity. This Bassano native has spent several decades immersed in the Valbrenta zone where he translated his passion for adventure river sports into a career by founding Ivan Team, one of the most respected adventure outfitters in northeastern Italy. With a variety of river sports championship titles under his belt, Pontarollo acts as a guide as well. Ivan Team offers participants a wide variety of activities from canoeing, rafting and hydrospeed to river trekking, bungee jumping and spelunking. They operate from April until October (the best season for river sports). Some activities are appropriate for children, including *battello*, a cruising raft that navigates the Brenta. Their locations include the river house, Casa sul Fiume in Solagna, and their headquarters at the Grotte di Oliero, where they operate boat trips to the caverns. Inquire about individual lessons and the Fly Day, River Day, Adrena

Day and Crazy Day adventure programs that combine a variety of adventure activities. Participants are provided with activity-appropriate equipment, including wet suits and life jackets, but should come prepared with their own water shoes, bathing suits, towels and active clothing.

Onda Selvaggia (Località Merlo, San Nazario, ☎ 0424-99581, www.ondaselvaggia.com) specializes in river sports in the Valbrenta zone, including canoeing and rafting as well as free climbing and hiking in the Brenta Valley. They also have a large presence in Italy's Valle d'Aosta region if your itinerary takes you there.

Adventures

Grotte di Oliero (Valstagna, ☎ 0424-558250, www.grottedioliero.it; Oct-Apr, Sun only; May, June and Sept, Wed-Mon; July and Aug, open daily; park hours 9 am-7 pm; weekday hours 9:30 am-noon and 2-5 pm; Sun 9 am-5 pm; park only €2, boat ride and park €6). Begin your adventure by embarking on a half-hour boat ride and guided visit to the Grotte di Oliero, said to be among Europe's largest Karst springs. After visiting the caves that were discovered in the 1800s by Alberto Parolini, spend an hour or two exploring the rich flora and vegetation of the surrounding botanical park's nature paths that wind through the valley. **Directional Info:** To get to Oliero from Bassano, take the Valsugana (SS47) and continue north, following signs for the Grotte.

> **Note:** While traveling the park on foot, remain on the path and respect the environment. Do not collect wildflowers, touch the stalactites or throw rocks into the water.

On Bikes

Cycling Made in Italy (US ☎ 810-629-6435, Italy ☎ 0424-98671, www.bikeitaly.com). When American cyclist and tri-athlete Lisa Dolza first came to the Valbrenta zone to train more than a decade ago, she didn't expect to find a new home. But the Michigan native became so enamored with the richness of the zone and the diversity of the cycling that she founded her own cycling company in the Brenta river valley in the 1990s. Recreational and professional cyclists have profited from CMI's cycling holiday program that, unlike many others, has a fixed home base where participants return each night. From April through October local English-speaking guides lead groups of no greater than 10 cyclists on daily itineraries that range from 30-80 miles and can be tailored to the fitness and interest levels of clients. Most guided rides take place in the morning and participants are free to spend their afternoons sightseeing and engaging in other activities such as kayaking, white water rafting and paragliding. At time of publication the weeklong program cost for one person was €1,500 and included guided daily rides, use of high-performance road bikes and hybrid bikes, airport pick-up in Venice, lodging and two meals daily. CMI also caters to cyclists who prefer embarking on self-guided itineraries, providing them with all of the necessary route and itinerary guidance. Most programs are weeklong during high season, but Lisa will arrange abbreviated programs (for a minimum of three days) when scheduling permits.

On Foot

La Calà del Sasso. For centuries loggers transported their wood from the Asiago Plateau to the Brenta River valley by way of the Calà del Sasso, a trail with 4,444 stone steps and an adjacent chute. When they reached the Brenta River, logs were loaded onto rafts and carried downstream to Venice for boat construction purposes. Today this interesting hike is one of the most popular in the zone, both for its historical and natural aspects. **Timing:** Allow approximately two hours to ascend the steep trail and another two to descend. **Difficulty:** Ascending this trail is moderately difficult because of its steepness and proper hiking attire is necessary. **Caution:** Walking on slippery stones can be dangerous and it is not recommended to embark on this trail during wet periods (in the early spring when the land begins to thaw and during or following rain storms). The best time to explore the trail is from June until September. **Directional Info:** From Valstagna, follow signs toward Foza. Just out of the town center at the road's second curve you'll see a small parking area where the trail begins.

Nocturnal excursions are organized from spring through fall and depart from the hotel San Giovanni (Solagna, ☎ 0424-556008). These events often begin with a dinner and are followed by a nighttime exploration of the Colli Alti east of Valbrenta. Contact the hotel for a schedule.

Rock Climbing

Palestra di Roccia in Valle S. Felicità. One of the more popular spots in the zone for rock climbing is just a few miles outside of Bassano del Grappa near Romano d'Ezzelino in what's known as the Valle S. Felicità. Climbers should come prepared with their own equipment. **Directional Info:** The easiest way to find the rock-climbing wall is from the Cadorna Road, the primary route to Monte Grappa. From the traffic circle in Romano d'Ezzelino, follow signs for Cima Grappa (you can access the route for Borso del Grappa and Possagno from this same traffic circle). Follow this road for approximately 1½ km and when you reach the restaurant **Hostaria da Giuliano** at the first switchback, pull into the small parking lot and follow the yellow signs onto a narrow road behind the restaurant. At the end of this small road, turn left and follow the road about half a kilometer until you reach a gravel parking lot where the road dead ends. Just before reaching the parking lot is a popular restaurant and hotel **Dalla Mena** (Via Santa Felicità 14, Romano d'Ezzelino, ☎ 0424-36481, €€) that serves typical local dishes. Beyond the large parking lot you'll find a small yellow chapel and the rock wall. This is also an important trailhead where several trails of varying degrees of difficulty depart. These include *CAI 100* to Campo Croce and Cima Grappa and *CAI 54* to Colle Averto and Campo Solagna.

> **Note:** If you are having trouble finding the road in Romano d'Ezzelino that leads to the rock wall, stop and ask where the Cadorna road or Valle S. Felicità are and any local should be able to guide you in the right direction.

Driving

 The most scenic and direct route to Monte Grappa (see Treviso's *Monte Grappa and Environs*) is **La Strada Cadorna** that can be accessed by following signs in Romano d'Ezzelino for Cima Grappa. The road is steep and often narrow with many switchbacks but reveals magnificent vistas and is well-worth driving in pleasant weather.

Dining Out

 There are a handful of places in the Valbrenta area where visitors can enjoy simple homestyle cooking, including **Cornale** (Valsugana Highway, SS47, ☎ 0424-92554, www.cornale.com; closed Mon; €), a Bavarian-style restaurant and birreria, and **Al Gargana** (Via Oliero di Sotto 73, Valstagna, ☎ 0424-98666; closed Mon; €€), a restaurant and pizzeria specializing in fish. Nearby Bassano del Grappa offers a wider range of dining options.

Accommodations

 Contarini (Via Contarini 112, Campolongo sul Brenta, ☎ 0424-558164, www.contarini.it; €€) and **Ai Cavallini** (Via Trento 38, Solagna, ☎ 0424-558005; €€) are small, comfortable hotels a few miles outside of Bassano del Grappa and are popular choices for travelers who come to the Valbrenta zone to engage in outdoor activities.

Local Resources

Comunità Montana del Brenta
Carpane di San Nazario
☎ 0424-99906

Consorzio Pro Loco Grappa Valbrenta
Via Foscolo
Romano d'Ezzelino
☎ 0424-99221

■ Asiago e l'Altopiano dei Sette Comuni

Less than 40 miles from Vicenza but worlds away in landscape, tradition and spirit sits the distinctly Alpine Altopiano di Asiago (Asiago Plateau), a territory that has straddled Italian and Germanic cultures for years and continues to reflect the influence of the Cimbrian people (of Germanic origin) who inhabited the area in the Middle Ages.

Asiago, the plateau's capital town and principle holiday destination, is surrounded by the *sette comuni* (seven communities): Conco, Enego, Foza, Gallio, Lusiana, Roana and Rotzo.

Aat about 1,000 meters/2,800 feet above sea level near the Trentino-Alto Adige region, the Asiago plateau is sheltered by surrounding mountains that protect it from extreme weather conditions. Asiago's fair climate year-round and its average of eight-nine hours of sunshine daily make it a great destination to practice a variety of summer and winter sports.

Although the plateau is a lively, well-equipped tourist resort today, it suffered terrible losses and destruction in the 20th century. During World War I, the plateau was on the Italian-Austrian front and was tremendously scarred by bombings and bloody battles that left indelible marks and destroyed much of the local culture and architecture.

And, while trenches, forts and old trails still remind visitors of the zone's role in history, most find an unparalleled serenity and beauty in the land, the culture and the people.

Getting There

 By Car: Take the **A4** from Venice or Verona and then pick up the **A31** near Vicenza. Continue on A31 and exit at Piovene Rocchette, following signs for Asiago. From Bassano, take the provincial scenic road that winds through the hills to the Asiago Plateau. The most convenient way to explore Asiago and its neighboring towns is definitely by car.

 By Bus: FTV (www.ftv.vi.it) buses travel to Asiago from both Vicenza and Bassano but only a few times daily, so plan accordingly. It takes approximately one hour to reach Asiago from Bassano by bus, and two hours from Vicenza.

 By Train: The nearest train stations are in Vicenza, Thiene and Bassano del Grappa. From here, connect to Asiago by bus.

 By Plane: The nearest major airport to Asiago with domestic and international flights daily is **Venice's Marco Polo**. From here visitors have the option of continuing on to Asiago by train or by bus. For details: www.veniceairport.it.

Sightseeing

 Sacrario Militare (Viale degli Eroi, ☎ 0424-463088; mid-May through Sept, 9 am-noon and 3-6 pm; Jan through mid-May, 9 am-noon and 2-5 pm; free admission). This impressive World War I memorial erected in the 1930s in honor of the soldiers who died in the bloody battles fought on the Altopiano di Asiago is considered one of the most important monuments in the zone. More than 51,000 soldiers are buried here and there is a small museum located within the memorial that contains photos, documents, weaponry and, one of the more chilling objects, a letter from a soldier to his family written only a few hours before his death.

Osservatorio Astrofisico di Asiago (Via dell'Osservatorio 8, Località Pennar, ☎ 0424-462221, www.pd.astro.it; open year-round). This observatory is one of the most important of its kind in Italy and controls the country's largest optical telescope. Call ahead to arrange a guided visit of the observatory and see their advanced equipment used to observe the sun, planets and galaxies.

Adventures

In Winter

Nordic Skiing

 Asiago is considered by many to be the Nordic (cross-country) ski capital of the world, with nearly 500 km/300 miles of trails that wind their way through the tranquil pastures and wooded zones of the plateau. It has seven cross-country skiing centers (*centro fondo*), and well-marked trails of varying degrees of difficulty, plus ski schools, lodges, equipment rentals and night time skiing.

Campolongo Rotzo (☎ 0424-66487, 100+ km of skiing, ski school, equipment rentals, lodge with bar and restaurant, trails ranging from easy to difficult).

Gallio (☎ 0424-445115, www.centrofondo-gallio.com, 150 km of skiing, Rifugio Base-Campomulo and Rifugio Adriana, bars, restaurants and lodging, ski school, equipment rentals, sledding, trails from easy to difficult).

Enego (☎ 0424-490267, 100 km of trails, bar and restaurant, some equipment rentals, trails from easy to difficult).

Cesuna (☎ 0424-67308, nearest to the plain, 40 km of trails through woods and pastures, interconnected with those of Centro Fondo Asiago, ski school, equipment rental, trails from easy to difficult).

Asiago (☎ 348-5920744, www.centrofondoasiago.it, 45 km of trails, hosted the Sci Nordico junior world championships in 1996 and 1999, near Asiago's golf course, ski school, equipment rental, bar, trails from easy through medium).

Monte Corno Lusiana (☎ 0424-406396, 50 km of trails, some nighttime skiing, equipment rental, restaurant, easy and medium trails).

Fontanella Lusiana/Asiago (☎ 0424-64241, snow shoe trails, ski school, equipment rentals, bar/restaurant, interconnected with Monte Corno's trails, trails from easy through difficult).

Alpine Skiing

Although Asiago is primarily a cross-country ski zone, there are approximately 100 km/60 miles of Alpine (downhill) skiing in the zone and more than 50 ski lifts. Most of Asiago's downhill facilities consist of lodges, ski schools and ski and snowboard rental shops, with the largest centers in Asiago (13 ski lifts), Gallio (14 ski lifts), Enego (eight ski lifts) and Mezzaselva (three ski lifts).

Ice Skating

Stadio Odegar (Piazzale della Stazione, Asiago, ☎ 0424-64580; summer and Christmas holidays, daily 10 am-noon, 3-6 pm and 9-11 pm; low season,

Mon, Wed and Fri 10 am-noon, Tue and Thurs 10 am-noon and 3-4:45 pm, Sat 10 am-noon, 3:30-5:30 pm and 9-11 pm, Sun 10 am-noon and 2:30-6 pm; closed May and June). Asiago's indoor ice stadium is open to the general public for ice skating at designated times throughout the year, and is also the site of many figure skating events and Asiago's Serie A ice hockey team's games.

In Summer

On Foot

 If you have some time to spare in Asiago and are interested in exploring the territory on foot, stop into the tourist information center and pick up a *Passeggiate ed Escursioni sul Altopiano* map that details the 31 CAI (Club Alpino Italiano, www.caiasiago.it) trails in the zone. The trails range from *facile (easy)* to *media difficoltà* (average difficulty) to *impegnativo* (difficult). The map also indicates the average time needed for the hike, *solo andata* (one-way) and *andata e ritorno* (roundtrip). Trails pass through old World War I forts, mule trails and trenches.

On Bikes

 There are hundreds of km of unpaved paths and roads throughout the Asiago plateau that date back to World War I and now serve as popular trails for mountain bikers. While some cross-country ski trails do become mountain bike trails in summer, there are others that are exclusively for hikers, as well as pastures and fields. Ask the Consorzio (see below) for details about the Gran Tour dell'Altopiano, a 260-km/156-mile trail that traverses the plateau.

> **Tip:** Contact the **Consorzio Turistico Asiago 7 Comuni** (☎ 0424-464137), for more information about mountain biking, horseback riding, gastronomical and historical excursions. The Consorzio often organizes weekend itineraries such as *Tutto Mountain Bike, A Cavallo delle Emozioni, Le Grandi Battaglie, Natura e Fantasia, Funghi che Passione* and *Le Gioie del Palato* – all inexpensive packages that generally include accommodations, meals and activities.

On Horseback

 Centro Ippico Orthal Kaberlaba (Kaberlaba, ☎ 0424-462119) offers lessons and guided excursions from Asiago's scenic Kaberlaba zone year-round. Call ahead to arrange excursions.

Golf

 Golf Club Asiago (Via Meltar 2, Asiago, ☎ 0424-462721; May-Oct). Despite its setting, Asiago's picturesque 18-hole golf course is relatively level and is transformed into a cross-country ski course in winter.

Culinary Adventures

Malghe Tour

Most of the *malghe* (mountain dairies) are only active for 90-120 days each year, generally open to the public from June through September. Surrounded by expansive pastures, these dairies are interesting to visit, particularly to sample and purchase unique varieties of local cheeses. While you will find many more on your travels through the Asiago plateau, here are a few of the larger, better-known dairies that often give guided tours (albeit in Italian) to visitors. There is also an official **Via delle Malghe**, a route that winds through Asiago's plateau with signs indicating the zone's 87 malghe. Visit the **Comunità Montana** (Spettabilie Reggenza dei Sette Comuni, Via Stazione 1, Asiago, ☎ 0424-63700) for a guide with a map and details about the 16 itineraries.

Malga Galmararetta (Località Galmara, Comune di Camporovere, ☎ 0424-63815; open June-Sept). Between two of the plateau's seven communities, Asiago and Roana, this dairy produces and sells Asiago cheese and gives tours and tastings upon request.

Malga Dosso di Sotto (Località Cima Larici, Asiago, ☎ 348-3234119; open daily June-Sept). Not far from Asiago's town center, this dairy produces Asiago d'Allevo, ricotta and butter.

Malga Busafonda-Campomulo (Via Melette, Località Campomulo, Gallio, ☎ 0445-621295; open June-Sept). In a small fraction of Gallio, this dairy produces several different varieties of Asiago cheese in addition to butter, caciotta and ricotta cheese. Tastings are possible.

Malga Fiara (Strada per l'Ortigara, Località Fiara, Roana, ☎ 360-246248; June-Sept). This malga near Gallio sells fresh and aged sheep's milk cheeses, including Pecorino and ricotta.

Malga Biancoia (Località Biancoia, Conco, ☎ 360-344025). This dairy in the plateau community of Conco sells Asiago pressato, Asiago d'Allevo, caciotta, ricotta and tasella cheeses, as well as butter.

Festivities

La Grande Rogazione di Asiago (Giro del Mondo). Thousands of locals gather annually on the day before the Ascension in May for the Great Tour of Asiago, a solemn 30-km/18-mile procession through the Asiago landscape. Locals give thanks for having escaped the 17th-century plague. One of the stops along the procession route is in the town of Lazzaretto, where many of the plague victims were buried. As a sign of continued life, it is tradition for women to present men with colored eggs on this day.

Dining Out

With such a large concentration of dairies on the Asiago plateau producing the celebrated Asiago D.O.P. cheese, there are numerous varieties that all have distinctly different flavors. A number of factors affect the cheese's essence and texture, including maturation and the type of milk used in production. Some Asiago varieties include La Dolcezza di Asiago, Asiago Allevo, Asiago Pressato, Stravecchio and Mazzano.

The Asiago plateau is also well-known for its production of various honeys and herb and honey flavored grappas and liquors such as Kumetto, Amaro Asiago, Amaro Cimbro and Kranebet. Locally produced meats include speck, pancetta and sopressa. *Patate* (potatoes) from Rotzo are used to make gnocchi and bread, and *sedano* (celery) from Rubbio and *funghi* (mushrooms) are also particularly good in the Asiago zone.

Some of Asiago's traditional dishes include *fan frich* (a type of omelet made with cheese and potatoes) and the *torta ortigara* (a dessert).

Casa Rossa (Via Kaberlaba 19, Asiago, ☎ 0424-462017, www.ristorantecasarossa.it; closed Thurs in low season and a few weeks in June; €€-€€€). Owned by the Dal Sasso family since 1923, this restaurant in Asiago's rural Kaberlaba area is in a picturesque setting surrounded by gently rolling hills and is one of the best places around to enjoy local mountain cuisine. For a good sampling of traditional cuisine, try one of the cheese-based dishes like the *Asiago fuso con funghi e polenta* (baked Asiago cheese and mushrooms served with polenta). If the weather is nice, request a table on the terrace. Otherwise, settle into a table in the upstairs dining rooms. The panoramic windows offer views almost as fantastic as the food.

Agriturismo Grüuntaal (Via Valle 69, Asiago, ☎ 0424-692798, www.gruuntaal.com; July-Sept, open daily; Oct-June, open weekends only; €€). Named for the green valley that surrounds it, Grüuntaal welcomes guests into its farmhouse whether they're coming for a meal, to stay in one of the apartments open year-round, or to purchase their products. The agriturismo owners raise rabbits, ducks, chickens, cows and pigs and serve their homemade products, including salumi, cheese and honey. Meats on the spit are a specialty.

Pasticceria Carli (Piazza Mazzini 2, Asiago, ☎ 0424-462143) is famous for the *Torta Ortigara*, a cake invented here in the 1920s that is prepared with fresh locally produced butter and has since become an Asiago favorite. This pastry shop has a good selection of other delicious sweets as well.

Accommodations

 Sporting Residence Hotel (Corso IV Novembre 77, Asiago, ☎ 0424-462177, www.sportingasiago.com, €€€). One of the more popular sleeps in town, the Sporting Residence in Asiago's pedestrian zone offers guests spacious, comfortably furnished apartments year-round, making it a convenient choice especially for low-season travel. One of its best rooms is #110, with a terrace overlooking the piazza. The hotel also arranges guided excursions to mountain dairies as well as horseback riding excursions. Its facilities include an indoor pool, a gym, and a restaurant.

La Baitina (Via Kaberlaba 35, Asiago, ☎ 0424-462149, www.labaitina.com; closed Tue and in Nov; €€). This friendly Alpine-style hotel and restaurant has a fine setting in Asiago's Kaberlaba area, overlooking the rolling landscape. Rooms are modest and most have private balconies. The restaurant serves traditional local dishes.

Shopping

Many shops in Asiago are open year-round, every day of the week, including Saturday and Sunday. Unusual as this may be, it is particularly nice if you're traveling through Asiago during low season. The pedestrian zone, Corso IV Novembre, is Asiago's main street, lined by attractive boutiques, shops and cafés with outdoor tables. Many shops sell locally produced cheese, honey, herb liquors and grappa-soaked fruits.

The **general market** takes place in Asiago's Piazza Martiri della Libertà each Saturday morning.

Antica Apicoltura Kaberlaba (Via Partut 1, ☎ 0424-462386; closed Sun, Via Lobbia 2, ☎ 0424-460009; closed Sun and Mon; major credit cards accepted). Honey-based cosmetics, honey candles, honey soaps, honey honey. You name it, and this small shop with one location in town and another in the Kaberlaba zone probably sells it. Products are made from locally produced honey.

Tutti i Frutti del Bosco (Corso IV Novembre 78, ☎ 0424-463896). This shop in the town center sells honey, marmalades and other locally produced specialty products.

Local Resources

IAT
Via Stazione 5
Asiago
☎ 0424-462221

Consorzio Turistico
Viale Trento e Trieste 19

Asiago
☎ 0424-464137

Websites

www.asiago7comuni.com
www.ascom.vi.it/asiago
www.caiasiago.it
www.altopiano-asiago.com

VOCABULARY	
Malghe	dairies
Sciare	to ski

> **Note:** You'll probably notice the name *Rigoni* more than once during your stay in Asiago. This is a very popular local name (the likes of Smith) and you'll see it in shops, restaurants and other public places.

Vicenza

Appendix

■ Additional Reading

The World of Venice by Jan Morris

The Architectural History of Venice by Deborah Howard

Stones of Venice by John Ruskin

A History of Venice by John Julius Norwich

Watermark by Joseph Brodsky

Art and Life in Renaissance Venice by Patricia Fortini Brown

Venice Revealed by Paolo Barbaro

The Merchant of Venice by William Shakespeare

Death in Venice by Thomas Mann

Across the River and Into the Trees by Ernest Hemingway

A Venetian Affair by Andrea Di Robilant

Various books by Donna Leon

■ Venice on Screen

Death in Venice (1971)

Casanova (1976)

Indiana Jones and the Temple of Doom (1984)

Everyone Says I Love You (1996)

The Talented Mr. Ripley (1999)

Pane e Tulipani (Bread and Tulips, 2000)

■ Helpful Websites

http://turismo.regione.veneto.it – Veneto tourism

www.italconsulnyc.org – Italian Consulate

www.italtrade.com – Italian Trade Commission

www.globalrefund.com – VAT (Value Added Tax) info

www.trenitalia.com – Railway information

www.autostrade.it – Italian highway information

www.agriturismo.com – Farm holidays in Italy

www.casa.it – Buy and rent houses in Italy

www.museionline.com – Museums in Italy

■ Bringing the Veneto to Your Kitchen

Pasta e Fasoi (Pasta and Bean Soup)

1 16 oz. bag pinto beans
1 large carrot
1 celery stalk
1 small potato
1 small yellow onion
olive oil
½ lb. tubetti, ditalini or other small pasta

Soak the beans for several hours or overnight, changing the water frequently. Add beans to a large pot of water, adding sliced carrot, celery and potato. Cover, bring to a boil, then lower heat to medium and cook for one hour. While the soup is cooking, sauté the onion in oil until golden and set aside. In a separate pot, boil water and cook pasta.

When the soup is done, add the onions, salt and pepper and stir well. Remove about a third of liquid and purée remainder in a blender. Return liquid to soup purée, mix well and ladle into bowls with pasta. Drizzle with extra virgin olive oil and top with grated cheese if desired.

Risi e Bisi (Rice and Peas)

Risi e Bisi is a traditional dish from the Veneto, commonly served on the feast day of St. Mark, Venice's patron saint.

2-3 large garlic cloves
1 small yellow onion
2-3 cups chicken or vegetable broth
1 cup peas (preferably fresh)
1 cup Arborio rice
2 tbsp. butter
Grated Parmesan

Sauté the onion and garlic in oil and butter until golden. Then add the peas and ½ cup of broth, then cook on medium-high heat for about 10 minutes.

Add the rice and 1½ cups of broth. Allow to cook over medium heat for about 30 minutes, stirring occasionally and adding more broth if necessary to achieve a thick consistency. Before removing from heat, add cheese and freshly ground black pepper. Serve immediately.

Fritelle

Fritelle are delicious sweets served in Venice and throughout the Veneto during the Carnevale period. These are sometimes filled with pastry cream, zabaglione or jams, but the most traditional recipe calls for raisins.

1 cup water
¼ cup butter (half a stick)
pinch of salt

1½ cups flour
¼ cup granulated sugar
1 tsp. pure vanilla
dash of lemon extract (optional)
3 large eggs
2 tsp. baking powder
½ cup raisins
powdered sugar for dusting
canola oil for frying (heated to 375°)

Bring water, butter and salt to a boil and remove from the stovetop. Add flour and mix well with a wooden spoon until the dough becomes a smooth ball.

Place back on the heat for about one minute, continuing to mix. Put the warm dough in a glass bowl, adding granulated sugar, pure vanilla, lemon extract and one egg at a time, mixing until the dough becomes somewhat shiny and forms points when dropped from a spoon. Allow to cool.

When cooled, incorporate the baking powder and raisins, mixing well. With the help of two teaspoons, form the fritelle and drop into a large pot of the heated oil.

After a few minutes flip the fritelle so they are golden on all sides. Remove from the oil and place on sheets of paper towel to drain the oil. When cool, dust with powdered sugar.

Bellini

This cocktail was invented in Harry's Bar in Venice by Giuseppe Cipriani, who had a particular love for white peaches.

1 part white peach nectar

3 parts sparkling Prosecco

■ Associations

Esagono (www.esagonoring.com). Six of the Veneto's art towns between Treviso, Padua and Vicenza are united in an association called Esagono (Hexagon) in an effort to promote their cultural heritage and tourism – Asolo, Castelfranco Veneto, Cittadella, Bassano del Grappa, Marostica and Possagno. Stop into a tourist office in any of the above towns for brochures that highlight the sights, restaurants and hotel linked together by this initiative.

Bandiera Arancione (www.touringclub.it/bandierearancioni). The Associazione Paesi Bandiera Arancione was established in 2002 in association with the Touring Club Italiano in order to unite Italian communities on the basis of various cultural, historical, gastronomic and environmental factors and help to promote tourism in these small towns. The Veneto's Bandiera Arancione towns are: Arquà Petrarca, Mel, Montagnana, Portobuffolé and Soave.

■ Language Guide

Basic Vocabulary & Expressions

Si: . . . . Yes

No: . . . . No

Dov'é: . . . . Where is?

Quando: . . . . When?

Che cos'é: . . . . What is it?

Chi: . . . . Who?

Come: . . . . How?

Quanto: . . . . How much?

Quanto costa: . . . . How much does it cost?

Perché: . . . . Why/because
Questo / Quello: . . . . This/That
Qui / Qua: . . . . Here
Li / La: . . . . There
Buon giorno: . . . . Good day/Good morning
Buona sera: . . . . Good afternoon/evening
Buona notte: . . . . Goodnight
Ciao: . . . . Hello/goodbye (informal)
Pronto: . . . . Hello (phone)
Arrivederci: . . . . Goodbye (informal)
Arrivederla: . . . . Goodbye (polite)
Signore: . . . . Mr.
Signora: . . . . Mrs.
Signorina: . . . . Miss
Piacere: . . . . Pleased to meet you
Come sta?: . . . . How are you? (formal, polite)
Come va?: . . . . How's it going? (informal, familiar)
Molto bene / Bene grazie: . . . . Very well/Fine thanks
Come si chiama: . . . . What is your name?
Mi chiamo: . . . . My name is
Grazie / No Grazie: . . . . Thank you/No thank you
Scusa: . . . . Excuse me
Per piacere / per favore: . . . . Please
Permesso: . . . . Excuse me/pardon me, passing through
Prego: . . . . You're welcome/please
Più lentamente: . . . . More slowly
Parla inglese: . . . . Do you speak English?
Non parlo italiano: . . . . I don't speak Italian
Non capisco / Non ho capito: . . . . . I don't/I didn't understand
Non lo so: . . . . I don't know
Vorrei: . . . . I would like
Vorrei pagare il conto: . . . . I would like to pay the check
Può portare il conto: . . . . Can you bring the check?
Vorrei comprare: . . . . I would like to buy
Vorrei mangiare: . . . . I would like to eat
Ho fame / Ho sete: . . . . I'm hungry/I'm thirsty
Mi dispiace: . . . . I'm sorry
Entrata / ingresso: . . . . Entrance
Uscita: . . . . Exit
Ho bisogno: . . . . I need
Poco / tanto: . . . . A little/a lot
Più / meno: . . . . More/less

Può aiutarmi: . . . . Can you help me? (polite, formal)
A destra: . . . . To the right
A sinistra: . . . . To the left
Sempre dritto: . . . . Straight ahead
Vicino: . . . . Close
Lontano: . . . . Far

Days & Time

Oggi: . . . . Today
Domani: . . . . Tomorrow
Ieri: . . . . Yesterday
Mattina: . . . . Morning
Pomeriggio: . . . . Afternoon
Stasera: . . . . Tonight
Lunedì: . . . . Monday
Martedì: . . . . Tuesday
Mercoledì: . . . . Wednesday
Giovedì: . . . . Thursday
Venerdì: . . . . Friday
Sabato: . . . . Saturday
Domenica: . . . . Sunday
Che ora é? / Che ore sono?: . . . . What time is it?
A che ora: . . . . At what time?
Un mezz'ora: . . . . A half hour
Un'ora: . . . . An hour

Numbers

Uno: . . . . One
Due: . . . . Two
Tre: . . . . Three
Quattro: . . . . Four
Cinque: . . . . Five
Sei: . . . . Six
Sette: . . . . Seven
Otto: . . . . Eight
Nove: . . . . Nine
Dieci: . . . . Ten
Unidici: . . . . Eleven
Dodici: . . . . Twelve
Tredici: . . . . Thirteen
Quattordici: . . . . Fourteen
Quindici: . . . . Fifteen

Sedici: . . . . Sixteen
Diciasette: . . . . Seventeen
Diciotto: . . . . Eighteen
Diciannove: . . . . Nineteen
Venti: . . . . Twenty
Ventuno: . . . . Twenty-One
Trenta: . . . . Thirty
Quaranta: . . . . Forty
Cinquanta: . . . . Fifty
Sessanta: . . . . Sixty
Settanta: . . . . Seventy
Ottanta: . . . . Eighty
Novanta: . . . . ninety
Cento: . . . . One hundred
Mille: . . . . One thousand

Weather

Tempo: . . . . Weather
Fa caldo: . . . . Warm
Fa freddo: . . . . Cold
Fa fresco: . . . . Cool
Tira vento: . . . . It's windy
É nuvoloso: . . . . It's cloudy
C'é nebbia: . . . . There's fog
Neve: . . . . Snow
Pioggia: . . . . Rain
Piove: . . . . It's raining
C'é sole: . . . . It's sunny
Che tempo fa: . . . . How's the weather?
Fa bel tempo: . . . . The weather is nice

Transportation

Macchina / auto: . . . . Car
Cintura: . . . . Seat belt
Semaforo: . . . . Stoplight
Benzina: . . . . Gas
Strada: . . . . Street
Carta stradale: Street map
Treno: . . . . Train
Binario: . . . . Track (train)
Stazione: . . . . Station
Andata: . . . . One-way

Appendix

Andata e ritorno: . . . . Roundtrip
La nave: . . . . Boat
Il Pullman: . . . . Extraurban bus
L'autobus: . . . . Urban bus
Fermata: . . . . Stop (bus stop)
Biglietto: . . . . Ticket
Aeroplano / aero: . . . . Airplane
Aeroporto: . . . . Airport
Passaporto: . . . . Passport
A che ora parte / arriva il treno?: . . . .
. . . . What time does the train leave/arrive?

Shopping

Mercato: . . . . Market
Padrone: . . . . Owner
Scontrino: . . . . Receipt
Prezzo: . . . . Price
Banca: . . . . Bank
Aperto: . . . . Open
Chiuso: . . . . Closed
Gratuito: . . . . Free of charge
Sconto: . . . . Discount

Emergencies

Ospedale: . . . . Hospital
Pronto soccorso: . . . . First aid station
Aiuto: . . . . Help
Fire: . . . . Fuoco
Medico / dottore: . . . . Doctor
Polizia: . . . . Police
Ho bisogno: . . . . I need

Accommodations

Albergo: . . . . Hotel
Piano: . . . . Floor (of a building)
Finestra: . . . . Window
Porta: . . . . Door
Camere: . . . . Rooms
Aria condizionata: . . . . Air conditioning
Con bagno: . . . . With bath
Con doccia: . . . . With shower?
Lenzuolo: . . . . Sheets
Televisione: . . . . TV

Telefono: . . . . Telephone
La chiave: . . . . The key
Prenotazione: . . . . Reservation
Fumatori / non-fumatori: . . . . Smoking/non-smoking

Restaurants

Riposo settimanale: . . . . Weekly rest day
Chiuso per ferie: . . . . Closed for vacation
Mancia: . . . . Tip
Conto: . . . . Bill
Fumatori / non-fumatori: . . . . Smokers/non-smokers
Sono vegetariano: . . . . I'm a vegetarian
Tavola: . . . . Table
Forchetta: . . . . Fork
Cucchaio / cucchaino: . . . . Tablespoon/teaspoon
Coltello: . . . . Knife
Bicchiere: . . . . Glass
Bottiglia: . . . . Bottle
Tazza: . . . . Cup
Piatto: . . . . Plate
La prima colazione: . . . . Breakfast
Il Pranzo: . . . . Lunch
La Cena: . . . . Dinner
Vorrei ordinare: . . . . I'd like to order
Menu / lista: . . . . Menu
Tovagliolo: . . . . Napkin
Sale e pepe: . . . . Salt & pepper
Zucchero: . . . . Sugar
Cameriere / cameriera: . . . . Waiter/waitress
Menu a prezzo fisso: . . . . Fixed price menu
Di stagione: . . . . In season
Coperto: . . . . Cover charge
Specialità: . . . . Specialty
Vorrei riservare/prenotare: . . . . I would like to reserve

Menu Guide

Antipasto: . . . . Appetizer
Primo Piatto: . . . . First course
Secondo piatto: . . . . Second course
Contorno: . . . . Side dish
Dolce: . . . . Dessert
Apperitivo: . . . . Aperitif

Vino:	Wine
Digestivo:	Digestive
Caffè:	Coffee
Tè:	Tea
Aqua naturale:	Still water
Aqua gazzata / frizzante / minerale:	Mineral/bubbly water
Degustazione:	Tasting (wine or food)
Cantina:	Wine cellar
Vino bianco:	White wine
Vino rosso:	Red wine
Panino / tramezzino:	Sandwich
Pane:	Bread
Pesce:	Fish
Carne:	Meat
Manzo:	Beef
Pollo:	Chicken
Anatra:	Duck
Salsicce:	Sausage
Bistecca:	Steak
Agnello:	Lamb
Cinghiale:	Boar
Frutta:	Fruit
Verdure:	Vegetables
Uove:	Eggs
Olio:	Oil
Aceto:	Vinegar
Bollito:	Boiled
Grigliata:	Grilled
Fritto:	Fried
Arrosto:	Roasted
Ripieno:	Stuffed
Affumicato:	Smoked
Al Forno:	Baked
Burro:	Butter
Formaggio:	Cheese
Miele:	Honey
Cornetto:	Croissant
Risotto:	Rice
Sugo / pomodoro:	Tomato sauce
Ragù:	Tomato-based meat sauce
Gelato:	Ice cream
Minestra / zuppa / broeto:	Soup

Index

ADVENTURE GUIDES
from Hunter Publishing

This signature Hunter series targets travelers eager to explore the destination. Extensively researched and offering the very latest information, Adventure Guides are written by knowledgeable, experienced authors. The focus is on outdoor activities – hiking, biking, rock climbing, horseback riding, downhill skiing, parasailing, scuba diving, backpacking, and waterskiing, among others – and these user-friendly books provide all the details you need, including prices. The best local outfitters are listed, along with contact numbers, addresses, e-mail and website information, and recommendations. A comprehensive introductory section provides background on history, geography, climate, culture, when to go, transportation and planning. These very readable guides then take a region-by-region approach, plunging into the very heart of each area and the adventures offered, giving a full range of accommodations, shopping, restaurants for every budget, and festivals. All books have town and regional maps; color photos. Fully indexed.

THE BAHAMAS
3rd Edition, Blair Howard

Fully updated reports for Grand Bahama, Freeport, Eleuthera, Bimini, Andros, the Exumas, Nassau, New Providence Island, plus new sections on San Salvador, Long Island, Cat Island, the Acklins, the Inaguas and the Berry Islands. Mailboat schedules, package vacations and snorkeling trips by Jean-Michel Cousteau.

6 x 9 pbk, 384 pp, $18.99, 1-58843-318-9

BELIZE

5th Edition, Vivien Lougheed

"Down-to-earth advice.... An excellent travel guide." – *Library Journal*

Extensive coverage of the country's political, social and economic history, along with the plant and animal life. Encouraging you to mingle with the locals, Entices you with descriptions of local dishes and festivals. Maps, color photos.

6 x 9 pbk, 400 pp, $18.95, 1-58843-289-0

ANGUILLA, ST. MARTIN, ST. BARTS, ST. KITTS, NEVIS, ANTIGUA, BARBUDA

2nd Edition, Paris Permenter & John Bigley

Far outdistances other guides. Recommended operators for day sails, island-hopping excursions, scuba dives, unique rainforest treks on verdant mountain slopes, and rugged four-wheel-drive trails. Previously called the *Adventure Guide to the Leeward Islands.*

6 x 9 pbk, 288 pp, $17.99, 1-55650-909-X

ARUBA, BONAIRE & CURACAO

Lynne Sullivan

By the author of our top-selling Virgin Islands Adventure Guide, here is the latest and most detailed guide to the three fascinating islands of the Dutch Caribbean. Diving, sailing, hiking, golf and horseback riding are excellent here. Enjoy gourmet cuisine, charming small inns and superb five-star resorts. Duty-free stores and unique island crafts makes the islands a shopper's delight. All of them are fully explored, with details on the history and culture that makes each one so appealing. Color photos.

6 x 9 pbk, 288 pp, $18.99, 1-58843-320-X

BERMUDA

3rd Edition, Blair Howard

Botanical gardens, pink sand beaches, historic houses, 17th-century forts, tennis clubs and a decidedly British air await! Bermuda retains much of its legndary charm even as a major tourist destination. Its golf courses are some of the best in the world, drawing an upscale crowd year-round.

6 x 9 pbk, 240 pp, $18.99, 1-58843-392-7

THE CAYMAN ISLANDS

2nd Edition, Paris Permenter & John Bigley

The only comprehensive guidebook to Grand
Cayman, Cayman Brac and Little Cayman.
Encyclopedic listings of dive/snorkel operators,
along with the best sites. Enjoy nighttime pony
rides on a glorious beach, visit the turtle farms,
prepare to get wet at staggering blowholes or
just laze on a white sand beach. Color photos.

6 x 9 pbk, 320pp, $18.99, 1-55650-915-4

COSTA RICA

5th Edition, Bruce & June Conord

"... most comprehensive... Excellent sections on
national parks, flora, fauna & history." –
CompuServe Travel Forum

Incredible detail on culture, plants, animals,
where to stay & eat, as well as practicalities of
travel. E-mail and website directory.

6 x 9 pbk, 384 pp, $17.99, 1-58843-502-4

DOMINICAN REPUBLIC

4th Edition, Fe Liza Bencosme & Clark Norton

Virgin beaches, 16th-century Spanish ruins, the
Caribbean's highest mountain, exotic wildlife,
vast forests. Visit Santa Domingo, revel in
Sosúa's European sophistication or explore the
Samaná Peninsula's jungle. Color photos.

6 x 9 pbk, 360 pp, $17.99, 1-58843-402-8

DOMINICA & ST. LUCIA

Lynne Sullivan

An in-depth guide to these highly popular English-speaking Caribbean islands by the author of
our top-selling Virgin Islands Adventure Guide.
Dominica is unique in that it was never farmed
over; it remains jungle-covered, mountainous
and the only island still occupied by the original
Carib Indians. St. Lucia is more developed, but
is breathtaking in its beauty, with high peaks
and azure-blue bays dotted with colorful boats.

Town and regional maps, color photos,
6 x 9 pbk, 244 pp, $16.99, 1-58843-393-5

THE FLORIDA KEYS & EVERGLADES NATIONAL PARK

4th Edition, Bruce Morris

"... vastly informative, absolutely user-friendly, chock full of information..." – Dr. Susan Cropper

"Practical & easy to use." – *Wilderness Southeast*

Canoe trails, airboat rides, nature hikes, Key West, diving, sailing, fishing. Color.

6 x 9 pbk, 344 pp, $18.99, 1-558843-403-6

PUERTO RICO

4th Edition, Kurt Pitzer

"A quality book that covers all aspects... it's all here & well done." – *The San Diego Tribune*

"... well researched. They include helpful facts... filled with insightful tips." – *Shoestring Traveler*

Crumbling watchtowers and fascinating folklore enchant visitors. Color photos.

6 x 9 pbk, 432 pp, $18.95, 1-558843-116-9

THE VIRGIN ISLANDS

5th Edition, Lynne Sullivan

Comprehensive coverage of both the US and British Virgin Islands, including St. Thomas, St. John, St. Croix, Tortola, Virgin Gorda, Jost Van Dyke, and more. Intriguing historical, ecological, and cultural facts bring the islands and their residents to life, while practical information smoothes the way for a stress-free vacation. Extensive coverage of the islands' protected natural areas both on land and underwater.

6 x 9 pbk, 400 pp, $19.99, 1-55650-907-3

THE YUCATAN, Cancún & Cozumel

3rd Edition, Bruce & June Conord

"This in-depth travel guide opens the doors to our enchanted Yucatán" – Mexico Ministry of Tourism. "A valuable resource." – *Travel & Leisure* magazine

Takes you to places not covered in competing guides. Take to the mountain trails, swim in hidden cenotes, watch the sun rise on a beach near the ancient Maya port of Polé (where the authors celebrated the dawn of the new millennium). Visit Bohemian Playa del Carmen, or history-rich Cozumel.

6 x 9 pbk, 456 pp, $19.99, 1-558843-370-6

TAMPA BAY & FLORIDA'S WEST COAST

3rd Edition, Chelle Koster Walton

Covers all of Tampa Bay/St. Petersburg and north to Withlacoochee State Forest, and south to Sanibel Island, Naples and Everglades National Park. Canoeing the Everglades, fishing on Marco Island, biking in Boca Grande, diving with manatees in Crystal River, sailing along St. Pete Beach, theater-going in Sarasota, shopping the sponge markets of Greek-flavored Tarpon Springs, exploring the history of Tampa's Latin Ybor City - it's all here! Town and regional maps. Fully indexed. Color photos.

6 x 9 pbk, 320 pp, $18.99, 1-58843-350-1

TUSCANY & UMBRIA

Emma Jones

This history-rich region offers some of Italy's classic landscapes – pole-straight cypress trees lining dusty farm roads, rolling hills that stretch as far as the eye can see, fields of vibrant sunflowers, medieval villages perched on rocky spurs above crashing surf. Visit them all with this comprehensive guide that helps you explore the very best places. A largely untouched coastline and protected wild areas only add to the appeal of this top vacation destination. Town and regional maps, color photos, fully indexed.

6 x 9 pbk, 500 pp, $19.99, 1-58843-399-4

SWITZERLAND

Kimberly Rinker

With azure-blue lakes that shine brilliantly against the greenest slopes of the surrounding Alps, its picturesque villages and chic towns are accessible via high-speed trains, though many opt to travel by longboat on some of the country's tranquil waterways. It is one of the world's most advanced industrialized nations, yet its towns and cities are incredibly clean. Part-time Swiss resident Kimberly Rinker has lived and worked here for years. She tells of little-known attractions as well as major tourist draws and everything in-between. Color photos.

6 X 9 pbk, 528 pp, $17.99, 1-58843-369-2

ST. MARTIN & ST. BARTS
Lynne Sullivan

Half-French, half-Dutch, St. Martin offers Orient Bay; duty-free shopping in Philipsburg; Marigot, with chic French boutiques and superb food; and Restaurant Row in Grand Case, with great eateries in charming Creole houses. St. Barts has few buildings higher than one story, no large hotels, memorable food and 22 beautiful beaches along turquoise seas. Lynne Sullivan, author of our best-selling Adventure Guide to the Virgin Islands and several other guides, shows you how to discover and enjoy these islands to the fullest, with island tours, shopping tips, historic sightseeing, watersports and hundreds of places to stay and eat.

6 x 9 pbk, 240 pp, $19.99, 1-58843-348-X

SPAIN
Kelly Lipscomb

A resident of Spain, the author delves into every province and town. He tells of the history and culture, and provides innumerableuseful traveling tips. Everything is explored – the cities, the parks, the islands, the mountains, the foods – plus walking tours, bike trips, sightseeing, hotels, restaurants. Covers the entire country, from Ibiza to Granada, Andalucia, Barcelona, Madrid and Toledo. Town and regional maps, color photos, fully indexed.

6 x 9 pbk, 730 pp, $21.99, 1-58843-398-6

SCOTLAND
Martin Li

The definitive guide to every aspect of Scotland – the legends, the clans, the castles and romantic hotels, the Highland games and, of course, the whisky. This long-time Scotland resident takes us from Edinburgh to Glasgow, Argyll and the Isles, Loch Lomond, the Highlands and to the Outer Isles. Fascinating details on the Loch Ness monster, Shakespeare's "Macbeth" castle, Mary Queen of Scots, the Viking legacy, Burns Night and the royal castles. This book covers it all, and has color photos, maps and index.

6 x 9 pbk, 750 pp, $21.99, 1-58843-406-0

PANAMA

Mother nature has bequeathed Panama with some stunning spots, rich soils and a vast biodiversity. White- and black-sand beaches alternate with mangrove mazes along the coast. Sparkling wild rivers overflowing with trout run through jungle-clad canyons filled with colorful flowers. Mist-crowned Baru Volcano towers above them all. This book explores every region from tip to toe, including the San Blas Islands, offshore Barro Colorado, and urban Panama City, gateway for visitors. Walking tours visit historic forts, gold museums, classic city parks and bustling crafts markets. Special attention is given to the national parks.
6 x 9 pbk, 360 pp, $19.99, 1-58843-368-4

GRENADA, ST. VINCENT & THE GRENADINES

Cindy Kilgore & Alan Moore

Unspoiled islands at the southern end of the Caribbean chain just now being discovered by tourists. St. Vincent, with the oldest botanical garden in the Americas, is dominated by a huge volcano. The Grenadines include Bequia, Mustigue, Mayreau. Grenada, with its pristine reefs, is the source for a third of the world's nutmeg. Full details on accommodations and restaurants, getting around, sightseeing, climate, history and geography.
6 x 9 pbk, 352 pp, $18.99, 1-58843-349-8

GERMANY

Henk Bekker

Bavaria, the Mosel Valley, the Rhine region, the Black Forest, Dresden, Berlin, Hamburg – this highly detailed guide covers every part of the country in depth. The author, a German resident, shows you how to experience the best, through town walks, drives in the countryside and immersing yourself in the entertainment, the sights, the history and culture. Hundreds of hotel and restaurant reviews.
6 x 9 pbk, 550 pp, $19.99, 1-58843-503-2

All Hunter titles are available at bookstores nationwide or from the publisher. To order direct, send a check for the total of the book(s) ordered plus $3 shipping and handling to Hunter Publishing, 130 Campus Drive, Edison NJ 08818. Secure credit card orders may be made at the Hunter website, where you will also find in-depth descriptions of the hundreds of travel guides we offer.

ORDER FORM

Yes! Send the following *Adventure Guides*:

TITLE	ISBN #	PRICE	QUANTITY	TOTAL
SUBTOTAL				
SHIPPING & HANDLING (United States only) (1-2 books, $3; 3-5 books, $5; 6-10 books, $8)				
ENCLOSED IS MY CHECK FOR				

NAME:	
ADDRESS:	
CITY:	STATE: ZIP:
PHONE:	